ETHNOMETHODOLOGICAL CONVERSATION ANALYSIS IN MOTION

T0386442

This volume discusses current and emerging trends in Ethnomethodological Conversation Analysis (EMCA). Focusing on step-by-step procedures of talk and interaction in real time, EMCA explores how people – through locally-produced, public, and common-sensical practices – accomplish activities together and thereby make sense and create social order as part of their everyday lives.

The volume is divided into four parts, and it provides a timely methodological contribution by exploring new questions, settings, and recording technologies in EMCA for the study of social interaction. It addresses the methodical diversity in EMCA, including current practices as well as those testing its boundaries, and paves the way for the development of future interaction research. At the same time, the book offers readers a glimpse into the ways in which human and non-human participants operate with each other and make sense of the world around them. The authors represent diverse fields of research, such as language studies, sociology, social psychology, human-computer interaction, and cognitive science. Ultimately, the book is a conversation opener that invites critical and constructive dialogue on how EMCA's methodology and toolbox could be developed for the purpose of acquiring richer perspectives on endogenous social action.

This is key reading for researchers and advanced students on a range of courses on conversation analysis, language in interaction, discourse studies, multimodality, and more.

Pentti Haddington is Professor of English Language at the University of Oulu, Finland.

Tiina Eilittä is a doctoral researcher at the Research Unit for Languages and Literature at the University of Oulu, Finland.

Antti Kamunen is a postdoctoral researcher at the Research Unit for Languages and Literature at the University of Oulu, Finland.

Laura Kohonen-Aho is a postdoctoral researcher at the Research Unit for Languages and Literature at the University of Oulu, Finland.

Tuire Oittinen is a postdoctoral researcher at the Research Unit for Languages and Literature at the University of Oulu, Finland.

Iira Rautiainen is a postdoctoral researcher at the Research Unit for Languages and Literature at the University of Oulu, Finland.

Anna Vatanen is a researcher at the Department of Finnish, Finno-Ugrian, and Scandinavian Studies, University of Helsinki, Finland, and also affiliated with the Research Unit for Languages and Literature at the University of Oulu, Finland.

ETHNOMETHODOLOGICAL CONVERSATION ANALYSIS IN MOTION

Emerging Methods and New Technologies

Edited by Pentti Haddington, Tiina Eilittä,
Antti Kamunen, Laura Kohonen-Aho,
Tuire Oittinen, Iira Rautiainen and Anna Vatanen

Routledge
Taylor & Francis Group

LONDON AND NEW YORK

Designed cover image: © Getty Images | Orbon Alija

First published 2024
by Routledge
4 Park Square, Milton Park, Abingdon, Oxon OX14 4RN

and by Routledge
605 Third Avenue, New York, NY 10158

Routledge is an imprint of the Taylor & Francis Group, an informa business

British Library Cataloguing-in-Publication Data
A catalogue record for this book is available from the British Library

ISBN: 978-1-032-54441-0 (hbk)
ISBN: 978-1-032-52255-5 (pbk)
ISBN: 978-1-003-42488-8 (ebk)

DOI: 10.4324/9781003424888

Typeset in Times New Roman
by Deanta Global Publishing Services, Chennai, India

CONTENTS

List of contributors   *viii*
Acknowledgements   *xiii*

1   Ethnomethodological conversation analysis in motion:
An introduction   1
Tiina Eilittä, Pentti Haddington, Antti Kamunen,
Laura Kohonen-Aho, Tuire Oittinen, Iira Rautiainen,
and Anna Vatanen

PART 1
Exploring "being a member"   **19**

2   How to study interactional history in non-human animals?
Challenges and opportunities   21
Federico Rossano

3   Transcribing human–robot interaction: Methodological
implications of participating machines   42
Hannah Pelikan

4   Ocularcentric participation frameworks: Dealing with a blind
member's perspective   63
Brian L. Due

PART 2
Broadening the analyst's access to a member's perspective by using various video materials   83

5 Collecting and analysing multi-source video data: Grasping the opacity of smartphone use in face-to-face encounters   85
Iuliia Avgustis and Florence Oloff

6 From distributed ecologies to distributed bodies in interaction: Capturing and analysing "dual embodiment" in virtual environments   111
Laura Kohonen-Aho and Pentti Haddington

7 360-cameras used by a team participating in a mobile gathering   132
Pirkko Raudaskoski

PART 3
Augmenting analyses of the member's perspective with multiple research materials and methods   151

8 Inductive approach in EMCA: The role of accumulated ethnographic knowledge and video-based observations in studying military crisis management training   153
Antti Kamunen, Tuire Oittinen, Iira Rautiainen, and Pentti Haddington

9 A satellite view of spatial points in conversation   171
Joe Blythe, Francesco Possemato, Josua Dahmen, Caroline de Dear, Rod Gardner, and Lesley Stirling

10 EMCA informed experimentation as a way of investigating (also) "non-accountable" interactional phenomena   199
Melisa Stevanovic

PART 4
Enhancing transparency of analytical processes   219

11 Beyond video: Using practice-based VolCap analysis to understand analytical practices volumetrically   221
Paul McIlvenny and Jacob Davidsen

12 Recurrent problems and recent experiments in
    transcribing video: Live transcribing in data sessions and
    depicting perspective   245
    Eric Laurier and Tobias Boelt Back

Index   *265*

LIST OF CONTRIBUTORS

Iuliia Avgustis is a doctoral researcher at the Research Unit for Languages and Literature and the Research Unit INTERACT: Human Computer Interaction and Human Centred Development at the University of Oulu, Finland, and a member of the project Smart Communication.

Her interdisciplinary video-based research combines methodological insights from ethnomethodology, multimodal conversation analysis, phenomenology, sociology, and human-computer interaction. In her doctoral dissertation, she focuses on collocated and collaborative smartphone use in the context of everyday face-to-face interactions.

Tobias Boelt Back is Assistant Professor in the Department of Culture and Learning at Aalborg University, Denmark, and member of the Centre for Discourses in Transition (C-DiT).

His research focuses on risk and inequality as barriers for transitions towards more environmentally sustainable mobilities. He uses graphic transcription and ethnomethodological membership categorisation analysis to explicate the categorial moral order of public transport settings as captured by 360-degree recording devices. Back is part of the Travelling Together project (2021–2023).

Joe Blythe is Associate Professor of Linguistics at Macquarie University, Australia.

Blythe is an interactional linguist specialising in Australian Indigenous languages. He leads the comparative project Conversational Interaction in Aboriginal and Remote Australia and is an investigator on OzSpace: Language and Landscape in Indigenous Australia, a project examining topography and spatial grammar in Australian Indigenous languages.

Josua Dahmen is an interactional linguist at Macquarie University, Australia, and at the Australian National University, Canberra, and a researcher in the comparative projects Conversational Interaction in Aboriginal and Remote Australia (CIARA) and Body, Language and Socialisation Across Cultures.

His research focuses on Australian Aboriginal languages and he conducts fieldwork on Jaru, an endangered language of Western Australia. His doctoral dissertation takes an interactional-linguistic approach to language documentation by investigating the recruitment of linguistic and embodied resources for the accomplishment of social actions in casual conversations in Jaru.

Jacob Davidsen is Associate Professor in the Department of Communication and Psychology at Aalborg University, Denmark.

He is co-founder of the Video Research Lab (VILA), the Big Video Manifesto, the QuiViRR journal, and the BigSoftVideo team who develop software tools to enhance qualitative video research. He is currently working with collaborative immersive environments for learning, participation, and collaboration.

Caroline de Dear is a doctoral researcher at Macquarie University, Australia, where she studies Gija, an endangered Australian Aboriginal language of Western Australia.

Her research interests include Australian Indigenous languages, gestures, and multimodal communication. Her doctoral dissertation adopts an interactional perspective on canonical and non-canonical questions in multiparty Gija conversations. Caroline is a researcher in the comparative project Conversational Interaction in Aboriginal and Remote Australia (CIARA).

Brian L. Due is Associate Professor of Communication at the Department of Nordic Studies and Linguistics at the University of Copenhagen, Denmark.

He is the co-editor of *Social Interaction. Video-Based Studies of Human Sociality*. He uses video ethnography and ethnomethodological conversation analysis to study humans interacting with animals and in material-technological settings. Currently, he studies perception as practical and distributed action. He builds connections between ethnomethodology, semiotics, and science and technology studies.

Tiina Eilittä is a doctoral researcher at the Research Unit for Languages and Literature at the University of Oulu, Finland.

She uses conversation analysis to study everyday adult–child interactions. Her research data consist of Finnish and English video recordings in families and early childhood education. She has published in the *Journal of Pragmatics and Gesprächsforschung*, works as an editor in the *Finnish Journal of Linguistics*, and co-edits the book *Complexity of Interaction*.

Rod Gardner is Honorary Associate Professor at the University of Queensland, Australia, and a member of the CIARA team.

He studies First Nations and remote English conversation in Australia using conversation analysis and interactional linguistic methods, focusing on turn-taking, epistemics, storytelling, and place and person reference. He has also studied classroom interaction and published the book *Effective Task Instruction in the First Year of Schooling* with Ilana Mushin.

Pentti Haddington is Professor of English Language at the University of Oulu, Finland.

He uses video methods and conversation analysis to study talk and multimodal conduct in social interaction. He has published, for example, in the *Journal of Pragmatics* and *Language in Society*, and co-edited several books and special issues. His current interests include interaction in multinational crisis management training, digital action, and multiactivity.

Antti Kamunen is a postdoctoral researcher at the Research Unit for Languages and Literature at the University of Oulu, Finland.

In his research, Kamunen uses conversation analysis to study the various embodied and multimodal practices in social interaction. Kamunen has worked as an editor in the *SKY Journal of Linguistics* and is currently co-editing the book *Complexity of Interaction*. His research interest concerns talk and interaction in multinational crisis management training.

Laura Kohonen-Aho is a postdoctoral researcher at the Research Unit for Languages and Literature at the University of Oulu, Finland.

She uses multimodal conversation analysis to study mediated social interaction. Her current research focuses on practices of multimodal participation in social virtual reality. Her research has been published, for example, in *Presence* and in the *Proceedings of HICSS* and *ICIS*. She is currently co-editing the book *Complexity of Interaction*.

Eric Laurier is Reader in Geography and Interaction at the University of Edinburgh, School of GeoSciences, UK.

Eric has had the good fortune to work with illustrators in developing forms of transcribing embodied action. He is interested in practical reasoning, mobility, public space, and social relationships. Using video, he analyses action in places like cafes, cars, city streets, editing suites, and moorlands.

Paul McIlvenny is Professor in the Department of Culture and Learning at Aalborg University, Denmark, and research leader of the Centre for Discourses in Transition (C-DiT).

He is co-founder of the Video Research Lab (VILA), the *QuiViRR* journal, and the BigSoftVideo team who develop software tools enhancing qualitative video research.

Florence Oloff is Professor of German Linguistics and Multimodal Interaction at the Leibniz-Institute for the German Language, Germany, and Affiliated Researcher at the Research Unit of Languages and Literature at the University of Oulu, Finland.

Using multimodal conversation analysis, she has worked on embodied practices related to turn-taking, simultaneous talk, and joint utterance formulation in various languages, on multilingual practices in professional settings, or object use and space in social interaction. More recently, she has focused on the role of mundane technologies in face-to-face interaction.

Tuire Oittinen is a postdoctoral researcher at the Research Unit for Languages and Literature at the University of Oulu, Finland.

She uses video-recorded data and multimodal conversation analysis to investigate social interaction in multilingual work and educational settings. Currently, she analyses inclusive teamwork practices in remote crisis management training. Her work has been published in academic journals, such as the *Journal of Pragmatics* and *Social Interaction. Video-Based Studies on Human Sociality.*

Hannah Pelikan is an incoming postdoctoral researcher in the division for Language, Culture, and Interaction at Linköping University, Sweden.

She studies how humans make sense of robot behaviour from an ethnomethodology and conversation analysis (EMCA) stance, with a particular interest in robot sound. Combining EMCA with interaction design, she also develops methods for designing human–robot interaction that embrace the situated and sequential nature of human interaction.

Francesco Possemato is a postdoctoral researcher at the Department of Communicative Disorders and Sciences at the State University of New York at Buffalo, USA.

He uses the methods of conversation analysis and interactional linguistics to investigate interactions between speakers with complex communication needs and their partners. Francesco has worked for the Conversational Interaction in Aboriginal and Remote Australia, and has published on Italian L2 teaching, atypical interaction, and pragmatic typology.

Pirkko Raudaskoski is Professor of Material-Discursive Practices at the Department of Communication and Psychology at the University of Aalborg, Denmark.

She uses multimodal interaction analysis to study how people make sense of each other and their surroundings through language and other forms of meaning-making, and how they orient to and involve the material setting in that work. Her recent focus is team camera work as a method to enhance participatory research.

Iira Rautiainen is a postdoctoral researcher at the Research Unit for Languages and Literature at the University of Oulu, Finland.

She combines ethnomethodology, conversation analysis, and ethnography to study social interaction in multinational crisis management training. Currently, she examines interactional practices in collaborative situations. She has published in the *Journal of Pragmatics*, co-edited the *Finnish Association of Applied Linguistics (AFinLA) yearbook 2020*, and is currently co-editing the book *Complexity of Interaction*.

Federico Rossano is Associate Professor in the Cognitive Science Department at UC San Diego, USA, and the director of the Comparative Cognition Lab.

His current research adopts a comparative perspective on social cognition (cross-ages, cross-cultures, and cross-species) and is focused on the development of communicative abilities and social norms in human and non-human animals (in particular non-human primates, dogs, and cats).

Melisa Stevanovic is a tenure track researcher in Social Psychology at the Faculty of Social Sciences at Tampere University, Finland.

Stevanovic has investigated deontic authority and joint decision-making in both naturally occurring interactions and experimental settings. Currently, Stevanovic leads an Academy-of-Finland-funded project on the interface of interactional and meta-interactional practices, focusing on the paradoxes, biases, and inequalities in people's possibilities to account for their problematic interactional experiences.

Lesley Stirling is Professor of Linguistics and Head of the School of Languages and Linguistics at the University of Melbourne, Australia.

Stirling has published in descriptive and typological linguistics, semantics, psycholinguistics, discourse analysis, and conversation analysis. She is a CI on the Conversational Interaction in Aboriginal and Remote Australia (CIARA) project, investigating turn-taking, epistemics, and storytelling among Aboriginal and non-Aboriginal speakers in remote regions of Australia.

Anna Vatanen is a researcher at the Department of Finnish, Finno-Ugrian, and Scandinavian Studies at the University of Helsinki, Finland, and also affiliated with the Research Unit for Languages and Literature at the University of Oulu, Finland.

Vatanen is an interactional linguist and conversation analyst who works on video-recorded Finnish and Estonian conversational data. She has investigated, for example, family interaction, turn-taking organisation, silences in interaction, various units of language, social actions, and multiactivity. Her research has been published in several high-quality journals and edited volumes.

ACKNOWLEDGEMENTS

We are grateful to the publisher Routledge and especially Senior Publisher Louisa Semlyen for her faith in the book from the very beginning. We also thank Senior Editorial Assistant Talitha Duncan-Todd for the vital help, support, and advice during the typesetting process. It has been a pleasure to work with both of you. We also thank the contributing authors for their hard work and patience with the process and us editors. We could not have done this without you.

This book would not have been possible without the help of many colleagues around the world. We want to thank Liz Stokoe for a critical piece of advice and collegial support at a moment when it was most needed. We also want to thank our colleagues in the COACT research community at the University of Oulu for providing an inspirational environment for exploring questions related, among so many other things, to methods and methodologies for studying social interaction. We are extremely grateful to our colleagues – both authors in the book and external readers – who have generously given their time and support when reading and reviewing the chapters and providing critical feedback and advice. Your help has been invaluable. We are grateful also to three scholars who reviewed the book proposal and made helpful suggestions that have developed the book in many ways. We also want to thank Melisa Stevanovic and Sylvaine Tuncer for carefully reading the book's introductory chapter and giving critical remarks and suggestions for improving it.

This book would not have been possible without the funding we have received for two projects, iTask: Linguistic and Embodied Features of Interactional Multitasking and PeaceTalk: Talk and Interaction in Multinational Crisis Management Training. Both projects have been funded by the Academy of

Finland (decision numbers 287219 and 322199) and the Eudaimonia Institute at the University of Oulu. We gratefully acknowledge the support by both of them.

We are privileged to be able to belong to the world-wide EMCA community and explore the world from the perspectives of talk and interaction, and we acknowledge our debt to the EMCA community, whose research continues to be a constant inspiration and source of joy to us. We hope that this volume will be a source of new ideas and inspiration for the study of social interaction in the EMCA community. We look forward to the future of EMCA. Lastly, we want to thank our families, friends, and other close ones for their interest, support, and understanding along the way.

1

ETHNOMETHODOLOGICAL CONVERSATION ANALYSIS IN MOTION

An introduction

*Tiina Eilittä, Pentti Haddington, Antti Kamunen,
Laura Kohonen-Aho, Tuire Oittinen, Iira Rautiainen,
and Anna Vatanen*

Introduction

Ethnomethodology (EM; e.g., Arminen, 2006; Garfinkel, 1967, 2002; Heritage, 1984) and Conversation Analysis (CA; e.g., Sacks, 1992; Schegloff, 2007; Sidnell & Stivers, 2013) are both approaches to the study of social action. Their theoretical and methodological backgrounds can be traced back to a common historical and intellectual origin, particularly to Garfinkel's re-reading of Talcott Parsons's sociological theory and the idea of actors' subordination to the social system, as well as the phenomenological philosophy of Edmund Husserl, Aron Gurwitch and Alfred Schütz (e.g., Heritage, 1984; Housley, 2021; Maynard, 2013). EM is not considered a method, nor does it use a specific method to achieve its analytical objectives; rather, it uses and relies on different qualitative and descriptive tools to help access and analyse participants' reasoning procedures and practical actions that constitute and order their everyday lives.

EM has had a strong influence on the inception and development of CA. CA is often considered a rigorous method for the study of the organisation of social interaction as it is accomplished by participants through talk and multimodal conduct. While CA focuses on social actions as they are produced in sequences of social interaction and relies on audio-video recordings of naturally occurring interaction, EM also uses methods such as (auto-)ethnography, observation and re-enactments, and studies the perception of the social world (e.g., Coulter & Parsons, 1990), rule-following and practical reasoning (e.g., Livingston, 1987; Sormani, 2014), and technology (e.g., Dourish, 2001), among others. For scholars in both EM and CA, the intelligibility and accountability of action emerge from the actions and activities themselves and can be traced back to and evidenced by the participants' own conduct (e.g., natural language use or embodied behaviour). Through this approach,

DOI: 10.4324/9781003424888-1

it is possible to identify and analyse members' competences and knowledge that they rely on to make sense of and create social order as part of their everyday lives.

Despite the common intellectual background, the relationship between EM's roots and the practices of "doing CA" is not unproblematic and has sparked off debates. Sometimes, for example, they have been considered to have diverged from the early days, CA drifting away from its theoretical and conceptual roots in EM, losing its social relevance or the sight of "macro", and turning into a technical method that is just used to accompany other methods (e.g., Arminen, 2006; Button et al., 2022; Macbeth, 2020). Furthermore, one field's influence on the other has varied, which is reflected in the nomenclature referring to their co-existence – "Ethnomethodology/Conversation Analysis" (Sacks, 1984, p. 21), "Ethnomethodologically Informed Conversation Analysis" (e.g., Haddington et al., 2014, p. 13), "Ethnomethodological Conversation Analysis" (e.g., Carlin, 2020, p. 33; Nevile et al., 2014, p. 9; Potter & Hepburn, 2010, p. 52), or "Ethnomethodology and Conversation Analysis" (e.g., Button et al., 2022; Llewellyn & Hindmarsh, 2010; Mlynář et al., 2018) – and the acronyms that are used to refer to them: EMCA, EM/CA, or (EM)CA.

In this volume, we use the title Ethnomethodological Conversation Analysis (EMCA). We are aware of the problems connected with the label, but we use it deliberately to emphasise the importance of the ethnomethodological roots for doing conversation analysis. Together, they are considered to form an analytic mentality and approach for studying the construction of action, activities, and social order. EMCA is a qualitative, inductive, and empirical approach that aims to uncover the ordinary practices, reasoning procedures, and methods that participants employ to accomplish activities together. It grounds its analyses on participants' actual talk and embodied conduct, as they are produced moment to moment in social interaction and witnessed in audio and/or video recordings of naturally occurring interactions. The evidence for analytic claims is gleaned from the design of participants' verbal, vocal, and embodied conduct (*the composition of action*) and the sequential location of that conduct within the broader course of action (*the position of action*). In particular, an action is seen to set up an interactional context for subsequent interactional moves, and a recipient's response is treated as the source of evidence through what is called the "next-turn proof procedure". The response thus displays, in and through its shape, the recipient's interpretation and understanding of the first action (e.g., Levinson, 2013; Sacks et al., 1974; Schegloff, 2007; Sidnell, 2010). At these moments participants orient to, establish, and maintain social order and normativity. This proof procedure is thus the fundamental analytic practice that provides evidence of the "member's (emic) perspective" in interaction, thus fulfilling the analytic objective of EMCA; only those aspects of interaction are considered relevant for analysis that interactants orient to and that are mutually accessible to them. By building on this analytic mentality, EMCA has successfully studied details of practices by which social order is created and maintained in and through multimodal social interaction.

This book takes the above as its starting point, but it also explores possible new methods, solutions, and proof procedures for uncovering participants' common-sense knowledge, practices, and reasoning procedures that they use to accomplish activities in interaction, which to us is in line with ethnomethodological thinking. This book has its origins in an affiliated edited volume that explores the constitution of joint action and shared understanding in complex interactions (Haddington et al., in press). While preparing the volume, we learned that studying the complexity of interaction involves new questions about how participants' backgrounds and the rich material and multimodal contexts contribute to the joint constitution of action and social order. We were also struck by how responding to the demands of studying social action in previously understudied settings involved the use of new methods and solutions for capturing and analysing interactions, and that video corpora were becoming exceedingly rich and diverse. Along with the richer datasets and more detailed focus on the multimodal details of interaction, the analysis and visual representations of video data were taking new forms. The affiliated volume taught us that there are unanswered questions and new methodical approaches that seem to be pushing the boundaries of EMCA. These issues and questions are now explored in this book.

At the outset, we approached colleagues who were using video-based methods and exploring new avenues in EMCA and asked: What aspects of their research had guided them towards creative methodological thinking? What traditional and new solutions had they used, and to what ends? As a result, the following question began to emerge and unite the current book's chapters: What can be treated as evidence for analytic claims in EMCA, and how can such evidence be analysed and represented? This question connects with EMCA's analytic mentality and ties firmly with Garfinkel's notion of "unique adequacy requirement", referring to the analyst's "vulgar" competence in the studied activity (Garfinkel, 2002; Garfinkel & Wieder, 1992). In EMCA, the member's perspective becomes evident and is mobilised in a technical sense with the next-turn proof procedure.

This volume studies how EMCA's robust approach to analyse social action and activity could be supported with new methods, without losing or compromising its strictly empirical roots. It explores how unique adequacy and common-sense knowledge could be uncovered, for example, by accompanying the next-turn proof procedure with other "proof procedures", such as ethnographic tools and knowledge about the studied community. From quite a different methodological perspective, the chapters also discuss the possibility of acquiring access to members' *private actions* and how it could contribute to the analysts' understanding of members' reasoning procedures and the joint constitution of action, activity, and social order, and what implications it may have for analysis. This book is a conversation opener, inviting critical and constructive dialogue on how EMCA's methodology and toolbox could be developed for the purpose of acquiring richer perspectives on endogenous social action. The next section positions this book alongside the history and development of EMCA and its evolution from the analysis of talk-as-action to the consideration of multimodal, visual, and multi-sensorial aspects of social (inter)action.

21st-century developments in EMCA research and methodology

EMCA has its roots in sociology in the 1950s and 1960s, and the works of two scholars, Harold Garfinkel and Erving Goffman. For Goffman, "interaction order" – that is, how the everyday interactions form existing social structures (e.g., Goffman, 1955, 1963, 1983) – was a substantive social institution that should be studied systematically through microanalysis. Garfinkel's ethnomethodology was based on his notion of not treating members' common-sense knowledge and practical reasoning as resources for studying how societies work, but rather as things to be studied in their own right (Garfinkel, 1967). CA – and here we deliberately use CA to refer to the analysis of "talk-in-interaction" and "talk-as-action" – emerged from this background with a special focus on the use of recordings from naturally occurring interactions and the emphasis on the *situated* accountability of actions (see Arminen, 2006). The initial steps in CA were taken first by Harvey Sacks, and later together with Gail Jefferson and Emanuel Schegloff, who highlighted the importance of the systematic analysis of the moment-by-moment organisation of talk-in-interaction (Sacks et al., 1974; Schegloff & Sacks, 1973). CA's early focus on audio-recorded talk made possible its development into a rigorous, methodical tool for investigating the systematic ways in which turns, actions, and sequences are organised in talk-in-interaction (Sacks et al., 1974; Schegloff, 2007). Nevertheless, as the main objective of CA was never to study language *per se*, but social action (Sacks, 1984; Sacks & Schegloff, 2002), the focus soon also embraced multimodal aspects of interaction. As the possibilities for collecting and playing video recordings developed in the early 1980s, pioneering researchers, such as Charles Goodwin (1980, 1981), Marjorie Goodwin (1980), and Christian Heath (1982, 1986), began to study bodily conduct as an equally important resource for the accomplishment of joint action in face-to-face encounters.

Since the beginning of the 21st century, the use of video recordings as data (e.g., Heath et al., 2010; Knoblauch et al., 2006; Nevile, 2004) has become increasingly common in EMCA. Investigations have, in addition to talk, focused more on the multimodal features of social interaction both in mundane and institutional contexts (Deppermann, 2013; Mondada, 2014, 2016a, 2016b, 2019b). Analyses have focused on, for example, gestures, gaze behaviour, facial expressions, body postures, object manipulations, movement in space (Deppermann, 2013; C. Goodwin, 2017; Nevile, 2015; Streeck et al., 2011), and, more recently, on "sensoriality" (e.g., Cekaite, 2015; M.H. Goodwin, 2017; Mondada, 2019a, 2020). These developments have been characterised as different "turns": the *visual turn* (Mondada, 2013), the *embodied turn* (Nevile, 2015), and the *material turn* (Nevile et al., 2014). Despite the term, these "turns" have never represented specific methodological or epistemological discoveries in EMCA, occurring at a particular moment in time. For example, many interactional phenomena on "embodiment" were highlighted – with the same methodology – by, for example, Charles and Marjorie Goodwin and Christian Heath already in the 1980s. This book also does not aim to give a full account of these "turns" or their conceptual or historical background, but rather reflects on the organic evolution and development of EMCA over time as evidenced by developing research interests and foci.

An important and rapidly evolving area of study within EMCA concerns the organisation of social conduct in "technologised" interaction contexts (e.g., Hutchby, 2001). Since Lucy Suchman's work in the 1980s on corporate technology design, which used EM and CA alongside other fields, research has touched upon asynchronous, quasi-synchronous, and synchronous interactions. The increasing interest in interactions in professional and workplace settings led to the development of new and distinct areas of study, including Computer-Supported Cooperative Work (CSCW; e.g., Heath et al., 2002) and Human-Computer Interaction (HCI; e.g., Reeves, 2019). In them, EMCA has been used for detailed analyses of video-mediated interaction (e.g., Due et al., 2019; Licoppe, 2017; Mlynář et al., 2018; Oittinen, 2020), and recently, for the investigation of 3D virtual environments (Bennerstedt & Ivarsson, 2010; Hindmarsh et al., 2006; Kohonen-Aho & Haddington, this volume; Kohonen-Aho & Vatanen, 2021). These studies highlight EMCA as a powerful methodological tool for studying how technologies feature in the collaborative accomplishment of social actions and activities (e.g., Arminen et al., 2016; Heath et al., 2000; Heath & Luff, 2000; Suchman, 1987). They have also invested in improving aspects of institutional practice and technology design (e.g., Reeves, 2019).

Additionally, the development of digital recording technology and solutions has enabled new approaches to data collection and analysis in EMCA. The availability of high-end recording devices, such as small, portable action cameras and 360-degree cameras, has offered the possibility to collect high-quality recordings that capture the rich, multimodal details of interaction in complex settings, such as operating rooms, outdoor activities, and car interiors (Avgusts & Oloff, this volume; Broth & Mondada, 2013; Haddington et al., 2013; Keisanen et al., 2017; Mondada, 2009, 2012; Raudaskoski, this volume). Such devices also make possible the collection of video recordings from different perspectives, including not only those of participants but also researchers (e.g., Edmonds, 2021). However, concerns regarding the use of high-end recording technologies have also been raised, for example, in relation to managing large corpora and analysing materials so that they subscribe to the EMCA's analytic mentality and ensure access to the participants' – or members' – *emic* perspective. Large video databases have still been considered beneficial for EMCA since they pave the way for new research questions and foci. Emerging subfields include developmental CA, longitudinal CA, and micro-longitudinal CA, which explore change, development, and transformation in the interactions of individuals and groups over extended periods of time, such as years, weeks, or days (Deppermann & Pekarek-Doehler, 2021;

Ishino, 2018; Rossano, this volume; Wagner et al., 2018). Longitudinal perspective has been used to explore such topics as socialisation processes and second and foreign language learning (Pekarek Doehler & Balaman, 2021; Pekarek Doehler & Berger, 2016). This is illustrative of the richness and flexibility of EMCA as a methodology and the possibility to develop it in new directions.

Moreover, new video data and methodological developments have inspired EMCA scholars to improve existing or design completely new ways to annotate, visualise, and represent research materials. This need has been prompted by the richness of multimodal data, which often defy simple and straightforward modes of representation. Recent excellent examples include the Laurierian comic strip visualisations (Laurier, 2013, 2019; Laurier & Back, this volume; see also Skedsmo, 2021), the combination of traditional transcripts and affective computing annotations (Rollet & Clavel, 2020), and the embedding of audio or video clips into online publications (Blythe et al., this volume; Mortensen & Due, 2018; Greer, 2018; Nevile, 2018). The new annotation and visualisation methods complement the commonly used systems, such as the Jeffersonian system (Jefferson, 2004), which is used to transcribe the details of talk, and the Mondadian system (Mondada, 2016a), which is used to transcribe multimodal conduct. New digital solutions for analysis have also had a profound impact on the EMCA methodology. A good example is a system by McIlvenny and Davidsen (2017; McIlvenny, 2019; McIlvenny & Davidsen, this volume) that allows new forms of collaborative analysis across distances and institutional barriers.

An important step within EMCA has been to extend its analytic scope beyond video recordings and the field itself as a single-method approach and to explore the value of other methods for the analysis of social action. This step has been partly inspired by the increasing interest in encounters involving, for example, babies (e.g., Kidwell, 2009) and people living with intellectual disabilities (e.g., Antaki & Crompton, 2015), non-human participants (primates or other animals; e.g., Mondémé, 2022; Rossano & Liebal, 2014), or non-sentient participants (robots; e.g., Due, 2021, 2022; Pelikan, this volume; Pelikan & Broth, 2016; Pitsch, 2020; artificial intelligence systems; e.g., Porcheron et al., 2018; Reeves et al., 2018). The interaction order in the groups and communities involving these participants may not only be beyond what research has described but also the analysis and interpretation of social conduct and endogenous action in them may require new forms of data. Important methodological questions follow: How much can the analyses involving the above kinds of participants be claimed to be based on the participants' own orientations? What does being a *member* (or a researcher) in these settings mean? What is required to achieve the "unique adequacy requirement" for conducting analysis in these settings (Garfinkel, 2002; Garfinkel & Wieder, 1992; Jenkings, 2018)?

Furthermore, research on workplace activities (e.g., Heath & Luff, 2000; Luff et al., 2000; Whalen & Vinkhuyzen, 2000), influenced by Lucy Suchman's (1987) work, has relied on ethnographic knowledge gleaned from the studied settings.

Consequently, the relationship between ethnography and EMCA has begun to receive an increasing amount of attention (see Maynard, 2006; Rawls & Lynch, 2022; see also Kamunen et al., this volume): Initiatives have been made to rethink the role of the researcher in the field and as part of the research process, from being a mere observer to obtaining a more participatory role in the setting (see Katila et al., 2021).

EMCA scholars have also called for "methodological pluralism" (Kendrick, 2017), "mixed methods" approaches (Stivers, 2015), and the fusion of EMCA and methods from experimental psychology (Alač, 2011; Hollander, 2015; Wooffitt, 2007). This is suggestive of the possibilities to validate EMCA research results with other methods and thereby extend its original scope. For example, EMCA has traditionally refrained from – or considered it to be against its fundamental tenet – using data from pre-arranged or simulated situations to test hypotheses or to deploy quantitative methods. Nevertheless, the possible benefits of experimentation, observation, and coding have been raised (e.g., Kendrick, 2017; Stevanovic, 2016; Stivers, 2015). Additionally, some contexts, such as those involving the design and implementation of technological innovations (e.g., eye-tracking tools), require experimental settings and a usage-based approach (Luff et al., 2014; Stukenbrock & Dao, 2019). Specific situations also call for collecting and using lab-induced biometric data (e.g., Peräkylä et al., 2015; Voutilainen et al., 2014). These methodological approaches stretch the boundaries of EMCA's long-standing naturalistic research design (see, e.g., Stevanovic et al., 2017), but the question remains what their role may be in the future of EMCA. However, the calls for experimental and pluralistic methods have also encountered resistance (e.g., Button et al., 2022; Macbeth, 2020).

The current volume engages with existing EMCA research and highlights its importance in three ways. First, EMCA is an established methodology and a *mentality* that is constantly developed by emerging trends and directions in the field. Second, the current understanding of EMCA and its applications have resulted from an organic evolution impacted by digitalisation and societal changes. Third, EMCA's role and relation to neighbouring fields and methodologies (e.g., in sociology, communication studies, anthropology, psychology, and linguistics) merit further exploration and discussion. This book reflects on the directions and broader evolution(s) within EMCA, along with its diverse "branches", and initiates discussion on the rich range of possibilities to study interaction and endogenous social action and activity.

Aim of the book

This volume aims to reflect on and deepen our understanding of the current and emerging methodological trends and transitions in EMCA. The chapters address the following themes and questions:

1. **Members' private actions**. What is the relevance of private actions – that is, actions that are not available to the co-participants nor often explicitly

accounted for – in/for understanding the social organisation of actions and activities? How can access to members' (private) actions be gained? How can private actions be studied?

2. **The analyst's access to a member's perspective.** How and why do some contexts require the use of novel methods, as well as diverse video and other research materials, to broaden the analyst's access to the members' perspective and endogenous social action?

3. **The affordances, limitations, and emerging trends of the EMCA methodology.** How can EMCA analyses and research processes be augmented and validated by innovative methodological solutions?

The chapters in this volume discuss whether and how creative ways of studying social actions and activities could, in fact, be part of EMCA's questions and support the achievement of EMCA's fundamental aim: the study of the intelligibility of situated social action from the perspective of the participants themselves. The volume converses the boundaries of EMCA, what the methodology can be considered to comprehend, and the various ways in which it can be utilised.

Contributions to the volume: Introducing the key themes

The book is divided into four thematic areas. Part 1 discusses the meaning of being a "member" in atypical situations, and how research can be carried out on participants whose perspectives the researcher does not share, such as people with disabilities, or non-human and even non-sentient participants. Part 2 explores how access to a member's perspective can be broadened by different analytical solutions. Part 3 focuses on the use of multiple materials and methods and their integration into the EMCA approach, which is sometimes needed to reveal the orderliness of interaction in very specialised settings or situations. Part 4 addresses the relevance of enhancing the transparency of analytical processes, illustrating how this can mean, for example, "inhabiting" the data and creating a 3D experience when analysing video-recorded situations.

Part 1: Exploring "being a member"

Traditionally, EMCA has mainly focused on ocularcentric analyses of sentient human participants, which has also guided the development of field-specific trends and terminology. Part 1 introduces studies in which participation and membership in certain groups have been difficult to access with EMCA methods. It explores the membership status of non-sentient participants (e.g., robots) and non-human species (e.g., primates) and studies interactions that are underexplored in EMCA, such as interactions between visually impaired and seeing participants (see, however, e.g., Hirvonen & Schmitt, 2018; Simone & Galatolo, 2020,

2021). The chapters extend the notion of members' perspective and discuss what it means to study interaction in under-researched settings or with non-traditional participants.

Rossano explores the importance of interactional histories in encounters between non-human animals. By focusing on sign–meaning relationships, he identifies change in the communicative practices of mother-infant bonobo dyads. The chapter shows how bonobo infants' gestures change over time and highlights how such a signal change can be investigated systematically. The chapter expands the notion of interactional histories to social interactions between non-human animals.

Similarly, Pelikan examines participants whose perspective has previously been unattainable. She studies robots as participants in social interaction and discusses how human interlocutors support and scaffold robots in their role as participants. Pelikan reflects on how the examination of human-robot interactions transforms aspects of the EMCA transcription process and illustrates how detailed transcriptions can make perspicuous the robots' participation and perspective in interaction.

Due focuses on interactions involving both seeing and visually impaired participants (VIPs), highlighting the role of ocularcentrism in the situated organisation of actions. The resources the VIPs use to engage in joint activity and to achieve membership in a participation framework are also discussed and raised as methodological issues when conducting analyses on these settings. Overall, the chapters in Part 1 contribute to a better understanding of the affordances and limitations of the traditional EMCA methodology and how the (lack of) access to a member's perspective can be addressed in the overall research process.

Part 2: Broadening the analyst's access to a member's perspective by using various video materials

Prior EMCA work has considered the visibility of participants' actions essential for making claims about the ongoing interaction from a member's perspective. The chapters in Part 2 discuss how various video materials can help the analyst explain and understand the context, the social situation, and the member's perspective, even when they are not explicitly accounted for. The chapters combine different types of video data to grasp a more holistic picture of the setting or situation, introducing new solutions for overcoming "opaque" interactional phenomena in video recordings.

The chapter by Avgustis and Oloff describes complementing video data (recorded with static and wearable cameras) with screen captures from mobile devices to study the "analytical opacity" of the devices. The combination of views allows the analyst to examine the participants' public actions but also to obtain a deeper understanding of the members' perspectives by seeing what the participants are doing privately with their mobile phones.

Similarly, Kohonen-Aho and Haddington argue that when studying technology-mediated interaction in virtual environments, the analyst gains a better understanding of the participants' actions if the interactions are recorded both in the participants' physical and virtual environment. This is shown to provide the researcher with access to the participants' private actions in both worlds, which is needed to validate the analysis of joint activities.

Raudaskoski explores the simultaneous use of mobile 360-degree video cameras and traditional video cameras for recording an event. She discusses how they together facilitate the analyst's understanding of the participants' orientation to their surroundings during nature hikes. The analysis shows how combining different video data allows the analyst to detect participants' courses of action and trace the occurrences of action sequences within the setting. She also discusses the added benefit of transparency as regards the analyst's ethnographic participation in the studied setting. On the whole, Part 2 thus shows how the analysis of private actions or phenomena that occur outside the reach of cameras may be relevant for gaining a thorough understanding of the setting and the endogenously emerging actions.

Part 3: Augmenting analyses of the member's perspective with multiple research materials and methods

EMCA has mostly been used as a methodology on its own, but recently it has also been used with accompanying (other) research approaches. Part 3 expands this line of work and introduces solutions and strategies to analyse talk, bodily-visual conduct, and multisensoriality when traditional EMCA methods are insufficient for capturing the interactional phenomena under scrutiny.

Kamunen, Oittinen, Rautiainen, and Haddington discuss how close collaboration with the studied community and ethnographic knowledge provide a deeper understanding of the setting and participants' locally produced actions. The authors also propose that the researchers' lived experiences during fieldwork and a multiphase data collection process function as proto-data that can inform the analyses, providing an in-depth understanding of the social context as well as the members' perspective.

Blythe, Possemato, Dahmen, de Dear, Gardner and Stirling present their research on the Australian Aboriginal languages of Gija, Murrinhpatha, and Jaru, and Australian English. The speakers of these languages use pointing gestures to refer to locations that are not in their immediate spatial proximity, and due to their distance, the targets of these points cannot be captured in the recordings. The chapter suggests that complementing audio-video data with geospatial information allows the analysts to uncover the relationship between locational gestures, language, and interaction with the wider environment, and to examine what this relationship reveals about the participants' spatial cognition.

Stevanovic addresses "ontological muteness" in EMCA and explores the types of "non-accountable" actions that are typically left outside its scope, such as prereflective human mirroring mechanisms (e.g., body movement synchrony, prosodic matching) and the physiological underpinnings of social interaction. Stevanovic describes both the benefits and concerns involved in complementing video-recorded data with experimental methods and invites more discussion on the potential avenues for developing this line of work in EMCA.

Part 4: Enhancing transparency of analytical processes

Part 4 explores ways to adjust or even renew traditional analytic processes and publishing methods to represent multimodal, multi-layered, or setting-specific features of interaction. The chapters illustrate creative ways to view and analyse research materials and to represent analyses, highlighting new and emerging practices in the field.

McIlvenny and Davidsen suggest that the growing use and development of new recording technologies create a need for novel ways to view, analyse, and annotate data. They propose an approach called *practice-based volumetric capture (VolCap) analysis*. The approach allows researchers to immerse themselves in the video data in a virtual reality (VR) environment. It also allows researcher collaboration within the VR environment in the form of viewing and manipulating complex audio-visual data and developing joint analyses. The approach provides the analysts with a richer understanding of the member's perspective and their actions, resembling the re-enactment method used in EM.

Laurier and Back similarly introduce novel ways of analysing and illustrating video data. They show how comic strip illustrations can be used to provide rich visual representations of participants' embodied actions and thus complement the traditional Jeffersonian and Mondadian annotation systems (see also Pelikan, this volume). The authors propose that comic strips provide a rich visual representation of data that can make the analysis and transcriptions more approachable to broader audiences. Finally, they introduce how comic strips can be used to support collaborative analysis (e.g., data sessions) for dealing with methodological complexities of embodiment and material environments in the data. This, they argue, supports and makes possible more reliable analyses.

Conclusion and discussion

This book aims to act as a conversation opener and inspire discussion on the possible development of the EMCA methodology. The chapters shed light on recent developments in EMCA, including the use of new digital recording technologies, complementary methods, and novel approaches in the research process. On the one hand, the discussion centres around interactional phenomena that can be studied with EMCA, while on the other hand, the focus is on the interface of methods and methodological diversity. All these can be seen to afford researchers with potentially more extended and versatile perspectives on human behaviour and on the local organisation of social actions from a *member's perspective*. Understanding not only the sequential but also the contextual environment of actions and their situated interpretation, as well as keeping up with societal changes, such as digitalisation and the ubiquitous use of technological devices, have been recognised as methodological challenges and are raised as key in the contributions. Furthermore, the contributions illustrate how an increasing amount of EMCA research may benefit and be motivated by a more open, innovative, and collaborative research process.

This volume discusses methodological and analytical questions that cut through the phases in the EMCA research process. It invites scholars to rethink EMCA concepts and terminology, such as participation, embodiment, perspective, and member. The contributions address changes and challenges in data collection. Not only is the researcher's role shifting from a mere observer to a participant in the field, but also the tools for making recordings are constantly developing. Furthermore, new types of access to interactional environments and phenomena create fresh, more versatile perspectives on human conduct and the organisation of social actions. Is the methodology keeping up with such rapid changes? The same question applies to the processes of transcribing, annotating, and visualising video data. The practice of transcribing is an integral part of EMCA's analytical process, but as video data become more and more complex, new challenges (and, possibly, biases) are recognised and require solutions. What new ways for data analysis and representation can be brought forth through adaptive and innovative solutions for transcribing?

Finally, the chapters explore diverse topics concerning data analysis. Given the EMCA researchers' expanding access to new research environments, and thus to new, context-specific interactional phenomena, the discussion of the validity of tools (both methodological and technical) that scholars in the same field can use (e.g., statistics, ethnographic observations, satellite geolocation) is timely and necessary. How can current methods in EMCA be complemented and supported with new methods without losing sight of EMCA's methodological principles and core strengths?

We understand that some of the views expressed in the chapters of this book may and will trigger debate. However, our aim has been to explore possible new methods and analytic practices for doing EMCA without, however, forgetting its main tenet and objective, that the focus must be on the accomplishment of human activity and social order from the member's own perspective. Consequently, we see this volume as a possibility to review the methodology and *mentality* of EMCA, calling for constructive dialogue on its varying possibilities and potentials. Along with digitalisation and (other) societal and global changes, new contexts for EMCA exploration will continue to emerge, and we need to address the demands for methodological development also in the future. In this respect, this book takes one step towards considering the many opportunities we have for refining our thinking as scholars in the analysis of human sociality and conduct. The future will show which ideas and solutions presented in this book will stand the test of time and EMCA's principles, and take the field further.

References

Alač, M. (2011). *Handling digital brains: A laboratory study of multimodal semiotic interaction in the age of computers*. MIT Press.
Antaki, C., & Crompton, R. J. (2015). Conversational practices promoting a discourse of agency for adults with intellectual disabilities. *Discourse and Society, 26*(6), 645–661.
Arminen, I. (2006). Ethnomethodology and conversation analysis. In C. Bryant & D. Peck (Eds.), *The handbook of the 21st century sociology* (pp. 8–16). Sage.
Arminen, I., Licoppe, C., & Spagnolli, A. (2016). Respecifying mediated interaction. *Research on Language and Social Interaction, 49*(4), 290–309.
Bennerstedt, U., & Ivarsson, J. (2010). Knowing the way: Managing epistemic topologies in virtual game worlds. *Computer Supported Cooperative Work (CSCW), 19*(2), 201–230.
Broth, M., & Mondada, L. (2013). Walking away: The embodied achievement of activity closings in mobile interaction. *Journal of Pragmatics, 47*(1), 41–58.
Button, G., Lynch, M., & Sharrock, W. (2022). *Ethnomethodology, conversation analysis and constructive analysis*. Routledge.
Carlin, P. (2020). Sacks' plenum: The inscription of social orders. In R. J. Smith, R. Fitzgerald, & W. Housley (Eds.), *On Sacks: Methodology, materials, and inspirations* (pp. 32–46). Routledge.
Cekaite, A. (2015). The coordination of talk and touch in adults' directives to children: Touch and social control. *Research on Language and Social Interaction, 48*(2), 152–175.
Coulter, J., & Parsons, E. D. (1990). The praxiology of perception: Visual orientations and practical action. *Inquiry, 33*(3), 251–272.
Deppermann, A. (2013). Multimodal interaction from a conversation analytic perspective. *Journal of Pragmatics, 46*(1), 1–7.
Deppermann, A., & Pekarek Doehler, S. (2021). Longitudinal conversation analysis - Introduction to the special issue. *Research on Language and Social Interaction, 54*(2), 127–141.
Dourish, P. (2001). *Where the action is: The foundations of embodied interaction*. The MIT Press.
Due, B. L. (2021). Distributed perception: Co-operation between sense-able, actionable, and accountable semiotic agents. *Symbolic Interaction, 44*(1), 134–162.
Due, B. L. (2022). Guide dog versus robot dog: Assembling visually impaired people with non-human agents and achieving assisted mobility through distributed co-constructed perception. *Mobilities, 18*(1), 148–166.
Due, B. L., Lange, S. B., Nielsen, M. F., & Jarlskov, C. (2019). Mimicable embodied demonstration in a decomposed sequence: Two aspects of recipient design in professionals' video-mediated encounters. *Journal of Pragmatics, 152*, 13–27.
Edmonds, R. (2021). Balancing research goals and community expectations: The affordances of body cameras and participant observation in the study of wildlife conservation. *Social Interaction: Video-Based Studies of Human Sociality, 4*(2). https://doi.org/10.7146/si.v4i2.127193
Garfinkel, H. (1967). *Studies in ethnomethodology*. Prentice-Hall.
Garfinkel, H. (2002). *Ethnomethodology's program: Working out Durkheim's aphorism*. Rowman & Littlefield.
Garfinkel, H., & Wieder, D. L. (1992). Two incommensurable, asymmetrically alternate technologies of social analysis. In G. Watson & R. M. Seiler (Eds.), *Text in context: Contributions to ethnomethodology* (pp. 175–206). Sage.

Goffman, E. (1955). On face-work: An analysis of ritual elements in social interaction. *Psychiatry, 18*(3), 213–231.

Goffman, E. (1963). *Behavior in public places: Notes on the social organization of gatherings.* Free Press.

Goffman, E. (1983). The interaction order: American Sociological Association, 1982 presidential address. *American Sociological Review, 48*(1), 1–17.

Goodwin, C. (1980). Restarts, pauses, and the achievement of a state of mutual gaze at turn-beginning. *Sociological Inquiry, 50*(3–4), 272–302.

Goodwin, C. (1981). *Conversational organization: Interaction between speakers and hearers.* Academic Press.

Goodwin, C. (2017). *Co-operative action.* Cambridge University Press.

Goodwin, M. H. (1980). Processes of mutual monitoring implicated in the production of description sequences. *Sociological Inquiry, 50*(3–4), 303–317.

Goodwin, M. H. (2017). Haptic sociality: The embodied interactive construction of intimacy through touch. In C. Meyer, J. Streeck, & J. S. Jordan (Eds.), *Intercorporeality: Beyond the body* (pp. 73–102). Oxford University Press.

Greer, T. (2018). Learning to say grace. *Social Interaction: Video-Based Studies of Human Sociality, 1*(1). https://doi.org/10.7146/si.v1i1.105499

Haddington, P., Eilittä, T., Kamunen, A., Kohonen-Aho, L., Rautiainen, I., & Vatanen, A. (Eds.). (in press). *Complexity of interaction: Studies in multimodal conversation analysis.* Palgrave Macmillan.

Haddington, P., Keisanen, T., Mondada, L., & Nevile, M. (2014). Towards multiactivity as a social and interactional phenomenon. In P. Haddington, T. Keisanen, L. Mondada, & M. Nevile (Eds.), *Multiactivity in social interaction: Beyond multitasking* (pp. 3–32). John Benjamins.

Haddington, P., Mondada, L., & Nevile, M. (2013). Being mobile: Interaction on the move. In P. Haddington, L. Mondada, & M. Nevile (Eds.), *Interaction and mobility: Language and the body in motion* (pp. 3–61). Walter de Gruyter.

Heath, C. (1982). The display of recipiency: An instance of sequential relationship in speech and body movement. *Semiotica, 42*(2–4), 27–42.

Heath, C. (1986). *Body movement and speech in medical interaction.* Cambridge University Press.

Heath, C., Hindmarsh, J., & Luff, P. (2010). *Video in qualitative research.* Sage.

Heath, C., Knoblauch, H., & Luff, P. (2000). Technology and social interaction: The emergence of 'workplace studies'. *British Journal of Sociology, 51*(2), 299–320.

Heath, C., & Luff, P. (2000). *Technology in action.* Cambridge University Press.

Heath, C., Svensson, M. S., Hindmarsh, J., Luff, P., & Vom Lehn, D. (2002). Configuring awareness. *Computer Supported Cooperative Work (CSCW), 11*(3–4), 317–347.

Heritage, J. (1984). *Garfinkel and ethnomethodology.* Polity Press.

Hindmarsh, J., Heath, C., & Fraser, M. (2006). (Im)materiality, virtual reality and interaction: Grounding the 'virtual' in studies of technology in action. *The Sociological Review, 54*(4), 795–817.

Hirvonen, M., & Schmitt, R. (2018). Blindheit als Ressource: Zur professionellen Kompetenz eines blinden Teammitglieds bei der gemeinsamen Anfertigung einer Audiodeskription. *Gesprächsforschung, 19,* 449–477. http://www.gespraechsforschung-online.de/2018.html

Hollander, M. (2015). The repertoire of resistance: Non-compliance with directives in Milgram's 'obedience' experiments. *British Journal of Social Psychology, 54*(3), 425–444.

Housley, W. (2021). *Society in the digital age: An interactionist perspective.* Sage.

Hutchby, I. (2001). *Conversation and technology: From the telephone to the Internet.* Polity Press.

Ishino, M. (2018). Micro-longitudinal conversation analysis in examining co-teachers' reflection-in-action. *System, 78,* 130–147.

Jefferson, G. (2004). Glossary of transcript symbols with an introduction. In G. Lerner (Ed.), *Conversation analysis: Studies from the first generation* (pp. 13–31). John Benjamins.

Jenkings, N. (2018). 'Unique adequacy' in Studies of the military, militarism and militarisation. *Ethnographic Studies, 15,* 38–57.

Katila, J., Gan, Y., Goico, S., & Goodwin, M. H. (2021). Special issue: Researchers participation roles in video-based fieldwork. *Social Interaction: Video-Based Studies of Human Sociality, 4*(2). https://tidsskrift.dk/socialinteraction/issue/view/9243

Keisanen, T., Rauniomaa, M., & Siitonen, P. (2017). Transitions as sites of socialization in family interaction outdoors. *Learning, Culture and Social Interaction, 14,* 24–37.

Kendrick, K. H. (2017). Using conversation analysis in the lab. *Research on Language and Social Interaction, 50*(1), 1–11.

Kidwell, M. (2009). Gaze shift as an interactional resource for very young children. *Discourse Processes, 46*(2–3), 145–160.

Knoblauch, H., Schnettler, B., Raab, J., & Söffner, H.-G. (2006). *Video-analysis: Methodology and methods.* Lang-Verlag.

Kohonen-Aho, L., & Vatanen, A. (2021). (Re-)Opening an encounter in the virtual world of second life: On types of joint presence in avatar interaction. *Journal for Media Linguistics - Journal für Medienlinguistik, 4*(2), 14–51.

Laurier, E. (2013). Before in and after: Cars making their way through roundabouts. In P. Haddington, L. Mondada & M. Nevile (Eds.), *Interaction and mobility: Language and the body in motion* (pp. 210–242). De Gruyter.

Laurier, E. (2019). The panel show: Further experiments with graphic transcripts and vignettes. *Social Interaction: Video-Based Studies of Human Sociality, 2*(1). https://doi.org/10.7146/si.v2i1.113968

Levinson, S. (2013). Action formation and ascription. In J. Sidnell & T. Stivers (Eds.), *The handbook of conversation analysis* (pp. 103–130). Wiley-Blackwell.

Licoppe, C. (2017). Showing objects in Skype video-mediated conversations: From showing gestures to showing sequences. *Journal of Pragmatics, 110,* 63–82.

Livingston, E. (1987). *Making sense of ethnomethodology.* Routledge and Paul Kegan.

Llewellyn, N., &, Hindmarsh, J. (2010). Work and organisation in real time: An introduction. In J. Hindmarsh & N. Llewellyn (Eds.), *Organisation, interaction and practice: Studies of ethnomethodology and conversation analysis* (pp. 3–23). Cambridge University Press.

Luff, P., Hindmarsh, J., & Heath, C. (2000). *Workplace studies: Recovering work practice and informing system design.* Cambridge University Press.

Luff, P., Patel, M., Kuzuoka, H., & Heath, C. (2014). Assembling collaboration: Informing the design of interaction spaces. *Research on Language and Social Interaction, 47*(3), 317–329.

Macbeth, D. (2020). CA and its heresies. *Ethnographic Studies, 17,* 125–142.

Maynard, D. (2013). Everyone and no one to turn to: Intellectual roots and contexts for conversation analysis. In J. Sidnell & T. Stivers (Eds.), *The handbook of conversation analysis* (pp. 11–31). Wiley-Blackwell.

Maynard, D. W. (2006). Ethnography and conversation analysis. In S. N. Hesse-Biber & P. Leavy (Eds.), *Emergent methods in social research* (pp. 55–94). Sage.

McIlvenny, P. B. (2019). Inhabiting spatial video and audio data: Towards a scenographic turn in the analysis of social interaction. *Social Interaction: Video-based Studies of Human Sociality*, *2*(1). https://doi.org/10.7146/si.v2i1.110409

McIlvenny, P. B., & Davidsen, J. (2017). A big video manifesto: Re-sensing video and audio. *Nordicom-Information*, *39*, 15–21.

Mlynář, J., González-Martínez, E., & Lalanne, D. (2018). Situated organization of video-mediated interaction: A review of ethnomethodological and conversation analytic studies. *Interacting with Computers*, *30*(2), 73–84.

Mondada, L. (2009). Emergent focused interactions in public places: A systematic analysis of the multimodal achievement of a common interactional space. *Journal of Pragmatics*, *41*(10), 1977–1997.

Mondada, L. (2012). Talking and driving: Multiactivity in the car. *Semiotica*, *191*(1/4), 223–256.

Mondada, L. (2013). Video as a tool in the social sciences. In C. Müller, A. Cienki, E. Fricke, S. Ladewig, D. McNeill, & S. Tessendorf (Eds.), *Body - language – communication: An international handbook on multimodality in human interaction* (pp. 982–992). De Gruyter Mouton.

Mondada, L. (2014). The local constitution of multimodal resources for social interaction. *Journal of Pragmatics*, *65*, 137–156.

Mondada, L. (2016a). Conventions for multimodal transcription. https://franzoesistik .philhist.unibas.ch/fileadmin/user_upload/franzoesistik/mondada_multimodal_ conventions.pdf

Mondada, L. (2016b). Challenges of multimodality: Language and the body in social interaction. *Journal of Sociolinguistics*, *20*(3), 336–366.

Mondada, L. (2019a). Contemporary issues in conversation analysis: Embodiment and materiality, multimodality and multisensoriality in social interaction. *Journal of Pragmatics*, *145*, 47–62.

Mondada, L. (2019b). Transcribing silent actions: A multimodal approach of sequence organization. *Social Interaction: Video-Based Studies of Human Sociality*, *2*(1). https:// doi.org/10.7146/si.v2i1.113150

Mondada, L. (2020). Orchestrating multi-sensoriality in tasting sessions: Sensing bodies, normativity, and language. *Symbolic Interaction*, *44*(1), 63–86.

Mondémé, C. (2022). Why study turn-taking sequences in interspecies interactions? *Journal for the Theory of Social Behaviour*, *52*(1), 67–85.

Mortensen, K., & Due, B. L. (2018). Editorial. *Social Interaction: Video-Based Studies of Human Sociality*, *1*(1). https://doi.org/10.7146/si.v1i1.105495

Nevile, M. (2004). *Beyond the black box: Talk-in-interaction in the airline cockpit*. Ashgate.

Nevile, M. (2015). The embodied turn in research on language and social interaction. *Research on Language and Social Interaction*, *48*(2), 121–151.

Nevile, M. (2018). Configuring materiality, mobility, and multiactivity: Interactions with objects in cars. *Social Interaction: Video-Based Studies of Human Sociality*, *1*(1). https://doi.org/10.7146/si.v1i1.105497

Nevile, M., Haddington, P., Heinemann, T., & Rauniomaa, M. (2014). On the interactional ecology of objects. In M. Nevile, P. Haddington, T. Heinemann, & M. Rauniomaa (Eds.), *Interacting with objects: Language, materiality, and social activity* (pp. 3–26). John Benjamins.

Oittinen, T. (2020). Noticing-prefaced recoveries of the interactional space in a video-mediated business meeting. *Social Interaction: Video-based Studies of Human Sociality, 3*(3). https://doi.org/10.7146/si.v3i3.122781

Pekarek Doehler, S., & Balaman, U. (2021). The routinization of grammar as a social action format: A longitudinal study of video-mediated interactions. *Research on Language and Social Interaction, 54*(2), 183–202.

Pekarek Doehler, S., & Berger, E. (2016). L2 interactional competence as increased ability for context-sensitive conduct: A longitudinal study of story-openings. *Applied Linguistics, 39*(4), 555–578.

Pelikan, H., & Broth, M. (2016). Why that Nao? How humans adapt to a conventional humanoid robot in taking turns-at-talk. In *Proceedings of the 2016 CHI conference on human factors in computing systems*, San Jose, California, USA.

Peräkylä, A., Henttonen, P., Voutilainen, L., Kahri, M., Stevanovic, M., Sams, M., & Ravaja, N. (2015). Sharing the emotional load: Recipient affiliation calms down the storyteller. *Social Psychology Quarterly, 78*(4), 301–323.

Pitsch, K. (2020). Answering a robot's questions: Participation dynamics of adult-child-groups in encounters with a museum guide robot. *Réseaux, 220–221*(2), 113–150. https://www.cairn-int.info/article-E_RES_220_0113--.htm

Porcheron, M., Fischer, J. E., Reeves, S., & Sharples, S. (2018). Voice interfaces in everyday life. *CHI 2018: CHI Conference on Human Factors in Computing Systems* (1-12). https://doi.org/10.1145/3173574.3174214

Potter, J., & Hepburn, A. (2010). A kind of governance: Rules, time and psychology in organisations. In J. Hindmarsh & N. Llewellyn (Eds.), *Organisation, interaction and practice: Studies of ethnomethodology and conversation analysis* (pp. 49–73). Cambridge University Press.

Rawls, A. W., & Lynch, M. (2022). Ethnography in ethnomethodology and conversation analysis: Both, neither, or something else altogether? *Qualitative Research, 0*(0), 1–29. https://doi.org/10.1177/14687941221138410

Reeves, S. (2019). How UX practitioners produce findings in usability testing. *ACM Transactions on Computer-Human Interaction, 26*(1), 1–38.

Reeves, S., Porcheron, M., & Fischer, J. (2018). 'This is not what we wanted': Designing for conversation with voice interfaces. *Interactions, 25*(1), 46–51.

Rollet, N., & Clavel, C. (2020). "Talk to you later": Doing social robotics with conversation analysis: Towards the development of an automatic system for the prediction of disengagement. *Interaction Studies, 21*(2), 268–292.

Rossano, F., & Liebal, K. (2014). Requests' and 'offers' in orangutans and human infants. In P. Drew & E. Couper-Kuhlen (Eds.), *Requesting in social interaction* (pp. 333–362). John Benjamins.

Sacks, H. (1984). Notes on methodology. In J. M. Atkinson & J. Heritage (Eds.), *Structures of social action* (pp. 21–27). Cambridge University Press.

Sacks, H. (1992). *Lectures on conversation: Volume I*. Blackwell.

Sacks, H., & Schegloff, E. A. (1973). Opening up closings. *Semiotica, 8*(4), 289–327.

Sacks, H., & Schegloff, E. A. (2002). Home position. *Gesture, 2*(2), 133–146.

Sacks, H., Schegloff, E. A., & Jefferson, G. (1974). A simplest systematics for the organization of turn taking for conversation. *Language, 50*(4), 696–735.

Schegloff, E. A. (2007). *Sequence organization in interaction: A primer in conversation analysis I*. Cambridge University Press.

Sidnell, J. (2010). *Conversation analysis: An introduction*. Wiley-Blackwell.

Sidnell, J., & Stivers, T. (2013). *The handbook of conversation analysis.* Wiley-Blackwell.

Simone, M., & Galatolo, R. (2020). Climbing as a pair: Instructions and instructed body movements in indoor climbing with visually impaired athletes. *Journal of Pragmatics, 155,* 286–302.

Simone, M., & Galatolo, R. (2021). Timing and prosody of lexical repetition: How repeated instructions assist visually impaired athletes' navigation in sport climbing. *Research on Language and Social Interaction, 54*(4), 397–419.

Skedsmo, K. (2021). How to use comic-strip graphics to represent signed conversation. *Research on Language and Social Interaction, 54*(3), 241–260.

Sormani, P. (2014). *Respecifying lab ethnography: An ethnomethodological study of experimental physics.* Ashgate.

Stevanovic, M. (2016). Keskustelunanalyysi ja kokeellinen vuorovaikutustutkimus. In M. Stevanovic & C. Lindholm (Eds.), *Keskustelunanalyysi: Kuinka tutkia sosiaalista toimintaa ja vuorovaikutusta* (pp. 390–409). Vastapaino.

Stevanovic, M., Himberg, T., Niinisalo, M., Kahri, M., Peräkylä, A., Sams, M., &, Hari, R. (2017). Sequentiality, mutual visibility, and behavioral matching: Body sway and pitch register during joint decision making. *Research on Language and Social Interaction, 50*(1), 33–53.

Stivers, T. (2015). Coding social interaction: A heretical approach in conversation analysis? *Research on Language and Social Interaction, 48*(1), 1–19.

Streeck, J., Goodwin, C., &, LeBaron, C. (Eds.). (2011). *Embodied interaction: Language and body in the material world.* Cambridge University Press.

Stukenbrock, A., &, Dao, A. N. (2019). Joint attention in passing: What dual mobile eye tracking reveals about gaze in coordinating embodied activities at a market. In E. Reber & C. Gerhardt (Eds.), *Embodied activities in face-to-face and mediated settings* (pp. 177–213). Palgrave Macmillan.

Suchman, L. (1987). *Plans and situated action: The problem of human-machine communication.* Cambridge University Press.

Voutilainen, L., Henttonen, P., Kahri, M., Kivioja, M., Ravaja, N., Sams, M., & Peräkylä, A. (2014). Affective stance, ambivalence, and psychophysiological responses during conversational storytelling. *Journal of Pragmatics, 68,* 1–24.

Wagner, J., Pekarek Doehler, S., & González-Martínez, E. (2018). Longitudinal research on the organization of social interaction: Current developments and methodological challenges. In S. Pekarek DoehlerS.,, J. Wagner & E. González-Martínez (Eds.), *Longitudinal studies on the organization of social interaction* (pp. 3–35). Palgrave Macmillan.

Whalen, J., & Vinkhuyzen, E. (2000). Expert systems in (inter)action: diagnosing document machine problems over the telephone. In P. Luff, J. Hindmarsh & C. Heath (Eds.), *Workplace studies: Recovering work practice and informing systems design* (pp. 92–140). Cambridge University Press.

Wooffitt, R. (2007). Communication and laboratory performance in parapsychology experiments: Demand characteristics and the social organization of interaction. *British Journal of Social Psychology, 46*(3), 477–498.

PART 1

Exploring "being a member"

2

HOW TO STUDY INTERACTIONAL HISTORY IN NON-HUMAN ANIMALS? CHALLENGES AND OPPORTUNITIES

Federico Rossano

There is a special map at the Austrian National Library in Vienna, hidden from the public and protected by UNESCO: the Tabula Peutingeriana (the Peutinger Map). It is the only remaining map representing the ancient road network in the Roman Empire between the Atlantic Ocean and India. It is a parchment scroll one foot high and 22 feet long (0.3 × 6.7 metres) with an iconic resemblance to the shape of a road. It is a precursor of topological maps such as subway maps, in that it does not represent any detailed geographical information but rather depicts routes and distances between cities connected by roads. The proportions and actual geographical orientation are not precise (e.g., Italy is presented as elongated horizontally, west to east, rather than north to south). Moreover, the map does not represent the state of the road network at any specific moment in time. For example, on the map, one can simultaneously find Pompei (destroyed in 79 AD) and Constantinople (founded in 328 AD). Yet the tabula does serve its purpose: to provide information about the roads that connect different cities. What it does not show is *the process* through which those roads were built and the cities got connected, and how those roads might have changed over time. In other words, it reminds us that maps are static and timeless. Time is not part of the picture.

Similarly, several disciplines investigating human communication have traditionally investigated communicative practices as having unchangeable, timeless relationships with the social actions they stand for. Conversation Analysis is no exception (though see Deppermann & Pekarek Doehler, 2021 and Pekarek Doehler et al., 2018 for recent work on longitudinal conversation analysis). Variations are accounted via individual differences, community/cultural differences, or contextual factors that might have modified how a communicative act should be interpreted. The way communicative practices change over time is usually not

DOI: 10.4324/9781003424888-3

a concern for scholarly investigations. Moreover, when the focus is on how an individual modifies the practices used to implement the same social action, this is seen as a learning or developmental change (i.e., over time an individual matures into adulthood or becomes an expert) where there is a model that the participant is attempting to match. Variation is caused by changes that are external to the individual, in the environment.

When we look at Ethology, the study of animal behaviour, the timeline is often even longer, so that change can be detected on a phylogenetic scale, but within an individual changes are only happening because of learning. There is a correct, final action X (a *signal*) that a young member of a species is learning to reproduce: something that we could build typologies on and prepare ethograms about. To this end, any variation that does not match the final action, usually produced by an adult, is just an imperfect attempt or evidence of some trauma in the rearing of the individual.

Inspired by both Conversation Analysis and Ethology, this chapter presents an approach that aims to identify changes in the communicative practices of a non-human animal that occur within a short time frame and through repeated interactions with the same partners. The chapter contributes to the recent literature on the role of interactional histories in action formation (e.g., by Broth, 2017; Deppermann, 2018a). In recent years, the traditional focus on recipient design (the tailoring of a communicative practice to a specific audience) has been expanded to operate not just on variables such as profession, status, or relationship but also on what has been termed interactional history (the fact that the participants have had previous social interactions) and how participants orient to this shared history. Moreover, this chapter adds a new type of key subject: non-human primates (specifically, infant bonobos). This presents an opportunity and a critical challenge. The opportunity concerns expanding our current pool of possible subjects for interactional analysis. The challenge concerns determining how to properly capture the member's practices, given the impossibility for human scholars to know for a fact that a specific behaviour counts as a social action for members of that species. Being members of two different species (human vs. bonobo) represents a key barrier to the "unique adequacy requirement" (the idea that an analyst should be able to function as an ordinary member of the population studied) for ethnomethodological investigations (Garfinkel, 2002). I propose that combining Ethology and Conversation Analysis can help us meet such a challenge.

An interactionist approach to communication

At the same time in which ethologists such as Tinbergen (1963) and Hinde (1966) were inviting scholars of animal behaviour to reconcile, on the one hand, observations and experimentation and, on the other hand, evolutionary and developmental questions, scholars studying human behaviour were realising that the previous obsession with language and linguistic structures had masked the importance of what was achieved via language: communication and social interaction.

Conversation Analysis (CA) emerged in sociology in the 1960s as a micro-analytical approach to the organisation of social action in social interaction (Sacks et al., 1974; Schegloff, 2007; Sidnell & Stivers, 2012). The initial goal of CA was to create an account of how two people who do not know each other (especially in institutional settings, e.g., a therapist and a patient, a 911 dispatcher and a caller, a physician and a patient) could manage to successfully engage in social interaction and make sense of each other. Accordingly, the assumption was that human communication is orderly and that participants engage in social interaction by relying on a machinery that can be studied partly, independently of its users.

In CA, the key units are the social actions produced by participants in interaction (e.g., requesting, offering, complaining, inviting). The production of social actions usually makes relevant responsive behaviour. Even remaining silent, when responding would be relevant, can be considered a responsive action (Schegloff, 2007). The intelligibility of social action is required for the accomplishment of mutual understanding, which provides for successful engagement in cooperative interactions.

In analysing and labelling what social actions are being produced during a conversation, conversation analysts tend to adopt an *emic* perspective (a participant's perspective, see Pike, 1966), and, thus, have developed a procedure for it that has been called the "next-turn proof procedure" (Sacks et al., 1974). The claim is that the interactional nature of conversation provides an obligation among participants to display to each other their understanding of the previous conversational turn. Given the obligation for B to convey how they have understood A's prior turn, if B's turn conveys a misunderstanding of A's turn, then A can correct herself, and if no correction occurs, then the assumption should be that B has correctly understood A, and, therefore, that A's turn was aimed at eliciting the kind of response that B produced. This procedure has been labelled the "central methodological resource for the investigation of conversation" (Sacks et al., 1974, p. 728).

Erving Goffman famously rejected the idea that this proof procedure would be sufficient to account for the design and structure of social action in social interaction by raising an interesting issue: "[A]n account of second utterances in terms of their contingency on a first leaves unexplained how there could be any firsts; after all, from where could they draw their design? Conversation could never begin" (1983, p. 50). To put it differently, while one major concern in CA is to provide evidence intrinsic to the interaction that members were treating practice X as implementing social action Y, Goffman was asking the question: how did practice X come to be associated with such social action so that a participant can recognise it and make sense of it in context? How do we choose the words that we choose when we calibrate a request? Is there a specific relationship between the format of a specific communicative practice and the social action it is implementing? Goffman's concern is even more poignant when we consider the development of non-human primates' gestural communication (i.e., nonverbal communication) and the way it has been investigated up to now. Is there a direct, recognisable relationship between a hand shape or a limb movement and what it is trying to communicate? It is precisely the next-turn proof procedure that can help the analyst to gain some access to the member's perspective also in the primate data and therefore tackle the membership issue previously discussed.

Communication in great apes

Since the 1970s, much has been written on gestural and vocal communication in non-human primates, partly aiming to document the extent and flexibility of their repertoire, and partly to compare these repertoires with the evolution of language in humans. The general claim is that non-human primates' vocalisations are innate and mostly inflexible (they can partly control the intensity and when to produce vocalisations but cannot learn new ones, see Crockford et al., 2012; Schel et al., 2013; Seyfarth & Cheney, 2003) while their gestural communication is flexible, under full intentional control, and at least in part it is learned (Call & Tomasello, 2007; Halina et al., 2013; Schneider et al., 2012). Their gestural repertoire has therefore received particular attention in recent years.

The term "gesture" in non-human great apes usually includes not only *visible* behaviour (like in humans), but also *tactile* and *auditory* signals, such as touching another interactional participant's body or making noise by hitting the ground (see Call & Tomasello, 2007). Moreover, assessing what counts as a gesture as opposed to a non-communicative physical action has been widely debated and considered a key methodological problem. In addressing this issue, for example, Liebal and Call (2012) have suggested that visible gestures and physical actions are not discrete categories but may in fact be arranged on a continuum. Certain features – such as mechanical ineffectiveness, gazing at each other, and waiting for a response – can help determine where on this continuum between action and gesture certain behaviours may lie.

Previous studies on gestural communication in great apes have focused on establishing the gestural "lexicon" for each species (i.e., the number and type of different gestures produced within a species) rather than "grammars" of their communicative behaviours (e.g., Call & Tomasello, 2007; Cartmill & Byrne, 2010; Genty et al., 2009; Graham et al., 2016; Hobaiter & Byrne, 2014;). Lexicons have been investigated by identifying specific behavioural forms that could count as signals and then inferring their functions by looking at their general context of use. In most previous studies, contexts of use have been categorised very broadly as sex, travel, nursing, feeding, play, agonistic (e.g., fighting), and affiliative (e.g., grooming) (e.g., Call & Tomasello, 2007; Genty et al., 2009; Pika et al., 2005), and the claim is that all social actions of great apes can be characterised according to these categories or functions.

More recently, Hobaiter and Byrne (2014) have focused on the meaning of gestural signals by relying on what they have called an "apparently satisfactory outcome" (ASO). The idea is that if the response to a signal was not satisfactory, the signaller would pursue the original intended goal and convey that the response obtained was inadequate. The outcome of the gesture (i.e., the response of the recipient) becomes the meaning of the gesture. The focus is on the signaller, who has to appear satisfied by the response. This approach also does not consider that a lack of a response might count as a sufficient response on some occasions (i.e., it could count as a "no" signal). More generally, this approach does not consider whether the behaviour of the other participant is simply stochastic (i.e., it coincidentally just happens next, like it would be in human interaction if B started drinking a glass of water after A had said "I am tired") or whether it is an appropriate second pair part to the initial first pair part (i.e., like it would be in human interaction if B provided a glass of water after A's "I am thirsty") (see Mondeme, 2022 and Schegloff, 2007 on the issue of "nextness").

This simplification arises when starting from forms and inferring functions, rather than from the specific social activities primates engage in and the social goals they try to achieve, and then identifying how those activities are initiated and negotiated via embodied communicative behaviour. Recent work has begun to move in the latter direction by focusing on primates' behaviour within a singular activity: co-locomotion via ventral or dorsal carry (Fröhlich et al., 2016a; Halina et al., 2013; Hutchins & Johnson, 2009), engagement in social play (Fröhlich et al., 2016b), or reciprocal greetings (Luef & Pika, 2017). Yet there has been no longitudinal investigation on gesture development, specifically assessing signal change over time, or the developmental relationship of different signals (i.e., whether signals are independent of each other, or rather that a signal developed through the modification of another one). While signal repertoires for each social action have been identified and data has been collected over weeks, or even months, the general goal of these studies has not been to investigate how individuals modify their signals over time. Rather, the aim of extended data collection has been to give the authors more chances to capture the full repertoire of the individuals observed.

There is an open debate about how gestures develop in great apes and how likely it is that most of their gestures are innate or learnt. Scholars who support the *biological inheritance hypothesis* suggest that the gestural repertoire of great apes is genetically pre-determined (Byrne et al., 2017; Genty et al., 2009; Graham et al., 2016; Hobaiter & Byrne, 2011), while those who support the *ontogenetic ritualisation hypothesis* posit that gestures are progressively ritualised through repeated dyadic interactions and that individual repertoires may vary (Halina et al., 2013; Tomasello et al., 1994; Tomasello et al., 1997). A third hypothesis, *the cultural learning hypothesis*, suggests that gestures are acquired by imitating those of others in the group (Russon & Galdikas, 1993; Tanner et al., 2006); however, there is no clear empirical support for this claim given the poor imitative skills of non-human primates (Tennie et al., 2006).

The actual interactional dynamics that lead to "ontogenetic ritualisation" remain hypotheses, with no empirical evidence. There is no detailed investigation of change, if not to say that at age X the apes do Y and at age X + Number of months, the same apes do Y and Z. The main reason for this gap in the literature is that scholars do not collect sufficient longitudinal video data at each age to capture enough instances of the same activities and the gestures that initiate them. The vast majority of studies rely on data amounting to 10–25 hours of video data of focal sampling per subject over many months, often collected in bouts of 3–4 hours on a single day, and each bout of focal data collection might be separated by weeks, or even months.

By showing how gestures can change through time, this paper aims to highlight ways of investigating how communicative practices change over time and to expand the notion of longitudinal change and interactional histories to social interactions between non-human animals. The proposal is to focus on the sequential unfolding of a communicative exchange between two primates and acknowledge that for animals that live together and communicate on a daily basis, interactional histories are likely to play a critical role in the calibration of communicative acts. While the scholar has no direct access to the animal's internal representations of what is going on (i.e., the member's perspective), it is possible to rely on behavioural displays to reconstruct how the animal is possibly interpreting the situation. As such, we can rely on the structure of social interaction to gain some insights into non-human animals' perspectives, and therefore expand the EMCA pool of potential subjects of empirical investigations.

Data

The following examples come from a larger project developed by Halina et al. (2013) that analysed 1173 infant carries in 410 hours of video recordings of ten different mother–infant bonobo dyads from six different zoos, during the infants' second year of life. Specifically, Halina et al. investigated these data in terms of actions and gestures leading to mother–infant carries and showed that, in each dyad, infants had developed a variable number of gesture types through ontogenetic ritualisation to get the mothers to engage in a carry. This study provided three key pieces of evidence in support of ontogenetic ritualisation:

1) Idiosyncratic gestures existed in the infant primates' repertoire.
2) The gesture types were correlated with the role played by that individual in that interaction (i.e., mother and infant gestures were not the same).
3) Different individuals showed partly different gestural repertoires.

Crucially, Halina et al.'s study did not provide evidence that the gestural signals change over time. Evidence of change over time is the goal of this chapter.

Carries in bonobos

Engaging in a carry in non-human primates can be considered a joint action (Clark, 1996), whereby each participant plays a specific role in bringing the action about. For example, the infant usually holds onto the mother's body while the mother moves, which is different from human infants. Nonetheless, a carry does not always play out as a ratified joint action. Indeed, mothers can force infants into a carry by grabbing them and holding them onto their venter with one arm. The opposite situation is not possible; that is, an infant cannot force the mother into a carry. This makes it particularly interesting to investigate asymmetric roles in these interactions, because if the infant wants to move, then s/he is posed with the problem of how to get the mother to engage in a carry. In general, carries are a frequent means for co-locomotion through the environment (on average, carries occur about five times per hour, see Halina et al., 2013).

Considering the body configuration that allows the baby to be carried around by the mother, either ventrally or dorsally, there are a few key features relevant to the following analysis:

1) The baby tends to hold onto the mother's hair by grabbing her hair on both sides of the body, a few inches below the mother's armpits.
2) The baby's arms are usually open wide and extended while holding onto the mother's body, in a hugging position.
3) The baby's legs are similarly open wide and wrapped around the mother's body.

In this paper, I show examples of infant requests to be carried that are performed by two female bonobos (L and K) in their second year of life. (They are representative of practices identified in other dyads.) All infants were born and live in captivity (L at Leipzig Zoo and K at San Diego Zoo) and were raised by their own mothers. As to L, the extracts come from 36 hours of data (122 carry events), and K's come from 29 hours of data (137 carry events). In the following analysis, the sequence-initiating move by the infant (i.e., the first sequential attempt to elicit a carry) will be considered the base First Pair Part (FPP). On the other hand, the behavioural response by the mother that makes the carry possible will be considered the Second Pair Part (SPP). Usually, the SPP involves the mother approaching the infant, placing a hand/arm behind the infant's back, slightly scooping her up, and getting up from the ground before the carry is actually performed.

All instances have been identified not by searching for specific gestures but by identifying instances of successful carries and then analysing the behavioural moves by both participants that led to the successful achievement of the joint activity. From a CA perspective, what I am suggesting here corresponds to what some scholars have done by focusing on social actions and attempting to identify different ways in which these actions can be accomplished in conversation (e.g., Golato [2005] on compliments; Fox & Heinemann [2017] on requests; Pillet-Shore [2012] on greetings).

In what follows, I present examples of two mechanisms that lead to the formation of communicative signals by which baby bonobos request to be carried. They are:

1) Originally responsive action produced in the first position
2) Shortening and speeding up

Originally responsive action produced in the first position

A way of developing a gesture consists of using a responsive behaviour (SPP) in the first position (i.e., as an FPP). Rossano and Liebal (2014) have shown how a male orangutan offers food to the females using behaviour that is identical to previous behaviour he used when giving them food after they had requested it. In other words, behaviourally, an offer corresponds to the SPP to a request. This suggests that requests came first compared to offers from a gesture development point of view.

Without using CA terminology on sequence organisation, Lock (1978) has similarly analysed the development of the arm raise signal in human infants that they use to request to be picked up by a caregiver. Lock describes the lifting of the arms by the infant as an initially responsive action that then begins to be produced in anticipation when the mother moves towards picking up the baby, and ultimately is produced in pursuit of the goal of being picked up (i.e., as a request). While recent CA work on how caregivers pick up and carry young children has highlighted different ways in which the initiation, the carry proper, and the release are implemented (see Cekaite et al., 2021), this study focuses solely on the initiation and the communicative practices deployed that allow the two bodies of mother and infant come together to initiate a carry.

In Excerpt 1, the carry is initiated by the mother via a present venter gesture (see Halina et al., 2013), yet what we are interested in is the way infant L responds to the gesture behaviourally.

1) Open legs in second position: Infant L

In Figure 2.1a, the mother is standing on a branch, leaning slightly backwards, facing, and displaying her venter towards L. Presenting her venter while looking at the infant is one way in which the mother can invite the infant to get on her venter, to then be carried (the FPP). L responds to this by moving towards the mother while holding onto a rope with her upper arms. In order to propel herself forward, L approaches the mother while opening her legs wide apart and swinging from a rope. Once in proximity to the mother's body, L opens her legs wide while looking at the mother, and then wraps her legs around the mother's body (1c). The key point here is that at this point, the opening of the legs is not a gesture. Indeed,

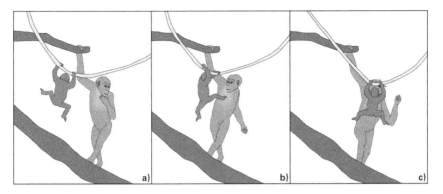

FIGURE 2.1 The infant spreads her legs in response to the mother's present venter gesture.

it is used both while moving through space to get to the mother faster, and most importantly it is the last behavioural move implemented in order for the infant to wrap her legs around the mother's body while holding her hands onto a rope.

In Excerpt 2, we can see how L initiates a carry sequence through an arm raise gesture but opens her legs wide in anticipation of the mother's arrival to pick her up.

2) Open legs in anticipation: Infant L

Figure 2.2a begins with L and the mother looking at each other across a distance of about three metres. L begins moving towards the mother and extends her right arm towards the mother to request to be carried (FPP). The mother begins moving forward towards L, whereupon L spreads her legs wide open (see 2a) in

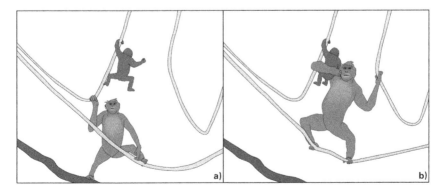

FIGURE 2.2 Infant spreads her legs in anticipation of the mother's arrival (to then carry her away).

anticipation of the mother's approach. Differently from the previous example, at the time L spreads her legs, L is no longer using the rope to propel herself; rather she is static and still holding her right arm extended towards the mother (see 2a). Furthermore, the mother is not directly in front of L when L spreads her legs open but still a couple of metres away. Indeed, the mother ends up grabbing L's entire body with her right arm (see 2b) rather than letting L wrap her legs onto her venter. The spreading of the legs, crucially, does not occur as part of L's responsive action (SPP) since L is the one actually requesting to be carried. Instead, L spreads her legs simultaneously with the mother's responsive move (to L's reach to be carried), in anticipation of the interlocking of the bodies needed for the carry to occur.

In Excerpt 3, we can see how the spreading of the legs while looking at the mother ultimately gets used in the first position by L to request to get carried.

3) Spread legs in first position: Infant L

The mother is sitting on a branch holding another branch with her right hand, while L begins to move down a rope towards her. The mother is not looking at L, and seems to be in a resting position. By the time L stops in front of the mother, the mother is looking away, towards her left side, while holding her knees bent in front of her venter (i.e., making it impossible for L to simply climb on or wrap her legs onto her venter). L is holding onto a rope and has already begun to spread her legs by the time she positions herself in front of the mother. Instead of stopping the signal and moving into the line of sight of the mother, L holds the leg spread signal (Figure 2.3a) for 2.5 seconds while also looking towards the mother. L persists until the mother engages in a carry. Note that L's body configuration requires sustained effort since it involves keeping the legs both lifted and spread while directing them (and her gaze) towards the mother (Figure 2.3a).

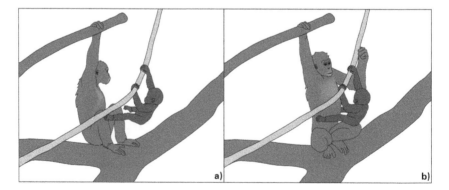

FIGURE 2.3 The infant spreads her legs in first position and waits until the mother can perceive the signal and respond with a carry.

Excerpts 1–3 show how behaviour that was originally part of the responsive actions performed by the infant bonobo evolved into a first position move across time. The transformation occurred when the mother began to anticipate and orient to L's responsive behaviour, and then L realised that she, herself, could initiate and elicit a carry by producing, in first position, her responsive behaviour. The time that passed between Excerpts 1 and 3 was three weeks. Thus, in less than a month, a behaviour that was not used to elicit a carry becomes a reliable intentional signal within this dyad. Notably, in the 36 hours of footage investigated for this dyad, there is no evidence of the existence of the gesture produced in Excerpt 3 until the date on which Excerpt 3 was documented. Interestingly, the steps through which this process occurred mirror those that have been claimed to take place for human infants' gesture of raising their arms to be picked up (Lock, 1978).

Shortening and speeding up

There is a second mechanism for the change of a communicative practice that can be identified within the bonobo data: shortening and speeding up. It consists of a series of steps outlined Excerpts 4–7, which take place over the course of 25 days. It ultimately leads to the development of an idiosyncratic signal (a spin) that is used by the infant to request to be carried and on the surface appears completely arbitrary. By looking at the longitudinal data and relying on the method previously outlined (i.e., starting from the activity the animals successfully engage in [e.g., a carry] and going back in time to look at the behaviours used to achieve that), it is instead possible to show how the spin gesture develops through the modification of a sequence of instrumental actions previously deployed by the same infant to elicit a carry.

4) Moving out, turning, moving back, and touching side: Infant K

In Figure 2.4a, while the mother monitors K, K begins moving away. After about three steps, K turns around and moves back towards the mother (Figure 2.4b), while raising her right arm (Figure 2.4c). It appears that K is moving her arm to touch/grab the mother's side. While doing so, the mother simultaneously moves her hand towards K's back and begins pulling K closer to her while K is touching the mother's side (Figure 2.4d). Ultimately, K lifts herself up to the mother's venter and the mother begins the carry. In this example, the actual signal is the moving towards the mother while reaching towards her side. Yet, the walking out and then turning to monitor the mother's behaviour could be interpreted already as a desire to move in a specific direction. Indeed, when the mother carries K, she moves in the same direction in which K was headed when initially moving away from the mother (Figure 2.4a).

Excerpt 5 shows the first shortening of the original sequence of behaviours performed by K to solicit a carry.

FIGURE 2.4   Infant K moves out, turns, returns to the mother, and begins the touch side
gesture to elicit a carry.

5) Moving out, turning, not coming back: Infant K

Following the movement of another adult female that was originally sitting beside
the mother and K, K moves one step in front of the mother (Figure 2.5a). After
the step, K turns towards the mother (Figure 2.5b) and looks at her (Figure 2.5c).

FIGURE 2.5   Infant K moves out, turns, but does not return to the mother and rather
waits for the mother to pick her up.

Before K moves further, the mother begins moving towards K and grabs her
back, pulling K towards herself (i.e., conveying that the mother is going to carry
her). K gets on the mother's venter (Figure 2.5e), and the mother follows the path
of the adult female that was previously sitting beside them. In this excerpt, the
infant's original moving out by three steps (as seen in Excerpt 4) and then returning towards the mother to touch/grab her side is now reduced to moving out only
one step and not moving back towards the mother. The key behaviour that so far is
conserved across time, and that signals to the mother the infant's wish to be carried is the first moving out in front of the mother and then turning.

Excerpt 6 shows how this two-step process (first moving and then turning) is further transformed and condensed.

6) Turning while moving out: Infant K

K begins to turn while simultaneously moving out in front of the mother (Figures 2.6a and 2.6b). In other words, the infant collapses the original two steps – moving out and then turning to monitor the mother – into a single movement, where the boundary between the two steps as seen in the previous two excerpts is less clear.

FIGURE 2.6 Infant K turns while moving out and produces a slow spin.

The articulation of the signal is not completely smooth and the moving out is still noticeable, only the turning begins while the infant throws herself out. The mother moves her arm to tap the infant's back before the infant has completed the spin (6c and 6e), and the infant gets onto the mother's venter while the mother begins the carry.

In Excerpt 7, we can see the final gesture emerging from the shortening and speeding up of the steps initially present in Excerpt 4. Only 25 days have gone by between Excerpts 4 and 7.

7) The spin: Infant K

K is already sitting in front of the mother when another female that was sitting beside the mother begins to move away (Figure 2.7a). K produces a 360° spin that brings her back to the same position (Figures 2.7b–2.7c), in front of the mother. While continuing to look at the mother, K waits for approximately one second for the mother to respond. The mother then leans forward towards K, and raises herself off the ground while placing her right hand on K's back (Figure 2.7d), thus, engaging in a carry (Figure 2.7e). While carrying K, the mother now moves in the same direction as the other female. K's spinning move has successfully garnered the mother's carry through the smooth spinning. However, without the steps moving out in a specific direction, K's move seems to lose the indexical (directional) information concerning the desired course of movement, which was evident in Excerpts 4 and 5, and partly, also, in Excerpt 6. A mere spin in front of the mother simply leads to the mother's forward movement (or the recent direction and movement of other adult females).

In sum, Excerpts 4–7 illustrate the steps through which K's spin gesture emerges via ritualisation:

1) Excerpt 4: moving out 3 steps, turning, returning to mother, touching side;
2) Excerpt 5: moving out 1 step, turning, not moving back;
3) Excerpt 6: combining moving out and turning into a single action in slow motion turn; and
4) Excerpt 7: first looking at the mother, then producing a 360° spin, then waiting for a response.

The spin, therefore, is not an arbitrary signal developed by K but a contraction and speeding up of the previous steps that she had used to solicit a successful carry. This process is analogous to what was described by Deppermann (2018b), concerning instructions in driving lessons that over time become shorter, less complex, and more condensed. Critically, the contraction of the signal is not done by the infant in a vacuum; rather, she relies on the mother's ability to project what she is trying to accomplish/communicate and to cooperatively respond by granting such request (Rossano, 2018). Without the mother's inferential projection, the

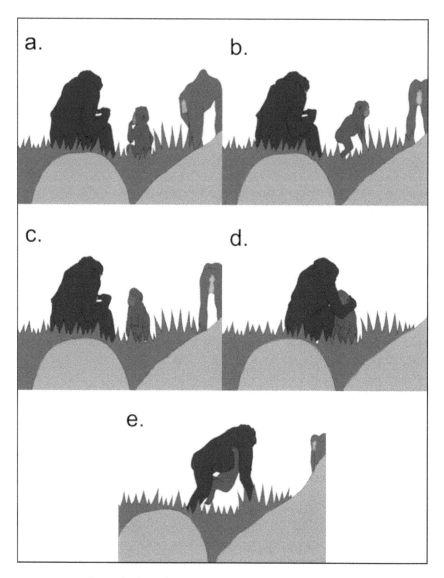

FIGURE 2.7   Infant K looks at the mother, produces a spin and then waits for a response from the mother.

communicative practice could not be compressed because the recipient would systematically fail to respond to any behaviour different from the original one. Similar to the first practice, the time that the process of ritualisation takes in bonobos is rather brief. The recordings of Excerpts 4 and 7 are 25 days apart, and Excerpts 5 and 7 only 11 days apart. In other words, the transformative process through which the spin signal emerges does not require an extensive amount of time.

Discussion

In this paper, I have relied on sequence organisation and next-turn proof procedure as two key tools to analyse not only how animals communicate, but also how their communicative signals might change over time. As shown, they provide access to the participant's perspective also in the primate data. By applying a CA perspective, I have shown how communicative gestures that infant bonobos use to request their mothers to carry them change over time, and through repeated interactions, becoming part of their interactional history. In particular, I have outlined two mechanisms through which behavioural practices can change while retaining some similarities with the original behaviour produced by the same individuals: 1) Responsive action produced in the first position, and 2) Shortening and speeding up. This is not an exhaustive list and most likely other mechanisms exist.

I have also shown how the process through which a responsive behaviour transforms into an initiating action does not require months or years, but rather a few weeks at most. The estimate is likely exaggerated since we did not collect data 24 hours a day; therefore, it is possible that the signal became ritualised even faster. The finding that ritualisation takes three weeks or less within the context of carry is critical because it addresses recent criticisms (e.g., Byrne et al., 2017) about the implausibility of ontogenetic ritualisation as a mechanism to acquire new gestures, given how long it would take to do so.

This study does not meet the criteria for investigating interactional histories (Deppermann, 2018a), that is, to capture interactions "from the beginning without a gap". Yet, the analysis builds on a significantly broader dataset focusing on the same individuals than any other prior study on gesture development in non-human primates. The current standard of collecting primate data has proven prohibitive to fully capturing the process of behavioural change. Primate data is often biased towards live observations and the use of ethograms (at the expense of video recordings), and even when video recordings are made, they are usually not collected on a daily basis but sporadically, for limited durations. Thus, it should not be too surprising that the methodological constraints of the current standard for data collection have hindered the possibility to fully capture behaviour that is malleable and quickly transforming. As we have long learned from the notion of recipient design (Sacks et al., 1974), the psycholinguistic work on lexical choice by Brennan and Clark (1996) and the work by Schegloff (1986) on the routine as achievement, repeated interactions with familiar others affect the way we communicate and calibrate our signals. The knowledge of who we are for each other and what we know about each other affects the signal selection, especially if the interaction is a routine one.

This study proposes a new perspective to the study of interactional histories. Instead of detecting a practice in earlier interactions and tracking how it changes over time, here we propose to start from activities (i.e., social actions) and look backwards to identify the behavioural practices that could have been used to implement them (for a similar type of analysis, see Skogmyr Marian, 2021 on complaints in L2). This is in contrast to the strategy of starting from behavioural forms, and then inferring which social actions they are implementing (relying on the next-turn proof procedure). Taking seriously Goffman's (1983) concern about the origin of the design of first turns means identifying all possible signals that a non-human primate can rely on to elicit a specific response, and figuring out what factors affect their implementation. Taking Goffman's remark seriously also means attempting to identify the history of a signal, its origins and development, and integrating it with the relational history of the interacting individuals. This would allow us to see and identify the origins of the signal's design and what is necessary for its development.

Furthermore, this work has important implications for the study of communicative development in human infants. Apart from the work by Lock (1978) and Clark (1978) and the original work on gesture acquisition in young infants (Bates et al., 1975), the focus of psychological research on human infants' remarkable imitative abilities (Gergely et al., 2002; Meltzoff, 1995) has led to a general neglect of alternative ways of learning and developing communicative signals in children (see, however, Cekaite, 2007; Gardner & Forrester, 2009; and Wootton, 1997, for exceptions). A recent article by Marentette and Nicoladis (2012), for example, has failed to find evidence for ontogenetic ritualisation in the gestural development of human infants less than one year old. Unfortunately, methodologically, their study corresponds to existing research on non-human primate gestures: they used infrequent and short recordings collected every few weeks and a coding scheme that looks for fully formed gestures to begin with, rather than starting from social activities and looking backwards at the non-gesture-like behaviours that the infants produced to elicit the social activities.

As to current questions in the CA community, this study reminds us that building typologies of social actions or practices should not come at the cost of detecting how actions and practices change. They might change because the individuals change (e.g., individuals grow older and their ability to communicate transforms) or because the relational history between interactional partners affects the recognisability of specific behaviours, facilitating ritualisation and the use of idiosyncratic expressions. The ability to make sense of each other while using modified communicative practices is one of the key reasons investigating interactional histories is gaining popularity within the field (e.g., Deppermann & Pekarek Doehler, 2021). We can now aim at tracking their role in the calibration of communicative practices also in non-human primates.

Acknowledgements

I want to thank the Wolfgang Köhler Primate Research Centre and Christine Johnson for generously allowing me to access their video data for the purpose of this project and Marike Schreiber, Catherine Eng and Paulina Lee for producing the drawings contained in this paper. I also want to thank Marta Halina for the many helpful discussions about gestures in primates and carries in bonobos.

References

Bates, E., Camaioni, L., & Volterra, V. (1975). The acquisition of performatives prior to speech. *Merrill-Palmer Quarterly of Behavior and Development, 21*(3), 205–226.

Brennan, S. E., & Clark, H. H. (1996). Conceptual pacts and lexical choice in conversation. *Journal of Experimental Psychology: Learning, Memory, and Cognition, 22*(6), 1482.

Broth, M. (2017). Starting out as a driver: Progression in instructed pedal work. In Å. Mäkitalo, P. Linell, & R. Säljö (Eds.), *Memory practices and learning: Interactional, institutional and sociocultural perspectives* (pp. 115–152). Information Age Publishing.

Byrne, R. W., Cartmill, E., Genty, E., Graham, K. E., Hobaiter, C., & Tanner, J. (2017). Great ape gestures: Intentional communication with a rich set of innate signals. *Animal Cognition, 20,* 755-769.

Call, J., & Tomasello, M. (2007). *The gestural communication of apes and monkeys.* Lawrence Erlbaum Associates.

Cartmill, E. A., & Byrne, R. W. (2010). Semantics of primate gestures: Intentional meanings of orangutan gestures. *Animal Cognition, 13*(6), 793–804.

Cekaite, A. (2007). A child's development of interactional competence in a Swedish L2 classroom. *The Modern Language Journal, 91*(1), 45–62.

Cekaite, A., Keisanen, T., Rauniomaa, M., & Siitonen, P. (2021). Human-assisted mobility as an interactional accomplishment. *Gesprächsforschung - Online-Zeitschrift zur Verbalen Interaktion, 2,* 469–475.

Clark, H. H. (1996). *Using language.* Cambridge University Press.

Clark, R. A. (1978). The transition from action to gesture. In A.E. Lock (Ed.), *Action, gesture and symbol* (pp. 231-257). Academic Press.

Crockford, C., Wittig, R. M., Mundry, R., & Zuberbuehler, K. (2012). Wild chimpanzees inform ignorant group members of danger. *Current Biology, 22*(2), 142–146.

Deppermann, A. (2018a). Changes in turn-design over interactional histories - The case of instructions in driving school lessons. In A. Deppermann & J. Streeck (Eds.), *Time in embodied interaction: Synchronicity and sequentiality of multimodal resources* (pp. 293–324). John Benjamins.

Deppermann, A. (2018b). Instruction practices in German driving lessons: Differential uses of declaratives and imperatives. *International Journal of Applied Linguistics, 28*(2), 265–282.

Deppermann, A., & Pekarek Doehler, S. (2021). Longitudinal conversation analysis-introduction to the special issue. *Research on Language and Social Interaction, 54*(2), 127–141.

Fox, B. A., & Heinemann, T. (2017). Issues in action formation: Requests and the problem with x. *Open Linguistics, 3*(1), 31–64.

Fröhlich, M., Wittig, R. M., & Pika, S. (2016a). Should I stay or should I go? Initiation of joint travel in mother–infant dyads of two chimpanzee communities in the wild. *Animal Cognition, 19*(3), 483–500.

Fröhlich, M., Wittig, R. M., & Pika, S. (2016b). Play-solicitation gestures in chimpanzees in the wild: Flexible adjustment to social circumstances and individual matrices. *Open Science, 3*(8), 160278.

Gardner, H., & Forrester, M. (Eds.). (2009). *Analysing interactions in childhood: Insights from conversation analysis.* John Wiley & Sons.

Garfinkel, H. (2002). *Ethnomethodology's program: Working out Durkheim's aphorism.* Rowman & Littlefield.

Genty, E., Breuer, T., Hobaiter, C., & Byrne, R. W. (2009). Gestural communication of the gorilla (Gorilla gorilla): Repertoire, intentionality and possible origins. *Animal Cognition, 12*(3), 527–546.

Gergely, G., Bekkering, H., & Király, I. (2002). Developmental psychology: Rational imitation in preverbal infants. *Nature, 415*(6873), 755–755.

Goffman, E. (1983). Felicity's condition. *American Journal of Sociology, 89*(1), 1–53.

Golato, A. (2005). *Compliments and compliment responses: Grammatical structure and sequential organization.* John Benjamins.

Graham, K. E., Furuichi, T., & Byrne, R. W. (2016). The gestural repertoire of the wild bonobo (Pan paniscus): A mutually understood communication system. *Animal Cognition, 20*(2), 171–177.

Halina, M., Rossano, F., & Tomasello, M. (2013). The ontogenetic ritualization of bonobo gestures. *Animal Cognition, 16*(4), 653–666.

Hinde, R. A. (1966). *Animal behavior: A synthesis of ethology and comparative psychology.* McGraw-Hill.

Hobaiter, C., & Byrne, R. W. (2011). The gestural repertoire of the wild chimpanzee. *Animal Cognition, 14*(5), 745–767.

Hobaiter, C., & Byrne, R. W. (2014). The meanings of chimpanzee gestures. *Current Biology, 24*(14), 1596–1600.

Hutchins, E., & Johnson, C. M. (2009). Modeling the emergence of language as an embodied collective cognitive activity. *Topics in Cognitive Science, 1*(3), 523–546.

Liebal, K., & Call, J. (2012). The origins of hon-human primates' manual gestures. *Philosophical Transactions of the Royal Society of London Series B, 367*(1585), 118–128.

Lock, A. (1978). The emergence of language. In A. Lock (Ed.), *Action, gesture and symbol: The emergence of language* (pp. 1–21). Academic Press.

Luef, E. M., & Pika, S. (2017). Reciprocal greeting in chimpanzees (Pan troglodytes) at the Ngogo community. *Journal of Neurolinguistics, 43*, 263–273.

Marentette, P., & Nicoladis, E. (2012). Does ontogenetic ritualization explain early communicative gestures in human infants. *Developments in Primate Gesture Research, 6*, 33.

Meltzoff, A. N. (1995). Understanding the intentions of others: Re-enactment of intended acts by 18-month-old children. *Developmental Psychology, 31*(5), 838.

Mondémé, C. (2022). Why study turn-taking sequences in interspecies interactions? *Journal for the Theory of Social Behaviour, 52*(1), 67–85.

Pekarek Doehler, S., Wagner, J., & González-Martínez, E. (Eds.). (2018). *Longitudinal studies on the organization of social interaction.* Palgrave Macmillan.

Pika, S., Liebal, K., & Tomasello, M. (2005). Gestural communication in subadult bonobos (Pan paniscus): Repertoire and use. *American Journal of Primatology, 65*(1), 39–61.

Pike, K. L. (1966). Etic and emic standpoints for the description of behaviour. In A. G. Smith (Ed.), *Communication and culture* (pp. 152–163). Holt Rinehart & Winston.

Pillet-Shore, D. (2012). Greeting: Displaying stance through prosodic recipient design. *Research on Language and Social Interaction, 45*(4), 375–398.

Rossano, F. (2018). Social manipulation, turn-taking and cooperation in apes: Implications for the evolution of language-based interaction in humans. *Interaction Studies, 19*(1–2), 151–166.

Rossano, F., & Liebal, K. (2014). Requests' and 'offers' in orangutans and human infants. In P. Drew & E. Couper-Kuhlen (Eds.), *Requesting in social interaction* (pp. 333–362). John Benjamins.

Russon, A. E., & Galdikas, B. M. (1993). Imitation in free-ranging rehabilitant orangutans (Pongo pygmaeus). *Journal of Comparative Psychology, 107*(2), 147–147.

Sacks, H., Schegloff, E. A., & Jefferson, G. (1974). A simplest systematics for the organization of turn-taking for conversation. *Language, 50*(4), 696–735.

Schegloff, E. A. (1986). The routine as achievement. *Human Studies, 9*(2–3), 111–151.

Schegloff, E. A. (2007). *Sequence organization in interaction: A primer in conversation analysis.* Cambridge University Press.

Schel, A. M., Machanda, Z., Townsend, S. W., Zuberbuhler, K., & Slocombe, K. E. (2013). Chimpanzee food calls are directed at specific individuals. *Animal Behaviour, 86*(5), 955–965.

Schneider, C., Call, C., & Liebal, K. (2012). What role do mothers play in the gestural acquisition of bonobos (Pan paniscus) and chimpanzees (Pan troglodytes). *International Journal of Primatology, 33*(1), 246–262.

Seyfarth, R. M., & Cheney, D. L. (2003). Signalers and receivers in animal communication. *Annual Review of Psychology, 54*, 145–173.

Sidnell, J., & Stivers, T. (Eds.). (2012). *The handbook of conversation analysis.* John Wiley & Sons.

Skogmyr Marian, K. (2021). Initiating a complaint: Change over time in French L2 speakers' practices. *Research on Language and Social Interaction, 54*(2), 163–182.

Tanner, J. E., Patterson, F. G., & Byrne, R. W. (2006). The development of spontaneous gestures in zoo-living gorillas and sign-taught gorillas: From action and location to object representation. *Journal of Developmental Processes, 1*, 69–102.

Tennie, C., Call, J., & Tomasello, M. (2006). Push or pull: Imitation vs. emulation in great apes and human children. *Ethology, 112*(12), 1159–1169.

Tinbergen, N. (1963). On aims and methods of ethology. *Ethology, 20*(4), 410–433.

Tomasello, M., Call, J., Nagell, C., Olguin, R., & Carpenter, M. (1994). The learning and use of gestural signals by young chimpanzees: A trans-generational study. *Primates, 35*(2), 137–154.

Tomasello, M., Call, J., Warren, J., Frost, G. T., Carpenter, M., & Nagell, K. (1997). The ontogeny of chimpanzee gestural signals: A comparison across groups and generations. *Evolution of Communication, 1*(2), 223–259.

Wootton, A. J. (1997). *Interaction and the development of mind.* Cambridge University Press.

3

TRANSCRIBING HUMAN–ROBOT INTERACTION

Methodological implications of participating machines

Hannah Pelikan

Introduction

Transcription is a crucial part of the workflow in the ethnomethodological and conversation analytic (EMCA) tradition, as it supports re-inspection and re-analysis of the data (Laurier, 2014). Besides standard practices for transcribing speech (Jefferson, 2004; Selting et al., 2011) and multimodal and embodied actions (Mondada, 2019), EMCA researchers have developed practices for representing interaction with material artefacts and interaction in complex (technological) environments (see e.g., Laurier & Reeves, 2014; Licoppe et al., 2017; Luff et al., 2013). While robots are increasingly gaining interest within the EMCA community (see e.g., Alač et al., 2011; Due et al., 2019; Fischer, 2016; Pelikan & Broth, 2016; Pitsch, 2016; Tuncer et al., 2023; Yamazaki et al., 2010), to date there is no systematic discussion of how to transcribe human–robot interaction. Should robot behaviour be transcribed like that of humans or of material objects? What adjustments and considerations may be necessary to capture the differences between humans and robots? What does transcription tell us about the interactional status of a robot?

Since "transcribing is an analytic process" (Roberts, 2012, p. 1), it is necessarily shaped and informed by the theoretical and subjective goals of the researcher (see e.g., Bucholtz, 2000; Jenks, 2013; Ochs, 1979). In the case of robots, it may matter considerably whether one is interested in how humans interact in the presence of a robot or whether one is focusing on the robot as a potential participant (Goffman, 1981; Goodwin & Goodwin, 2005) in interaction. In line with common definitions in robotics (see e.g., Bekey, 2005), I define robots as physically embodied machines that can sense and act in the material world with a degree of autonomy. As this opens opportunities for joint actions, this chapter will focus

DOI: 10.4324/9781003424888-4

on robots as potential participants, rather than mere tools. Gesturing, turning their heads, and sometimes even speaking, robots may appear to behave similarly to humans. At the same time, they are not acting independently but animate (Goffman, 1981) what human programmers and interaction designers instructed them to do. Their interactional possibilities are crucially shaped by their sensors and actuators. Sometimes, a robot cannot provide an appropriate next turn because it has not detected a relevant aspect of the interaction or because the required action is not part of its behavioural repertoire. Transcribing robots' interactional moves helps to shed light on their interactional role and dynamically changing participation status.

Drawing on studies with robots in lab, home, and public settings, this chapter highlights how aspects of the EMCA transcription process need to be adjusted when studying robots in social interaction. I start by illustrating how multimodal robot behaviour can be transcribed, particularly focusing on non-lexical sounds, its auditory means beyond speech. Subsequently, I discuss how to represent "repeated" actions, and how to strike a balance between the script that gives rise to robot behaviour and its situated interpretation by human participants. Moving towards analysis, I demonstrate how the next-turn proof procedure (Sacks et al., 1974) may reveal differences in how humans and robots understand previous actions. I show how humans *scaffold* robots by setting up sequential contexts in which robot actions appear as relevant and by adapting their actions to a machine-recognisable format, making up for the robots' limited interactional abilities. The chapter makes two major contributions: First, it reflects on how to transcribe video recordings of human–robot interaction from an EMCA perspective. Second, it illustrates how detailed transcription can shed light on the role that robots take in interaction, necessarily as more or less scaffolded participants.

Transcribing interaction with technology

EMCA has had an affinity for technology since the early days. Technical equipment plays a crucial role in documenting interaction (see e.g., Broth et al., 2014) and increasingly also in automated transcription (Housley et al., 2019; Moore, 2015). More importantly, technology often takes a constitutive role in the studied activity, such as when participants interact over the phone (see e.g., Garfinkel & Wieder, 1992; Schegloff, 1968), or through video calls (see e.g., Gan et al., 2020; Licoppe et al., 2017).

Studying human–robot interaction, the analytical interest focuses on how humans interact with a particular robot. One may argue that, like for interactions involving material objects, machine conduct should only be transcribed when participants orient to it. However, as Lucy Suchman (1987/2007) demonstrates in her work on interaction with copying machines, careful transcription of both human and machine actions may lead to new insights about the status of these machines and can uncover potential sources of trouble and misunderstanding. Suchman

(1987/2007) transcribes machine actions carefully, but in addition to *machine effects available to the user* she also includes the *design rationale* in her transcripts. Further, she distinguishes participants' actions into *user actions available to the machine* and *user actions not available to the machine*. Suchman (1987/2007, p. 123) argues that "the framework proved invaluable for taking seriously the idea that user and machine were interacting". In other words, to study interaction between humans and robots, it may be necessary to consider the robot's perspective to identify where "mutual intelligibility or shared understanding" (Suchman, 1987/2007, p. 34), or at least some form of recognition of human actions by the robot could actually arise. This has crucial implications also for participation, as it can help to understand whether the machine is only coincidentally producing fitting turns (see e.g., Pelikan et al., 2020) or whether the machine's actions are actual re-actions to a previously registered action, fine-tuned to the ongoing interactional context.

The interactional role of robots

The interactional role of machines has been critically discussed in EMCA. Early work suggested that computers (controlled through keyboards and screens) could be analysed as having the role of an interactant (see e.g., McIlvenny, 1990; Norman & Thomas, 1991), while others problematised the view of computers as being able to engage in conversation (Button, 1990). The rise of voice user interfaces has revived this debate and the question whether machines can be participants in interaction has resurfaced. Contemporary EMCA work argues that talking to voice interfaces is not a conversation because the turns by the interface are scripted rather than interactionally unfolding (Porcheron et al., 2018). Virtual agents (Krummheuer, 2009) and robots (Pitsch, 2016) have been pointed out not to interact on equal grounds with humans. Pitsch (2016) instead regards robots and humans as part of an "interactional system" that is jointly solving interactional tasks. These works point to a possible tension. On the one hand, machines may have a potential for being a participant, on the other hand, they are clearly different from humans. Reconsidering how EMCA defines participation may shed some light on this issue.

Goffman's notion of footing (1981) highlights that there may be varying degrees of participation, which is also increasingly recognised in the field of human–robot interaction (see e.g., Mutlu et al., 2009; Skantze, 2017). The EMCA notion of participation extends this perspective and highlights the joint and dynamic element in participation, focusing on how "different kinds of parties build actions together" (Goodwin & Goodwin, 2005, p. 225), for instance, when one person modifies an emerging action in response to what other participants are doing. Participation is thereby tied to the dynamic capability to contribute to joint activities (Goodwin & Goodwin, 2005; Krummheuer, 2015). Animals can also be considered as participants and EMCA analysis can nuance what type of participant an animal is (Mondémé, 2016; see also Rossano, this volume). Multimodal transcription can uncover changes in participation status not only for humans and animals but also for robots (see also Pelikan et al., 2022).

With their ability to speak and act autonomously, robots are not only potential participants but may even fall under the ethnomethodological concept of a "member", as introduced by Garfinkel and Sacks (1970, p. 342, emphasis in original):

> The notion of **member** is at the heart of the matter. We do not use the term to refer to a person. It refers instead to mastery of natural language, which we understand in the following way. We offer the observation that persons, because of the fact that they are heard to be speaking a natural language, **somehow** are heard to be engaged in the objective production and objective display of commonsense knowledge of everyday activities as observable and reportable [...] that is **account-able** phenomena

If membership is based on mastery of natural language, a robot that produces natural language could in principle qualify as a member. At the same time, Garfinkel and Sacks highlight crucial challenges: If a robot is speaking a natural language, it will be heard to display and engage in the production of common-sense knowledge of everyday activities and its actions will be treated as accountable. This is perhaps the crux of participating machines. Humans may be willing to treat robots as members, but in turn expect that they contribute recognisable and explainable actions. In other words, robots are held accountable for behaving in line with common-sense knowledge of how social activities are to be accomplished and organised.

The materialised presence of robots further complicates this. While much of the early EMCA work focused on talk, the embodied turn (Nevile, 2015) has led to the insight that everyday activities are accomplished multimodally. Recent work demonstrates that language is not only comprised of words, but of other vocalisations that characteristically occur in combination with embodied displays (Keevallik & Ogden, 2020). From this perspective, robots are an especially interesting case. Physically embodied, they can potentially participate in fine-tuning of actions and engage in everyday interaction through various modalities. At the same time, they are machines that animate scripted actions, and technically lack common sense about interaction. This raises interesting methodological questions, which this chapter will discuss.

The data

The chapter features three different robots that I recorded in different settings. Table 3.1 offers an overview of the data.

TABLE 3.1 The robots referred to in this chapter, including information about the setting, participants, and further details about the respective studies

Robot (manufacturer)	Robot type	Setting	Participants	Country/language	Details about data material
Nao (Aldebaran)	60 cm tall humanoid robot that can perform complex gestures	Lab (charade game)	13 university students	Sweden/English (native & non-native)	Pelikan and Broth (2016)
Cozmo (Anki)	Palm-sized toy robot with forklift that can pick up toy cubes, animated display face	Home (free play)	6 families, 4 adult pairs	Sweden/Swedish, Germany/ German	Pelikan et al. (2020)
Autonomous shuttle bus (Navya)	Autonomous vehicle for public transport (15 passengers)	Public roads	Safety drivers, traffic participants	Sweden/Swedish (native & non-native)	Pelikan (2021)

Transcribing video recordings of human–robot interaction

The EMCA focus on what is observable is inherently user-centred. Studying participants' understanding, EMCA focuses on how humans (robot users) interpret robot actions rather than what causes them. This perspective allows the analyst to ignore the underlying code (i.e., why something is happening from the technical point of view) when starting to transcribe human–robot interaction.

A robot's multimodal resources

Most present-day robots rely on physical hardware that is significantly more rigid than human joints and tendons. Therefore, robotic movement is often restricted to a specific dimension in space, allowing for a limited degree of freedom (e.g., up–down but not left–right). This may make transcription easier, as trajectories are often more straightforward and therefore easier to capture. However, robots may also use non-human resources, such as vibration or lights. When treated as relevant for the interaction, they should also be transcribed.

More importantly, a robot's audio track may sound quite different from human interaction, which poses challenges for transcription. While synthetic voice generators are getting more human-like and robotic speech may be captured through practices established for human talk, robots also emit a range of other sounds. Robots use beeps to communicate, play musical sequences to amplify their presence, and utter gibberish speech (Yilmayildiz et al., 2016). Some robots produce sounds that may recall human or animal vocalisations. A robot's physical embodiment in the world may lead to sounds as well, such as motor noise or rolling on a surface. Work in human–robot interaction explores, for instance, whether motor sounds can be designed to communicate (Moore et al., 2020). While such sounds are typically not the main focus of interaction, they may be oriented to by humans (Pelikan & Hofstetter, 2022). Following Sacks (1984), nothing should be excluded a priori from the analysis, so all these sounds can be potential resources for interaction. Especially robots for end-customers (including vehicles), may be designed by professionals (see e.g., Robinson et al., 2022a). Sound designers often experiment with their own voice in *vocal sketching* (Panariello et al., 2019), take inspiration from movies (Latupeirissa et al., 2019), or draw on musical theory (Robinson et al., 2022b). Translating the virtuous work of sound designers back into transcripts requires careful listening.

Transcribing robot sound

Humans have conventional ways of capturing non-human sounds in everyday speech: Animal and machine sounds are often lexicalised in the form of onomatopoeia, and some languages describe sensory qualities through ideophones (Dingemanse, 2014; Keevallik & Ogden, 2020). Bird watchers spell out bird song in syllables (see e.g., ten Have, 2002). Similarly, participants in everyday settings usually do not describe robot sound by reporting that the robot emitted a one-second tone at 440 Hz, but by putting it into words. Consider for instance the following transcript in which a safety driver on an autonomous shuttle bus formulates a rendering of the bus' sounds in anticipation of a break. The transcription style is adapted from Jefferson (2004) and Mondada (2019).

Excerpt 1   Pling pling. NY-f-2020-09-02. B-Huset.

```
01 ((pedestrians in front of bus are slowing down))
02 DRI   pling pling
03 BUS   ding (1.0) ding
```

The bus is driving a few metres behind a pair of pedestrians. When they slow down (l. 01), the safety driver who is monitoring the situation utters "pling pling" (l. 02). A moment later, the bus indeed produces two metallic bell sounds (l. 03), which are usually triggered before braking, when the bus detects an obstacle. The example demonstrates that such sounds are relevant for participants who demonstrate their understanding by producing onomatopoeic renderings of the sounds. This can also guide the analyst in capturing these sounds.

When trying to put sounds into words, we may imitate a car engine with a "vroom", and a honk with a "beep" (Laurier et al., 2020). However, as these examples illustrate, by rendering a written version of them, we present them in a particular language: The same sounds above would be written as "brumm" and "tuut", respectively, in German for example. This highlights that as soon as we decide to transcribe sounds, we are "translating" them into a particular language and its sign system. This can pose a challenge for transcription: Should robot sounds be transcribed in the language of the participants, the native language of the analyst, or in the language of the design team? Differences in orthographic representation may make it impossible to compare transcripts across languages. Since transcripts should be understandable, I found transcribing robot sound in the language that the paper is written in the most practical solution (if only to avoid translation lines).

Representing robotic sound from an emic perspective

Representing non-lexical sound in the transcript allows initial analysis of whether and how it is reacted to by the participants. More nuanced transcription can deepen analytic understanding and may uncover participants' orientation to slight differences in length or pitch (see e.g., Barth-Weingarten et al., 2020; Keevallik, 2021). For example, humanoid robot Nao plays characteristic sounds, which have been transcribed as "dadup sound" (Arend et al., 2017), "da↑dup" and "da↓dap" (Pelikan & Broth, 2016), or "da ↑dap" and "da ↓dap" (Jarske et al., 2022) in the literature. Although all three studies include the sounds in their transcripts, there are differences in spelling and two studies distinguish the sounds with raising ("da↑dup"/"da↑dap") from those with falling intonation ("da↓dap"). The following transcript illustrates a typical moment in which the robot plays these sounds.

Participant Rachel is seated on a carpet in a robot lab and is about to play a charade game with humanoid robot Nao. The robot just introduced itself and the game and is now asking Rachel whether she is ready to play.

Excerpt 2   Are you ready? BDMV_13 [2:12-2:23]

```
01 Nao   are you ready?
02 Rac   i'[m ready ]
03 Nao     [da·dup::]
04         (5.4)
05 Rac   YES I'm ready
06         (0.6)
07 Nao   da↓dap
08         (0.7)
09 Nao   good.
```

In the excerpt, the robot asks whether Rachel is ready (l. 01) and she immediately produces the preferred response, indicating that she is indeed ready (l. 02). Her utterance overlaps with a sound that the robot plays (l. 03). After a significant amount of silence (l. 04), she repeats and extends her utterance, saying "yes, I am ready" (l. 05). The robot plays another sound (l. 07) before responding "good" (l. 09). Transcribing these sounds (in whatever lexicalised form) enables a temporal analysis, demonstrating for instance that the first sound (l. 03) occurs in overlap with Rachel's utterance.

Analysing the sounds more carefully, I noticed that they typically occur after the robot has asked a question and that there are usually two sounds occurring in close proximity: A sound with rising intonation (l. 03) will be followed by a sound with falling intonation (l. 07). Human utterances that occur in overlap with or before the robot's sound will not be reacted to by the robot. In fact, the sounds mark a time window during which the robot is recognising the participant's speech. Distinguishing between the sound that indicates that the robot is now starting or stopping to listen thus informed my subsequent analysis. While I sometimes include the intended meaning in a comment such as ((speech recognition on/off)), participants may not necessarily have been aware of what the sounds meant. Since analysts cannot look inside participants' heads to verify whether they understand the underlying technological function of a sound, transcribing sound in an onomatopoeic way is a more neutral option.

While "dadap" is clearly robotic, sounds inspired by human vocalisations raise different challenges for transcription. They require careful balancing between transcribing in a way that is *realistic* (staying true to how it actually sounds, capturing the details of the robotic production) and *recognisable* (making the transcript readable and preserving the associated meaning potentials) (ten Have, 2002). Excerpt 3 illustrates this through an early transcript draft, which I include here to highlight problems with capturing key elements of the sound in line 28. A German couple, Petra and Robert, are playing with toy robot Cozmo at the dinner table in their home. Making use of its face recognition component, Cozmo just learnt to recognise Petra's face and is now able to greet her by name whenever her face appears in its camera view. With some effort, she has managed to orient the palm-sized robot away from her own face towards Robert, who is leaning towards it, waiting for the robot to also learn his name. While the researcher manually typed both names into a phone app that launches the activity, Cozmo now autonomously performs a sequence of moves.

Excerpt 3   Um. Cozmo-A1 [04:28-04:35]. Early transcript draft.

```
22 ROB   •         ha•llo
                   hello
   coz   •turns away•
23        •   (0.5)  •(1.2)•     (0.3)    •(.)
   coz   •turns back•     •drives forward•
24 ROB   [m]
25 COZ   [o]wa:odidi
26 ROB   mog[st mi ned
         don't (you) like me? ((Bavarian dialect))
27 COZ      [dr::r::r::r::
28 COZ   ä:::
         uh
29    ((Petra and researcher laugh))
```

Just when Robert greets the robot, Cozmo turns away again (l. 22). When the robot turns back (l. 23) and plays a squeaky beep sound (l. 25), Robert asks "don't you like me" (l. 26). Cozmo produces a cog-like machine sound in overlap (l. 27), followed by a human-inspired vocalisation uttered in a robot voice (l. 28), which evokes associations with a hesitating "uh". Robert's wife and the researcher acknowledge this interpretation with a few brief laughter particles (l. 29).

While I initially transcribed Cozmo's sound in line 28 with the German hesitation marker "ä", the sound is extensively stretched, which makes it more ambiguous than a typical human version. It was challenging to strike a balance between capturing the meaning potential (Linell, 2009) while also highlighting the robotic-ness of the sound. This is especially relevant as I am working on collections of repeated sequences, in which the sound may or may not be oriented to as carrying a particular meaning. In later stages of transcription, I rendered the sound as "uUUUUUUHH" following English spelling conventions (see Figure 3.1 image 3). This version captures the potential hearing as "uh" while it also highlights the difference to a typical human hesitation maker and a slight shift in how it sounds at its onset, as compared to the prolonged duration.

FIGURE 3.1 Cozmo's face learning script (Pelikan & Hofstetter, 2022).

As Cozmo's sounds have been designed by a professional sound designer, they are relatively complex. Being interested in how family members make sense of the different sounds, I transcribed them at a high level of detail, which made me notice fine differences between them. Excerpt 4 features a more thorough transcription of the same robot sounds as in Excerpt 3 (l. 02 corresponds to Excerpt 3, l. 25 and line 05 to Excerpt 3, l. 27–28). In this excerpt, Cozmo is in a Swedish family home with Nellie and her mother and performs the same face learning activity, which has been launched by the mother through the Cozmo app on her phone. Robot turns are highlighted for easier identification.

Excerpt 4   Face learning. Cozmo-FAM5. Day 1 (*Pelikan & Hofstetter, 2022*). Cozmo's
pre-programmed turns are highlighted in grey.

```
01 MOM    så du får no krypa ner lite dö+
          so you probably have to crawl down a bit, you
   nel                                      +moves backwards-->
02 COZ    o[Ade-e]
03 NEL     [okehe]j
           okay
04         (0.1)+(0.9)
   nel    -->+lies down on belly-->
05 COZ    rrrrrrrrrrrrr aa+Aaaaaaaoooo
   nel                  -->+
06 COZ    rrrrr[rrrrrrrr          ]
07 NEL         [tänk om (h)(h)han]
               imagine if      he
08 NEL    (la::: sig) på [mig]
          (          ) on me
09 COZ                   [ rr]rrrrrr
10 NEL    va [ö-]
          what er
11 COZ    [di]ng:::::[:::        ]
12 MOM              [>nu får du<] va tyst
                    now you have to be quiet
13        (0.6)
14 COZ    a↑Aaaooooooo
15        (1.0)
16 COZ    nellie?
17        (0.5)
18 MOM    .hhhh hhi[hihi   ]
19 COZ             [ahaaaa]aow
20        (0.2)
21 NEL    khehe k[HA]
22 COZ           [ne]llie.
23 NEL    han sa mitt namn
          he said my name
```

Repeatedly watching the videos in a collection of face learning sequences,
I started to see that the robot kept repeating certain multimodal moves, which
seemed to be part of the general sequence. It turned out that the "oAde-e" sound
(Excerpt 4, l. 02) seemed to be present in all cases, apparently indicating the
beginning of the sequence. Including the sound systematically in all transcripts
provides evidence of when this sequence starts – even if it is often ignored by
the participants. The attempt to create a generalised version to compare to provided deeper insight into the "rrr" sounds. These can be adjusted flexibly in duration and may be repeated when the robot is still scanning the visual scene for a
face. Depending on the situated context, the scripted element of cog-like "rrr"
sounds may thus be deployed slightly differently, potentially leading to different
outcomes. More importantly, the attempt to create a general reference transcription revealed that the "aaAaaaaaaaoooo" sound (l. 05) is different from the "ä"
(or rather "uUUUUUHH") in Excerpt 3 (l. 28). While the "aaAaaaaaaaoooo"

can also be heard as "uh", its meaning potential as hesitation marker seems to be slightly weaker.

A recording of the robot in a silent environment proved particularly helpful when creating a reference transcription. Tools for prosodic analysis like Praat and Audacity supported scrutiny and comparison of the individual sounds. Sometimes adjustments to situated hearing were necessary, for instance when a sound lingered on longer (cf. Excerpt 2, l. 03 for an example), or when the onset of the sound was drowned out in overlapping talk. Similarly, dealing with many repetitions of the same multimodal behaviour across different recordings, I noticed that certain elements (e.g., a small movement paired with a sound) may be treated as relevant in some situations and ignored in others. One way to present this is to provide a detailed multimodal transcription of the "idealised" robot animation (see Figure 3.1) and to use a version that is reduced to what is relevant for the situated scene in the transcripts (Pelikan et al., 2020; Pelikan & Hofstetter, 2022). In other cases, I decided to keep certain elements in all transcripts, even if a clear orientation to them is absent, as one would perhaps do with babbling babies. For instance, the listening sounds described in Extract 2 with Nao provide an important insight into what the robot is doing – which is available to those with prior experience of talking to machines and those with programming knowledge.

Identifying the script

It is not only the analyst who will be confronted with repetition: When repeatedly interacting with a robot, participants also recognise regularities and may construct their own actions in anticipation of specific robot behaviour. For example, family members familiar with Cozmo's face learning sequence position their own hands in anticipation of the robot's raised forklift arms, so that it appears as if Cozmo were high fiving them. Even without knowing the exact programming, safety drivers and regular commuters anticipate that the autonomous bus will start braking when getting close to a potential obstacle such as a pedestrian or cyclist.

I use the term *script* (see also Clinkenbeard, 2018) to denote these recognisable patterns – not the actual code that elicits a robot's actions but rather the general algorithm, set of rules, or plan (Suchman, 1987/2007) that determines how a robot should generally react given certain inputs. In contrast to the specific lines of code, the script is an abstraction that could be represented in the form of a flow chart. The robot can animate the script again and again in virtually identical form. These repetitions provide an exceptionally regular ground for building collections. It is usually comparatively easy to find many (if not all) repetitions of the same part of the script in the recorded situated interactions, especially if one has access to the robot's log files. However, the repetitions pose new challenges for transcription. How to balance between the scripted actions and situated hearing/watching, in which repetitions may be very similar but not identical?

While robots may be able to react differently depending on a range of different inputs, they ultimately cannot deviate from their part of the script. They may flexibly react to changes in the environment or read out sentences that have not been written by their designers, but even these reactions are constrained to what they have been pre-programmed to do by a human programmer/interaction designer (cf. Porcheron et al., 2018). Compared to the arguably infinite set of human multimodal actions, robot action is limited and the underlying general scheme can often be identified after just a few interactions, both by participants and the analyst.

The general script may be represented in the form of text including the aspects that are crucial for the respective analysis (Pelikan & Broth, 2016, p. 4923). Alternatively, the script may be represented in the form of a reference transcription that highlights features in the robot behaviour crucial for the respective analysis, such as in Figure 3.1: The Cozmo robot displays squinted "eyes" and plays a sound indicating the beginning of the sequence, followed by cog-like "rrr" sounds of flexible length. Often this is combined with an "aAaaoooooooo" vocalisation (frame 1). Once this is finished, Cozmo plays a "ding" sound (frame 2). After a brief silence, the robot produces a sound that is reminiscent of "uh" (frame 3), and after further silence reads the name that users have previously entered into the robot's app interface. This is followed by a sound that reminds one of "wow" (frame 4) and a repetition of the username (frame 5). Finally, the robot displays smiley eyes and waves its arms, while it plays a prolonged musical sound (frame 6).

Dealing with the script in a systematic way strengthens the analysis by shedding light on whether the timing of a robot action is consistent throughout a collection, or just a coincidence. When taking Figure 3.1 as a reference during analysis of a collection of face learning sequences, it became relatively easy to recognise interruptions in the script, such as moments when the sequence failed (possibly due to technical errors, timeouts in detecting a relevant input, etc.). Depending on the research question one may then treat these deviant cases with special care. Looking very carefully, one may even discover twitches and delays that are not intended by the designers and will not be in the code but are part of the robot's regular behaviour. Small deviations in timing may occur when software is translated to motors, and network delays can turn a short silence into a problematic lapse. This highlights that while log data, code, and interviews with the designers (see e.g., Pelikan et al., 2020) may give a general insight into the rationale behind machine behaviour (Suchman, 1987/2007), they cannot replace analysing the robot's actions carefully from the perspective of the participants in the interaction.

The interactional role of robots

Considering each robot move as possibly meaningful action that should be transcribed, robots have been systematically treated as (potential) participants in the previous section. When transitioning towards analysis, the robot's status as an object needs to be taken seriously (Alač, 2016): The differences between humans

and robots have implications for the applicability of the next-turn proof procedure (Sacks et al., 1974), in which the recipient's understanding of a current turn
becomes observable for speaker and analyst in the next turn. Taking the term
"participant understanding" seriously, a robot is also displaying its understanding,
but the particulars may differ significantly from those of the human participants.

Consider for instance Excerpt 5 below, in which participant Gary is just starting to interact with Nao. While the initial turns do not appear problematic, the
question in line 10 points to a mismatch between how Gary understood the previous turns and how they are treated by the robot.

Excerpt 5   I'm Gary. Nexus_3. [00:43-01:25] (*Pelikan & Broth, 2016*).

```
01 Nao  +(0.6) he̲llo:
   nao  +waving-->
02      (0.4)
03 Gar  >hi<
04 Nao  (0.5) i'm nao.
05      (0.8)
06 Gar  i'm+ gar[y]
   nao  -->+
07 Nao          ↑[i]'m a ro̲:bot
08 Nao  (0.4) an i'm four ↑years ↓old
09 Nao  (0.9) I come from fra:nce
10 Nao  (0.9) ↑what's ↓your name?
11 Nao  (0.4) da↑dup
12 Gar  (0.7) >gary<
13 Nao  (0.9) da↓dap
14 Nao  (0.3) ni̲ce to ↑meet ↓you (0.2) g̲ary,
15 Nao  (1.6) I ↑lo̲ve games,
```

Nao greets Gary (l. 01), and Gary produces the second pair part to the greeting
(l. 03). Nao then proceeds by introducing its name (l. 04) and again, Gary fills the
slot with a relevant next action (l. 06). Nao continues and provides more information (l. 08–09). However, when the robot asks, "what's your name?" (l. 10), it
becomes evident that the robot has not registered Gary's name and Gary has to
repeat it (l. 12), speaking in the window marked by the previously analysed sounds
(l. 11 and l. 13).

From Nao's perspective, no input was registered outside its audio recording time frame, so the robot does not respond to Gary until after the beep
sounds (l. 14). The utterance "I'm Nao" (l. 04) is not displaying understanding
of Gary's previous turn as a return greeting. Instead, at that moment, the robot
shares similarities with automata like washing machines, juke boxes, or vend-
ing machines that, once triggered, perform a series of actions *no matter what.*
Relying on its sensors and processing capabilities, the robot's understanding is
severely limited. This raises questions about who displays what kind of understanding at what point in time and highlights the asymmetry between Gary and
the robot.

While initially orienting to Nao as a competent member, Gary repeats his
name calmly and without asking for an account. He thereby treats the robot like

a machine that requires certain input, like answering machines that only register what is said after a beep or websites that only accept text strings of a certain length. The excerpt highlights that while a robot may be momentarily treated as a member that displays common sense knowledge, it may lose that status in the next moment when it demonstrates lack of that knowledge, such as following through a typical greeting sequence. Studying interaction with robots as potential (though limited) members also raises questions about how we describe human practices, and what it means to be a competent member in interaction.

Robots as scaffolded participants

While robots may contribute to joint actions, they are simultaneously limited in their interactional capabilities and are usually scaffolded by humans in their status as participants, often someone with experience with the robot. In semi-experimental settings, the scaffolding role is taken by experimenters and roboticists, who frame the robot's behaviour as relevant and instruct others how to make sense of it (Alač et al., 2011). Researchers may end up saving the robot from failure by proposing new opportunities for interaction that are within the robot's capabilities. Excerpt 6 illustrates an example of this from my early data collection with Cozmo. As participants are increasingly getting frustrated with the robot, the researcher proposes a new activity demonstrating Cozmo's capabilities.

Excerpt 6   Cozmo at the dinner table. A2 [2:20–2:28].

```
01 ULR   hallo antworten
         hello, respond!
02 COZ   me↓oooooo
03 ULR   ja (.) was is denn das für ne antwort
         well what kind of a response is that
04       (0.9)
05 RES   wollt ihr dass er eure namen lernt?
         would you like him to learn your names?
06 COZ   oai?
07       (0.9)
08 HOS?  [ja:  ]
         yes
09 ULR   [ich h]eiße ulrich
         my name is ulrich
```

Participant Ulrich (ULR) commands a response (l. 01) and subsequently displays dissatisfaction with Cozmo's reaction (l. 02–03). Since the robot does not have speech recognition, it has no means to appropriately answer. During an ensuing silence (l. 04), which might have ended with participants abandoning the robot, the researcher proposes a new activity (l. 05), saving Cozmo from a moment in which it is unable to provide further relevant actions. At the same time, she frames a new context in which the robot can contribute competently during the clearly structured face learning sequence.

While the scaffolding role of researchers requires special scrutiny, this way of supporting the robot is common even in their absence. In my second round of data collection, Cozmo stayed with families for several days. Parents and siblings led each other through activities, and sometimes selected specific actions in the app to compensate for missing responses from the robot. Naturally, technologically more experienced participants took the lead, shaping how the others experienced the robot (for an example, see Pelikan et al., 2022). The recorded data consequently reveals not only the scaffolded status of the robot, but also the variable degrees of the participants' robotic expertise.

Scaffolding occurs not only in groups but can also be observed in one-on-one interaction between humans and robots. Adapting to the robot and producing utterances that can be handled by the machine (see Excerpt 5, Pelikan & Broth, 2016), humans permit the robot to smoothly advance through the interactional sequence that it is capable of – scaffolding by removing complexities that the robot may not be able to handle. These examples highlight that robots can be considered participants, albeit with limited capabilities. Their participation status may dynamically change from one moment to the next.

Concluding discussion

As I have illustrated in this chapter, transcribing robot behaviour in detail sheds light on the role robots take in interaction. However, since robot action repertoires differ from those of humans, transcription practices need to be adjusted, particularly with respect to non-lexical sound. Transcribing non-human utterances in letter combinations enables deep analysis but also poses challenges, as one necessarily renders them in a specific language. Capturing ambiguity and meaning potentials (Linell, 2009) that participants may or may not orient to requires careful consideration of transcription choices. Further, when dealing with repetitions of complex robot behaviour, creating a reference transcription may prove valuable. This may be created for individual utterances/interactional moves or for longer sequences. Aggregating situated transcriptions into a generalised script pays off particularly when one aims to demonstrate a robot's interactional flaws. Suggestions for improvement of the robot's interaction design can be demonstrated by adjusting the identified script, pointing out alternative sequential trajectories that will be easier to follow from the perspective of human users (see e.g., Pelikan & Broth, 2016; Pelikan et al., 2020; Pelikan & Hofstetter, 2022).

In the second part of the chapter, I have argued for paying particular attention to the robot's understanding in later stages of the analysis. EMCA analysis heavily draws on the next-turn proof procedure (Sacks et al., 1974), identifying how a next turn displays understanding of the previous. To analyse what understanding a robot is displaying at a given moment, it may be important to determine whether a robot is actually in a reactive mode. Suchman (1987/2007) for instance notes for each human action in her transcripts whether it is registered by the copying machine. Engaging with the way a robot locally produces its actions can be compared with gaining vulgar competence (Garfinkel & Wieder, 1992) in the perspective of the robot. If we want to treat or develop robots as potential participants whose perspective is different from that of humans, we may want to consider carefully what researchers need to know about this perspective. Ultimately, looking at what behaviour is unavailable to the machine and where the machine is scaffolded provides a sobering perspective on the state of the art of human–robot interaction.

Finally, empirically analysing video recordings enables EMCA researchers to shed light onto the role that robots take in interaction. Transcription supports documentation of embodied actions and changing participation frameworks. As robots are increasingly able to dynamically react to people's actions, such as their movement in space (cf. Excerpt 4, in which the robot is extending the scanning process in response to the moving participant), one may argue that robots can be considered participants in specific moments. Careful transcription can uncover how experienced co-participants project and scaffold a robot's next actions, creating contexts in which the robot's actions appear as competent. This chapter has demonstrated the continued relevance of early EMCA work on machines as interactants (McIlvenny, 1990; Norman & Thomas, 1991). However, in line with contemporary work (Pitsch, 2016), it also presents robots as participants that require (more or less) interactional support. Human co-participants treat robots as participants (and potential members) and robots can be analysed as such, but at the same time, one should not overlook the human scaffolding work that goes into achieving this participation status.

Acknowledgements

I am indebted to Leelo Keevallik and Mathias Broth for fruitful discussions and would like to thank Jenny Fu for commenting on an earlier draft. This work is funded by the Swedish Research Council (2016-00827).

Reference list

Alač, M. (2016). Social robots: Things or agents? *AI and Society, 31*(4), 519–535. https://doi .org/10.1007/s00146-015-0631-6

Alač, M., Movellan, J., & Tanaka, F. (2011). When a robot is social: Spatial arrangements and multimodal semiotic engagement in the practice of social robotics. *Social Studies of Science, 41*(6), 893–926.

Arend, B., Sunnen, P., & Caire, P. (2017). Investigating breakdowns in human robot interaction: A conversation analysis guided single case study of a human-robot communication in a museum environment. *International Journal of Mechanical and Mechatronics Engineering, 11*(5), 949–955. https://doi.org/10.5281/zenodo.1130169

Barth-Weingarten, D., Couper-Kuhlen, E., & Deppermann, A. (2020). Konstruktionsgrammatik und Prosodie: OH in englischer Alltagsinteraktion. In W.

Imo & J. P. Lanwer (Eds.), *Prosodie und Konstruktionsgrammatik* (pp. 35–74). De Gruyter. https://doi.org/10.1515/9783110637489-002

Bekey, G. A. (2005). *Autonomous robots: From biological inspiration to implementation and control.* MIT Press.

Broth, M., Laurier, E., & Mondada, L. (2014). Introducing video at work. In M. Broth, E. Laurier, & L. Mondada (Eds.), *Studies of video practices: Video at work* (pp. 1–29). Routledge.

Bucholtz, M. (2000). The politics of transcription. *Journal of Pragmatics, 32*(10), 1439–1465. https://doi.org/10.1016/S0378-2166(99)00094-6

Button, G. (1990). Going up a blind alley. In P. Luff, N. Gilbert, & D. B. T. Frohlich (Eds.), *Computers and conversation* (pp. 67–90). Elsevier.

Clinkenbeard, M. (2018). Multimodal conversation analysis and usability studies: Exploring human-technology interactions in multiparty contexts. *Communication Design Quarterly, 6*(2), 103–113. https://doi.org/10.1145/3282665.3282675

Dingemanse, M. (2014). Making new ideophones in Siwu: Creative depiction in conversation. *Pragmatics and Society, 5*(3), 384–405. https://doi.org/10.1075/ps.5.3.04din

Due, B. L., Lange, S. B., Femø Nielsen, M., Toft, T. L. W., Landgrebe, J., Nielsen, R., & Hassert, L. (2019). Den andens ansigt: Afdækning af deltagerorientering via multimodal interaktionsanalyse. *NyS, Nydanske Sprogstudier, 56*, 10–51. https://doi.org/10.7146/nys.v1i56.111286

Fischer, K. (2016). *Designing speech for a recipient: The roles of partner modeling, alignment and feedback in so-called 'simplified registers'* (Vol. 270). John Benjamins Publishing Company.

Gan, Y., Greiffenhagen, C., & Reeves, S. (2020). Connecting distributed families: Camera work for three-party mobile video calls. In *Proceedings of the 2020 CHI conference on human factors in computing systems* (pp. 1–12). Association for Computing Machinery. https://doi.org/10.1145/3313831.3376704

Garfinkel, H., & Sacks, H. (1970). On formal structures of practical actions. In J. C. McKinney & E. A. Tiryakian (Eds.), *Theoretical sociology: Perspectives and development* (pp. 337–366). Appleton-Century-Crofts.

Garfinkel, H., & Wieder, D. L. (1992). Two incommensurable, asymmetrically alternate technologies of social analysis. In G. Watson & R. M. Seiler (Eds.), *Text in context: Contributions to ethnomethodology* (pp. 175–206). Sage Publications.

Goffman, E. (1981). *Forms of talk.* University of Pennsylvania Press.

Goodwin, C., & Goodwin, M. H. (2005). Participation. In A. Duranti (Ed.), *A companion to linguistic anthropology* (pp. 222–244). Wiley. https://doi.org/10.1002/9780470996522.ch10

Housley, W., Albert, S., & Stokoe, E. (2019). Natural action processing. In *Proceedings of the halfway to the future symposium.* Association for Computing Machinery. https://doi.org/10.1145/3363384.3363478

Jarske, S., Raudaskoski, S., Kaipainen, K., & Väänänen, K. (2022). Making sense of robots together: Examining group interactions with Pepper. Reconfiguring HRI workshop. https://medien.informatik.tu-chemnitz.de/reconfig-hri/files/2022/03/05_Jarske.pdf

Jefferson, G. (2004). Glossary of transcript symbols with an introduction. In G. H. Lerner (Ed.), *Conversation Analysis: Studies from the first generation* (pp. 13–31). John Benjamins. https://doi.org/10.1075/pbns.125.02jef

Jenks, C. J. (2013). Working with transcripts: An abridged review of issues in transcription. *Language and Linguistics Compass, 7*(4), 251–261. https://doi.org/10.1111/lnc3.12023

Keevallik, L. (2021). Vocalizations in dance classes teach body knowledge. *Linguistics Vanguard*, *7*(s4), 20200098. https://doi.org/doi:10.1515/lingvan-2020-0098

Keevallik, L., & Ogden, R. (2020). Sounds on the margins of language at the heart of interaction. *Research on Language and Social Interaction*, *53*(1), 1–18.

Krummheuer, A. (2015). Performing an action one cannot do: Participation, scaffolding and embodied interaction. *Journal of Interactional Research in Communication Disorders*, *6*(2), 187–210. https://doi.org/10.1558/jircd.v6i2.26986

Krummheuer, A. L. (2009). Conversation analysis, video recordings, and human-computer interchanges. In U. T. Kissmann (Ed.), *Video interaction analysis* (pp. 59–83). Peter Lang.

Latupeirissa, A. B., Frid, E., & Bresin, R. (2019). Sonic characteristics of robots in films. In *Proceedings of the 16th sound and music computing conference*. http://smc2019.uma.es/articles/P2/P2_07_SMC2019_paper.pdf

Laurier, E. (2014). The graphic transcript: Poaching comic book grammar for inscribing the visual, spatial and temporal aspects of action. *Geography Compass*, *8*(4), 235–248. https://doi.org/10.1111/gec3.12123

Laurier, E., Muñoz, D., Miller, R., & Brown, B. (2020). A bip, a beeeep, and a beep beep: How horns are sounded in Chennai traffic. *Research on Language and Social Interaction*, *53*(3), 341–356. https://doi.org/10.1080/08351813.2020.1785775

Laurier, E., & Reeves, S. (2014). Cameras in video games: Comparing play in counterstrike and the doctor who adventures. In M. Broth, E. Laurier, & L. Mondada (Eds.), *Studies of video practices: Video at work* (pp. 181–207). Routledge.

Licoppe, C., Luff, P. K., Heath, C., Kuzuoka, H., Yamashita, N., & Tuncer, S. (2017). Showing objects: Holding and manipulating artefacts in video-mediated collaborative settings. In *Proceedings of the 2017 CHI conference on human factors in computing systems* (pp. 5295–5306). Association for Computing Machinery. https://doi.org/10.1145/3025453.3025848

Linell, P. (2009). *Rethinking language, mind, and world dialogically*. Information Age Publishing.

Luff, P., Jirotka, M., Yamashita, N., Kuzuoka, H., Heath, C., & Eden, G. (2013). Embedded interaction. *ACM Transactions on Computer-Human Interaction*, *20*(1), 1–22. https://doi.org/10.1145/2442106.2442112

McIlvenny, P. (1990). Communicative action and computers: Re-embodying conversation analysis? In P. Luff, N. Gilbert, & D. B. T. Frohlich (Eds.), *Computers and conversation* (pp. 91–132). Academic Press.

Mondada, L. (2019). Conventions for transcribing multimodality. https://www.lorenzamondada.net/multimodal-transcription

Mondémé, C. (2016). Extension de la question de «l'ordre social» aux interactions hommes / animaux. une approche ethnométhodologique. *L'Année Sociologique*, *66*(2), 319–350. https://doi.org/10.3917/anso.162.0319

Moore, D., Currano, R., & Sirkin, D. (2020). Sound decisions: How synthetic motor sounds improve autonomous vehicle-pedestrian interactions. In *12th international conference on automotive user interfaces and interactive vehicular applications* (pp. 94–103). Association for Computing Machinery. https://doi.org/10.1145/3409120.3410667

Moore, R. J. (2015). Automated transcription and conversation analysis. *Research on Language and Social Interaction*, *48*(3), 253–270. https://doi.org/10.1080/08351813.2015.1058600

Mutlu, B., Shiwa, T., Kanda, T., Ishiguro, H., & Hagita, N. (2009). Footing in human-robot conversations: How robots might shape participant roles using gaze cues. In *Proceedings of the 4th ACM/IEEE international conference on human robot interaction* (pp. 61–68). Association for Computing Machinery. https://doi.org/10.1145/1514095.1514109

Nevile, M. (2015). The embodied turn in research on language and social interaction. *Research on Language and Social Interaction, 48*(2), 121–151. https://doi.org/10.1080/08351813.2015.1025499

Norman, M. A., & Thomas, P. J. (1991). Informing HCI design through conversation analysis. *International Journal of Man-Machine Studies, 35*(2), 235–250.

Ochs, E. (1979). Transcription as theory. In E. Ochs & B. B. Schieffelin (Eds.), *Developmental pragmatics* (pp. 43–72). Academic Press.

Panariello, C., Sköld, M., Frid, E., & Bresin, R. (2019). From vocal sketching to sound models by means of a sound-based musical transcription system. In *Proceedings of the 16th sound and music computing conference.* https://www.smc2019.uma.es/articles/S2/S2_05_SMC2019_paper.pdf

Pelikan, H. R. M. (2021). Why autonomous driving is so hard: The social dimension of traffic. In *Companion of the 2021 ACM/IEEE international conference on human-robot interaction* (pp. 81–85). Association for Computing Machinery. https://doi.org/10.1145/3434074.3447133

Pelikan, H. R. M., & Broth, M. (2016). Why that Nao? How humans adapt to a conventional humanoid robot in taking turns-at-talk. In *Proceedings of the 2016 CHI conference on human factors in computing systems* (pp. 4921–4932). Association for Computing Machinery. https://doi.org/10.1145/2858036.2858478

Pelikan, H. R. M., Broth, M., & Keevallik, L. (2020). "Are you sad, Cozmo?": How humans make sense of a home robot's emotion displays. In *Proceedings of the 2020 ACM/IEEE international conference on human-robot interaction* (pp. 461–470). Association for Computing Machinery. https://doi.org/10.1145/3319502.3374814

Pelikan, H. R. M., Broth, M., & Keevallik, L. (2022). When a robot comes to life: The interactional achievement of agency as a transient phenomenon. *Social Interaction. Video-Based Studies of Human Sociality, 5*(3). https://doi.org/10.7146/si.v5i3.129915

Pelikan, H., & Hofstetter, E. (2022). Managing delays in human–robot interaction. *ACM Transactions on Computer–Human Interaction Just Accepted (October 2022).* https://doi.org/10.1145/3569890

Pitsch, K. (2016). Limits and opportunities for mathematizing communicational conduct for social robotics in the real world? Toward enabling a robot to make use of the human's competences. *AI and Society, 31*(4), 587–593. https://doi.org/10.1007/s00146-015-0629-0

Porcheron, M., Fischer, J. E., Reeves, S., & Sharples, S. (2018). Voice interfaces in everyday life. In *Proceedings of the 2018 CHI conference on human factors in computing systems* (pp. 640:1–640:12). Association for Computing Machinery. https://doi.org/10.1145/3173574.3174214

Roberts, F. (2012). Transcribing and transcription. In *The international encyclopedia of communication.* John Wiley & Sons, Ltd. https://doi.org/10.1002/9781405186407.wbiect056.pub2

Robinson, F. A., Bown, O., & Velonaki, M. (2022a). Designing sound for social robots: Candidate design principles. *International Journal of Social Robotics, 14*(6), 1507–1525. https://doi.org/10.1007/s12369-022-00891-0

Robinson, F., Velonaki, M., & Bown, O. (2022b). Crafting the language of robotic agents: A vision for electroacoustic music in human–robot interaction. *Organised Sound,* 1–13. https://doi.org/10.1017/S1355771822000358

Sacks, H. (1984). Notes on methodology. In J. Heritage & J. M. Atkinson (Ed.), *Structures of social action: Studies in conversation analysis* (pp. 21–27). Cambridge University Press.

Sacks, H., Schegloff, E. A., & Jefferson, G. (1974). A simplest systematics for the organization of Turn-Taking for conversation. *Language, 50*(4), 696. https://doi.org/10.2307/412243

Schegloff, E. A. (1968). Sequencing in conversational openings. *American Anthropologist, 70*(6), 1075–1095.

Selting, M., Auer, P., Barth-Weingarten, D., Bergmann, J., Bergmann, P., Birkner, K., Couper-Kuhlen, E., Meyer, C., Oberzaucher, F., & Uhmann, S. (2011). A system for transcribing talk-in-interaction: GAT 2. *Gesprächsforschung: Online-Zeitschrift Zur Verbalen Interaktion, 12*, 1–51.

Skantze, G. (2017). Predicting and regulating participation equality in human-robot conversations. In *Proceedings of the 2017 ACM/IEEE International Conference on Human-Robot Interaction* (pp. 196–204). Association for Computing Machinery. https://doi.org/10.1145/2909824.3020210

Suchman, L. A. (2007). *Human-machine reconfigurations: Plans and situated actions* (2nd ed.). Cambridge University Press. (Original work published 1987).

ten Have, P. (2002). Reflections on transcription. *Cahiers de Praxématique, 39*, 21–43. https://doi.org/10.4000/praxematique.1833

Tuncer, S., Licoppe, C., Luff, P., & Heath, C. (2023). Recipient design in human–robot interaction: The emergent assessment of a robot's competence. *AI and Society*. https://doi.org/10.1007/s00146-022-01608-7

Yamazaki, A., Yamazaki, K., Burdelski, M., Kuno, Y., & Fukushima, M. (2010). Coordination of verbal and non-verbal actions in human–robot interaction at museums and exhibitions. *Journal of Pragmatics, 42*(9), 2398–2414. https://doi.org/10.1016/j.pragma.2009.12.023

Yilmazyildiz, S., Read, R., Belpeame, T., & Verhelst, W. (2016). Review of semantic-free utterances in social human–robot interaction. *International Journal of Human–Computer Interaction, 32*(1), 63–85. https://doi.org/10.1080/10447318.2015.1093856

making co-participants see what the viewer is seeing (Nishizaka, 2018) or what a participant wants somebody else to see (Due et al., 2019), or different perceptions of what other participants are seeing (Goodwin, 1995). However, these kinds of studies anticipate sight as a common sensory resource. Organising participation frameworks in which one or more individuals are recognised as VIPs prompts a reconfiguration of the social, spatial, multimodal, and multisensorial organisation. As I will also reflect upon: Providing analytical insights on such types of configurations can be troublesome for any researcher who might also anticipate vision as a common resource.

Participation frameworks are built around participants, whom ethnomethodology considers members of a cultural society. Ten Have (2002) describes how "members use and rely on a corpus of practical knowledge which they assume is shared at least in part with others". As Garfinkel (1967) originally conceived, this membership knowledge is a "seen but unnoticed" resource in interaction. A member is not an individual or person but a collection of a specific set of cultural, epistemic, and language competences involved in being a member of a particular group (Garfinkel & Sacks, 1970). Participants in interaction mostly take for granted visual resources, just as most EMCA researchers assume the member's visual perspective when collecting and analysing data. As such, ocularcentrism has an invisible moral orderliness that becomes apparent in troublesome cases (cf. Garfinkel's study of a "transsexual" (1967, p. 116ff)). In this chapter, I adopt Garfinkel's approach to studies of perspicuous settings for close examination of sense-making activities, where the taken-for-granted vision becomes prominent.

EMCA research into settings with people with visual impairment

EMCA research on visual impairment has, in particular, focused on wayfinding, mobility, and navigation (Due & Lange, 2018b, 2018c; Psathas, 1976, 1992; Quéré & Relieu, 2001), but also on the guide dog (Due & Lange, 2018a; Mondémé, 2020), objects (Kreplak & Mondémé, 2014; Lehn, 2010), and technologies (Due et al., 2017; Hirvonen & Schmitt, 2018; Reyes-Cruz et al., 2020). Other studies have explored VIPs in local spatial settings in schools (Abrahamson et al., 2019; Avital & Streeck, 2011) or indoor climbing settings (Simone & Galatolo, 2020). These different studies of visual impairment have demonstrated aspects of how the world is ocularcentric, i.e. designed by and for sighted people. The studies reveal some of the taken-for-granted knowledge and practices that form part of our everyday activities and how they relate specifically to aspects of multisensoriality and perception. However, they do not deal with the social and embodied organisation of ocularcentric participation frameworks, in which the inclusion of VIPs becomes an accountable accomplishment. This chapter contributes new knowledge by bringing to the forefront the obvious existence and potentially excluding nature of ocularcentric participation frameworks.

Data and method

In a study of ocularcentric participation frameworks, we could, in principle, choose any type of data in which a visually impaired person interacts with a group of seeing participants. In this chapter, I have chosen an example that clearly highlights the difference between seeing participants and how their visual ecology and use of deictic terms naturally excludes the VIP, as well as how the shift away from ocularcentric sensory resources and toward a haptic sociality enables inclusion. We will examine in close detail the initiation of an experiment in which the VIP is supposed to eventually navigate from A to B with the commercial robot Spot, manufactured by Boston Dynamics. However, I do *not* focus on the experiment or on how the VIP accomplishes navigating along with the robot (for those analyses see Due (2022a, 2022b, 2023)). Rather, I unpack the ecology of initiating the experiment when participants with different statuses are involved. Of particular interest is the way in which visual impairment becomes relevant for the organisation of the pre-experiment. Image 1 illustrates the complexity of the participation framework.

The Spot robot is the main organisational hub at the centre of this F-formation (Kendon, 1976). There are two visually impaired people (VIPs). PAR1 owns the dog and is the subject who will walk with the robot in this experiment. Both PAR1 and PAR2 are completely blind. Also present are three researchers from the university. RES2 is the project leader, who is not recording. RES5 and RES6 (an instructor for blind people) are located on each side of the setting and are recording using GoPros. There are four participants from the technical institute that owns the robot. RES1 is an assistant, who is responsible for public relations. She is also a participant in the experiment (as a human "obstacle" around which the VIP + robot will eventually have to navigate). RES3 is the supervisor, who also performs

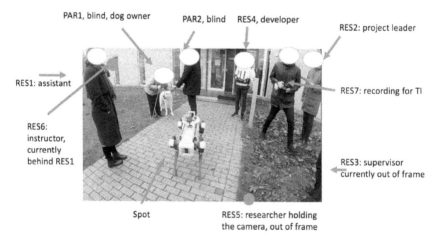

IMAGE 1 The setting, consisting of nine human agents and two non-human agents (dog and robot).

a role as a human "obstacle". RES4 is the software developer who operates Spot. RES7 also works in public relations for the institute and is taking close-up recordings for the project. This analysis follows the unfolding of this single case as the experiment is about to begin. The example is divided into four fragments: 1) getting ready to move as a blind person alone; 2) taking – and accounting for the lack of – a member's perspective; 3) verbally including the VIP in the ocularcentric participation framework; and 4) fracturing the ocularcentric participation framework by shifting to a haptic sociality. The guiding analytical questions concern problematic aspects associated with taking a member's perspective, as well as the construction and deconstruction of the ocularcentric participation framework.

Analysis

It is observable how PAR1, PAR2, and the dog form a micro-territory (Scheflen, 1975), with the dog as the focal point (Figures 13–15), and that they are standing slightly apart from the others. While PAR1, who owns the dog, is standing with her face and front towards the robot and the other participants, PAR2 is squatting at an intimate distance with the dog (Hall, 1976). PAR1 is bodily displaying an orientation to the main activity: the other participants and the robot. She has just handed the dog's leash to PAR2, and it is noticeable how she minimally initiates a movement with her left leg toward the operator and the robot (Figure 13). It is not a complete movement as she is still holding the cane in a resting position with a closed fist, and the stick falls perpendicularly to the ground. By comparing Figure 13 with 14, it is noticeable how she reorients her body away from the dog and

FRAGMENT 1   Getting ready to move as a blind person alone.

#13 / 00.28   #14 / 00.29   #15 / 00.30

#13b / 00.28   #15b / 00.30

18. RES4: test nummer et med spot robotten#13
          test number one with the spot robot
19.   #14(0.5)#15(0.5)

PAR2 and towards the robot, but she then stands still in a waiting position (Figure 15). This reorientation can be seen as a response to the more formalised initiation of the experiment produced by RES4: "test number one with the spot robot" (l. 18). This turn is a response to a prior interaction between RES4 and RES3 concerning the recording equipment. These sighted members of the situation – and I as the analyst – recognise how the turn in line 18 is directed to the recording device as a kind of "start-the-test-documentary", as there is no visual orientation to another human recipient (Figure 14–16). However, without this access to RES4's visual orientation, the turn can also be interpreted as a common initiation of the experiment, in which PAR1 is supposed to walk with the robot. This situation is a manifestation of the *ocularcentric participation framework*, where a sighted participant produces a turn with no extra verbal references or other indexical cues or multisensorial signs that make its recipiency understandable by sensory means other than sight alone. The intelligibility lies solely in the visibility of the speaker's body, head, and gaze direction that is *not* projected towards a human recipient (RES4, Figure 15). So far, the visually impaired person is reorienting and displaying "getting ready to move" (Broth & Keevallik, 2014) but is left standing alone in a waiting position with no display of understanding of whether she was projected as the next person to do something or not.

From a visual perspective, however, the VIP seems marginalised as she orients away from the dog and PAR2 and still is not bodily included in the new configuration. But from a visually impaired perspective, this might not be the case since no one accounts for the identity of the "true" recipient of RES4 utterance. As such, dealing with a blind member's perspective seems to be infused with a paradox: namely, that the visual analysis shows how a blind person is left in a waiting position with no clear understanding of the next actions due to a "wrong" understanding of recipiency, but at the same time the VIP herself does not account for this as a problem, as she has no perception of it. PAR1 is displaying an orientation towards the robot but is standing still in a waiting position and exhibiting a bodily monitoring stance, probably waiting for a more directive instruction. In the next fragment, we see how this isolated waiting becomes accountable.

RES6 seems to recognise PAR1's bodily orientation towards the robot, as she now produces a request to "someone" (l.20): "I am thinking someone should give you a clue about where it is (.) Tina" (l. 20–22). RES6's verbal action can be taken as an accountable response to the fact that PAR1 is displaying readiness but has received no verbal direction or guidance of any sort. Thus, RES6 is taking another member's perspective by verbally addressing the need for guidance, something she presumably infers from PAR1's bodily orientation, which projects the trajectory. However, while PAR1 is standing in an isolated waiting position, RES4 is engaged in a different conversation. He is addressing the other participants (see image 1) with task-specific talk regarding the experiment (l. 21-26). The talk is produced in overlap, and there is no response to RES6's request to assist PAR1. RES4 is bodily orienting away from the VIP and toward RES2, and

FRAGMENT 2   Taking – and accounting for the lack of – a member's perspective.

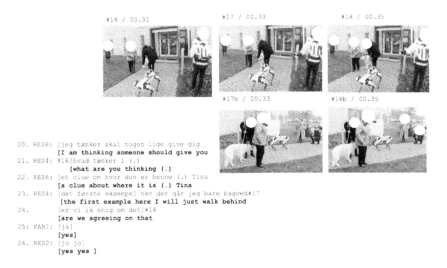

```
20. RES6: [jeg tænker skal nogen lige give dig
           [I am thinking someone should give you
21. RES4: #16[hvad tænker i (.)
              [what are you thinking (.)
22. RES6: [et clue om hvor den er henne (.) Tina
           [a clue about where it is (.) Tina
23. RES4: [det første eksempel her der går jeg bare bagved#17
           [the first example here I will just walk behind
24.        [er vi ik enig om det]#18
           [are we agreeing on that
25: PAR1: [ja]
           [yes]
26. RES2: [jo jo]
           [yes yes ]
```

then RES3 and RES5 (Figure 18b), as he explicates his understanding of what he will do in the experiment: "the first experiment here I will just walk behind are we agreeing on that" (l. 23–24). RES2 responds to this question design with a minimal aligning "yes, yes". It is also noticeable that PAR1, the VIP responds with a "yes" (l.25). A purely linguistics analysis could lead to the interpretation that this is an aligning response to RES4, similar to RES2. However, a multi-modal analysis encourages the interpretation that PAR1s response is a confirmation of the RES6 prior turn. Figures 17b–18b shows how PAR1 is turning her head and directing her response designed with a smile to the person standing behind her (RES6), which can be interpreted as a visual display of PAR1's recipiency of RES6's previous turn (l. 22). This "yes" is thus not just a minimal response but rather displaying emotional affiliation and strong agreement with the suggestion that "someone should give you a clue about where it is" (l. 20–22). So, two distinct participation frameworks appear to be active concurrently, one including RES6 and PAR1 and the other including RES4, RES3 and RES5. The talk about aspects of the experiment does not seem to be produced with PAR1 as a recipient. The other seeing participants recognise this from RES4 turning his torso, head and gaze to project them as recipients (Figure 16–18), and I, in the role of analyst, recognise this from observing the video recordings. At the same time, RES6 and PAR1 are co-constructing the need for guidance. We will see how this is done in the next excerpt.

RES6 seems to recognise the visually impaired person's (PAR1) orientation to the main activity. By taking the blind member's non-visual perspective, she produces further verbal actions aimed at including PAR1 in the participation

FRAGMENT 3   Verbally including the VIP in the ocularcentric participation framework.

```
27. RES6: jeg tror liige I skal    [guide Tina over til (.) spot #19
          I just think you should [guide Tina towards spot
28. RES4:                          [JA (.) Tina (.) [kom med her#20 (.) den kommer lige her#21
                                   [YES (.) Tina (.) come with me (.) it is just here
29. PAR2:                                           [må jeg få en godbid
                                                    [can I have a dog treat
30: PAR1: det må du#22b
          yes you may
```

```
31. RES4: du har robotten#25 til venstre for dig
          you have the robot on your left side
32. PAR1: jaa#26
          yees
```

framework, which can be heard as an upgraded account produced in a sequential environment where there has been no uptake on the prior call for guidance: "I just think you should guide Tina towards spot" (l. 27). Although the word choice "I think" is grammatically and epistemically weak, it only functions as a mitigating *pre* before the unfolding of the project within this turn, which is: "you should guide Tina". Merged into this directive turn-design (Potter & Craven, 2010) is a moral obligation ("you should") that builds on the contextual and indexical knowledge of PAR1 being blind, and thus the difficulties of understanding spatial relations and accomplishing "simple" navigational tasks such as walking toward the robot.

At this point in the analysis, we must include prior knowledge of the different participants' experiences and epistemic stances (Heritage, 2012) in relation to visual impairment. Whereas RES6 displays a transportable identity (Zimmerman, 1998) of being knowledgeable about blindness, as is observable in her adopting the blind member's perspective (she is an instructor in a blindness organisation), RES4 displays a situated and transportable identity of being a novice in terms of blindness. Therefore, it seems obvious that RES6 is enacting the membership category "blindness-knowing" by practically orienting toward issues of assistance, mobility, and navigation for PAR1, whereas RES4, being a novice in blindness, but an expert in robotics, orients to the procedures of the experiment.

As this upgraded moral obligation ("you should") is built into the design of the turn produced by RES6, it is unsurprising that RES4 responds immediately and in overlap. When RES6 finishes her turn ("guide Tina towards Spot" (l. 27)), RES4 simultaneously produces a strong affiliation with the moral obligation, which can be heard through the prompt responding "YES", produced with high volume, followed by a request to Tina to approach the Spot robot: "Tina (.) come with me (.) it is just here" (l. 28).

If PAR1 were a sighted person with visual access to the robot and the sociotechnical ecology, there would be no problems with this simple verbal request, which is designed as a declarative using deixis, to produce an indexical reference to a point in space ("it is just here"). This is produced while RES4 simultaneously seems to reach out to Tina with his right hand, as if projecting a haptic guidance (Fig. 20/20b), but such embodied action is aborted because immediately afterwards Tina turns to PAR2 to give him a dog treat following his overlapping request (l. 29). Then, RES6 uses the index finger to produce a simple pointing gesture to the robot ("it is just here") (Figure 21). As we know from previous studies of pointing practices (e.g. Goodwin, 2003), to point is to project something as understandable from a visual point of view. Pointing is a basic aspect of human sociality and the evolution of language (Tomasello, 2008) but loses its concrete meaning in the context of blindness (Saerberg, 2010). Pointing is a prime example of the organisation of ocularcentric participation frameworks, as its semiotic meaning is purely visually indexical.

RES4 then changes action formation toward a more explanatory description of the object's position in space. While pointing (Figure 25), he produces a spatial description, the pragmatic features of which could also be an instruction: "you have the robot on your left side" (l. 31). Compared to the prior turn, this turn is significantly more indexical in terms of preparing for the VIP's "perception-related actions" (Due, 2021). This is recognisable through the reversed point of view ("on your") and the location-specific indexical word choice ("left side"). Such words

FRAGMENT 4   Fracturing the ocularcentric participation framework through intercorporeality.

33. RES4: lidt længere til venstre#27
       a little further to the left
34. PAR1: ja; (.) nu har jeg kun min blindestok#28 med i dag#29
       yes ¡(.) I only have my cane with me today
35. RES4: jaa (.) så kommer den (.) liige #30
       yees (.) here it comes (.) juust

36. RES4: må jeg kan du mærke#31 din hånd her#32 (.) yes#33
       may I can you feel your hand here (.) yes
37. PAR1: der var den ja#34
       there it was yes

can be employed effectively to provide a blind recipient with instructions during navigational tasks, for instance, this has been shown in previous analyses of para-climbing with visually impaired climbers (Simone & Galatolo, 2021). But they are not effective in this context as there is no shared understanding of the procedures for the activity. Whereas RES6 requested that someone "should guide Tina" (l. 27), possibly implying that this guiding should be bodily and tactile, RES4 approaches it as a verbal, descriptive practice. PAR1 (Tina) is reaching out her left arm (Figure 26), which is sequentially positioned following the description or possible direction given by RES4 ("you have the robot on your left side" (l. 31). In this environment, the embodied action of reaching out the arm both displays an understanding of RES4's prior turn as an instruction to grab the robot and an invitation to be haptically guided by RES4.

In many situations within ordinary taken-for-granted ocularcentric participation frameworks, verbal descriptions work finely as "seen but unnoticed" (Garfinkel, 1967) guiding actions, but they are revealed as accountable phenomena when visually impaired people are part of the framework in contexts where co-participants do not have a member's knowledge of how to act in coordination with visually impaired people. Figure 27 illustrates an uncooperative moment. The VIP reaches out, either grabbing the robot and/or receiving bodily guiding and assistance, thus seeking to break the configuration of the participation framework as solely being visually organised. However, instead of responding with the body or with further detailed verbal instructions, RES4 points toward the robot with a palm hand. There is no fracture of the ocularcentric organisation, which prompts PAR1 to produce a verbal account that almost works as an excuse for not being able to find the robot: "yes (.) I only have my cane with me today" (l. 34). This turn, in this sequential environment, functions as an explanation of the trouble involved in locating the whereabouts of the robot and the failure to receive bodily guidance based on verbal descriptions alone. Only a member of "the culture of visual impairment" would know the difference between a long white cane and a short guide cane. A long white cane is the "norm" used for navigation. The short guide cane is used to identify any immediate obstacles, and it is not used for navigation in the way that the white cane is used. The differences between the canes are made interactionally relevant in this context as a kind of excuse for not easily navigating towards and locating the robot. This indexical membership knowledge is used as an explanation that makes the category of being blind explicitly and morally relevant, but there is no uptake from RES4. This may be because he has no knowledge of the differences between canes, and their consequences for navigation and the practices of achieving understanding of object–space relations in the situation, and thus his inability to adopt that kind of membership perspective.

While PAR1 produces the account (l. 34), she simultaneously makes an observable change in her bodily stance, from reaching out (Figure 27), thereby bodily recruiting assistance (Kendrick & Drew, 2016), to standing still, with her arm bent (Figure 28). One of the "official" practices for guiding visually impaired people is to let them hold on to the elbow or forearm (EverydaySight, 2018), which PAR1 can be seen to invite in Figure 27. As RES4 does not orient to this practical morality of attending to the consequences of visual impairment, PAR1 changes her bodily position, now more clearly offering her left arm (elbow) to be grabbed – an action that seems to be mirrored by RES4 (Figure 28). As RES4 still does not engage in a haptic sociality (Cekaite et al., 2020) with PAR1, she reaches her arm out towards the presumed position of the robot, while RES4 continues to produce verbal descriptions of the robot's position in space (l. 35).

For sighted people, and in the visual analysis, it seems that PAR1 is almost touching the robot. However, as the robot is producing no non-visual sensory signs, its position in space is not recognisable for PAR1. In effect, she can be close to touching it while at the same time being "far away" from succeeding. Finally, RES4 seems to recognise that verbal descriptions are insufficient in guiding PAR1 into the midst of the participation framework and toward a physical encounter with the robot – specifically, grabbing the harness attached to it. Consequently, RES4 first touches PAR1 on the left elbow (Figure 30) and then accounts for it: "may I can you feel your hand here (.) yes" (l. 36). Touching and achieving an intercorporeal (Meyer et al., 2017) relation with PAR1 is thus not unnoticeably accomplished but treated as something that requires permission. The first part of the turn, "may I", is a question associated with politeness, which displays an orientation toward the morality of attending to the sensory impairment as a reason for crossing the boundary of another person's intimate space. However, as RES4 has already touched PAR1, the turn-constructional unit has no real pragmatic effect. This is observable because PAR1 does not respond, and RES4 continues, with no intraturn space produced for a response. As RES4 has already touched PAR1, he continues with the bodily directed description "can you feel" (l. 36) while observably grabbing PAR1's arm more firmly and pulling it down (Figure 31), and then says, "your hand here" (l. 36), as he pulls her arm all the way down to the harness, which is hanging from the robot (Figure 32). The deictic word "here" is produced at the exact moment PAR1 touches the harness (Figure 32), and RES4 lets go of PAR1's arm (Figure 33). He accounts for the fact that PAR1 has now touched the robot and grabbed the harness with a confirming verbal attachment: "yes" (l. 36). PAR1 responds with affiliation (Steensig, 2013): "there it was yes" (l. 37, Figure 34). The deictic "there" referring to the harness's spatial position, combined with the affiliation, confirms that common ground and a mutual perceptual field have been established. This excerpt neatly illustrates the possible "awkwardness" and "uncertainty" participants may experience and display in interaction with people with disabilities. These kinds of social encounters require attention to what is otherwise taken for granted, and the analysis has shown how this requires extra communicative work to fracture the otherwise taken-for-granted ocularcentric participation framework.

Conclusion

For a visually impaired person, moving two metres towards a robodog and grabbing its harness requires a complex organisation of participation status, requests, bodily displays of recruitment, verbal descriptions and instructions, and the final organisation of a haptic sociality as an apparatus for fracturing the ocularcentric organisation of the participation framework. Orienting to the robot is, as the analysis has shown, only a "simple task", for all practical purposes, when participants can easily see and have a shared perception of the object to which attention is directed. However, the situation is very different when one of the participants is visually impaired, which makes this a perspicuous case for exploring the seen but unnoticed visual aspects of ocularcentric participation frameworks. The analysis showed the overall sequential process of 1) getting ready to move as a blind person alone, and 2) how a competent member (RES6) then verbally adopts a member's perspective and accounts for the possible social exclusion. The analysis then showed 3) how RES4 reorients and takes a member's perspective and displays recognition for the need for guiding actions, but then produces these as verbal descriptions, using ocularcentric indexical terminology. As such, ocularcentric participation frameworks seem to be defined by actions that privilege vision and the use of deictics in face-formations over other senses and thus practices of seeing, looking, and gazing as a member's taken-for-granted resource for ordinary interactional projects. Finally, 4) the analysis showed how the ocularcentric participation framework becomes an observable, accountable form of contextual configuration when the visual primacy is fractured, and intersubjectivity is achieved through other sensory resources – specifically, haptics and touch, as the key sensory resource for distribution of perception-related actions (Due, 2021). The shift in sensory resource was enacted as a change from deictic terms ("here", "there") to touching the VIP, but only after the VIP (PAR1) produced recruiting actions (Drew & Kendrick, 2018) (bodily positioning and verbal excuses). There was then a stepwise transition from indexical verbal descriptions with pointing practices to a haptic sociality. Cekaite and Mondada have shown how touch can be used as "a communicative resource to coordinate social interaction and various courses of action" (2021, p. 10). In this analysis, steering and coordination through the use of "body techniques" (Mauss, 1935) are not treated interactionally as an intervention but as effective means for accomplishing the activity.

This chapter described the shift in sensory resources for communication as not just joint attention but a *morality of attention* towards sensory impairment, most explicitly accounted for by the word "should" (l. 22 and 24). This directive turn-design in that sequential environment has a moral obligation toward guiding. Belonging to the category of being visually impaired involves aspects of help and assistance. These category devices have a cultural association, which Sacks calls standardised relational pairs. Housley (2021, p. 211) states that

> one of the key features of these forms of membership categorization is that they exercise descriptive and moral control of who or what is allocated where. In addition, standardized relational pairs can be seen to be operative within particular situations, such as the activity of giving or providing help [...] In situations where help is required, the absence of one of these categories from these types of pairing is recognizable and morally notable.

There is a distributed form of responsibility for accomplishing the mobility of PAR1 in and through both her own actions and the actions of RES4 and RES6, making the pairing of "guiding help" + "VIP" a relevant moral concern that is embedded within the unfolding ecology of the situation as an ocularcentric participation framework.

For sighted people, spatial positions and the unfolding of activities are understandable via interpretations of bodily positions, head movements, and gaze directions, which function as projecting devices (Streeck, 1995). A sighted person can see what is going on, and they are able to infer relevance and meaning from this. This is clearly not possible for a VIP. This analysis prompts deeper reflections on membership understandings. On the one hand, we could easily compare being blindfolded with visual impairment, as Garfinkel had his students do in a breaching project on the use of "inverting lenses", which impair vision by reversing left/right and up/down. Robillard (1999, p. 155) describes how Garfinkel's students found it impossible to write their names on a blackboard while wearing these lenses. Via this experiment, Garfinkel demonstrated how mundane tasks such as writing are founded on the assumption of normal eyesight. However, this kind of experiment is not really providing knowledge about visually impaired members' experiences. As the blind researcher Saerberg argues, we need to shift the conception of blindness as loss of sight (a deficit) to a conception that sees blindness "as an own style of perception" based on a "different organization of sensory and bodily orientation and practice" (Saerberg, 2015, pp. 582–583). Adopting a blind member's perspective on an issue as fundamental as sensory access to the world might therefore require deeper understandings of perception and membership experiences as displayed in social interaction. As the analysis showed, orienting to a "world of blindness" (Hull, 1997) was performed very differently by RES6 (knowledgeable about blindness) and RES4 (novice in terms of blindness), thus showing how membership is always membership of some (sub-)culture with specific forms of knowledge territory (Goffman, 1971). RES6 displayed a transportable identity of concern for, and knowledge of, visual impairment. RES4, on the other hand, displayed a transportable identity of being the operator of the robot. These different membership categories were also shown to be pertinent in situ as different ways of adopting a blind member's perspective.

One principle in EMCA research is to study *witnessable, observable, exhibited,* and *displayable* phenomena as they are and as they occur as practical action in everyday situations (Garfinkel & Sacks, 1970). This is clearly visually biased terminology. Consequently, it could be argued that a visual bias is embedded within some EMCA research. This is due, in part, to our society's more general ocularcentrism. However, it may also relate, in a more methodological sense, to original observations in ethnomethodology concerning the *visibility* (etc.) of action. What I would suggest calling the *visibility bias* relates to the fact that EMCA has largely focused on visual resources and actions. Even in the growing literature available on multisensoriality, visual sensation remains primordial (e.g. Edmonds & Greiffenhagen, 2020; Pillet-Shore, 2020) – exceptions being taste (Fele & Liberman, 2020; Wiggins & Keevallik, 2020) and smell (Mondada, 2021) – but still in a context of an anticipated common visual orientation. Studying VIPs prompts a respecification of sociality as being more than "simply" visually organised. The visibility bias thus also requires a respecification of the categories used to describe practices. Consequently, it might be argued that learning about a VIP's being-in-the-world could require methods other than video recordings. Such forms of analysis may entail conceivable biases and inherent problems, in that the researcher is analysing a world that is simply too foreign and strange to them, and because the sighted, video-recording researcher is unable truly to inhabit the member's perspective. One way to counter and address these challenges is by drawing on both ethnographic and interview material, as well as the principles of EMCA's *descriptive* action-oriented analysis.

In this chapter, I have attempted to strike a balance between, on the one hand, the need to find evidence for each claim within the data itself without invoking unnecessary further contextual knowledge (Schegloff, 1987) and on the other, an acknowledgement that insightful analysis is only possible when it involves some form of member's competence, i.e. ethnographic knowledge (Heath & Hindmarsh, 2002; Moerman, 1988) of who the participants are, their situational identities, and their epistemic status on the issue of blindness. Garfinkel called for the "quiddity" (just whatness) and "haecceity" (just thisness) (Lynch, 1993) of what makes up a particular situation and wrote that in order to achieve this, the researcher should develop a deep competence in the particular field. What Garfinkel and Wieder (1992, p. 182) called the "unique adequacy requirement of methods" refers to how the researcher must be "vulgarly competent in the local production and reflexively natural accountability of the phenomenon of order he is 'studying'". On this basis, ethnomethodologists have explored, in depth and from the inside, phenomena such as learning to play the piano (Sudnow, 1978), doing advanced mathematics (Livingston, 1986), or living with impairment (Robillard, 1999), to name but a few. However, as I have tried to show in this chapter, a member's perspective is not sufficient for, nor a guarantee of a more truthful analysis. The idea that you must have – and exhibit in analysis – a vulgar competence in "the local production of the phenomenon of order" (Garfinkel & Wieder, 1992) is not the same as maintaining any such local member's perspective throughout the analytical work. The analysis of this perspicuous case of how a blind person is only slowly included in a participation framework as its ocularcentrism becomes fractured shows not only the situated members' problems in terms of adopting a blind perspective but also the analyst's paradox of trying to hear the world from a blind perspective, while still seeing how hearing is not sufficient for the member's timely inclusion.

As a seeing researcher, I cannot fully adopt a blind perspective on the world, but neither can other situated participants. I could have chosen only to conduct this analysis by listening to the audio from the camera closest to the VIP, which would have enabled a deeper blind member's perspective on the situation. However, I would then have missed precisely what blind people often miss – namely, the visual organisation that excludes blind people, even though they might not observe it or account for it. This observation is not reproducing the problem of constructing blindness as a deficit, as sometimes found in disability studies, but argues that practical interactions with VIPs require different organisations of sensory and bodily practices. Future studies of not just visually impaired people in interactions with seeing participants but also ordinary ocularcentric participation frameworks could pay more attention to multisensoriality and moderate the usually strong focus on the audio–visual organisation of interaction and the taken-for-granted nature of the individual's own membership perspective.

References

Abrahamson, D., Flood, V. J., Miele, J. A., & Siu, Y.-T. (2019). Enactivism and ethnomethodological conversation analysis as tools for expanding universal design for learning: The case of visually impaired mathematics students. *ZDM, 51*(2), 291–303. https://doi.org/10.1007/s11858-018-0998-1

Avital, S., & Streeck, J. (2011). Terra incognita: Social interaction among blind children. In J. Streeck, C. Goodwin, & C. D. LeBaron (Eds.), *Embodied interaction: Language and body in the material world* (pp. 169–181). Cambridge University Press.

Broth, M., & Keevallik, L. (2014). Getting ready to move as a couple accomplishing mobile formations in a dance class. *Space and Culture, 17*(2), 107–121. https://doi.org/10.1177/1206331213508483

Cekaite, A., & Mondada, L. (2021) (eds.). Towards an interactional approach to touch in social encounters. In *Touch in social interaction: Touch, language, and body* (pp. 1–27). Routledge.

Cekaite, A., Mondada, L., & Mondada, L. (2020). *Touch in social interaction: Touch, language, and body*. Routledge. https://doi.org/10.4324/9781003026631

Drew, P., & Kendrick, K. H. (2018). Searching for trouble: Recruiting assistance through embodied action. *Social Interaction: Video-Based Studies of Human Sociality, 1*(1). https://doi.org/10.7146/si.v1i1.105496

Due, B. L. (2021). Distributed perception: Co-operation between Sense-Able, actionable, and accountable semiotic agents. *Symbolic Interaction, 44*(1), 134–162. https://doi.org/10.1002/symb.538

Due, B. L. (2022a). The haecceity of assembling by distributing perception. *Academic Medicine/IEEE HRI 2022*. 17th annual ACM/IEEE international conference on human-robot interaction (HRI 2022)!, Online Originaly Sapporo, Hokkaido, Japan.

Due, B. L. (2022b). Guide dog versus robot dog: Assembling visually impaired people with non-human agents and achieving assisted mobility through distributed co-constructed perception. *Mobilities, 0*(0), 1–19. https://doi.org/10.1080/17450101.2022.2086059

Due, B. L. (2023). A walk in the park with Robodog: Navigating around pedestrians using a Spot robot as a 'guide dog.' *Space and Culture*. DOI:10.1177/12063312231159215

Due, B. L., Kupers, R., Lange, S. B., & Ptito, M. (2017). Technology enhanced vision in blind and visually impaired individuals. Synoptik Foundation Research project. *Circd Working Papers in Social Interaction, 3, 1*, 1–31.

Due, B. L., & Lange, S. B. (2018a). Semiotic resources for navigation: A video ethnographic study of blind people's uses of the white cane and a guide dog for navigating in urban areas. *Semiotica, 222,* 287–312. https://doi.org/10.1515/sem-2016-0196

Due, B. L., & Lange, S. B. (2018b). The Moses effect: The spatial hierarchy and joint accomplishment of a blind person navigating. *Space and Culture, 21*(2), 129–144. https://doi.org/10.1177/1206331217734541

Due, B. L., & Lange, S. B. (2018c). Troublesome objects: Unpacking ocular-centrism in urban environments by studying blind navigation using video ethnography and ethnomethodology. *Sociological Research Online, 24*(4), 475–495. https://doi.org/10.1177/1360780418811963

Due, B. L., Lange, S. B., Nielsen, M. F., & Jarlskov, C. (2019). Mimicable embodied demonstration in a decomposed sequence: Two aspects of recipient design in professionals' video-mediated encounters. *Journal of Pragmatics, 152,* 13–27. https://doi.org/10.1016/j.pragma.2019.07.015

Edmonds, D. M., & Greiffenhagen, C. (2020). Configuring prospective sensations: Experimenters preparing participants for what they might feel. *Symbolic Interaction, n/a*(n/a). https://doi.org/10.1002/symb.485

EverydaySight. (2018, November 27). How to guide a person who is visually impaired or blind: 12 tips for sighted guide. *Everyday Sight.* https://www.everydaysight.com/how-to-guide-a-person-who-is-visually-impaired/

Fele, G., & Liberman, K. (2020). Some discovered practices of lay coffee drinkers. *Symbolic Interaction, online first.* https://doi.org/10.1002/symb.486

Garfinkel, H. (1963). A conception of and experiments with '"trust"' as a condition of stable concerted actions. In O. J. Harvey (Ed.), *Motivation and social interaction: Cognitive determinants* (pp. 187–138). The Ronald Press Company.

Garfinkel, H. (1967). *Studies in ethnomethodology.* Prentice Hall.

Garfinkel, H., & Sacks, H. L. (1970). On formal structures of practical actions. In J. C. McKinney & E. A. Tiryakian (Eds.), *Theoretical sociology: Perspectives and developments* (pp. 338–366). Appleton Century Crofts.

Garfinkel, H., & Wieder, D. L. (1992). Two incommensurable, asymmetrically alternate technologies of social analysis. In G. Watson & R. M. Seiler (Eds.), *Text in context: Studies in ethnomethodology* (pp. 175–206). Sage.

Goffman, E. (1971). *Relations in public: Microstudies of the public order.* Harper and Row.

Goffman, E. (1981). *Forms of talk.* University of Pennsylvania Press.

Goodwin, C. (1980). Restarts, pauses, and the achievement of a state of mutual gaze at turn-beginning. *Sociological Inquiry, 50*(3–4), 272–302.

Goodwin, C. (1994). Professional vision. *American Anthropologist, 96*(3), 606–633.

Goodwin, C. (1995). Seeing in depth. *Social Studies of Science, 25*(2), 237–274.

Goodwin, C. (2003). Pointing as situated practice. In S. Kita (Ed.), *Pointing: Where language, culture and cognition meet* (pp. 217–241). Erlbaum.

Goodwin, C. (2007). Participation, stance and affect in the organization of activities. *Discourse and Society, 18*(1), 53–74.

Goodwin, C., & Goodwin, M. H. (2005). Participation. In A. Duranti (Ed.), *A companion to linguistic anthropology.*(pp. 222-244) Blackwell.

Hall, E. T. (1976). *Beyond culture.* Anchor. http://www.amazon.com/Beyond-Culture-Edward-T-Hall/dp/0385124740

Have, P. T. (2002). The notion of member is the heart of the matter: On the role of membership knowledge in ethnomethodological inquiry. *Forum Qualitative Sozialforschung: Forum:*

Qualitative Social Research, *3*(3). http://www.qualitative-research.net/index.php/fqs/article/view/834

Heath, C. (1984). Participation in the medical consultation: The co-ordination of verbal and nonverbal behaviour between the doctor and patient. *Sociology of Health and Illness*, *6*(3), 311–388. https://doi.org/10.1111/1467-9566.ep10491964

Heath, C., & Hindmarsh, J. (2002). Analysing interaction: Video, ethnography and situated conduct. In T. May (Ed.), *Qualitative research in action* (pp. 99–121). http://citeseerx.ist.psu.edu/viewdoc/summary?doi=10.1.1.111.5096

Heritage, J. (2012). The epistemic engine: Sequence organization and territories of knowledge. *Research on Language and Social Interaction*, *45*(1), 30–52. https://doi.org/10.1080/08351813.2012.646685

Hirvonen, M. I., & Schmitt, R. (2018). Blindheit als Ressource: Zur professionellen Kompetenz eines blinden Teammitglieds bei der gemeinsamen Anfertigung einer Audiodeskription. *Gesprächsforschung*, *19*, 449–477.

Housley, W. (2021). Harvey Sacks, membership categorization and social media. In O. Sacks (Ed.), *Methodology, materials, and inspirations* (pp. 208–221). Routledge.

Hull, J. M. (1997). *On sight & insight: A journey into the world of blindness*. Oneworld.

Jay, M. (1994). *Downcast eyes: The denigration of vision in twentieth-century French thought*. University of California Press.

Kendon, A., Harris, R. M., & Key, M. R. (1975). *Organization of behavior in face-to-face interaction*. Walter de Gruyter.

Kendon, A. (1976). The F-Formation System: The Spatial Organization of Social Encounters. *Man-Environment Systems*, *6*, 291–296.

Kendrick, K. H., & Drew, P. (2016). Recruitment: Offers, requests, and the organization of assistance in interaction. *Research on Language and Social Interaction*, *49*(1), 1–19. https://doi.org/10.1080/08351813.2016.1126436

Kreplak, Y., & Mondémé, C. (2014). Artworks as touchable objects. In M. Nevile, P. Haddington, T. Heinemann, & M. Rauniomaa (Eds.), *Interacting with Objects: Language, materiality, and social activity* (pp. 295–318). John Benjamins Publishing. https://benjamins.com/#catalog/books/z.186.13kre/details

Livingston, E. (1986). *The ethnomethodological foundations of mathematics*. Routledge & Kegan Paul.

Lynch, M. (1993). *Scientific practice and ordinary action: Ethnomethodology and social studies of science*. Cambridge University Press.

Mauss, M. (1935). Les techniques du corps = bodily techniques. *Journal de Psychologie Normale et Pathologique*, *32*, 271–293.

Maynard, D. (2005). Social actions, gestalt coherence, and designations of disability: Lessons from and about autism. *Social Problems*, *52*(4), 499–524. https://doi.org/10.1525/SP.2005.52.4.499

Meyer, C., Streeck, J., & Jordan, J. S. (2017). *Intercorporeality: Emerging socialities in interaction*. Oxford University Press.

Moerman, M. (1988). *Talking culture: Ethnography and conversation analysis*. University of Pennsylvania Press.

Mondada, L. (Ed.). (2021). Sensing in social interaction. In *Sensing in social interaction: The taste for cheese in gourmet shops* (pp. i–ii). Cambridge University Press. https://www.cambridge.org/core/books/sensing-in-social-interaction/sensing-in-social-interaction/920F3437C1F1630D2C2D547627F92E69

Mondémé, C. (2020). *La socialité interspécifique: Une analyse multimodale des interactions homme-chien*. Lambert-Lucas.

Nishizaka, A. (2018). Aspect-seeing in the interactional organization of activities. *Tartu Semiotics Library*, *19*, 345–354.

Pillet-Shore, D. (2020). When to make the sensory social: Registering in face-to-face openings. *Symbolic Interaction*, *n/a*(n/a). https://doi.org/10.1002/symb.481

Potter, J., & Craven, A. (2010). Directives: Entitlement and contingency in action. *Discourse Studies*. http://journals.sagepub.com/doi/10.1177/1461445610370126

Psathas, G. (1976). Mobility, orientation, and navigation: Conceptual and theoretical considerations. *New Outlook for the Blind*, *70*(9), 385–391.

Psathas, G. (1992). The study of extended sequences: The case of the garden lesson. In G. Watson & R. M. Seiler (Eds.), *Text in context: Contributions to ethnomethodology* (pp. 99–122). Sage.

Quéré, L., & Relieu, M. (2001). *Modes de locomotion et inscription spatiale des inégalités. Les déplacements des personnes atteintes de handicaps visuels et moteurs dans l'esplace public*. RAPPORT DE RECHERCHE Convention Ecole des Hautes Etudes en Sciences Sociales/Ministère de l'équipement, du transport et du logement-Direction générale de l'urbanisme, de l'habitat et de la construction

Rawls, A. W., Whitehead, K. A., & Duck, W. (Eds.). (2020). *Black lives matter—Ethnomethodological and conversation analytic studies of Race and systemic racism in everyday interaction*. Routledge.

Raymond, G., & Heritage, J. (2006). The epistemics of social relations: Owning grandchildren. *Language in Society*, *35*(05), 677–705. https://doi.org/10.1017/S0047404506060325

Reyes-Cruz, G., Fischer, J. E., & Reeves, S. (2020). Reframing disability as competency: Unpacking everyday technology practices of people with visual impairments. In *Proceedings of the 2020 CHI conference on human factors in computing systems* (pp. 1–13). https://doi.org/10.1145/3313831.3376767

Robillard, A. B. (1999). *Meaning of a disability: The lived experience of paralysis*. Temple University Press.

Sacks, H. L. (1989). Lecture six: The M.I.R. membership categorization device. *Human Studies*, *12*(3/4), 271–281.

Saerberg, S. (2010). Just go straight ahead. *The Senses and Society*, *5*(3), 364–381. https://doi.org/10.2752/174589210X12753842356124

Saerberg, S. (2015). Chewing accidents a phenomenology of visible and invisible everyday accomplishments. *Journal of Contemporary Ethnography*, *44*(5), 580–597. https://doi.org/10.1177/0891241615587380

Scheflen, A. E. (1975). Micro-territories in human interaction. In A. Kendon, R. M. Harris, & M. R. Key (Eds.), *Organization of behavior in face-to-face interaction* (pp. 159–174). Mouton; Chicago.

Schegloff, E. A. (1987). Between micro and micro: Contexts and other connections. In J. Alexander, B. Giesen, R. Munch, & N. Smelser (Eds.), *The micro-macro link* (pp. 207–234). University of California Press.

Simone, M., & Galatolo, R. (2020). Climbing as a pair: Instructions and instructed body movements in indoor climbing with visually impaired athletes. *Journal of Pragmatics*, *155*, 286–302. https://doi.org/10.1016/j.pragma.2019.09.008

Simone, M., & Galatolo, R. (2021). Timing and prosody of lexical repetition: How repeated instructions assist visually impaired athletes' navigation in sport climbing. *Research on Language and Social Interaction*, *54*(4), 397–419. https://doi.org/10.1080/08351813.2021.1974742

Steensig, J. (2013). Conversation analysis and affiliation and alignment. In C. A. Chapelle (Ed.), *The encyclopedia of applied linguistics* (pp. 944–948). Wiley-Blackwell.

Streeck, J. (1995). On projection. In E. Goody (Ed.), *Social intelligence and interaction* (pp. 87–110). Cambridge University Press.

Sudnow, D. (1978). *Ways of the hand.* The MIT Press.

Tomasello, M. (2008). *Origins of human communication.* MIT Press.

Vom Lehn, D. (2010). Discovering 'experience-ables': Socially including visually impaired people in art museums. *Journal of Marketing Management, 26*(7–8), 749–769. https://doi.org/10.1080/02672571003780155

Wiggins, S., & Keevallik, L. (2020). Enacting gustatory pleasure on behalf of another: The multimodal coordination of infant tasting practices. *Symbolic Interaction, n/a*(n/a). https://doi.org/10.1002/symb.527

Yamazaki, A., Yamazaki, K., Kuno, Y., Burdelski, M., Kawashima, M., & Kuzuoka, H. (2008). Precision timing in human-robot interaction: Coordination of head movement and utterance. In *Proceedings of the SIGCHI conference on human factors in computing systems* (pp. 131–140). https://doi.org/10.1145/1357054.1357077

Zimmerman, D. H. (1998). Identity, context and interaction. In C. Antaki & S. Widdicombe (Eds.), *Identities in talk.* (pp. 87–106). Sage Publications.

PART 2

Broadening the analyst's access to a member's perspective by using various video materials

5

COLLECTING AND ANALYSING MULTI-SOURCE VIDEO DATA

Grasping the opacity of smartphone use in face-to-face encounters

Iuliia Avgustis and Florence Oloff

Introduction

This chapter will discuss how additional types of recording hardware and software (that is, wearable cameras and screen capture) can reveal – or sometimes modify – analytical objects when investigating smartphone use in face-to-face interactions. Within the framework of ethnomethodological conversation analysis, the observability of social actions in naturally occurring interactions is the basis of social order, thus making it available to both the participants themselves and to the researchers recording them (Sacks, 1984). The increasing interest in the coordination of talk, embodied actions, object use, and interactional space in recent decades has gone hand in hand with the systematic use of video recordings, leading to the currently well-established multimodal approach to social interaction (e.g., Goodwin, 1981; Streeck et al., 2011). It has been widely acknowledged that different recording set-ups can reveal different aspects of the temporal and sequential organisation and unfolding of social interaction (Mondada, 2013; see also Kohonen-Aho & Haddington, this volume; McIlvenny & Davidsen, this volume; Raudaskoski, this volume). The ubiquity of mobile devices, typically smartphones, in a large variety of contemporary interactional settings represents a further challenge to the observability of participants' actions. Due to their inherent multi-functionality and mobility, smartphones can be used in a variety of individual and joint actions, which are often of low visibility to co-present others. While mundane technology use does not usually suffer from "opaqueness" in the overall setting (Goodwin, 2000, p. 1508), there is a twofold opacity that is related to the technological object itself, namely participant opacity (or "bystander ignorance", Raudaskoski et al., 2017) and analytical opacity.

DOI: 10.4324/9781003424888-7

Our focus is on the latter, analytical opacity, as a situation that researchers may encounter during analysis, and which can potentially become a hindrance to making analytical claims. This problem has been addressed via the use of additional recording equipment in previous interactional research on mobile device use. In the next three sub-sections, we will discuss how different recording set-ups have been motivated by different analytical foci. The opacity of smartphones has been acknowledged as being a challenge for both the participants in the interaction and for researchers. However, additional recording equipment might aggravate the long-standing and familiar issue regarding the naturalness of the recorded data. This theoretical consideration will be reflected in examples taken from video recordings of everyday encounters in Russian[1], which combine static cameras, individual wearable cameras, and dynamic screen captures on the mobile devices. In the following sub-sections, we will show how this combination provides access to additional details concerning how smartphone-related multiactivity unfolds and provides a different perspective on the sequential embeddedness of individual smartphone use. Moreover, this way of recording can lead to a better understanding of how multimodal actions relate to onscreen digital objects, leading to a refinement of well-known interactional phenomena such as assessments or pointing gestures. We will then discuss whether more invasive recording equipment can "contaminate" interactional phenomena by demonstrating that this mainly depends on the type of action under scrutiny (non-technologically related actions versus smartphone-related phenomena). Finally, we will address both the advantages and the challenges of complex recording set-ups for the analysis of mundane mobile device use in face-to-face interactions.

Using video recordings for analysing mobile device use in social interaction

This section provides an overview of previous research on situated mobile device use with a specific focus on the selected settings, the recording set-up, and the phenomena of interest. While the problem of the analytical opacity of smartphone use can be resolved via additional recording devices, this more complex way of collecting data also potentially impacts on the types of activities and the sequential organisation within the recorded encounters.

Video-based studies of mobile device use

Within the past decade, an increasing number of video-based studies have been interested in mobile device use in face-to-face interaction. The three types of recording set-ups that can be identified in these studies are static cameras only, wearable cameras/screen capture only, and a combination of both. The choice of the technology used for data collection is intrinsically related to the main analytical focus. In the case of video recordings of overall social encounters, researchers are mainly interested in verbal phenomena or conversation-centred activities. For example, mobile device use was studied as a resource for inviting assessments (Raclaw et al., 2016) or as an activity that could interfere with social norms of availability (Mantere & Raudaskoski, 2017). Previous research has also revealed how participants shift between conversations with distant and co-present participants (DiDomenico & Boase, 2013; DiDomenico et al., 2020), how they accomplish other mobile-related activities during co-present conversations (Porcheron et al., 2016, 2017), and how they account for mobile phone use (Robles et al., 2018).

The interest in device-related phenomena has led researchers to use different recording hardware (chest- or head-mounted cameras, or camera-glasses) and software (screen captures). Research that does not rely on static cameras often focuses on single users and their mobile device use. Licoppe and Figeac (2018) studied how smartphone users alternated between smartphone-related and other activities in transport situations. Camera-glasses and the concurrent screen capture made the temporal patterns of gaze switching toward and away from the mobile device visible. This type of recording equipment has also allowed researchers to analyse how gestures on touch screens acted as both interface and interactional gestures (Brown et al., 2013), how walking was connected to actions in map applications (Laurier et al., 2016), how the organisation of search results on the phone's screen affected on-going co-present conversations (Brown et al., 2015), and how the content of messages could become a part of co-present interactions (Brown et al., 2018). Even if these data reveal how mobile device use is intertwined with collocated interactions, embodied resources or specifics of the material environment are often not available for the analysis (Brown et al., 2018, p. 23). Therefore, the possible range of analytical foci is limited.

A combination of static and wearable cameras/screen capture has been used less frequently, particularly in educational or other task-related settings. Hellerman et al. (2017) combined a hand-held camera and head-mounted cameras to record English-language learners playing an augmented reality mobile game. While the wearable camera provided access to the original text in the game, the external view allowed the researchers to analyse when the participants chose to read aloud, how they paraphrased the original text, and how this reading could be accomplished based on the participants' environment. In Asplund et al.'s (2018) study of classroom interactions, screen capture recordings were used to identify moments of information seeking, and the general view of the participants allowed the researchers to analyse information seeking as an embodied and often collaborative activity. Sahlström et al. (2019) used traditional static and screen recordings to study how smartphone users shifted their focus of attention between the classroom interaction and the smartphone-related activity. While the screen captures gave them access to the specifics of smartphones as semiotic artefacts, the general view allowed them to track changes in the participation framework. Therefore, the combination of these recordings provided access to a greater variety of resources and contingencies, which could potentially be opaque for a researcher using only one angle of vision.

The opacity of smartphone use as a practical problem for participants and analysts

The opacity of smartphone-related activities has been discussed in previous research as posing a problem for co-present participants. The effect of the invisibility of phone users' actions has been studied, for example, in interactions between parents and children (Mantere et al., 2018; Raudaskoski et al., 2017). Various aspects, such as the phase and the category of action of the smartphone user's activity, can be opaque for co-present participants, the reason being the large variety of possible actions on a smartphone's screen in combination with the small amount of visual and auditory information available to the co-present participants (Mantere et al., 2018). This feature was also addressed in classroom settings, in which different students' phone-related activities can appear very similar to both teachers and peers (Sahlström et al., 2019).

The limited visibility of device-related actions is a major practical concern for the participants, and smartphone users often find ways to make their activities accountable for co-present others. For example, smartphone users can explain what they are doing on their mobile devices and why they are doing so (Hendry et al., 2016; Oloff, 2021; Porcheron et al., 2016), topicalise the content on the screen and/or share it with co-present others (Porcheron et al., 2016), read the content of text messages aloud (DiDomenico et al., 2020), or voice the writing process (Oloff, 2021; Porcheron et al., 2016). A smartphone holder's embodied conduct also makes their mobile device use at least partially observable and reportable (Porcheron et al., 2016). The type of onscreen actions (typing, scrolling, or swiping), as well as the body and gaze orientation, can give co-participants clues regarding the smartphone holder's involvement. In addition, co-present others can request an account by addressing the smartphone user directly (Hendry et al., 2016). Even though opacity is an intrinsic feature of mobile devices, it is not always problematic, as participants have ways of making their mobile device use observable and reportable. This also makes smartphone use observable for researchers; in this case, having one static camera is frequently sufficient for the analysis of a particular instance of mobile device use.

However, the opacity of mobile device use is not always addressed by the interacting participants. A smartphone user's individual involvement can neither be topicalised nor accounted for; therefore, it can be opaque both for the co-participants and for the researcher. Another potentially problematic situation from the researcher's perspective is joint smartphone use, as the digital content might be visible to all the participants while simultaneously being inaccessible to the researcher. Therefore, a smartphone user's involvement can be opaque for the researcher in situations of both convergent device use (that is, being connected to the on-going interaction) and divergent ones (that is, being separate from the joint interaction) (see Brown et al., 2013). This opacity can potentially problematise our understanding of members' sense-making practices. In this chapter, we will show how additional hardware and software used to record interactions around smartphones can overcome this analytical opacity, at least partially. However, the use of additional equipment might raise questions regarding the naturalness of recorded interactions.

The naturalness of video-recorded interactions

As long as voice recorders and video cameras have been used to record naturally occurring interactions, the question of the reliability and authenticity of these data have been relevant. Possible effects of cameras on the participants' conduct, and the differences between "natural" and "contaminated" data, have been discussed in previous work (e.g., Lomax & Casey, 1998; Potter, 2002; Speer, 2002; Speer & Hutchby, 2003). More recently, the participants' orientation towards recording equipment has been studied as a phenomenon in its own right. These studies have shown that participants can glance at cameras, "act up" for them, use them as a resource for laughter and jokes, or for completing different sequentially relevant actions (Heath et al., 2010; Hutchby et al., 2012; Laurier & Philo, 2006; Tuncer, 2016). Recording equipment has also been explored as a resource for identity work (Gordon, 2013; Hazel, 2016). Participants often orient towards cameras at particular moments in interaction, such as during "slack moments" (Heath et al., 2010, p. 48), or when a new participant enters the room (Heath et al., 2010, p. 48; Tuncer, 2016).

Researchers have emphasised that, despite this occasional orientation towards cameras, the quality of the entire data corpus is not affected by the presence of recording equipment. Heath et al. (2010) emphasised that participants still accomplished their activities in a way that was recognisable to others, including the researcher. Moreover, there is insufficient evidence to assume that the presence of cameras transforms the way in which these actions are achieved (Heath et al., 2010, p. 48). As the moments at which participants orient towards cameras are easily recognised, they can either be excluded from the data set (Laurier & Philo, 2006) or collected and analysed separately if the researcher focuses on the impact of this form of technology on the interaction (e.g., Hazel, 2016). In general, researchers agree that video-recorded interactions should not be considered to be "un-natural" a priori. Instead, the naturalness of recorded interactions should be addressed empirically by studying the participants' orientation towards the recording equipment (Heath et al., 2010; Laurier & Philo, 2006; Speer, 2002; Speer & Hutchby, 2003). In this chapter, the connection between a more complex recording set-up and the naturalness of social conduct will be empirically addressed.

Understanding the variety and temporality of smartphone uses through multi-source video data

The excerpts in this section will serve to illustrate how a combination of stationary cameras, wearable cameras, and dynamic screen capture allows for a further exploration of the situated use of the "most visible invisible computers" (Raudaskoski, 2009, p. 188). Standard camcorders on tripods and GoPro Hero action cameras with harnesses were used in the recording set-up. GoPro cameras were chosen from a variety of action- and spy-cameras due to having the best ratios of size, mounting options, the quality of the recordings, data processing possibilities, and data compatibility, usability, and price. The dynamic screen captures were recorded using integrated or freely downloadable applications. The participants themselves made the decisions regarding the number of participants they wished to invite, as well as the place and the time of the recording. The static recording set-up was arranged prior to the participants' arrival, and wearable cameras were placed on the participants at the beginning of the recording event. The participants were not instructed to use their phones or to do anything specific for the purposes of the research. The length of an average data collection event was 90 minutes to two hours. The participants in the data collection (data were collected in 2018 and 2019) all gave their consent for the scientific use of the recordings, including the use of unanonymised stills in scientific publications. All their names have been replaced by pseudonyms; the original talk in Russian was transliterated according to Bolden's (2004) guidelines, while the multimodal transcriptions follow Mondada's (2018, 2022) conventions.

Understanding smartphone-related multiactivity

When a participant begins to use their smartphone, the other participant(s) often continue to talk, which leads to a multiactivity (Haddington et al., 2014) situation for the smartphone user. Even though multiactivity itself is a visible and accountable phenomenon (Mondada 2014, p. 71), some important details concerning the concurrent activities may be invisible to the analyst. Even the individual manipulation of a smartphone builds on and is sensitive to the progressivity of the overall interaction. Individual activities, just as in the case of joint activities, are "informed by our membership of society and our social relationships with others" (Francis & Hester, 2004, p. 2); therefore, video recordings used in ethnomethodological and conversation analytic research should capture the conduct of all the participants, including device manipulation (Mondada, 2013, p. 47). The first excerpts demonstrate how multi-source recordings provide the researchers with the opportunity for better access to what the participants themselves perceive, thus enabling a better understanding of the members' perspectives, the temporal organisation of individual smartphone use, and its embeddedness in co-present interaction.

Prior to Excerpt 1, the three participants had been discussing people who inspired them, and Mihail (MIH) started talking about a journalist whose videos he found motivational. Tina (TIN) then asked him to send the link to this journalist's YouTube channel on the participants' group chat. As MIH began to look for the link, TIN initiated an individual activity of picture taking in which she would remain involved throughout the entire excerpt. In the meantime, Dana (DAN) continued the discussion about inspirational people. In the analysis of this excerpt, we will focus on the way in which MIH alternates between talk with DAN and his individual smartphone use. One way of managing simultaneous mobile phone use and co-present conversation is to occasionally display attention to the co-participants (DiDomenico et al., 2020; Porcheron et al., 2016). However, previous studies have not focused on the temporality of these shifts of attention. In the multimodal annotations, only MIH's embodied actions and his smartphone screen's content (spm, i.e., MIH's smartphone) have been transcribed. Note that the side-by-side seating arrangement was chosen by the participants themselves.

Excerpt 1   (181222_OwnWay_Ru)

```
01    DAN:   +naverno mne by xotelos' perenjat' kakie-to ↓cher+ty no::
             probably I would like   to adopt  some       ↓traits bu::t
      mih:   >>gaze SP->
      mih:   +chooses share option and VK--------------------+
02           (0.6)
03           @#mne by naverno:: vot xotelos' by::@+ vot,     +
             I would probably:: well want to well,
      spm:   @options on screen: post or PM------@Interface:Youtube to VK->
      mih:                                        +chooses PM+....->
      fig:   #fig.1.a-b
```

Figure 1.a-b.

```
04           chto+ vot#    [real'no] @xotelos'+ by+ eto,#
             what (I) would [really ] want is,
05    MIH:                  [mhm    ]
                            [mhm    ]
      mih:   >...+gaze DAN--------------------------+,,,+gaze SP->>
      spm:                               >@VK chats on screen->
      fig:            #fig.2a-b                          #fig.3a-b
```

Figure 2.a-b.

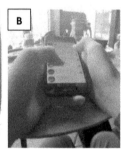

Figure 3.a-b.

```
06            (1.0)
07    DAN:    +perenjat' to vpechatlenie na ljudej
              to make the (same) impression on people
      mih:    +searches for the chat->>
08            kotoroe eti ljudi proizvodjat
              that these people make
```

The excerpt begins after MIH has found the YouTube channel he wants to share with his co-participants. He has been looking at his screen during the entire searching process and continues to do so at the beginning of the transcript. In line 1, he selects the "share" option on his phone; when his phone prompts options for sharing, he chooses the Russian social network Vkontakte (VK in the transcript). He then selects the option "send as a personal message" (Figure 1.b), and his phone's screen becomes white for several moments before the VK interface appears. During this interface switch, MIH raises his gaze from the phone, looks at DAN, and provides a minimal response token ("mhm", l. 05, Figures 2.a–b). He then quickly switches his gaze back to the smartphone on which the VK interface has appeared (Figures 3.a–b).

The temporal organisation of gaze switches from and to mobile devices has been studied previously in a non-interactional context. In their study of single commuters, Licoppe and Figeac (2018) showed that phone users switched their gaze from the phone to other activities at particular moments, for example, when a "progress bar icon" appeared on the screen. Thus, the "sequential texture" of the phone interfaces provides opportunities for changes in the phone user's focus of attention. In our excerpt, MIH carries out his smartphone use and participation in the on-going conversation as parallel, nonconflicting activities (Haddington et al., 2014), but he only shifts his gaze to DAN when his smartphone provides a sequential opportunity to switch to another activity; that is, when it is temporarily not usable. Hence, this can be described as "shifting the attention away from the phone" rather than "shifting the attention to the co-participant". It is at this moment that MIH provides a response to DAN, which demonstrates his commitment to the co-present interaction despite his involvement in an individual activity. However, his response is late in relation to DAN's prior turn suspension and is positioned in the middle of her next turn-constructional unit: MIH provides a pro forma rather than a fitted response (Oloff, 2021, p. 222). MIH's smartphone use is topically related to the on-going talk, but follows a different temporal order. Both activities have the potential to affect each other's progressivity; therefore, both should be recorded and considered in the analysis. While screen captures make the temporal order to which MIH orients clearly visible, the static camera captures the switches in his displayed attention.

In contrast to the previous excerpt in which the smartphone use is recognisably occasioned by talk, this only becomes evident in Excerpt 2 due to the screen capture recording. Prior to the excerpt, Maria (MAR) and Ekaterina (EKA) had been discussing when they were going to finish their lunch. In line 01, EKA tells MAR that they could finish lunch earlier, to which MAR responds with the Russian change-of-state token "a" (Heritage, 1984), indicating that this information is new. EKA then immediately starts a new sequence and topic by showing and commenting on her dish (l. 04–05). At the same time, MAR puts her fork down, picks up her phone (Figure 4), and unlocks it. MAR does not account for this action and it is not commented upon further. The screen capture provides empirical proof that MAR's phone use was occasioned by the previous talk and is linked to a practical concern, namely scheduling the next meeting. Therefore, having access to MAR's screen provides a better understanding of her perspective, as well as of the way in which she makes sense of and displays her sense-making of the situation.

Excerpt 2   (191227_Cilantro_RU)

```
01    EKA:   my zhe ran'she mozhem zakonchit'.
             we can finish earlier.
      mar:   >>picks up salad with a fork->
      mar:   >>gaze salad->
02           (0.3)
03    MAR:   a:: da?=
             o::h really?=
04    EKA:   =mne nravitsja mne: kinuli otdel'no perets,
             =I like (that they) threw me: a pepper separately,
05           vidimo esli +tebe nedostatoch+no (0.3) +↑ostro#
             apparently if for you (it's) not sufficiently (0.3) ↑hot
      mar:            ->+fork down-------+........+takes SP->
      mar:            ->+gaze pepper->
      fig:                                              #fig.4
```

Figure 4.

```
06           +(0.6)
      mar:   >+unlocks SP->
07    MAR:   >da +da da.<@
             >yeah yeah yeah.<
      mar:       ->+gaze spm->
      spm:                   @Instagram home page on the screen->
08           (0.9)+@(0.3)
      mar:        >+opens side bar
      spm:        >@
09    MAR:   u:hm+
      mar:       >+closes side bar->
10           (0.7)+    (1.0)    +    (0.8) + (0.5)
      mar:       >+opens messages+opens chat+opens keyboard->
11    EKA:   eto# +↑krevetka, eto kal'mar?
             is this a ↑shrimp, is this a squid?
      mar:       ->+types "Oh, no, I will be free earlier"->
      fig:       #fig.5.a-c
```

Figure 5.a-c.

```
12              (1.5)
13      EKA:    ja vizhu zdes' ˌkinzu.
                I see ˌcilantro here.
14              (2.5)+      (0.5)           +
        mar:       ->+sends the message+
15      MAR:    +ki:nzu+# v tom jame?
                ci:lantro in tom yum?
        mar:    >+.....+gaze EKA's soup->>
        fig:            #fig.6.a-c
```

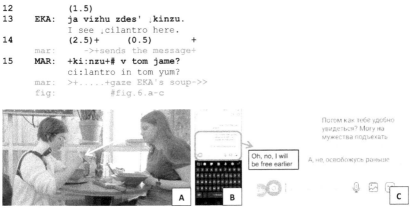

Figure 6.a-c.

After having picked up her phone, MAR provides a late-timed and somewhat unengaged response to EKA's comment regarding the food ("yeah yeah yeah", l. 07), thereby aiming to halt the course of EKA's action (Stivers, 2004). In fact, MAR starts to look at her smartphone after the first response token, while EKA begins to gaze down at her soup, and a lapse occurs (l. 08). Maria then continues to be involved in her smartphone-related activity until the end of the excerpt. Her "uhm" (l. 09) is related to her navigation process on the screen and simultaneously displays to EKA that she is involved in a phone-related activity. After MAR opens the chat in which she previously wrote that she would be free at 15:40 (l. 10, Figure 5.a–c), she begins to type ("Oh, no, I will be free earlier"), while EKA resumes her commentary on the food (l. 11). When preparing and sending the message, Maria does not show any audible or visible engagement with EKA, and several long periods of silence occur (l. 12, 14).

Without the screen capture, one would not be able to state definitively whether MAR's smartphone use is connected to the previous talk or not. However, the screen capture reveals that MAR's phone use is related to the practical task of planning her day, and that this message is clearly based on the new information (l. 01) that she has received (l. 03). MAR also returns to the co-present interaction as soon as the message has been sent (l. 15, Figures 6.a–c), which shows that her device-related activity was restricted to a precise task. Porcheron et al. (2016) analysed both conversation-related and conversation-unrelated occasions of mobile device use in their study of everyday conversations in pubs. However, they excluded situations in which the device use was not accounted for or topicalised. This might have been related to the fact that the authors only used fixed cameras to record the overall view of the interaction. Unaddressed device use remains analytically opaque in such a recording set-up, and it is not possible to determine whether such use is related or unrelated to the conversation. Accordingly, smartphone use that is not topicalised or explicitly accounted for remains largely underinvestigated. The use of additional hardware and software could allow researchers to explore when and how the participants prefer to conceal their smartphone-related activities (that is, relating the device use to "impression management"), or when they find it unnecessary to topicalise or account for their device use; that is, concerning the morality of smartphone use (see Robles et al., 2018).

This section has illustrated how a combination of stationary and wearable cameras/screen capture provides an opportunity to better understand the organisation of smartphone-related multiactivity. While wearable cameras and/or screen capture provide access to the temporal organisation of a smartphone user's individual activity, the static camera provides access to shifts in the smartphone user's gaze orientation. A multi-source recording can be used to understand not only how the progression of the interaction is affected by onscreen events (Excerpt 1), but also why the smartphone use was originally initiated (Excerpt 2). Even if the participants do not address a smartphone-based activity explicitly, the activity can still be relevant from an analytical point of view, as individual courses of action can become recognisably connected to previous or future joint courses of action.

Investigating the specificity of social actions related to the affordances of the device

Participants in face-to-face interaction regularly refer to visible and/or audible content on their mobile devices, such as digital images, videos, or text on webpages, in messages, or on social media postings (Oloff, 2019; Raclaw et al., 2016). In such showing sequences, the content on the screen is referred to by turns-at-talk that provide noticings, descriptions, or assessments (Excerpt 3), or by pointing to the display (Excerpt 4). In the absence of visible screens, the precise relationship of the digital content to these actions remains under-specified and inaccessible to the researcher (see also Kohonen-Aho & Haddington, this volume, on researchers' access to participants' private actions).

In Excerpt 3, Daria (DAR) had previously informed Igor (IGO) about Nikolai's and her plans to get a French bulldog. Following IGO's enquiry about the breed's appearance, DAR said that she would show a picture on her phone. After half a minute of searching, she finally locates a folder with a collection of dog pictures and selects it via a tapping gesture (l. 01). As the picture collection starts to become visible, IGO begins to look at her display (end of l. 01). He then produces a first assessment despite the selected showable not yet being fully on display (l. 04, Figure 7.b):

Excerpt 3   (181225_FrenchDog_Ru)

```
01    IGO:   (0.7)+(0.9)*(0.2)@(0.2)*(0.3)  @(0.2)
      dar:   >>gaze SPd---------------------->>
      dar:        +taps on folder/display
      spd:                    @..pics appear@visible>
      igo:             *..gaze NIK-*..SPd---------->
02    NIK:   +#.hf*::
      dar:   +taps on pic
      igo:         *..leans t/DAR->
      fig:   #fig.7.a-b
03           (0.2)
```

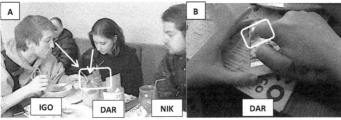

Figure 7.a-b.

```
04    IGO:   #m::::.*eto xoro+shen'[kij.]
             mh::: it (is)     pre[tty ]
05    DAR:                         [ vo:]:t *o@n.#
                                    [the:]:re it (is)
      dar:                     +taps on same pic
      spd:                               @..pic loads->
      igo:   >.....*leans t/DAR------------*..leans closer->>
      fig:   #fig.8.a-b                       #fig.9
06           (0.3)
07    IGO:   nu    eto uzhe  bol'shoj.
             well this (is)  already big.
```

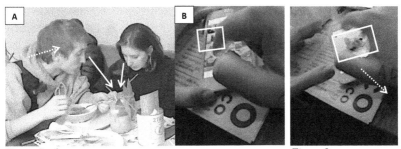

Figure 8.a-b.   *Figure 9.*

Digital content has to be retrieved on a smartphone prior to being able to show it. In this case, DAR first needs to locate the folder (l. 01), followed by searching for the picture she wants to show within the collection of pictures (l. 02, Figure 7.b). IGO looks at the display during this process and can therefore perceive the picture that Daria is selecting (Figures 7.a–b). He then begins to lean towards her but, as the interface does not respond to DAR's first tapping gesture, his first assessment appears to be premature (l. 04, Figures 8.a–b). This is also observable in DAR's next action: She taps on the picture a second time (l. 04) and, a micro-second later, produces a turn-constructional unit to present the showable ("there it is", l. 05). Her vowel lengthening takes the delay in the interface's response to the tapping into account, as the picture only begins to load towards the end of her turn (Figure 9). In response to her presentative turn and the picture finally appearing in a larger size, IGO again leans closer to her. He produces a second assessment of the dog's picture once DAR has completely withdrawn her right hand from the display and moved the device closer to him (l. 07).

The analytical access to the display reveals that assessments in smartphone-based showings can either be in response to the general visual accessibility of *some* content on the screen (l. 02), or to its explicit multimodal framing as *showable* (l. 05). This allows us to reflect on the interactional motivations of such double assessments. On the one hand, the first assessment could simply be understood as the result of a coordination problem, with the recipient anticipating an accidentally delayed showable. On the other hand, delays between the announcement of a digital showable and its actual presentation are a recurrent feature of smartphone-based showings. Thus, a double assessment could respond precisely to this temporality: The first assessment responds to the overall visual accessibility of the screen and displays the recipient's involvement, while the second assessment, which is often more specific, responds to the showing and inspection proper. While the latter interpretation has been suggested previously (Oloff, 2019), it can only be empirically substantiated if the data combine recordings of the overall setting and the device screens.

Speaking turns that refer to a showable on a smartphone screen are frequently accompanied by pointing gestures. While it is often clear from previous and subsequent talk what the participants are talking about, the concrete objects to which they are referring are usually not visible on stationary video recordings. This visual inaccessibility is linked to the position of the device (usually facing the participants) and the small size of both the screen and the showable. Research within the field of gesture studies has explored how different fingers or other body parts (e.g., Kendon, 2004, p. 199ff.), handshapes, and positions used for pointing are related to how the pointed-at objects are referred to in discourse. These findings have been based on settings in which the objects concerned are physical and three-dimensional, such as co-present persons, food, or buildings. However, when pointing at displays, the pointed-at objects are necessarily two-dimensional and are situated in a small, delimited space; thus, one might wonder how the act of referring to digital objects is systematically shaped by these material affordances, and how it compares to "non-digital pointings".

Excerpt 4 shows some possible variations of these "digital pointings". MAR and EKA are discussing the cast of the film series *Kingsman*. MAR has previously opened a list with the names and pictures of the cast on her smartphone display. She then enquires about one of the actor's roles, tilts the phone and the display in EKA's direction (Figures 10.a–b), and points at the picture of "Stanley Tucci" with her right index finger (see Figure 10.c, in Cyrillic script).

Excerpt 4   (191227_Merlin_Ru)

```
01    MAR:   *a eto sluchajno ne tot chuvak*kotoryj igral+:*#
             and isn't this by chance the guy who played:
      eka:   >>gaze own SP-------------------------------+..gaze SP_MAR->
      mar:   *...rHand off SP..index finger*pppp to actor on display->
             *...lHand tilts SP twd EKA...................*--->
      fig:                                                #fig.10.a-c
02           *u::hm       *°v takix zhe *ochk(h)ax?°=
             u::hm         °with the same glasses?°=
      mar:   *hovers finger*hovers hand--*,,retracts from display->
```

Figure 10.a-c.

```
03    EKA:   =eto Merlin.
             =this is Merlin.
04           (0.4)
05    MAR:   *da.
             yes.
      mar:   *,,,retracts hand
06           +(0.3)
      eka:   +...rHand&index to display->
07    MAR:   [+eto      #↑on     +byl?]
             [ was       it       him?]
08    EKA:   [      pod #nim    pod+pis]ano, + da*:.
             [below him (it's)  writt]en,    yes.
      eka:    +indexFinger pppp--+,,,,,,,,,,+touches pen>
      mar:   >--SP tilted twd EKA---------------*,,,
      fig:               #fig.11.a-b
```

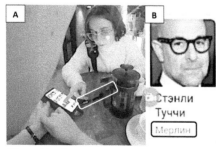

Figure 11.a-b.   *Figure 12.*

```
09              (0.6---)+(0.6)
       eka:    >touches+..moves pen to display->
10     EKA:    tut pod+#°p(h)is(h)+ano [bl(h)ja:t'°+]
               here (it's)  wr°itten  [dammit°     ]
11     MAR:                           [°mhehe°     ]
       eka:    >......+ppp w/pen--+,,,,
       eka:    >gaze display-----------------------+...looks up to MAR->
       fig:             #fig.12
12     MAR:    nu eto v fi- eto novyj fi:l'm tipa,
               well it's in the fi- this is a new fi:lm kinda,
```

The palm-down position of MAR's hand and her use of the local deictic *eto* "this" reveal her pointing to have the aim of identifying a specific object (Kendon, 2004, pp. 207–209). However, the lack of tension in her pointing finger and the hovering movement of her finger and hand over the display (l. 02) hint at a possible uncertainty, which is reflected in her incomplete turn and the hesitation particle. EKA then identifies the actor as having played the role of Merlin (l. 03). As this information is not fully endorsed by MAR (l. 04–05), EKA then moves her right hand and index finger to the display (l. 06) and points to the caption "Merlin" below the actor's picture (l. 08, Figures 11.a–b). MAR explicitly questions this information in overlap with this turn (l. 07). Shortly after the overlap has been resolved, EKA grasps the pen that is lying in the middle of the table (Figure 11.a), moves it towards the display, and uses it to point at the "Merlin" caption again (l. 09–10, Figure 12), thus reformulating and placing emphasis on her previous turn ("here it's written", l. 10).

Excerpt 4 illustrates that pointing to displays can be carried out in a variety of ways that, similar to pointing to non-digital objects, display the way in which the participants refer to the object in question, for example, an object about which a question is formulated, as something that can substantiate a claim (by referring to a visible detail such as the caption) or that substantiates a claim once again. Different types of resources are used in these instances, such as a finger versus a pen, tensed versus relaxed fingers, immobile versus hovering pointing, and so forth. The types and shapes of digital pointing are thus not deployed according to the objectively small size of the objects to which they refer, but are adapted to the contingencies of potentially static or dynamic objects and foci of attention, and to the assumed relevance of the object for the recipient.

While an overall view is indispensable for researchers in order to access the participants' bodily orientation towards the device and each other, the details of the pointing hands and the things that they are referring to generally remain invisible. Wearable cameras – ideally in combination with screen capture or otherwise accessible files of what is on the screen – can provide a valuable data base for investigating pointing gestures, as well as for assessments of the digital content on the screen. This allows for the understanding of how the establishment of joint attention, speaking turns, gestures, and digital objects are interconnected, and which aspects of the referring to and assessing of digital objects are similar or different with regard to non-digital settings. Moreover, it allows for the discovery of practices that appear to be specifically adapted to the affordances of the device and the handling thereof, such as in the event of double assessments. Partially overcoming the analytical opacity of smartphone use can thus contribute to revisiting basic social actions in light of new material features and affordances of the setting.

Understanding the participants' orientation towards wearable cameras and screen capture

This section will illustrate how participants can observably orient to additional recording equipment. As with any other object, recording devices might affect the interactional ecology to varying degrees depending on the number of cameras, their type, size, position, and distance from the participants. Representing a situated resource, cameras can be used by participants in different ways to accomplish different practical goals. In addition to orientations towards cameras mentioned in previous research (see the section "The naturalness of video-recorded interactions"), participants can orient towards wearable cameras and screen capture applications in new ways, as these devices enable different types of activities and actions.

As physical objects located on the participants' shoulders, the wearable cameras in our data often became the focus of photographs. Prior to Excerpt 5, TIN had taken several selfies from a low angle and shown two of them to her co-participants. DAN then started talking about the actor Mark Wahlberg who, according to her, is often filmed from a similar angle. She continues her multi-turn unit in lines 01–04. Meanwhile, TIN poses for yet another selfie and MIH continues to look at her smartphone's screen (Fig. 13).

Excerpt 5   (181222_AllCameras_Ru)

```
01    DAN:   koroche prosto fishka Δv tom chto::
             in short the point is tha::t
      tin:   >>poses for a pic->
      mih:   >>looks at TIN's SP->
      dan:   >>looks at TIN's SP---Δaway->
02           (0.5)
03    DAN:   uhm Δon ↑snjalsja-+# (0.8)
             uhm he ↑starred (0.8)
      dan:      ->ΔTIN's SP->
      mih:                        +leans towards TIN's phone->>
      fig:                        #fig.13
```

Figure 13.

```
04           v fil- fil'me moej# ljubimoj franshi-Δ#
             in a fil- film of my favourite fran-
      dan:                                Δ.....->
      fig:                  #fig.14          #fig.15
```

Figure 14.   Figure 15.

```
05           (1.0)
06    TIN:   [*Δda davajte vse chtob] vse ka:mery byli* vidny.*
             [yes let's all so that ] all cameras would be seen.
07    DAN:   [da davajte snimem      ]
             [yes let's take (a pic)]
      dan:   >Δstands and leans towards TIN's SP->>
      tin:   >*moves SP to the middle--------------------------*
```

Figure 16.

During DAN's turn, MIH leans towards TIN's phone, apparently to include himself in TIN's picture (l. 03, Figure 14). Shortly afterwards, DAN shifts her gaze to TIN's smartphone, then abandons her turn (l. 4), and also leans towards the phone (Figure 15). These embodied actions display an interest in joint picture taking, and TIN and DAN simultaneously suggest taking a picture in which the wearable cameras are visible (l. 06–07). After the excerpt ends, the participants continue to pose with and comment on the cameras as props. When the cameras are finally visible in the image section, TIN points to the camera and presses the shutter with her other hand (Figure 16, taken after the end of the excerpt). MIH then asks TIN to send the picture to their group chat, and DAN reinitiates her previous topic.

This excerpt shows one way in which participants can orient towards the presence of wearable cameras. Even though wearable cameras are now widely used in a variety of different settings in daily life, they are still associated with exciting and difficult activities (Chalfen, 2014). By taking pictures with wearable cameras, or "zooming in" on them when recording videos, the participants show their orientation towards this equipment as a potentially exceptional object in a cafe. However, as the wearable camera is simply another photographable object in this scenario, this excerpt could be included amongst other instances of situated picture taking with smartphones.

In the present data set, all of the participants agreed to use integrated or freely downloadable screen capture software. The participants usually activated the screen capture at the beginning of the event, and received a reminder about the on-going recording either via notifications or as a small icon on the display (see Excerpt 4, Figure 11.b). Unlike wearable cameras, the screen capture was rarely topicalised once the application had been installed and activated. However, the participants experienced problems with the software (the recording stopped every time the phone was locked) during one of the events, and decided to activate the screen capture manually every time they used their smartphones. Excerpt 6 shows an instance of Daria (DAR) reminding Nina (NIN) to activate the screen capture. DAR, a psychologist, is listing the mental disorders affecting the people whom she had previously counselled. This list construction, as part of an extended storytelling, has been going on for some time, and NIN picks up her smartphone at the beginning of the excerpt.

Excerpt 6   (181229_PanicAttacks_Ru)

```
01    DAR:   +a,+ nartsissicheskoe* rasstrojstvo*[lichn+os]ti
             oh, narcissistic personality     [ disord]er
02    NIN:                                     [mhm    ]
      dar:   +..+gaze NIN----------------------------+gaze SP->
      nin:   >>gaze DAR-----------------------*looks at SP->>
      nin:   >>grabs SP----------*unlocks phone*checks notifications->
03    DAR:   u Anny +Pavlovny kak by tozhe znakomo,+ aga?#
             of Anna Pavlovna is also familiar,     right?
      dar:          >+looks at NIN----------------+looks SP->
      fig:                                          #fig.17
04           (0.7)
05           kak by ja v kurse.*
             I am kinda aware.
      nin:              ->*checks apps->
06           (1.1)
07    NIN:   mhm
08           (0.3)
09    DAR:   ty vkljuchila?
             did you turn (it) on?
10           (0.5)
11    NIN:   *ja: idu vkljuchat'.#
             I: am going to turn (it) on.
      nin:   ->*opens screen capture app and turns it on->l.17
      fig:                  #fig.18
```

Figure 17.   Figure 18.

```
12           (1.4)
13    NIN:   °°hi hi ↑hih°°
14           (2.5)*(0.5)
      nin:      ->*opens messages->
15    DAR:   °mhm°
16           (0.6)
17    DAR:   @*.h:: i vo:t.+#
             .h:: and we:ll.
      spn:   @screen capture is recording->>
      nin:   >*opens a message window and reads->
      dar:              >+looks away->
      fig:              #fig.19
18           (2.7)
19    DAR:   .ts +tam+ byla takaja shtuka*+ kak+ panicheskie ataki.#
             .ts there was   such thing      as panic attacks.
      dar:     >+...+looks at NIN-------+SP--+looks at NIN->
      nin:                          >*opens keyboard and types->>
      fig:                                          #fig.20
```

Figure 19.   Figure 20.

After picking up her phone, NIN first checks her notifications and then scrolls through her applications (l. 01). In the meantime, DAR continues to talk about the disorders she had treated, but also shifts her gaze towards NIN's phone (l. 03, Figure 17). After closely monitoring NIN's phone, DAR asks NIN if she has turned on the screen capture (l. 9). NIN answers with a slightly modified other-repeat and laughs quietly (l. 11–13, Figure 18). She then locates the screen capture application and turns it on (l. 11). DAR's question about the screen capture demonstrates her momentary self-categorisation as a research participant. DAR also waits for confirmation that the screen capture has been activated before she resumes her suspended turn. DAR acknowledges this waiting process ("mhm", l. 15), observes the beginning of the recording, and only then returns to the previous topic (l. 17). A participant's orientation towards "doing being a research participant" can also be used to accomplish certain actions, such as to make jokes or to moralise about others' device use (see Robles et al., 2018). In this sense, DAR's reminder about the recording might also serve to emphasise that the suspension of her storytelling has been caused by NIN's smartphone use; also see DAR's gaze back to NIN (l. 19) and her facial expression (Figure 20).

By initiating a side sequence related to the recording application, DAR makes both the suspension of her telling (also see the gesture-hold of her left hand, Figures 17–19) and her monitoring of NIN's device-related activity publicly available. Apart from the fact that equipment-related sequences might implement multiple action types, this episode sequentially functions in the same way that any other side sequence would do in this environment, as it suspends the previously on-going telling. In this regard, this excerpt could be treated analytically as an instance of suspension and resumption practices (Helisten, 2017) in general, without having to specifically take its topical relationship to the recording set-up into account. However, if we observe the manipulation of the device itself closely, it can be seen that NIN switches from reading the notifications (l. 02) to searching for and activating the screen recording (l. 05), then goes back to open a messaging application (l. 14). This makes it more difficult to reconstruct the initially projected trajectory of NIN's phone use. Consequently, the activation of the recording application may interfere with the unrecorded use, as it might lead to different temporalities and types of navigation on the interface.

This section has illustrated how wearable cameras and screen capture can appear in the data as additional objects, topics, or activities. On the one hand, these can be considered to not contaminate the data, as the basic actions and activities are still accomplished in systematic and recognisable ways ("everything is a natural *something*", Hofstetter, 2021, p. 14). On the other hand, supplementary recording devices can also modify the sequential organisation of smartphone-based actions. A possible superimposed orientation towards the recording equipment can therefore render an occurrence of this specific action less typical. Accordingly, the analytical adequacy of certain types of video data depends on the phenomena under scrutiny, with some phenomena and actions being less prototypical. However, such topicalised interferences of the recording equipment are rare in our data. Furthermore, as they are largely traceable in the interactions, the specificity of these situations can be taken into account when analysing the data with regard to a particular phenomenon.

Discussion and conclusion

In this contribution, we focused on the impact of data collection methods on the study of mobile device use in face-to-face encounters. The inherent opacity of mobile devices has been acknowledged as both a focus of interest and as a methodological challenge within interactional research. Accordingly, previous studies have used supplementary recording equipment, such as wearable cameras and dynamic screen captures of the devices' displays. This was frequently motivated by an interest in mobility and specific task-related activities, and the traditional static camera has been often dismissed for both analytical and practical reasons. However, immobile settings have mainly been captured from an exclusive and overall view, thus revealing the researchers' focus on the connection between the device use and the conversation. Against the background of these two main lines of research, we introduced mobile recording techniques in stationary settings, and combined them with recordings of overall perspectives of the event. This combined recording set-up for the investigation of smartphone use has rarely been implemented to date and, in the few cases in which it has been used, the researchers usually targeted specific institutional and task-driven settings. We claim that this type of multi-source video data is also analytically beneficial when applied to smartphone use in situations of everyday socialising.

We presented three interrelated topics of interest with regard to this recording set-up, namely multiactivity, technological affordances, and the naturalness of the data. Once synchronised, the different video-recorded perspectives allowed us to counteract the inherent analytical opacity of smartphones. This is a prerequisite for understanding smartphone-related multiactivity in more detail: The smartphone user's coordination of manipulating the device and the on-going interaction becomes available for analysis, and their interactional motivation for engaging in individual device use can be explored. Joint smartphone-based activities, despite having been of primary interest in interactional research, have merely been shown to exist at present. A multi-camera perspective provides access to details of the sequential organisation, particularly if the specificity with regard to the affordances of the technological device is to be investigated in more detail. Standard social practices, such as those relating to assessments and deictic actions, can thus be linked to objects provided by the smartphone's interface, and can be understood as new forms of technology-supported joint actions. Recording devices that are close to the participants' bodies and to their personal objects raise the question of the possible contamination of the data. As is the case with more traditional fixed cameras, the participants' occasional orientations towards this supplementary equipment are visible and therefore analysable. While some of these instances can be understood as being simple variations of well-known social actions and activities, others might be more important in relation to the analysis, thus requiring increased attention to be paid to the assessment of their exceptional or prototypical sequential features.

Some objections could be raised with regard to the use of such a comparatively complex recording set-up. Wearable cameras and screen capture clearly interfere with the participants' privacy. The proximity of the recording equipment to the participants' bodies also introduces an institutional dimension into these everyday settings, as this visibly turns them into research settings. This leads to more frequent (self-)categorisation practices of the participants as research participants, which thus becomes of interest for future methodological reflections. More generally, wearable cameras and screen recordings are not a panacea for the analytical opacity of smartphone use. Due to the participants' flexible articulation of their bodies and mobile devices, action cameras might not always capture the desired angle of vision, and the lighting conditions might render the display invisible. Unless specifically designed for and used on the same model of a particular device, screen recording applications cannot meet the technical requirements of all the possible types of smartphones; the participants may need to adjust their device settings in various ways, and the recordings might simply fail due to technical reasons. Multi-source data are also considerably more time consuming due to the necessary processing, synchronisation, and anonymisation (for example, of personal information on the displays). Despite these diverse challenges, a combination of multiple recording devices is clearly beneficial to extend the range of analytical phenomena that can be related to everyday smartphone use. Maximally documenting the temporal and sequential unfolding of smartphone use enables us to correctly assess its meaning in our social routines and how it shapes our daily encounters.

Note

1 The data were collected as part of the project "Smart Communication: The situated practices of mobile technology and lifelong digital literacies" (funded by the Eudaimonia Institute, University of Oulu 2018–2022, and the Academy of Finland, 2019–2023, project number: 323848).

References

Asplund, S.-B., Olin-Scheller, C., & Tanner, M. (2018). Under the teacher's radar: Literacy practices in task-related smartphone use in the connected classroom. *L1-Educational Studies in Language and Literature*, *18*, 1–26. https://doi.org/10.17239/L1ESLL-2018 .18.01.03

Bolden, G. (2004). The quote and beyond: Defining boundaries of reported speech in conversational Russian. *Journal of Pragmatics*, *36*(6), 1071–1118. https://doi.org/10 .1016/j.pragma.2003.10.015

Brown, B., McGregor, M., & Laurier, E. (2013). *IPhone in vivo: Video analysis of mobile device use* (pp. 1031–1040). https://doi.org/10.1145/2470654.2466132

Brown, B., McGregor, M., & McMillan, D. (2015). *Searchable objects: Search in everyday conversation* (pp. 508–517). https://doi.org/10.1145/2675133.2675206

Brown, B., O'Hara, K., McGregor, M., & McMillan, D. (2018). Text in talk: Lightweight messages in co-present interaction. *ACM Transactions on Computer-Human Interaction, 24*(6), 42:1–42:25. https://doi.org/10.1145/3152419

Chalfen, R. (2014). 'Your panopticon or mine?' Incorporating wearable technology's Glass and GoPro into visual social science. *Visual Studies, 29*(3), 299–310. https://doi.org/10.1080/1472586X.2014.941547

DiDomenico, S. M., & Boase, J. (2013). Bringing mobiles into the conversation: Applying a conversation analytic approach to the study of mobiles in co-present interaction. In D. Tannen & A. Trester (Eds.), *Discourse 2.0: Language and new media* (pp. 119–131). Georgetown University Press.

DiDomenico, S. M., Raclaw, J., & Robles, J. S. (2020). Attending to the mobile text summons: Managing multiple communicative activities across physically copresent and technologically mediated interpersonal interactions. *Communication Research, 47*(5), 669–700. https://doi.org/10.1177/0093650218803537

Francis, D., & Hester, S. (2004). *An invitation to ethnomethodology: Language, society and social interaction.* Sage Publications. https://doi.org/10.4135/9781849208567

Goodwin, C. (1981). *Conversational organization: Interaction between speakers and hearers.* Academic Press.

Goodwin, C. (2000). Action and embodiment within situated human interaction. *Journal of Pragmatics, 32*(10), 1489–1522. https://doi.org/10.1016/S0378-2166(99)00096-X

Gordon, C. (2013). Beyond the observer's paradox: The audio-recorder as a resource for the display of identity. *Qualitative Research, 13*(3), 299–317. https://doi.org/10.1177/1468794112442771

Haddington, P., Keisanen, T., Mondada, L., & Nevile, M. (2014). Towards multiactivity as a social and interactional phenomenon. In P. Haddington, T. Keisanen, L. Mondada, & M. Nevile (Eds.), *Multiactivity in social interaction: Beyond multitasking* (pp. 3–32). John Benjamins. https://doi.org/10.1075/z.187.01had

Hazel, S. (2016). The paradox from within: Research participants doing-being-observed. *Qualitative Research, 16*(4), 446–467. https://doi.org/10.1177/1468794115596216

Heath, C., Hindmarsh, J., & Luff, P. (2010). *Video in qualitative research: Analysing social interaction in everyday life.* Sage. https://doi.org/10.4135/9781526435385

Helisten, M. (2017). Resumptions as multimodal achievements in conversational (story) tellings. *Journal of Pragmatics, 112*, 1–19. https://doi.org/10.1016/j.pragma.2017.01.014

Hellermann, J., Thorne, S. L., & Fodor, P. (2017). Mobile reading as social and embodied practice. *Classroom Discourse, 8*(2), 99–121. https://doi.org/10.1080/19463014.2017.1328703

Hendry, G., Wiggins, S., & Anderson, T. M. (2016). Are you still with us? Managing mobile phone use and group interaction in PBL. *Interdisciplinary Journal of Problem-Based Learning, 10*(2). https://doi.org/10.7771/1541-5015.1600

Heritage, J. (1984). A change-of-state token and aspects of its sequential placement. In J. M. Atkinson & J. Heritage (Eds.), *Structures of social action* (pp. 299–345). Cambridge University Press. https://doi.org/10.1017/CBO9780511665868.020

Hofstetter, E. (2021). Analyzing the researcher-participant in EMCA. *Social Interaction: Video-Based Studies of Human Sociality, 4*(2), Article 2. https://doi.org/10.7146/si.v4i2.127185

Hutchby, I., O'Reilly, M., & Parker, N. (2012). Ethics in praxis: Negotiating the presence and functions of a video camera in family therapy. *Discourse Studies*, *14*(6), 675–690. https://doi.org/10.1177/1461445612457487

Kendon, A. (2004). *Gesture: Visible action as utterance*. Cambridge University Press. https://doi.org/10.1017/CBO9780511807572

Laurier, E., Brown, B., & McGregor, M. (2016). Mediated pedestrian mobility: Walking and the map app. *Mobilities*, *11*(1), 117–134. https://doi.org/10.1080/17450101.2015 .1099900

Laurier, E., & Philo, C. (2006). Natural problems of naturalistic video data. In H. Knoblauch, B. Schnettler, J. Raab, & H.-G. Soeffner (Eds.), *Video-analysis methodology and methods, qualitative audiovisual data analysis in sociology* (pp. 183–192). Peter Lang.

Licoppe, C., & Figeac, J. (2018). Gaze patterns and the temporal organization of multiple activities in mobile smartphone uses. *Human–Computer Interaction*, *33*(5–6), 311–334. https://doi.org/10.1080/07370024.2017.1326008

Lomax, H., & Casey, N. (1998). Recording social life: Reflexivity and video methodology. *Sociological Research Online*, *3*(2), 121–146. https://doi.org/10.5153/sro.1372

Mantere, E., & Raudaskoski, S. (2017). The sticky media device. In A. R. Lahikainen, T. Mälkiä, & K. Repo (Eds.), *Media, family interaction and the digitalization of childhood* (pp. 135–154). Edward Elgar Publishing. https://doi.org/10.4337 /9781785366673.00018

Mantere, E., Raudaskoski, S., & Valkonen, S. (2018). Parental smartphone use and bystander ignorance on child development. In M. Loicq, S. Aude, & I. Féroc Dumez (Eds.), *Les cultures médiatiques de l'enfance et de la petite enfance* (pp. 98–113). Editions du Centre d'études sur les Jeunes et les Médias.

Mondada, L. (2013). The conversation analytic approach to data collection. In J. Sidnell & T. Stivers (Eds.), *The handbook of conversation analysis* (pp. 32–56). Wiley-Blackwell. https://doi.org/10.1002/9781118325001.ch3

Mondada, L. (2014). The temporal orders of multiactivity: Operating and demonstrating in the surgical theatre. In P. Haddington, T. Keisanen, L. Mondada, & M. Nevile (Eds.), *Multiactivity in social interaction: Beyond multitasking* (pp. 33–76). John Benjamins. https://doi.org/10.1075/z.187.02mon

Mondada, L. (2018). Multiple temporalities of language and body in interaction: Challenges for transcribing multimodality. *Research on Language and Social Interaction*, *51*(1), 85–106. https://doi.org/10.1080/08351813.2018.1413878

Mondada, L. (2022). *Conventions for multimodal transcription*. Online resource. https:// www.lorenzamondada.net/multimodal-transcription

Oloff, F. (2019). Das Smartphone als soziales Objekt: Eine multimodale Analyse von initialen Zeigesequenzen in Alltagsgesprächen. In K. Marx & A. Schmidt (Eds.), *Interaktion und Medien: Interaktionsanalytische Zugänge zu medienvermittelter Kommunikation* (pp. 191–218). Universitätsverlag Winter.

Oloff, F. (2021). Some systematic aspects of self-initiated mobile device use in face-to-face encounters. *Journal für Medienlinguistik*, *2*(2), 195–235. https://doi.org/10.21248/jfml .2019.21

Porcheron, M., Fischer, J. E., & Sharples, S. (2016). Using mobile phones in pub talk. In *CSCW '16: Proceedings of the 19th ACM conference on computer-supported cooperative work & social computing* (pp. 1649–1661). https://doi.org/10.1145/2818048.2820014

Porcheron, M., Fischer, J. E., & Sharples, S. (2017). "Do Animals Have Accents?" talking with agents in multi-party conversation. *Language and Communication, 60,* 207–219. https://doi.org/10.1145/2998181.2998298

Potter, J. (2002). Two kinds of natural. *Discourse Studies, 4*(4), 539–542. https://doi.org/10.1177/14614456020040040901

Raclaw, J., Robles, J. S., & DiDomenico, S. M. (2016). Providing epistemic support for assessments through mobile-supported sharing activities. *Research on Language and Social Interaction, 49*(4), 362–379. https://doi.org/10.1080/08351813.2016.1199089

Raudaskoski, S. (2009). *Tool and machine: The affordances of the mobile phone.* University of Tampere Press.

Raudaskoski, S., Mantere, E., & Vakonen, S. (2017). The influence of parental smartphone use, eye contact and 'bystander ignorance' on child development. In A. R. Lahikainen, T. Mälkiä, & K. Repo (Eds.), *Media, family interaction and the digitalization of childhood* (pp. 173–184). Edward Elgar. https://doi.org/10.4337/9781785366673.00021

Robles, J. S., DiDomenico, S., & Raclaw, J. (2020). Doing being an ordinary technology and social media user. *Language and Communication, 60,* 150–167. https://doi.org/10.1016/j.langcom.2018.03.002

Sacks, H. (1984). Notes on methodology. In J. M. Atkinson & J. Heritage (Eds.), *Structures of social action: Studies in conversation analysis* (pp. 21–27). Cambridge University Press.

Sahlström, F., Tanner, M., & Valasmo, V. (2019). Connected youth, connected classrooms: Smartphone use and student and teacher participation during plenary teaching. *Learning, Culture and Social Interaction, 21,* 311–331. https://doi.org/10.1016/j.lcsi.2019.03.008

Speer, S. A. (2002). 'Natural' and 'contrived' data: A sustainable distinction? *Discourse Studies, 4*(4), 511–525. https://doi.org/10.1177/14614456020040040601

Speer, S. A., & Hutchby, I. (2003). From ethics to analytics: Aspects of participants' orientations to the presence and relevance of recording devices. *Sociology, 37*(2), 315–337. https://doi.org/10.1177/0038038503037002006

Stivers, A. (2004). "No no no" and other types of multiple sayings in social interaction. *Human Communication Research, 30*(2), 260–293. https://doi.org/10.1111/j.1468-2958.2004.tb00733.x

Streeck, J., Goodwin, C., & LeBaron, C. (Eds.). (2011). *Embodied interaction. Language and body in the material world.* Cambridge University Press.

Tuncer, S. (2016). The effects of video recording on office workers' conduct, and the validity of video data for the study of naturally-occurring interactions. *Forum Qualitative Sozialforschung/Forum: Qualitative Social Research, 17*(3), Article 3. https://doi.org/10.17169/fqs-17.3.2604

6

FROM DISTRIBUTED ECOLOGIES TO DISTRIBUTED BODIES IN INTERACTION

Capturing and analysing "dual embodiment" in virtual environments

Laura Kohonen-Aho and Pentti Haddington

Introduction

The human body is an important resource for producing and ascribing meanings to social actions in face-to-face interaction. It constitutes an element – or a "semiotic field" – among others (talk with its language structure, the shapes and structures of the material environment, etc.) within emerging "contextual configurations" that participants use to build and interpret actions (Goodwin, 2000, p. 1490, 2018, p. 134). Embodied participation frameworks – that is, different kinds of constellations of human bodies in interaction – are embedded elements in contextual configurations. In them, the human body is used to accomplish joint focus to a referent or establish mutual orientation between participants. Hence, they are also frames for producing and interpreting social actions (Goodwin, 2018, p. 235).

Technology-mediated interactions provide their own contextual configurations for establishing embodied participant frameworks. This is because the technological platforms that are used for interaction provide setting-specific affordances for using embodied resources (e.g., eye contact, gestures, and body movements) and establishing joint focus and mutual orientation. This can lead to co-participants' fragmented and limited access to shared multimodal (embodied or material) resources, which in turn affects their use as resources for producing and interpreting social actions. For example, Heath and Luff (1992) and Luff et al. (2003) use the terms "communicative asymmetry" and "fractured ecologies" to analyse the problems involved in building a shared perspective in video-mediated interactions, when co-participants do not share a physical space.

Current graphical three-dimensional virtual environments (VEs), such as virtual worlds (VWs) and immersive virtual realities (VRs), are spaces where users can interact in shared virtual spaces and form embodied participation frameworks

DOI: 10.4324/9781003424888-8

with others by using a virtual body, an *avatar*. Contrary to the "living physical body", the avatar is an artificial virtual character. Still, participants orient to avatar bodies as interactional resources, for example, when (re-)opening encounters in VEs (Kohonen-Aho & Vatanen, 2021). In VEs, the participants inhabit two worlds: the physical world and the virtual world. They also operate with two bodies: the physical and the avatar body. This is a unique feature of VE interaction (Cleland, 2010; Strain, 1999). In this chapter, we use the term "dual embodiment" to refer to this phenomenon.

This chapter explores how dual embodiment features in the organisation of action in VEs. First, we analyse a case in which *a participant's virtual body is partly and momentarily inaccessible to the participant themselves while it remains accessible to the co-participants*. Second, we analyse a case in which *a participant's physical body is invisible and not accessible to the co-participants*. We show how fragmented or limited joint access to embodied resources caused by dual embodiment is consequential for the intelligibility and coordination of joint action. We also show how establishing joint access to an embodied resource for this or that social end may require the use of other resources, such as talk or the participants' private physical actions.

Finally, we highlight the importance of studying dual embodiment as a feature of joint action in VEs. We show how recording the participants' actions and interactions both in the virtual and physical environments provides the analyst access to new participant or "member's" perspectives. This introduces important theoretical and methodological questions for EMCA research, which are discussed at the end of the chapter.

Body and embodiment in VE interaction

In EMCA, "embodiment" refers to the non-verbal use of the body and its parts as a resource for participants to build mutually understandable and joint action (e.g., Goodwin, 2000, 2003). The body features in the accomplishment of action in two ways. First, social actions that involve the use of the body are not understandable in isolation; they become intelligible relative to features and structures in the environment (e.g., Goodwin, 2000, 2003, 2007). The body and the environment are symbiotic and mutually elaborate each other. Together, they constitute "a locally relevant array of semiotic fields that participants demonstrably orient to", which Goodwin (2000) calls "contextual configuration". Second, contextual configurations can include *the bodies of others*, so that several bodies together form embodied participation frameworks in which participants establish joint orientation to each other for accomplishing joint action (Goodwin, 2003, pp. 22–23).

In VEs, participants not only inhabit two environments (the virtual and the physical), but also two bodies (also the virtual and the physical). In the literature, this has been variously termed "extended body" or "dual embodiment" (e.g., Cleland, 2010; Strain, 1999). More specifically, dual embodiment has been used to refer to the extension of one's physical body and the interplay of the actions of the two bodies in VE contexts, rather than as the virtual body being separate from the physical body (Cleland, 2010; Strain, 1999). In this chapter, we argue that in VEs a social action's intelligibility can be contingent on dual embodiment; either manifestation of the body can be used as a resource for producing and ascribing meanings to social action.

The virtual bodies in VEs are called *avatars*, and they are operated by human users in real time. Depending on the VE, avatars have different appearances and embodied capabilities. In most VEs, users can modify their avatar's appearance, for example, by changing its skin and hair colour, body shape, and clothing. Most avatars can move, gesticulate, and change their facial expressions. Common avatar movements include walking, flying, jumping, and turning around.

Depending on the VE, avatar movements and gestures are produced with different devices. In desktop VWs, such as Second Life, typical avatar gestures include pointing, waving, and clapping. In some cases, users can use pre-defined gestures, "emblems", or facial expressions (e.g., smiling) that are selected from a library of avatar features. One challenge involved in the use of pre-defined gestures is the difficulty of controlling their timely production and duration (Moore et al., 2006). The avatar's movement is controlled by the mouse and specific keys on the keyboard. In immersive VR, gesticulation and movement are different. The system detects in real time the user's head, body, and hand movements (e.g., pointing and waving) from a head-mounted display (HMD) and hand-held controllers that the user is wearing and translates them into avatar movements. Consequently, they tend to appear more accurate in terms of direction, timing, and duration than in VWs. The controllers are also used to activate and manipulate virtual objects. Facial expressions, on the other hand, are often generated automatically by the system; for example, the avatar's lips move when the system recognises that the user speaks. More sophisticated motion-tracking gear, such as full-body motion capture suits, are also being developed. All in all, the user's actions with the physical devices usually have consequences for their avatar actions in the VE (Gamberini & Spagnolli, 2003).

Embodied avatar interaction has been a popular research topic since the first "blockie"-shaped avatars (Bowers et al., 1996). Even though the design purpose of most VEs has long been to develop avatars that realistically resemble human conduct, the (in)accuracy and (un)intelligibility of avatar actions has still raised the interest of researchers. Moore et al. (2006) note that despite the increasing visual realism of VEs, avatars still lack interactional sophistication in displaying the users' intentions or current state. For example, the way in which an avatar's gaze appears to others can differ from its user's actual view to the environment (Moore et al., 2006). This may have consequences for, or even disrupt, the accountability and intelligibility of actions (Robinson, 2016) in VEs.

These observations about interaction in VE were already raised by Hindmarsh et al. (2006). They analysed how the embodied features of avatars affect or

disrupt the organisation of interaction in VEs. First, they showed how VE interaction can become fragmented because, depending on the interactants' current
body and gaze direction, the VE is available for them in different ways. Second,
they showed that participants easily presuppose mutual accessibility and availability when interacting, while, in fact, their perspectives to one another and the
surrounding world are different. Third, they showed that because the VE technology fails to display the complete trajectory of an avatar's embodied action,
and part of the trajectory remains hidden, the interpretability of that action is
compromised. Finally, participants assume that their gestures are available to
their co-participants when appearing in their visual field, while they may not
see the gesture at all. In sum, witnessing, recognising, and ascribing meanings
to the visible features of co-participants' conduct in VEs seems to depend on
the avatar's exact body position and gaze direction (Hindmarsh et al., 2006).
Thus, it can be difficult for one participant to assess whether a co-participant
sees or does not see the gesture they have produced.[1] The next section discusses
the collection of parallel videos from the virtual and the physical environment
and argues for its importance to identify and analyse dual embodiment in VEs
interaction.

Solutions for capturing social interaction in VEs

Practices for collecting data in VEs have evolved over recent years. For example,
when conducting "virtual ethnography", researchers use participatory methods
and spend long time periods in online game environments and virtual communities to observe and document social practices and behaviours in them (Boellstorff,
2008). Their focus is on "the player's perspective" in VEs (Moore et al., 2006).
However, rather than studying the person at the keyboard, the analysis focuses on
the actions the user produces through the avatar.

The diversity and large number of VEs have also offered psychologists a setting for studying human behaviour with experimental methods. VEs provide a
possibility to design conditions that are impossible in real life due to ethical
or safety reasons (Blascovich et al., 2002). Research interest in interpersonal
interaction in VEs has also led to quasi-experimental studies where participants'
encounters in VEs are video-recorded for the purposes of analysing interactional
practices (e.g., Bowers et al., 1996; Hindmarsh et al., 2006; Kohonen-Aho &
Vatanen, 2021). From the perspective of EMCA, the collection and use of (video)
data from (quasi-)experimental settings breaches one of the methodological ide-
als in EMCA: The studied and recorded situation should occur naturally, regardless of the researcher's presence. (Quasi-)experiments are events organised for
research purposes and are thus not "natural" in the true EMCA sense of the word.
The benefit of them, however, is that they allow the simulation and study of, for
example, group work and collaboration, where participants are not instructed

to behave in a particular way but where interaction can unfold naturally within the given context, potentially providing novel insights into social interaction (Kendrick, 2017).

Yet another aspect of collecting video from VE interaction relates to the participants' simultaneous presence in parallel physical and virtual spaces. Gamberini and Spagnolli (2003) argue that it is necessary to capture all the digital, physical, and local resources that participants use when they operate technologies. EMCA researchers frequently use multiple cameras to capture the events of an interactional situation from different perspectives. However, multiple cameras are used within the same contextual configuration. As to VEs, on the other hand, Gamberini and Spagnolli (2003) propose the use of a "split-screen technique" where the video recording of the avatar is merged and synchronised with a recording of the user in the physical environment. The merged videos offer a possibility to analyse the connection between the users' physical movements with a keyboard or controllers and the avatar actions in the VE. In other words, they offer two perspectives of the "same" action in different contextual configurations which are not similarly accessible to all participants, thus offering the analyst a richer perspective to the shape and delivery of multimodal social action in VEs (for more examples of similar recording setups, see Hindmarsh et al., 2006; Kohonen-Aho & Alin, 2015; Steier, 2020). Next, we introduce the settings and data that were used to study dual embodiment. Then, we illustrate with two excerpts how the participants orient to their own physical body and each other's virtual bodies in VE interaction. We show how dual embodiment can be consequential for understanding bodily appearances and for producing and ascribing meanings to embodied actions in VEs.

Towards analysing the accountability and privacy of action in VEs

Research settings and data

The video data come from two VEs: Second Life and Rec Room. Both datasets include parallel recordings from the virtual environment (VE video) and the participants' physical environments (PE video). Second Life is a virtual world that offers both numerous public places and the possibility to create private places where participants can spend time and interact. The participants can interact by writing on public and private chats and talking to each other in real time through an audio connection. They can also use virtual objects and customisable avatars for interaction. Participants can operate their avatars either from a first-person or third-person perspective.

The Second Life recordings were collected in a quasi-experimental setting where 36 participants, divided into 12 three-member teams, were assigned to collaborate for completing different tasks. The collaboration space was built on a private island. Each team member used an avatar that was created for them by the researchers. All three avatars in a team had a customary male appearance. During the collaboration session, in the physical world, the three participants sat in adjacent rooms where they could not see or hear each other; they could only see one another's avatars on their computer displays and speak through an audio connection. The team members did not know each other, and they met face-to-face for the first time after the session. Before the session began, the participants were given instructions on how to move with the avatar.

Figure 6.1 illustrates the data collected in Second Life. We used screen capture software to record one VE video from the researcher's computer, recording all three avatars from a third-person perspective. This was made possible by placing the researcher's avatar in the virtual space with the participants but putting it out of sight under the floor. The three participants in the physical space were video recorded with remote-controlled cameras in three adjacent rooms. The cameras were positioned to the side from an angle that captured the computer displays on the video frame. An alternative solution for getting the participants' perspective on the VE would have been to use screen capture software for recording the events as they unfolded on their displays. However, this would have resulted in six recordings (three VE videos and three PE videos), making the analysis arduous. As a compromise, the PE videos provided access to each participant and their private perspective to the VE through the computer display, which turned out to be sufficient for the analysis.

Rec Room is a multiplayer virtual reality game environment with possibilities to play, for example, paintball, charades, or disc golf. The users can customise

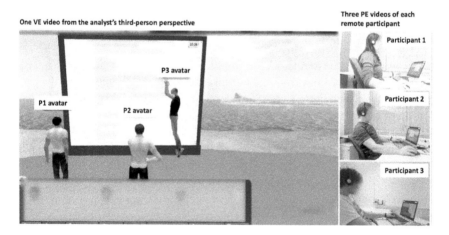

FIGURE 6.1 Parallel videos in the VW data in Second Life.

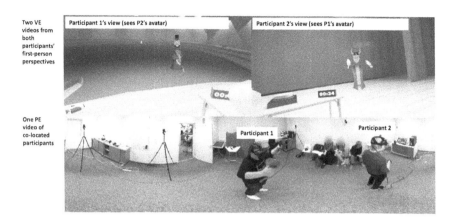

FIGURE 6.2   Parallel videos in the VR data in Rec Room.

their avatar appearance, but unlike in Second Life, the avatar body consists of a head, upper body, hands, and no lower body (see Figure 6.2). The players interact by moving and gesturing with their avatars, activating and moving objects, and talking in real-time through an audio connection. Facial expressions are generated automatically: The avatars' lips move when the user talks and the avatars frown when something hits their body or face. The avatars can be operated only from a first-person perspective.

The data were recorded as part of a university course on interaction analysis. Twelve volunteers were recruited (not students in the course), and they were divided into six pairs and instructed to stay together and freely interact and explore the environment. Both participants' first-person perspective in the VE (see the top frames in Figure 6.2) and the in-game stereoscopic sound were recorded separately with screen-capture software from two computers that ran the Rec Room game. The participants' talk was recorded from the microphones on the HMDs. Since the two participants were physically in the same space, only one PE recording was made with a 360-degree video camera and high-quality microphones. The participants move in the virtual space either by using a teleportation feature or the game's menu to select and move to a specific place in the game. In the physical space, the participants can move within a small and delimited area defined by the VR gear. Approaching the boundaries of the area triggers a grid on the HMD warning the user to not step over the boundary. In principle, this prevents the participants from entering each other's physical space. The HMDs were connected to a computer with a cable, which constrained the participants' movements. The users wore earphones to hear one another and the in-game sounds in Rec Room. Some participants chose to wear only one of the earphones to hear both the game sounds and the talk in the lab.

Two cases of dual embodiment and shared access to embodied action

In this section, we examine dual embodiment with two excerpts. First, we illustrate how in Second Life, a participant can lose visual access to their own avatar body. The lost access is then verbalised by the participant and becomes an issue that is solved by the participants together. Second, we examine an interactional episode in Rec Room where the participants – without them realising it – use the different bodies (virtual vs. physical) as resources for producing an embodied action and ascribing a meaning to it.

Dual embodiment as two perspectives to an avatar body in a virtual world

Entering a VE for the first time, especially with a pre-given avatar, can trigger from the participants such questions as "How do I look?" or "Does my avatar appear similarly to you as it does to me"? Excerpt 1, which comes from Second Life, illustrates how the participants' alternating perspectives to their own avatar body can become accountable. VE users have limited possibilities to perceive the appearance of their own avatar, especially in the first-person perspective. However, also the third-person perspective can create challenges; it may be challenging to see particular parts of one's own avatar body. The excerpt shows how dual embodiment becomes relevant when a participant has limited visual access to their own avatar body, while at the same time it remains visible and accessible to the co-participants. Thus, one body becomes "dual" by becoming visually accessible in different ways for different participants.

In Excerpt 1, the avatar appearances are first topicalised, after which one of the participants expresses lack of knowledge about the visual appearance of his avatar body and asks others to help understand it. In order to understand the circumstances in the excerpt, it is good to know that the participant has activated the third-person perspective. While the default mode is to view the avatar from behind, it is also possible to select a view from the front, top, or side. The view can be changed at any time. In the following episode, the participant has selected the default view, which also hides the front of the avatar. The excerpt shows how the participants jointly gain visual access to the front side of the avatar's body by relying on both shared resources in the VE and the participants' private resources in the PE.

Prior to the excerpt, Iiris, Antti, and Hugo have completed a collaborative task and have some leisure time before the next one. The excerpt begins when Antti produces a noticing about the shirts worn by the other avatars (line 1). In the beginning, the PE videos show that the participants are watching their avatars from the third-person perspective, behind their avatars. We refer to the participants with their pseudonyms (e.g., "Antti") and to their avatars by adding the letter A after the pseudonym (e.g., "Antti-A") (see also Kohonen-Aho & Vatanen, 2021).

Excerpt 1   VW Team 2, avatar shirts

```
01 ANT:    *+^teil on oikeen hienot ((yliopisto)) paidatkin tässä.
           *+^you have very nice ((university)) shirts here.
    iir:   *third-person perspective active->>
    ant:    +third-person perspective active->>
    hug:     ^third-person perspective active->
02 IIR:    joo. hh hh
           yes. hh hh
03 HUG:    ^:minkä värinen paita teil on niinku ittel kun mul
           ^:what color do you have on your shirts since to me it
    hug: -> ^third-person perspective active, uses WASD keys to
            move avatar->
    hug-A:  ^starts to walk->
04 HUG:    näyttää et täl ukol on val- musta paita.
           looks like this dude has a whi- black shirt.
05 ANT:    mul on ainaki  ^valkonen.
           I have at least ^white.
    hug-A:              ->^walks next to ant-A
06 IIR:    [mul on] valkonen kans.
           [I have] a white as well.
07 HUG:    [aijaa.]
           [oh.   ]
08 HUG:    ^lukeeks täs (.) ^#mustas paidas ((yliopisto)).
           ^does this       ^#black shirt read (.) ((university)).
    hug-A:  ^turns to face ant-a
    hug-A:                  ^backs away few steps->
    fig:                    #fig6.3
```

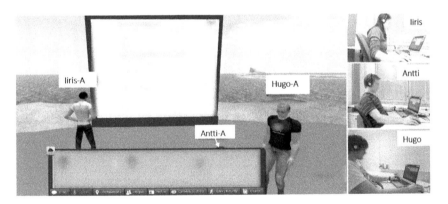

FIGURE 6.3   Hugo's avatar turns to Antti's avatar and takes a few steps back.

```
09 ANT:    ^no siin on ainakin se ((yliopisto)) logo ja-,
           ^well at least it has the ((university)) logo and-,
    hug: -> ^stops using WASD-keys
    hug-A:->^stops moving, facing ant-A
10 HUG:    okei. (.) [^miten °täs se ei     ]
           okay. (.) [^how °here it does not]
11 IIR:              [joo.                  ]
                     [yes.                  ]
    hug:              ^uses WASD keys-->
12 HUG:    ^käänny.° (.) .hh
           ^turn°. (.) .hh
    hug-A:  ^turns around 360 degrees and backs away from ant-A->
13         (0.5)
```

```
14 IIR:     se on tosi (.)
            it is really (.)
15          ^pienellä lukee ^#mut,
            ^small        ^#but,
  hug:   ->^presses alt key and moves mouse simultaneously
  hug-A:->^stops moving   ^stands still-->>
  hug:                    ^hugo-A's front side turns to the screen
  fig:                    #fig6.4
```

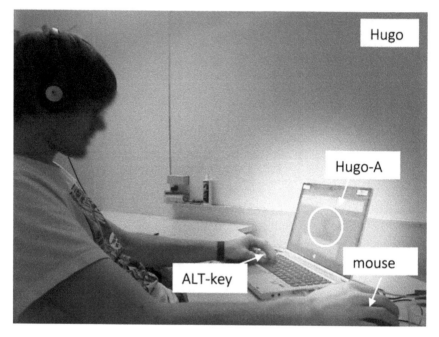

FIGURE 6.4 Hugo is controlling his avatar's movements.

```
16 HUG:     ai kato lukee siin ((yliopisto)).
            oh look it does read ((university)).
17 IIR:     joo.
            yes.
```

The excerpt shows an emerging dual embodiment problem. Following Antti's noticing and Iiris's response (lines 1–2), Hugo asks about the colours of the others' avatar shirts and tells them that his own shirt looks black (lines 3–4). Hugo starts to refer to his shirt as "white" but then corrects himself with a self-initiated repair (e.g., Kitzinger, 2013, pp. 232–233) by saying "black". Indeed, Hugo-A's shirt is black, while Iiris-A and Antti-A have white shirts. It is possible that Hugo asks the question to check if the colours appear similarly to all participants or differently depending on who is looking. As Hugo begins his question, he starts to move his avatar. Antti and Iiris confirm that they have white shirts. Following Antti's confirmation, and in overlap with Iiris' turn, Hugo says *aijaa* "oh", a change-of-state token (Heritage, 1984), treating the answer as news. It suggests that Hugo was expecting a different answer, for example, that the others also see their own shirts as black (lines 5–7). Then Hugo asks another question about the appearance of his shirt in line 8: *lukeeks täs (.) mustas paidas ((yliopisto))* "does this black shirt read ((university))". The question is motivated by the fact that while Hugo can see and read the text on his co-participants' shirts, he cannot see the front of his own shirt. This is a dual embodiment problem: Even though he is controlling the virtual body, he does not have visual access to the front of the avatar's body. With the question, he checks if the same information stands on all their shirts even though their colour is different. As he asks the question, to solve the dual embodiment problem, he positions Hugo-A's body so that it faces Antti-A, making the text on the shirt available to him (Figure 6.3). Antti confirms that the shirt has the university logo on it. The turn-final *ja-* "and-" suggests that he plans to continue the turn, but he then cuts it off (line 8). Hugo acknowledges Antti's description with *okei* "okay" in line 9, after which Iiris also confirms seeing the logo on Hugo-A's shirt (line 11).

Next, in overlap with Iiris' confirmation, Hugo moves on to turning his avatar around 360 degrees, possibly to see the front side of his avatar. This private action is another attempt and practice for solving the dual embodiment problem. Simultaneously, he verbalises his attempts in lines 10–12. Hugo's voice fades during the turn, indicating that the turn is produced as self-talk, indeed reflecting his private attempt to solve the issue, rather than as a genuine question to the others. This is also how Iiris and Antti interpret Hugo's turn, because they do not respond to it. After a 0.5-second pause (line 13), Iiris continues to talk about Hugo's shirt, stating that the text on it is small (lines 14–15). At the same time, Hugo finds a solution to see the front side of his own avatar and solves the dual embodiment problem. The PE video shows that by pressing the ALT-key and simultaneously moving his mouse, he is able to turn Hugo-A around so that it faces Hugo on the computer display (Figure 6.4). This confirms that his aim earlier was to face his avatar. At this point, Hugo has gained visual access to the text on his avatar's shirt, which is evidenced by his noticing turn *ai kato lukee siin ((yliopisto))* "oh look, it does read ((yliopisto))" in line 16. Iiris then confirms Hugo's discovery (line 17).

Excerpt 1 shows how in VE interaction a participant may lose visual access to (the full appearance of) their avatar's body. In VE interactions, this usually occurs with the first-person perspective but can also occur with the third-person perspective active, for example, when viewing one's avatar from behind. The analysis shows how Hugo attempts to solve the problem of not seeing a part of his avatar body by using verbal and social resources (i.e., asking the others for more information about the avatar's appearance) and by using private, embodied resources, to figure out the correct keyboard and mouse configurations to see the front of the avatar's body. The PE video shows why Hugo does not have access to his own avatar shirt: His own computer display does not show it. Additionally, the PE video reveals Hugo's orientation when he moves from asking his team-mates for help to trying to solve the dual embodiment problem himself by using the mouse and the keyboard to control his avatar. These actions are not visible in the VE video.

In sum, Excerpt 1 shows how dual embodiment in VE can become evident as limited visual access to one's own avatar body; the person steering the avatar can-not see their own avatar body in the same way as their co-participants can. This res-onates with the analysis on the intelligibility of pointing gestures and fragmented interaction in VR by Hindmarsh et al. (2006): The user's *perspective* may limit or prevent visual access to (parts of) their own avatar body, which in turn may lead to fragmented interaction. This has consequences for interaction: One cannot assume that one's co-participants have full visual access to the details and appearance of their own avatar even though that avatar is present and in use.

Dual embodiment as an orientation to different manifestations of one action in a virtual reality

In immersive VR, participants' own physical body movements are rendered as avatar movements. When a user walks, turns around, or points with their physical body, their avatar replicates the movement in VR. However, not all movements and gestures are replicated to the avatar exactly as they appear in the physical environment, which may lead to disrupted or incomplete trajectories of embodied actions (see Hindmarsh et al., 2006).

In Excerpt 2 from Rec Room, one of the participants produces a gesture that uses the hip and the waist area of the physical body as a resource for producing a meaning to the gesture (see Goodwin, 2007). However, while the recipient can see the gesture as the avatar's movement, he lacks access to the physical resource that is used to produce the gesture, as the avatars do not have a lower body. At the same time, because of the first-person perspective, the producer of the gesture has limited access to his own avatar body and how the gesture appears to the recipient. This constitutes the dual embodiment problem: the two participants momentar-ily orient to different bodies, the physical vs. the virtual, when producing and ascribing a meaning to the gesture. This leads to fragmented bodily orientation, is potentially misleading (see Hindmarsh et al., 2006), and has consequences for the intelligibility and recognisability of bodily actions and thus for the unfolding joint activity.

In Excerpt 2, Pertti and Heikki are playing the word-guessing game "charades". They are using English as a lingua franca. Although the official rules of the game discourage talking, they use talk to describe the drawings. Before the excerpt, Pertti has tried to draw the word "pocket" for Heikki using a virtual "pen." He has drawn two circles to both sides of his avatar body. Heikki has made two guesses:

ribs and life vest. At the beginning of the excerpt, Pertti changes his strategy: He throws away the existing drawings and produces a gesture next to his waist and verbally directs Heikki's attention to his pants.

Excerpt 2   VR Team 2, pocket

```
01 PER:     you know (.) *#pants.
   per:                  *tracing movement in front of his waist->
   per-A:                *hand/pen appearing and disappearing->
   fig:                  #fig6.5
```

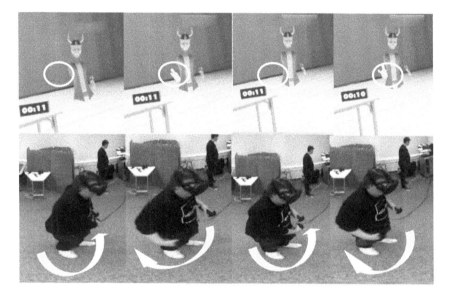

FIGURE 6.5   Pertti produces the gesture around his waist while at the same time the virtual pen and hand keep appearing and disappearing.

```
02 HEI:     ba[dge.]
03 PER:       [pan ]ts. (.) yeah*
   per:                       -*
   per-A:                     -*
04          (0.4)
05 HEI:     pants? (.) oh, pants.
06 PER:     I've got (.) uhh.
07          *(2.4)                          *
   per:     *shakes hands in the air, palms up*
   per-A:   *hands shaking-------------------*
08 PER:     *mhh
   per:     *drops hands down
   per-A:   *drops hands down
09 HEI:     I think I know what you mean,
10          but I can't remember the English word
```

```
11 PER:    *this (.) (you know) (.) this (into) this.
   per-A:  *grabs alarm
12         ((alarm sound + GAME OVER -shout in Rec Room))
13 HEI:    hhh. he he
14         (0.8)
15 PER:    the pocket man(h)hh.
16 HEI:    o::hh. (.) pocket?
17 PER:    pocket.=
18 HEI:    =that didn't look like a pocket.
19 PER:    he he. (.) I mean(h)-
20         *(1.1)
   per:    *shrugging
21 PER:    I was trying to *highlight [the areas.           ]*
22 HEI:                               [+no you- you just put these]
   per:                    *gestures circles in front of his waist *
   hei:                               +gestures circles->
23 HEI:    in here,+ I don't put pockets into my pants they're he he
   hei:            -+
24         already(h) he he
```

Pertti begins a new explanation sequence by directing Heikki's attention to his pants (line 1). The PE video shows that during his turn he produces a gesture that depicts the word "pocket". First, the gesture combines iconic (drawing the shape of a pocket) and deictic (pointing to the waist) elements. Second, the gesture is produced against his waist thus using it (as one usual location for pockets) as a resource for explaining the word "pocket" (Figure 6.5). However, Pertti-A's virtual gesturing is not equivalent to Pertti's physical gesture. The avatar's hand does not follow the trajectory of Pertti's hand movement, but rather keeps appearing and disappearing during the gesture. Moreover, the location of the gesture near Pertti's waist does not translate to VR because the avatar does not have a lower body. The symbiotic nature of Pertti's gesture – that is, how the gesture ties with an environmental feature (Goodwin, 2007) – is lost in VR. Due to the first-person perspective, Pertti also fails to recognise the incompleteness of his avatar movement as Heikki sees it; the only cue that Heikki has for guessing the word is Pertti's verbal *you know, pants*. Heikki's problems in ascribing a meaning to Pertti's previous turn becomes evident in his repair-initiator *pants* (line 2). Pertti's subsequent response and confirmation (line 3) is not sufficient, and Heikki repeats the repair-initiation before then verbalising a realisation in line 5 with a turn-initial change-of-state token *oh*. However, Heikki still does not guess the right word.

Pertti continues to try to explain the word but, as is evidenced by the 2.4-second silence during which he just shakes his hands, he has difficulties formulating or gesturing something new. He then drops down his hands and grunts as an indication of frustration and giving up (line 8). Heikki takes part of the responsibility for failing to guess the right word by acknowledging Pertti's attempts and blaming his own inability to remember the right word (lines 9–10). Pertti then begins to rely on a new explanation strategy and grabs a virtual clock that is counting the remaining time of their game and says *this (.) (you know) (.) this (into) this.* (line 11). However, they run out of time (line 12), to which Heikki reacts with laughter. Pertti responds by saying the word he was trying to draw (lines 13–15). Heikki expresses his surprise with the change-of-state token *ohh* and repeating the word *pocket?* Heikki's turn in line 18, =*that didn't look like a pocket,* is important, because it verbalises the problem of ascribing meaning to Pertti's gesture. After laughing and shrugging, Pertti explains the strategy he used to describe the target word *I was trying to highlight the areas* and reproduces the gesture he made earlier in front of his waist.

Excerpt 2 illustrates the possible interactional challenges involved in producing recognisable and intelligible embodied actions in VR. It shows how such challenges may be occasioned by the co-participants' orientation to different manifestations of the distributed bodies, the virtual or the physical. When Pertti uses his physical body as a reference point for the gesture, he builds on assumed equivalence between the appearances of his physical and virtual bodies. The form of Pertti's gesture, as shown in the PE video, reveals that it is designed with respect to his physical body (waist/pants). However, this is not intelligible to Heikki partly because the avatar lacks a lower body. Indeed, as Moore et al. (2006, p. 272) argue, in VR, it is not what one intends to do that matters but what is publicly displayed and becomes evident as a social action.

Moore et al. (2006) also suggest that avatar movements are less intelligible than physical ones because they are less sophisticated. However, Excerpt 2 shows that the challenge is not only related to the crudeness of the avatar body but is also deeply rooted in dual embodiment; despite being co-present in the physical and the virtual environments, the participants orient to different manifestations of their bodies: Pertti to his physical body and Heikki to Pertti's avatar body. Pertti's physical body remains inaccessible to Heikki, although it is precisely the physical body that would be needed for ascribing meaning to the gesture. Simultaneously, the motion capture technology used in VR seems to make it effortless for the participants to use their physical bodies, in rich and subtle ways, to produce embodied actions. Nevertheless, as Excerpt 2 shows, they can also lose access to how the technology replicates their movements and actions to the avatar.

Finally, the use of both VE and PE video made it possible for analysing the subtle features of embodied social action. PE video provided access to Pertti's physical body that produced the gesture within its "private" contextual configuration, while for Heikki, Pertti's gesture became intelligible only within the virtual contextual configuration and embodied participation framework that they both shared (Goodwin, 2000, 2007). In the following, we discuss how the above observations invite us to rethink some theoretical and methodological questions and principles in EMCA.

Discussion

From embodied participation frameworks and distributed ecologies to distributed bodies in VE interaction

New technologies provide new environments for human–human interaction and, therefore, new forms of "contextual configurations" (Goodwin, 2000) and new possibilities for establishing embodied participation frameworks (Goodwin, 2018;

see also Haddington & Oittinen, 2022). Moreover, in VEs, one participant inhabits two bodies simultaneously, the virtual and the physical. We showed how the two bodies function variously as interactional resources for action production and action ascription in VE interaction. Thus, we argue for the importance of considering "dual embodiment" and its relevance for understanding participants' procedures for making social action intelligible (i.e., accountable) in VEs. This said, dual embodiment cannot be treated as something that by default characterises VE interactions. Rather, VEs *afford* dual embodiment; it is a contingent phenomenon that may become relevant for the participants and consequential for the coordination of joint action. Dual embodiment may lead to divergent orientations of the body as a resource and influence a social action's intelligibility and accountability, requiring further interactional work to coordinate action.

We analysed two excerpts that illustrate how participants in VE may – due to dual embodiment – occasionally lose shared access to a body (part) that is relevant for the intelligibility of action. Excerpt 1 showed how participants may lose access to their own virtual body, which may in turn become an issue that needs a joint resolution. Excerpt 2 showed how the participants attended to the same embodied action (an iconic and indexical gesture) but oriented to different manifestations of the body when producing the action and ascribing a meaning to it: One of them to the physical body and the other to the virtual body. In the excerpts, dual embodiment disrupts the contextual configuration and the embodied participation framework between the participants, affecting the accountability and intelligibility of the embodied action, which is later resolved through talk.

These observations resonate more broadly with EMCA research on video-mediated technologies that afford interaction and collaboration across remote environments (e.g., Heath & Luff, 1992; Luff et al., 2003). The challenge that these environments – and their distributed ecologies – present for the intelligibility of embodied action originates in them being produced in a scene (physical environment) that is different from the scene in which they are received and interpreted (a computer display). They make possible situations where participants do not have equal access to the resources needed for joint action. In other words, they have divergent or fragmented contextual configurations (Goodwin, 2000) which can lead to communicative asymmetry and fractured interaction.

VEs add a new layer to this asymmetry and invite use to replenish the concept of "distributed ecology". In contrast to video-mediated settings, VEs create a shared ecology for distributed participants and provide them with an array of common resources that they can orient to and use for joint action. However, this shared ecology can be misleading; the fact that the participants still inhabit distributed ecologies becomes evident, as our analysis shows, in the form of dual embodiment. VEs provide an additional virtual body to the users that is controlled and operated by the physical body, sometimes from different perspectives (first-person and third-person perspectives). As a result, in VEs, actions and activities are produced and interpreted with *distributed bodies*. This can fragment, as we have seen in the analyses, embodied participation frameworks (Goodwin, 2018) and contextual configurations (Goodwin, 2000) with possible consequences for the mutual intelligibility and accountability of embodied action.

The practical solution we suggest for studying the "dual embodiment puzzle" in VEs is to make video recordings in both the virtual and the physical environment. While there are advantages of using recordings from both environments, the suggested solution also introduces important theoretical and methodological questions for EMCA, which have not been discussed before (see Gamberini & Spagnolli, 2003; Hindmarsh et al., 2006; Kohonen-Aho & Alin, 2015; Steier, 2020), but which we address in the next section.

Rethinking methodological principles in EMCA

The first methodological question that arises from the above suggestion concerns the source of evidence for analysis. Traditionally, EMCA has treated the recipient's response (usually a turn-at-talk) as the source of evidence for an analysis of what happened just before it (e.g., Levinson, 2013, p. 111; Sacks, Schegloff & Jefferson, 1974, p. 728; Sidnell, 2013, p. 79). Related to this "next-turn proof procedure" is Goodwin's (2000, pp. 1517–1518) idea of the public visibility of the body and how it allows co-participants to form interpretations of actions in their sequential context. In sum, in EMCA, only those features of action that are mutually accessible to participants are relevant for analysis.

By grounding the analytic observations on the recordings in VE, in which the participants have access to co-participants' previous verbal and (virtual) embodied actions, and PE, which is not accessible to the co-participants in the same way, we diverge from the next-turn proof procedure principle. We argue that the PE videos are instrumental for analysing joint interaction in distributed spaces where it is important to gain access to the participants' *private* actions. In our case, they were critical for discovering how dual embodiment features in the constitution and intelligibility of joint action. They revealed aspects of the fractured embodied participation frameworks and contextual configurations in VEs that would not have become evident in the VE recordings. They also showed how the participants restored mutual understanding when fragmentation occurred. Crucially for EMCA, they also revealed important aspects of "recipient design" (Sacks, 1992) by showing to whom an action is addressed and how that action is specifically designed for that recipient. This can provide important insights into the participants' tacit assumptions about what they share and what is mutually accessible to them.[2] Due to dual embodiment, these aspects may remain invisible in recordings made in VE. Nevertheless, the use of PE and VE videos side by side foregrounds the information gap between the member's and researcher's perspectives. Hence, PE videos should be used with caution. While any data that goes beyond what is available to interactants themselves (gleaned, for example, from multiple recordings, data logs, or eye tracking devices) can be useful, it is important for the analyst to not alienate themselves from the participants' social realities (Arminen et al., 2016).[3]

The second methodological question concerns the quasi-experimental nature of the studies in which the interactions were recorded and whether they reflect the endogenous organisation of social interaction between people who would meet "naturally" to play. The settings in both cases were partly the source of the participants' problems. In Excerpt 1, especially, the avatar appearances and the colours of the shirts were defined by the researchers. Thus, it is possible to argue that the interactional problem concerning the virtual body would not have arisen had the participants been recorded in a naturally occurring situation and created their own avatars. However, at the same time, the quasi-experiments showed the participants' orientation to their physical and virtual bodies, allowing the analysis to reveal the existence of dual embodiment and its relevance for joint social action. As different VE environments become more common in the future, these analyses can be complemented and verified with recordings made in naturally occurring situations.

Third, EMCA scholars who work with video are generally familiar with observing the participants from a third-person perspective, that is, "from the outside". In VEs – and especially in immersive VR (see Excerpt 2) – the recordings are made from a participant's first-person perspective. This has consequences for the analysis. On the one hand, the first-person perspective provides straightforward access to the recorded participant's perspective; the analyst shares the view of the recorded participant. At the same time, however, with the first-person perspective, the analyst may miss information about the broader context that a recording made from a third-person perspective would offer.[4] As to the VR data in this study, however, it is important to note that the recordings used for analysis are two-dimensional videos captured from computer screens. They differ greatly from and are not able to capture the participant's full experience of being immersed in VR (McIlvenny, 2020). An advanced solution for the analyst to access the participant's immersive experience is AVA360VR, a software tool designed for collecting and analysing "volumetric" data (see McIlvenny, 2019, 2020; McIlvenny & Davidsen, this volume). AVA360VR allows the analyst to "enter" a 360-degree recording with virtual glasses and experience the recorded situation from a first-person perspective that the participants had during their interaction.

To conclude, as long as existing and emerging VE technologies offer interactional affordances that diverge from the ones that are familiar to us from face-to-face interaction, such as the possibility of having two bodies (of which the physical one is constantly private for its user), the users of VE are likely to continue encountering situations where they cannot rely on the mechanisms of face-to-face interaction and hence come up with new setting-specific strategies to ensure the intelligibility of joint action (see, e.g., Bennerstedt & Ivarsson, 2010; Kohonen-Aho & Vatanen, 2021). Capturing these requires the development of the EMCA methodology in a direction such as the one we have proposed. Although parallel videos should be used with caution because they offer the analyst more information than the participants have themselves, we argue that they are necessary for complementing the analysis of multimodal interaction as well as for exploring the participants' orientation and mutual action in VEs.

Notes

1 One possible reason for not seeing a co-participant's embodied action may be related to the system: the field of vision with HMDs is narrower than human field of vision, which makes it more difficult to see from the corner of one's eye.
2 This opens a broader question related to what the participants can be expected to "know" about how the features of the virtual environment affect their actions. It is true that the more experience an individual has about operating in VEs the more they may be able to design their actions in view of the specific affordances in it. However, "knowledge" or "experience" does not necessarily translate into action. As to the dual embodiment puzzle in particular, even if one "knows" that their avatar does not have the lower part of the body, it does not mean that the individual stops using their real lower body as a resource for producing an embodied action in VE.
3 There is also another feature related to the information gap between analysis and participants that we have not addressed. In the Second Life data, the participants sat in separate rooms and did not have any sensory access to each other's bodies. In the Rec Room data, however, the participants were co-present in the same room. Although the HMD blocked their visual access to the physical appearance of their co-participant, it is impossible to prove, unless made explicit, if and when the participants could hear or sense each other's physical presence. For example, the participants may be able to hear talk and sounds from the physical environment through the earphones. Some participants also deliberately wore only one of the earphones to gain better auditory access to the physical environment.
4 One way to overcome this problem is that the researcher enters the same virtual environment with the recorded participants and follows their actions through the virtual glasses that are also used for capturing their interaction from a third-person perspective.

References

Arminen, I., Licoppe, C., & Spagnolli, A. (2016). Respecifying mediated interaction. *Research on Language and Social Interaction*, *49*(4), 290–309. https://doi.org/10.1080/08351813.2016.1234614

Bennerstedt, U., & Ivarsson, J. (2010). Knowing the way: Managing epistemic topologies in virtual game worlds. *Computer Supported Cooperative Work (CSCW)*, *19*(2), 201–230. https://doi.org/10.1007/s10606-010-9109-8

Blascovich, J., Loomis, J., Beall, A. C., Swinth, K. R., Hoyt, C. L., & Bailenson, J. N. (2002). Immersive virtual environment technology as a methodological tool for social psychology. *Psychological Inquiry*, *13*(2), 103–124.

Boellstorff, T. (2008). *Coming of age in second life*. Princeton University Press.

Bowers, J., Pycock, J., & O'brien, J. (1996). Talk and embodiment in collaborative virtual environments. In *Proceedings of the SIGCHI conference on human factors in computing systems* (pp. 58–65).

Cleland, K. (2010). Prostethic bodies and virtual cyborgs. *Second Nature: International Journal of Creative Media*, *2*, 74–101.

Gamberini, L., & Spagnolli, A. (2003). Display techniques and methods for cross-medial data analysis. *PsychNology Journal*, *1*(2), 131–140.

Goodwin, C. (2000). Action and embodiment within situated human interaction. *Journal of Pragmatics*, *32*(10), 1489–1522. https://doi.org/10.1016/S0378-2166(99)00096-X

Goodwin, C. (2003). The body in action. In J. Coupland & R. Gwyn (Eds.), *Discourse, the body and identity* (pp. 19–42). Palgrave Macmillan.

Goodwin, C. (2007). Environmentally coupled gestures. In S. D. Duncan, J. Cassell, & E. T. Levy (Eds.), *Gesture and the dynamic dimension of language: Essays in Honor of David McNeill* (pp. 195–212). John Benjamins Publishing.

Goodwin, C. (2018). *Co-operative action*. Cambridge University Press.

Haddington, P., & Oittinen, T. (2022). Interactional spaces in stationary, mobile, video-mediated and virtual encounters. In A. H. Jucker & H. Hausendorf (Eds.), *Pragmatics of space* (pp. 317–362). De Gruyter Mouton. https://doi.org/doi:10.1515/9783110693713-011

Heath, C., & Luff, P. (1992). Media space and communicative asymmetries: Preliminary observations of video-mediated interaction. *Human–Computer Interaction*, *7*(3), 315–346. https://doi.org/10.1207/s15327051hci0703_3

Heritage, J. (1984). A change-of-state token and aspects of its sequential placement. In J. M. Atkinson and J. Heritage (Eds), *Structures of Social Action: Studies in Conversation Analysis*, (pp. 299–345). Cambridge University Press.

Hindmarsh, J., Heath, C., & Fraser, M. (2006). (Im)materiality, virtual reality and interaction: Grounding the 'virtual' in studies of technology in action. *The Sociological Review*, *54*(4), 795–817. https://doi.org/10.1111/j.1467-954X.2006.00672.x

Kendrick, K. H. (2017). Using conversation analysis in the lab. *Research on Language and Social Interaction*, *50*(1), 1–11. https://doi.org/10.1080/08351813.2017.1267911

Kitzinger, C. (2013). Repair. In T. Stivers & J. Sidnell (Eds.), *The Handbook of Conversation Analysis*, (pp. 229–256). Wiley-Blackwell.

Kohonen-Aho, L., & Alin, P. (2015). Introducing a video-based strategy for theorizing social presence emergence in 3D virtual environments. *Presence: Teleoperators and Virtual Environments*, *24*(2), 113–131. https://doi.org/10.1162/PRES_a_00222

Kohonen-Aho, L., & Vatanen, A. (2021). (Re-)Opening an encounter in the virtual world of second life: On types of joint presence in avatar interaction. *Journal for Media Linguistics - Journal Für Medienlinguistik*, *4*(2), 14–51. https://doi.org/10.21248/jfml .2021.30

Levinson, S. (2013). Action formation and ascription. In J. Sidnell & T. Stivers (Eds.), *The handbook of conversation analysis* (pp. 103–130). Wiley-Blackwell.

Luff, P., Heath, C., Kuzuoka, H., Hindmarsh, J., Yamazaki, K., & Oyama, S. (2003). Fractured ecologies: Creating environments for collaboration. *Human-Computer Interaction*, *18*(1), 51–84. https://doi.org/10.1207/S15327051HCI1812_3

McIlvenny, P. (2019). Inhabiting spatial video and audio data: Towards a scenographic turn in the analysis of social interaction. *Social Interaction: Video-Based Studies of Human Sociality*, *2*(1), Article 1. https://doi.org/10.7146/si.v2i1.110409

McIlvenny, P. (2020). The future of 'video' in video-based qualitative research is not 'dumb' flat pixels! Exploring volumetric performance capture and immersive performative replay. *Qualitative Research*, *20*(6), 800–818. https://doi.org/10.1177 /1468794120905460

Moore, R. J., Ducheneaut, N., & Nickell, E. (2006). Doing virtually nothing: Awareness and accountability in massively multiplayer online worlds. *Computer Supported Cooperative Work (CSCW)*, *16*(3), 265–305. https://doi.org/10.1007/s10606-006-9021-4

Robinson, J. D. (2016). Accountability in social interaction. In J. D. Robinson (Ed.), *Accountability in social interaction* (pp. 1–44). Oxford University Press.

Sacks, H. (1992). *Lectures on conversation*. Blackwell Publishers.

Sacks, H., Schegloff, E. A., & Jefferson, G. (1974). A simplest systematics for the organization of Turn-Taking for conversation. *Language*, *50*(4), 696–735.

Sidnell, J. (2013). Basic conversation analytic methods. In J. Sidnell & T. Stivers (Eds.), *The handbook of conversation analysis* (pp. 77–99). Blackwell Publishing.

Steier, R. (2020). Designing for joint attention and co-presence across parallel realities. In *Proceedings of ICLS 2020* (pp. 1309–1316). https://repository.isls.org/bitstream/1/6330/1/1309-1316.pdf

Strain, E. (1999). Virtual VR. *Convergence*, *5*(2), 10–15.

7

360-CAMERAS USED BY A TEAM PARTICIPATING IN A MOBILE GATHERING

Pirkko Raudaskoski

Introduction: why and how to use 360-degree cameras

This chapter explores how a group of researchers in a mobile group (cf. Haddington et al., 2013) deployed (non-zoomable) 360-degree 2D cameras together with traditional (zoomable) 2D[1] (Lafruit & Teratani, 2022) video cameras to capture the participants' orientation to their surroundings as they moved through them and stopped from time to time. Such a combination of devices can help the analyst detect interesting courses of action undertaken by groups or by specific individuals and trace the occurrences of those action sequences throughout an event in its complex totality. Drawing on experiences from a guided nature hike that took place as part of an annual Danish nature event, this chapter discusses both the practical accomplishment of camerawork and the related methodological issues. The researchers took part in all the nature hikes in the national event that year and had participated in some the previous year. It has been interesting to follow how participants relate to the natural environment because climate change is rendering our relationship with nature increasingly pertinent.

Nature hikes with expert guides offer a learning experience in which guides explain what can be seen or heard in the environment. As they are present in the natural environment, participants also experience it through other senses. It is typical for a nature hike group to scatter along the path when moving from one site of interest to the next and to gather around the guides when a plant or other object becomes a focus of interest. A combination of 360-degree cameras and traditional video cameras not only increases the possibilities for analytical observation; it also renders transparent how data collection through ethnographic participation happens in practice because all nearby participants, camerapersons included, are visible in 360-degree footage. Participation represents a possibility for double membership, rather than interference, in the situation. All the participants display various types of

DOI: 10.4324/9781003424888-9

knowledge in their sayings and doings and in that the analyst gains access to a new, enlarged range of possibilities to produce new knowledge in a field of research. The nature hike in focus in the present chapter involved six guides and 14 participants visiting a local forest. The guides explained what could be seen or heard in the surroundings. The participants were also given a printed "bingo sheet quiz" to help them spot specific plants. While on the move, the participant-researchers spread out among the stretched-out group, typically with one of them in front, one around the middle, and one accompanying the slowest group. An analytically interesting situation was spotted in the footage when two guides offered participants two different sensory orientations (seeing, feeling) to inspecting the contents of a scientific tool: a rod with a soil sample. The chance to touch a sample of soil was generally welcomed by the participants. The "why that now" question surfaced when, stepping closer to the rod like those who wanted to touch it, one participant did not take a soil sample, but instead asked about its invisible contents (bacteria, acidity). This occurred while another participant standing next to him was touching two samples and discussing the feel of them with the guides. I looked through the combined footage from the entire hike to see whether they resorted to similar active participation in other situations. The chapter does not concentrate on the actual analysis (Raudaskoski, 2019) but uses the analytic interest to illustrate the benefits of the setup used to document the mobile and stretched-out group. My claim is that when the outputs of several camera and audio channels are collected as raw data on one screen (Figure 7.3 below) to allow closer study of the rendered versions of the 360-camera footage, this increases the possibility to follow the EMCA principle of attending to "the demonstrable indigenous import of the events and of their context for their participants (Schegloff, 1997, p. 184). The concluding remarks of the chapter also relate the study reported here to recent developments in ethnography.

Some background to multimodal data and its collection

Erickson (2004) explores the historical background of the analysis of interactions as multimodal in nature, as opposed to purely verbal. He emphasises the importance of the availability of film and video recording technology for the emergence of what has become the mainstream approach within EMCA and beyond. Erickson explains the divergent analytical interests among discourse and interaction analysts in terms of "differences in scholars' routine looking and listening practices which resulted from the differing affordances of different kinds of audiovisual reviewing equipment" (2004, p. 202). He also urges scholars to perform longitudinal multimodal analytic studies instead of just analysing short episodes. To do multimodal interaction analysis as comprehensively as possible, especially of complex mobile events, well-planned multiple camerawork (McIlvenny & Davidsen, 2017) offers the advantage of leaving few gaps, thus helping reduce the partial documentation that camera operators' motivated choices result in (cf. Cekaite & Goodwin, 2021). In a commentary to a special issue on researchers' participation roles in video-based fieldwork, Erickson (2021) also accentuates the inevitably participatory nature of video research (see Hofstetter, 2021 for another plea for researcher-participants). As 360-degree camera footage includes the camerawork, it enhances an openly participatory approach.

In recent EMCA studies, the moving and sensing body has become a central theme that has superseded the interest in gaze and gestures that video had made available to study. The EMCA repertoire has extended to mobility (e.g., McIlvenny et al., 2009), the sensory experiences of touch (e.g., Mondada & Cekaite, 2020), taste (e.g., Liberman, 2013), and sense of smell (e.g., Mondada, 2021). Being mobile in the world and sensing its various aspects require perception-in-action (e.g., Goodwin & Smith, 2020; McIlvenny, 2011; Raudaskoski, 2020; Smith, 2019). In particular, vision is a basic sensory and interactional ability allowing non-blind people to orient to their surroundings (e.g., Nishizaka, 2018). In some situations, such as patrolling (e.g., Kamunen et al., 2022), and in certain settings, such as airports (e.g., Goodwin & Goodwin, 1996), people concentrate on noticing actions or situations that do not seem quite right (e.g., Keisanen, 2012). All sensory experiences are, of course, inner in nature, but EMCA orients to them analytically through publicly observable talk and other actions.

When it comes to the analysis of data, the epistemological work of the multimodal interaction analyst requires video footage to do unmotivated looking and noticing. Sacks emphasized how this form of openness to the detection of a phenomenon should extend to openness in the next stage, thus resulting in "investigation in any direction that can be produced from it" (1984, p. 27). With 360-degree cameras as the latest addition to the recording technologies available, the footage literally improves investigation of "any direction". However, the footage has sometimes been regarded as too rich, especially when several 360-degree and traditional cameras are deployed to cover the ongoing event as comprehensively as possible. It is certainly true that there are more investigative avenues for analysts to follow, but the claim resembles complaints by some communication scholars that EMCA transcripts are too dense and complex. However, the situation they depict (as footage or as transcript) concentrates on the participant perspective, that is, how participants deal with their (often) effortless participation.

When gathering data with 2D handheld cameras, the researcher is involved in motivated looking and noticing (cf. protoanalysis; Mondada, 2014): A typical stance of the researcher-recorder is that of an observer (e.g., Mondada, 2014), and the camerawork requires constant orientation to capturing what might be most relevant in the situation for later analysis (Macbeth, 1999). Both Macbeth and Mondada report on one cameraperson doing the work of documenting a mobile group. This means that they follow the participants behind them to capture the group's ongoing orientation to each other and the surroundings. In the present case, the camerapersons are a team that are working from within the group whose practices they are interested in witnessing. They do that both when the group is moving and when they stop to gather, typically in a circular formation, to see and hear about a specific feature of the environment.

It is important to have a provisional division of labour for the camera crew, especially for a moving, often stretched-out group. When it stops, the camerapersons have to monitor each other to decide where to place themselves such that the crowd in its entity is captured. With handheld 2D cameras, that work also includes zooming in and out to record the details of artefacts used (camera *operator*). In complex situations, for instance with a moving group, that epistemic work becomes difficult as it is hard to follow the practice from the various participants' continuously changing perspectives (see Broth & Lundström, 2013). In complex data-gathering situations such as the ones reported in this chapter, a cameraperson will necessarily switch from the role of (detached) observer of an evolving action who is trying to make sense of it, to the role of a participant who orients to the situation with another type of instrumental stance (Goodwin, 2007). Since 360-degree cameras render the camerapersons' practices visible in the footage, it is possible to analyse their embodied participation. As mentioned, that participation should not be seen as problematic influencing but as one aspect of how the situation evolves as a specific configuration. The camerapersons monitor their concrete placement without seeing the exact result through a viewfinder, sometimes holding the camera at arm's length, if not further away with the help of a pole, or on a pole touching the ground next to them (cf. Figure 7.1). An almost continuously changing mobile formation requires an agile

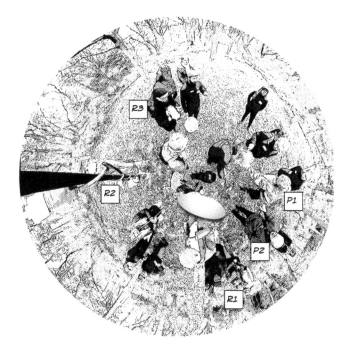

FIGURE 7.1   A one-lens 360-camera view from above

camera team. The cameraperson without a viewfinder view is fairly free to visibly orient to the ongoing situation, to become available to other participants, and thus to play a part in the ongoing action. They cannot see the exact camera view but concentrate on the action. In this way they behave like Garfinkel's ethnomethodologists:

> [O]ne has to be doing, as a competent participant or 'member,' what other members of a concrete setting are doing. It is only in this way that one can see what the practices are that make up the setting and that are features of it by being observable *as* features.
>
> *(Emibrayer & Maynard, 2011, p. 240)*

A comparable situation occurs when researchers participate in the interaction order under scrutiny with GoPro cameras attached to the body (e.g., Raudaskoski & Klemmensen, 2019).

The group effort enables a more thorough documentation of the participants' publicly available interpretations of the evolving situation: the ongoing documentary method of interpretation (Garfinkel, 1967). Using improved technological recording possibilities, EMCA has steadily expanded what counts in the depiction of meaningful action; what was originally restricted to the close analysis of audio data can now also draw on video-recorded evidence to encompass the importance of gaze and gestures (e.g., Stivers & Sidnell, 2005) and the specific texts or artefacts used (e.g., Suchman, 1987). In addition, the viewfinder has been enlarged both analytically and technologically to cover more of the seen but unnoticed (Garfinkel, 1967) nature of visible actions, and this requires consideration of what a 360-degree view might capture such that most of the ongoing event is covered in its details. EMCA is interested in showing how any activity is reflectively co-created as intelligible (or not) through continuous moral and normative work. The focus is on members' methods (Garfinkel, 1967) and not on individuals when, for instance, participants are relating sensory experiences to other participants (cf. Gibson & vom Lehn, 2021). A careful study of how episodic events relate to the total activity in question gives contextual knowledge (Arminen, 2005) and enables the investigation of specific members' habitual orientations. In the present case, the analytical interest turned out to be first-hand bodily sensory experiences versus abstractions and concepts, as they are different epistemological practices, turning the analytic gaze to participants-in-interaction.

The practical accomplishment of data gathering from the nature hike

Some members of the camera crew had attended nature hikes a year earlier, during the first national event to gain valuable practical experience of filming as a multiple camera (multi-cam) crew (McIlvenny & Davidsen, 2017). Participants' attention could suddenly switch from a plant on the ground to approaching horses or to a bird heard singing in the distance (Raudaskoski & McIlvenny, 2017). Whether the group was on the move or at a halt, the result was a variety of *withs* (Goffman, 1971). One of the successful local data gathering innovations was to attach a one-lens 360-degree[2] camera to a pole. Figure 7.1 below comes from footage from that camera, providing an overview shot from raw data. Another pole-mounted 360-degree camera was kept close to the ground to obtain a better view of bodily orientations to plants. Unfortunately, it malfunctioned during the nature hike that provided the data for this study.

The researchers asked the organisers of the nature event for general permission to collect data. As there were a number of scheduled activities, they also approached each arranger of a nature hike separately. The participant-researcher group arrived at the starting site of the nature hike (a carpark near a forest) in good time to be able to distribute and collect consent forms for the video recording. One participant who refused to be analysed has subsequently been blocked completely, even from otherwise pseudonymised images.

Figure 7.1 shows the three researchers (R) who gathered five recordings. They used an eight-lens 360-degree camera (R1), a one-lens 360-degree camera with a small 2D Olympus camera attached to a pole (R2), and a 2D Panasonic with the possibility of an extra picture-in-picture view (R3). The pole proved to be a useful extension, especially in situations where people circled around a common focus, as in Figure 7.1. The researcher could stay in a participant position while recording an overview of the situation. R1's and R2's recordings included the participation of all camerapersons, including R1 and R2 (cf. Mondada, 2014). With its view from the raw (not rendered) 360-camera footage, Figure 7.1 shows an example of this. It shows how R3 focuses on the viewfinder of the camera instead of attending to the action in question as an interested member of the group, whereas the 360-degree camera holders are open to contact. The most important data collection concern for them is where to place themselves in the group. However, they are not hiding that aspect of their participation either; they exhibit their *instrumental stance*: "the placement of entities in the ways that are required for the sign exchange processes necessary for the accomplishment of the activity in progress" (Goodwin, 2007, p. 70). They are free to look wherever they want. This freedom means that the camerapersons' actions can be analysed as having a double orientation: each cameraperson is an interested member who participates in the activity itself and at the same time orients to the camerawork. In other words, the camerapersons also worry about the present and future *epistemic stance*, "positioning participants so that they can appropriately experience, properly perceive, grasp and understand relevant features of the events they are engaged in" (Goodwin, 2007, p. 70). The way the instrumental and epistemic stances are entangled indicates the difficulty of distinguishing ontological and epistemological issues, as participation in all mobile and stationary situations requires knowing *how* (cf. Ryle, 2009). Therefore, it might be better to talk about onto-epistem-ology. The analyst can go back to the camerapersons' instrumental and epistemic choices but also observe more than they did *in situ*.

In Figure 7.1, the group has stopped and gathered around an object. Both R2 and R3 came to the scene later than R1, who seemed to have found an instrumentally best position to monitor what was going on with the earth sample. R2 and R3 first stopped to film a couple of metres to the left from R1, but after G1 introduced the rod with a soil sample asking what the group can see there, several participants moved towards the rod and so did R2 and R3. Even after settling for a position, they moved around, deciding where to place themselves in the changing configuration. This happened, in fact, when the group members' action trajectory changed from monitoring a guide's (G1) explanation of what they see to following another guide's (G2) offer to touch the soil sample (see below). As most group members moved to the rod, two camera team members had to adjust their positions, too: R2 moved around and closer to the rod and R3 moved to a squat position to get a better close-up of the hands and fingers at the rod. R2's footage shows that he glanced at the camera on the forward tilting pole, estimating its viewfinder's coverage, while R3 saw through the viewfinder to get the best possible shot. R1 stayed put, as she and the camera had a direct view to the rod; her own field of vision was approximately the same as the camera view.

Being a cameraperson was no less challenging when the group was a moving gestaltic configuration or Goffmanian plastic vehicular unit (cf. Mondada, 2014): The shape of the moving group would change continuously as participants adjusted their speed in the stretched-out mobile formation (McIlvenny, 2013a) while engaging in incipient talk. The only cameraperson orienting to filming "an entire recognizable configuration" (Mondada, 2014, p. 52) was the 2D camera operator, who concentrated on capturing the tail of the group.

The analytical affordances of 2D and 360-degree footage

McIlvenny (2013b) reminds us of David Sudnow's discussion about how reading a transcript of talk makes it possible to move back and forth in the text, whereas a video relies on the temporal unfolding of the actions and their recognisability *as* those evolving actions rather than as representations in text form. In other words, the hermeneutic circle is different in the two analytical situations. Sudnow was referring to 2D footage camera view that can be repeatedly watched on a flat screen. With 360-degree footage, the experience is different; rather than being confined to the frame and focus chosen by the cameraperson, it is possible to 'look around' and see how participants (including the cameraperson) are orienting to each other and their surroundings *in situ*. McIlvenny and Davidsen (this volume) report on an even more immersive, embodied participation experience in VR. I suffer from nausea in virtual reality, so my account of the camerawork is based on watching the footage on a 2D screen, with the additional possibility of looking around by moving the image rather than my head. The 360-degree freedom to choose where to look still gives a stronger feeling of being there, especially because recent developments in online data sessions (McIlvenny, 2020) mean that you can join as an avatar (head) in a non-VR mode, too. In the data session, you can also examine the data clip at your own pace during individual observation time without the others present. Data sessions and data inspection both afford experiences that approximate visiting the place, not just as "formerly present" (Laurier & Philo, 2006) but, rather, as something "situated", that is, more "here" and therefore also "now". The analyst can come closer to the ongoing documentary method of interpretation. In my case, I could engage in different ways of encountering and making sense of nature. For me, being able to track the participants throughout the hike occasioned an analytic stance to individual participants' orientations to nature in guided nature hikes.

My analytical EMCA observations of the data grew out of general interest in affect and agency studies (Raudaskoski, 2017a) and the usefulness of Goodwin's approach for socio-material analysis (Raudaskoski, 2017b). In both approaches, the analytical focus remained on situations where the guides invited participants to inspect the contents of a soil sample, offering a choice between what might be deemed two distinct referential practices: the embodied perception of vision, on the one hand, or touch on the other. In addition, what is visible in Figure 7.1 is also of interest: Two participants standing next to each other both take a step towards the soil sample but engage in different activities. P1 joins others in touching the soil to feel it, whereas P2 asks a question about its contents. The following cartoon strips (cf. Laurier, 2014; Laurier & Back, this volume) show how the footage was used to visualise the analytical interest in transcripts. (Movement is indicated with arrows, and transcribed talk in Danish lasts approximately as long as the action visible in the frame; talk corresponding to the duration of movement is highlighted).

1) Invitation to inspect: sight

G1: så skal vi prøve og se hvad vi har her=I   kan se igen vi har noget organisk stof heroppe
    so shall we try and see what we have here=you can see again we have some organic stuff up here

This camera view comes from the Panasonic 2D camera. The picture quality is high, which is important for closeups, showing the usefulness of zoomable 2D cameras. At this point in the data analysis, it was not just the invitation to watch and listen that was of interest, but also how the reference "organic stuff" gets constituted by the guide: The object is built while attending to it (cf. Smith, 2019), as opposed to reference or description acting as a separate representation of the object in the world (cf. Potter, 1996).

2) Invitation to inspect: touch

G2: (vil) I mærke på det? G3: he he he G2: det er sand, >d- det< det sjove er jo at mærke forskellen
   you (want to) feel it?   it is sand, t- the the funny thing is to feel the difference

The rod in this cartoon looks bent due to the chosen view from the one-lens 360-degree camera footage. The first frame also shows a closeup insert from the Panasonic footage which shows the detail of the guide's fingers on the rod.

The rendered version of the one-lens 360-camera footage also made it possible to zoom in on the group, as can be seen in the upper picture of Figure 7.2. The images below show the rendered version of R1's camera view at the same exact moment, starting from the view to the front. Under it are the images when the analyst turns the image to the left or right to inspect what is happening around R1 at that moment: to her left and behind, or to her right and behind. The blob in the left-hand side image at the bottom is the top of her head, showing how the camera placement slightly above her head did not block the view. (The images from R1's camera are cut-outs from the otherwise 360-degree possibility – only the camera itself and what was below it is invisible.)

Figure 7.2 shows the different orientations of the two participants of interest; P1 is touching the soil, and P2 is asking about it with a pointed finger. Both have just taken a step towards the rod, showing an interest in the topic. These two distinct orientations to the soil sample have made me think again about building reference and knowledge; while "subjective" haptic knowledge is based on life experiences and is available to all those who want to touch the soil (cf. Goodwin & Smith, 2020), "objective" scientific knowledge hints at "book" knowledge. Did resorting to the latter provide a way for P2 to do action-wise self-deselection (cf. Hoey, 2021) while still being active?

Instead of going through the analysis more closely (see Raudaskoski, in press, 2023), I have chosen to explain how the footage made it possible to follow the two participants throughout the hike. I did this to see if the participants showed similar "natural attitudes" to the material world during the rest of the hike. Raw footage from all five cameras was combined (see Figure 7.3), together with all the audio data that was available from the hike. The composite arrangement allowed comparison of the different camera views simultaneously to select views on which to concentrate, that is, the views which showed the participants who were the focus of interest. It also made it possible to choose the audio recording that was most relevant or clear. P1 and P2 were visible in all the used cameras when P1 was feeling the soil and P2 asking about it. In the rest of the footage, especially when they

FIGURE 7.2   Above: zoom in capture from the 360-camera on pole (the 8-lens camera marked on the right); Below: the 8-lens camera view straight ahead, to left and behind, to right and behind

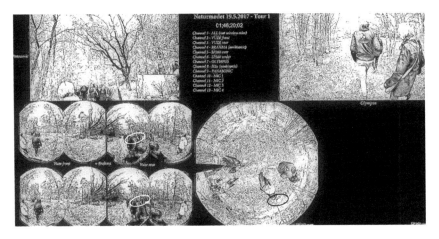

FIGURE 7.3   Simultaneous five camera views

were walking between sites, P1 and P2 were in separate subgroups but they could be followed from the different footages covering the entire stretched-out group (Figure 7.3). The 360-camera view from above helped in the detection of relevant occasions in the moving vehicular units (Goffman, 1971) and the view from the eight-lens camera enabled the detection of potentially interesting phenomena involving singles or participation units (Goffman, 1971; Figure 7.2).

The combined footage from the nature hike provided additional insight into the differences in orientation of the two participants. For instance, when the 2D camera operator was walking with the last grouping, which included P1 as a participant, P1 suddenly ran into the woods to fetch a twig from a beech tree, ate a leaf, and offered the twig to the rest of the group. This became a traceable action for the camera operator as, just seconds earlier, the group had visibly noticed (pointed at, looked at) the big "shiny" tree visible about 20 metres into the forest. Nevertheless, had shadowing a participant been the task, many actions and activities might have gone unnoticed by the 2D camera. This was the case when P1 shared another plant, this time in connection with the bingo sheet quiz. He was standing by the side of the path and then walked to another participant in the middle of the crowd, handing her a specimen. This action took place behind R1, but because she was bearing the eight-lens 360-degree camera in the middle of the group, it was detectable from her footage (P1 marked by white rings Figure 7.3) and analysable from the rendered version. The 2D cameraperson did not have to worry about whether or not P1's movements represented an important focus to follow. P2 is visible in the one-lens raw footage (marked with a black ring) in Figure 7.3. He was visibly surveying both sides of the path for specimens and could be detected at different places in the stretched-out mobile group, mostly in the middle. His only physical contact with specimens under scrutiny occurred when a guide instructed everybody to touch a fallen tree trunk. While at the rod, the same guide had only suggested that participants might touch it.

Summary

The general setup of the nature hike involved a visit to a forest habitat with experts. After an initial analytical "why that now?" question, the coverage from the multiple camera footage made it possible to follow two participants, P1 and P2, throughout the whole nature hike. The initial interest in the referential practice regarding a soil sample (vision, touch) turned out to be an example of individual "preference structures" in relation to the natural phenomena they encountered: P2 observed whereas P1 chose direct engagement.

Whether the participants are following instruction or making their own choices, the combined views capture how the participants' encounters with specimens constitute the objects, that is, how they "build the objects" while attending to them. The footage documents reference-making in both the "primary movement" and "secondary movement" (Broth et al., 2014, p. 17), providing materials to study the perspective of both movements and throughout the event. McIlvenny and Davidsen (this volume) show how the iterative co-analysis of the materials can also be recorded as practical work in the footage, providing analysts with ample opportunities not just to go back and check previous analytical observations, but also to immerse themselves and study EMCA (or other) analytical practices in vivo (cf. Greiffenhagen et al., 2015). For those researchers who suffer from nausea in VR, the important message from the present paper is that, after successful camera team work, the combined footage makes it possible to study the unfolding of the many scattered practices constituting an overall activity even outside the VR. The opportunities for analytical unmotivated looking also multiplied: Instead of only studying how different types of actions are formed through collections of similar cases (an important area of study, e.g., Levinson, 2012), analysis could trace the types of participants and – without a cameraperson having decided to shadow them – their orientations to each other and the natural habitat.

It is possible to make a comparison between the two types of orientations (P1 and P2) that the situation afforded to the camerapersons with the 2D and 360-degree cameras: While the 2D camera operator concentrated on epistemological concerns about collecting data for research (observing, finding the best point of view to capture; cf. P2), the other camerapersons were also able to participate or engage more freely in the ongoing event. When the group stops, the task becomes to ensure a configuration of camera positions that cover the group's practices. The work of the 360-cameraperson without a viewfinder requires a skill at envisioning what the camera on a pole or next to them captures of the participant perspectives of members of a group. In a moving group, a 360-camera can ensure that the footage also covers what goes on behind the cameraperson's field of vision. In this way, camerawork becomes more subtle as the cameraperson does not need to start walking backwards (with a 2D-camera) should their protoanalysis capture something interesting behind them. While stopping, the pole allows the 360-cameraperson to stand with others in a circular standing formation instead of (maybe awkwardly) in the middle, thus making it possible to participate through double membership. An added benefit is that the work of the camerapersons themselves becomes part of the footage, that is, the data collection work becomes directly documented (cf. Mondada, 2014).

The only footage that could be analytically equated with the cameraperson's potential viewpoint comes from the eight-lens 360-degree camera, as it captures everything else but the camera itself and what is below it; the cameraperson could turn around and look up or down while holding the camera located slightly above her head. The out of body (Raudaskoski, 2017a) version of the one-lens camera suggests an imagined viewpoint that the cameraperson has while holding the pole above the group. In any case, the camerapersons' practical work, their "practices of representing" (Barad, 2003, p. 804) while within the phenomenon they are studying, is available as part of the research data. The cameraperson holding a pole can quickly change from an overall "neutral" view (pole straight up) by turning the pole so that the camera faces a specific direction to capture a focused interaction (Goffman, 1963).

Discussion

Contemporary scholarship on ethnographic research methods criticises repre-sentationalism and advocates for reflexivity in qualitative research (e.g., Lynch & O'Mara, 2019). Macbeth (2001) suggests a division of the types of reflexivity encouraged in this movement into positional and textual reflexivities. Whereas positional reflexivity concentrates on the researcher's epistemic ponderings, tex-tual reflexivity treats written discourses as isolated entities. Macbeth goes on to explain the ethnomethodological take on reflexivity as a practical constitutive phenomenon, where texts are part of the accomplishment that can be analysed. The present chapter has built on the ethnomethodological point of departure, highlighting the possibilities that multiple data gathering affords to enlarge the analytical potentials of those constitutive practices and, importantly, to make the camerapersons' reflexive participation publicly available. This opens up new ana-lytical possibilities to study how researcher-participants manage to accomplish truly joint partnerships (see the ethnography of nexus analysis in Ingold, 2018; Raudaskoski, 2021; Scollon & Scollon, 2007). The practices covered by 360-cam-era data provide access to the concrete locatedness of researchers' positionings and enable analysts to "revisit" their situated positions. For the camera crew using multiple cameras in this study, the practical work was similar to the practices of any other person on the move: "the very observability of a scene is embedded in, endogenous to, and mutually elaborated with and for the observing members' ongoing activities, location, and context" (Smith, 2019, p. 38).

The group effort captures the participants' reflexive constitution of socio-mate-rial ontology during a (thoroughly documented) nature hike, enabling the analyst to shadow the actions and epistemologically revisit different aspects of that reflexive work. The contrastive pair formed by two participants orienting to a soil sample led to an analytical focus on types of participant-in-interaction, rather than solely on types of (multimodal) talk-in-interaction; in other words, the footage allowed a different type of EMCA collection. Here, it has allowed us to follow the constitu-tion of referents as members' practice, and the data has supported the sensation of revisiting events, rather than merely studying a closely corresponding 2D represen-tation. Since the camerapersons are visible in the footage, their ethno-methods or analytical work (both as participants and as researchers) is available for scrutiny. This allows access not just to the analytical practices, but also to the data collection aspect of "research as a practical enterprise" (Greiffenhagen et al., 2015, p. 480).

Conclusion

This chapter has addressed various issues involved in using a multi-cam crew (McIlvenny & Davidsen, 2017) and, more particularly, the benefits of a constella-tion of one 360-degree camera (with one-lens and with a small 2D camera attached to the pole), one (eight-lens) 360-degree camera, and a 2D camera (with the possi-bility of a picture-in-picture from an additional adjustable lens). The participation of a researcher team in a nature hike has served as an example of practical work, drawn upon in the discussion of the benefits of this type of research set-up.

The camera team should decide beforehand a rough division of labour for when the group is on the move. In our case this "preliminary protoanalysis" (Mondada, 2014, p. 34) was formed on the basis of our previous experiences from several nature hikes where we had tested the use of a combination of 360-degree and 2D cameras when trying to capture a situation with many mobile participants and their objects of interest. The ongoing protoanalysis while recording is not just about looking for the shifting attentions in the moving/stopping group, that is, what are the participants hearing and seeing, but also, based on the position and actions of the other members of the camera team, what is the camera's (approximate) field of vision, what are they looking at (cf. Macbeth, 1999). With big enough camera crew rehearsed in participating in mobile situations, this contingent protoanalysis can be smooth enough to produce footage with lesser gaps in the group's shifting interaction order(s). Skilful camerawork also contributes positively to the double membership of participant and documentarist. The worry about whether the cameras disturb/change a naturally occurring situation shifts to whether the camera crew manages a complex, necessarily to some extent improvised, instrumental choreography (cf. Whalen et al., 2003) such that none of the memberships disturbs the other in the team effort and the group trajectory.

The multi-cam footage involving 360-degree cameras increases the probability of tracing interesting phenomena, making it possible to check not just what seems to be of relevance at a specific moment but also, importantly, to go on to find further consistency in how people participate. When analysts are applying unmotivated looking to the "constitution of social-interactional reality" (Schegloff, 1997, p. 167) in all its material complexity, the array of footage allows them to notice or spot phenomena of interest to study further. The study discussed here was able to emphasise specific participants' ways of orienting to the natural habitat because their actions could be followed in the complex ecological huddle (Goffman, 1961) with changing contextual configurations. This made it possible to inspect participant perspective as a longitudinal, routinised affair, and not only as the best analytical approach for detecting how individuals show their orientation to the evolving situation, though that was the basis for detecting their accomplishment of local actions. The "pattern recognition" applied to the two participants is different from the standard collection of typified uses of language or gestures in EMCA, and it could also benefit the methodology of general practice studies (cf. Raudaskoski & Klemmensen, 2019).

Even if it requires more technical work than more straight-forward 2D footages, the practical analytical task of combining camera views and audio tracks together with rendering 360-camera footage to produce the split screen is definitely worth the trouble. The result was an increased awareness of "the object of study", that is, of the referent at more overall levels: 1) humans as embodied parts of the natural environments they visit and study through direct experiential sensory knowledge and indirect accumulated cultural knowledge; 2) researchers with cameras as participants in that situation rather than as disturbing elements. This means that sensing is entangled with sense-making, that rationality is entangled with affect, and that the footages bear concrete witness to both complex entanglements.

The footage provides ample opportunities to analyse how the participants achieve order at all points, in accordance with the basic claim of ethnomethodology (Sacks, 1984, p. 22). Adding 360-cameras to a group recording effort thus strengthens onto-epistemological reflexivity. This implies treating data collection not just as a technical issue involving equipment and (researcher) positioning; data collection must be treated with the same seriousness that Sacks treated the data collected with: "to see how it is that persons go about producing what they produce" (Sacks, 1992, p. 11). In other words, the data gathered make it possible to observe the participation trajectories of various participants (the researchers included), and the semiotic fields (Goodwin, 2000) that they use in the evolving situation. "Onto-" in onto-epistemological reflexivity refers to treating the situation as it is: the researchers' participation in the situation along with the other participants, whether as neutral observers or as fully-fledged participants. Consequently, this chapter problematises any strict demand for a "fly on the wall" approach to EMCA data collection in line with recent calls to move towards a more open and participatory ethnography.

The combined use of cameras comes close to mobile video ethnography (Büscher et al., 2011). However, as with 360-degree cameras, the quest is not for where to look but where to stand/walk. The camerapersons' attendance in the group differs thus from that of a 2D camera *operator* who focuses on the viewfinder. Multiple camerawork facilitates tracing events (almost) in their totality and thus supports a more longitudinal study of the basic EMCA interest, "what constitutes the relevant social [and material] context" (Schegloff, 1997, p. 170, my addition). The eight-lens 360-degree camera footage makes it possible not just to revisit the situation, but to re-choose the orientation of the cameraperson's *potential* here-and-now (participatory) and/or future-oriented (data collection) gaze from that perspectival point and, if necessary, to jump to another camera's perspectival point. The *out of body* view from the 360-degree camera above the group underlines the necessity of having a general view of the mobile group without making it into an abstracted "view from nowhere" (Haraway, 1988). Instead, while allowing the monitoring of the movements (and talk) of the members of a group in relation to each other, it also enables an analysis of how the data collection method is realised in practice.

As this chapter has indicated, I was able to revisit the situation, now as an analyst with a more "omnipresent" view than my own situated, embodied presence had permitted. The material, context-bound sensory and sense-making practices became available for inspection in a more all-inclusive way, thanks to the participants' and researchers' "ontological practices of knowledge production" (Childers, 2013, p. 603) captured closely in "the materiality of fieldwork" (ibid).

Notes

1 I will refer to the traditional (60/90-degree) video cameras as 2D-cameras in the rest of the chapter.
2 The one-lens camera was, in fact, a 220-degree one, but the sky that could not be seen was not of analytical interest.

References

Arminen, I. (2005). *Institutional interaction*. Ashgate.

Barad, K. (2003). Posthumanist performativity. *Signs, 28*(3), 801–831.

Broth, M., Laurier, E., & Mondada, L. (2014). Introducing video at work. In M. Broth, E. Laurier, & L. Mondada (Eds.), *Studies of video practices* (pp. 1–29). Routledge.

Broth, M., & Lundström, F. (2013). A walk on the pier: Establishing relevant places in mobile instruction. In P. Haddington, L. Mondada, & M. Nevile (Eds.), *Interaction and mobility* (pp. 91–122). De Gruyter.

Büscher, M., Urry, J., & Witchger, K. (Eds.). (2011). *Mobile methods*. Routledge.

Cekaite, A., & Goodwin, M. H. (2021). Researcher participation, ethics, and cameras in the field. *Social Interaction, 4*(2). DOI: https://doi.org/10.7146/si.v4i2.127215

Childers, S. M. (2013). The materiality of fieldwork: An ontology of feminist becoming. *International Journal of Qualitative Studies in Education, 26*(5), 599–609.

Emibrayer, M., & Maynard, D. W. (2011). Pragmatism and ethnomethodology. *Qualitative Sociology, 34*(1), 221–261.

Erickson, F. (2004). Origins: A brief intellectual and technological history of the emergence of multimodal discourse analysis. In P. Levine & R. Scollon (Eds.), *Discourse and technology* (pp. 196–207). Georgetown University Press.

Erickson, F. (2021). Co-operative participation, social ecology, and ethics in video-based ethnography. *Social Interaction, 4*(2). DOI: https://doi.org/10.7146/si.v4i2.127210

Garfinkel, H. (1967). *Studies in ethnomethodology*. Prentice Hall.

Gibson, W., & vom Lehn, K. (2021). The senses in social interaction. Special Issue. *Symbolic Interaction, 44*(1), 3–9.

Goffman, E. (1961). *Encounters: Two studies in the sociology of interaction*. Bobbs-Merrill.

Goffman, E. (1963). *Behavior in public places*. The Free Press.

Goffman, E. (1971). *Relations in public*. Penguin.

Goodwin, C. (2000). Action and embodiment within situated human interaction. *Journal of Pragmatics, 32*(10), 1489–1522.

Goodwin, C. (2007). Participation, stance and affect in the organization of activities. *Discourse and Society, 18*(1), 53–72.

Goodwin, C., & Goodwin, M. H. (1996). Seeing as situated activity. In Y. Engeström & D. Middleton (Eds.), *Cognition and communication at work* (pp. 61–95). CUP.

Goodwin, C., & Smith, M. S. (2020). Calibrating professional perception through touch in geological fieldwork. In L. Mondada & A. Cekaite (Eds.), *Touch in social interaction* (pp. 269–287). Routledge.

Greiffenhagen, C., Mair, M., & Sharrock, W. (2015). Methodological troubles as problems and phenomena. *British Journal of Sociology, 66*(3), 460–485.

Haddington, P., Mondada, L., & Nevile, M. (Eds.). (2013). *Interaction and mobility*. De Gruyter.

Haraway, D. (1988). Situated knowledges. *Feminist Studies, 14*(3), 575–599.

Hoey, E. M. (2021). Sacks and silence. In R. Smith, R. Fitzgerald, & W. Housley (Eds.), *On Sacks*. Routledge.

Hofstetter, E. (2021). Analyzing the researcher-participant in EMCA. *Social Interaction*, *4*(2). DOI: https://doi.org/10.7146/si.v4i2.127185

Ingold, T. (2018). *Anthropology and/as education*. Routledge.

Kamunen, A., Haddington, P., & Rautiainen, I. (2022). "It seems to be some kind of an accident": Perception and team decision-making in time critical situations. *Journal of Pragmatics*, *195*, 7–30.

Keisanen, T. (2012). 'Uh-oh, we were going there': Environmentally occasioned noticings of trouble in in-car interaction. *Semiotica*, *191*(1/4), 197–222.

Lafruit, G., & Teratani, M. (2022). *Virtual reality and light field immersive video technologies for real-world application*. The Institution of Engineering and Technology.

Laurier, E. (2014). The graphic transcript. *Geography Compass*, *8*(4), 235–248.

Laurier, E., & Philo, C. (2006). Natural problems of naturalistic video data. In H. Knoblauch, B. Schnettler, J. Raab, & H.-G. Soeffner (Eds.), *Video analysis* (pp. 183–192). Peter Lang.

Levinson, S. C. (2012). Action formation and ascription. In J. Sidnell & T. Stivers (Eds.), *The handbook of conversation analysis* (pp. 101–130). Blackwell.

Liberman, K. (2013). *More studies in ethnomethodology*. Suny.

Lynch, J., & O'Mara, J. (2019). Morphologies of knowing. In J. Lynch, J. Rowlands, T. Gale, & S. Parker (Eds.), *Practice methodologies in education research* (pp. 166–186). Taylor & Francis.

Macbeth, D. (1999). Glances, traces, and their relevance for a visual sociology. In P. L. Jalbert (Ed.), *Media studies: Ethnomethodological approaches* (pp. 135–170). University Press of America.

Macbeth, D. (2001). On "reflexivity" in qualitative research: Two readings, and a third. *Qualitative Inquiry*, *7*(1), 35–68.

McIlvenny, P. (2011). Video interventions in "everyday life": Semiotic and spatial practices of embedded video as a therapeutic tool in reality TV parenting programmes. *Social Semiotics*, *21*(2), 259–288.

McIlvenny, P. (2013a). The joy of biking together. *Mobilities*, *10*(1), 55–82.

McIlvenny, P. (2013b). Interacting outside the box: Between social interaction and mobilities. In P. Haddington, L. Mondada, & M. Nevile (Eds.), *Interaction and mobility* (pp. 409–417). De Gruyter.

McIlvenny, P. (2020). New technology and tools to enhance collaborative video analysis in live 'data sessions'. *QuiViRR: Qualitative Video Research Reports*, *1*(December), a0001. https://doi.org/10.5278/ojs.quivirr.v1.2020.a0001

McIlvenny, P., Broth, M., & Haddington, P. (2009). Communicating place, space and mobility. Special Issue. *Journal of Pragmatics*, *41*(10), 1879–1886.

McIlvenny, P., & Davidsen, J. (2017). A big video manifesto: Re-sensing video and audio. *Nordicom Information*, *39*(2), 15–21.

Mondada, L. (2014). Shooting as a research activity: The embodied production of video data. In M. Broth, E. Laurier, & L. Mondada (Eds.), *Studies of video practices* (pp. 33–62). Routledge.

Mondada, L. (2021). Orchestrating multi-sensoriality in tasting sessions: Sensing bodies, normativity, and language. *Symbolic Interaction*, *44*(1), 63–86.

Mondada, L., & Cekaite, A. (Eds.). (2020). *Touch in social interaction*. Routledge.

Nishizaka, A. (2018). Aspect-seeing in the interactional organization of activities. In D. Favareau (Ed.), *Co-operative engagements in Intertwined semiosis: Essays in Honor of Charles Goodwin* (pp. 345–354). University of Tartu Press.

Potter, J. (1996). *Representing reality.* Sage.

Raudaskoski, P. (2017a). Re-sensing in 360/3D: Better analytical sense of participants' perspective? Presentation given at Big Video Sprint symposium. Aalborg University, Denmark, November 22–24, 2017.

Raudaskoski, P. (2017b). Digging the nature: Inspecting the earth in a nature tour. Presentation given at Multimodal Day symposium. Copenhagen University, Denmark, October 6, 2017.

Raudaskoski, P. (2019). Analysing the complexity of nature hikes with 360-degree and stereoscopic video recordings. Presentation given at COACT conference interaction and discourse in flux: Changing landscapes of everyday life. Oulu University, Finland, April 24–26, 2019.

Raudaskoski, P. (2020). Participant status through touch-in-interaction in a residential home for people with acquired brain injury. *Social Interaction: Studies of Video-based Human Sociality, 3*(1). DOI: https://doi.org/10.7146/si.v3i1.120269

Raudaskoski, P. (2021). Discourse studies and the material turn: From representation (facts) to participation (concerns). *Zeitschrift für Diskursforschung/ Journal for Discourse Studies, 9*(2), 244–269.

Raudaskoski, P. (2023, in press). Learning in nature about nature. In P. Fossa & C. Cortés-Rivera (Eds.), *Affectivity and learning.* Springer Nature.

Raudaskoski, P., & Klemmensen, C. (2019). The entanglements of affect and participation. *Frontiers in Psychology, 10.* DOI: https://doi.org/10.3389/fpsyg.2019.02815

Raudaskoski, P., & McIlvenny, P. (2017). Encountering grasses, flowers and horses: Interaction in and with the 'natural world' on guided nature tours. Presentation given in 15th IPRA conference, Belfast July 16–21, 2017.

Ryle, G. (2009). *The concept of mind.* Routledge.

Sacks, H. (1984). Notes on methodology. In M. Atkinson & J. Heritage (Eds.), *Structures of social action: Studies in conversation analysis* (pp. 21–27). CUP.

Sacks, H. (1992). *Lectures* G. Jefferson (Ed.). Blackwell.

Schegloff, E. (1997). Whose text? Whose context? *Discourse and Society, 8*(2), 165–187.

Scollon, R., & Scollon, S. W. (2007). Nexus analysis: Refocusing ethnography of action. *Journal of Sociolinguistics, 11*(5), 608–625.

Smith, R. (2019). Visually available order, categorisation practices, and perception-in-action: A running commentary. *Visual Studies, 34*(1), 28–40.

Stivers, T., & Sidnell, J. (2005). Multimodal interaction. Special Issue. *Semiotica, 156*(1/4), 1–20.

Suchman, L. (1987). *Plans and situated actions.* CUP.

Whalen, J., Whalen, M., & Henderson, K. (2003). Improvisational choreography in teleservice work. *British Journal of Sociology, 53*(2), 239–258.

PART 3

Augmenting analyses of the member's perspective with multiple research materials and methods

8

INDUCTIVE APPROACH IN EMCA

The role of accumulated ethnographic
knowledge and video-based observations in
studying military crisis management training

*Antti Kamunen, Tuire Oittinen, Iira Rautiainen,
and Pentti Haddington*

Introduction

Ethnomethodological conversation analysis (EMCA) has a long-standing tradition
in investigating people's methods of "doing" and "being" in the world with each
other (Arminen, 2005, p. 9). It is based on the ethnomethodological aspiration to
understand human social conduct and on the systematic study of interaction as
the "primordial site of human sociality" (Schegloff, 1996). The latter forms the
tenets of conversation analysis (CA) which has two underlying assumptions: 1)
All interaction is orderly, and 2) This orderliness is oriented to, and made visible,
by the interlocutors *themselves* through their situated conduct and sense-making
practices (e.g., Stivers & Sidnell, 2005, p. 2). What has formed the core of EMCA
research is detecting micro-level interactional phenomena with a special focus on
the sequential organisation of actions. It has been taken as illustrative of the ways
in which interlocutors construct mutual understanding about their social realities and the situation in which they are engaging. The overarching aspiration has
been to unravel how situations unfold, and are experienced, from a *member's perspective*. The theoretical and methodological underpinnings of EMCA have been
employed by researchers working on both mundane and institutional interactions,
such as medical settings, courtrooms, classrooms, and diverse workplace contexts. Whereas the former has been characterised as the "purest" kind of CA, as it
tends to focus on the basic operations of sociality (e.g., Drew & Heritage, 1992; ten
Have, 2007), the latter has been often referred to as "applied CA", since it typically
deals with more specialised uses of language and other conduct with the potential
aim to improve some aspect(s) of institutional practice. However, the boundary
between these lines of work is not straightforward, since it is foremost a matter of

DOI: 10.4324/9781003424888-11

the overall research aims and the stance and viewpoint taken by scholars, that is, their researcher positionality (e.g., Day & Kjaerbeck, 2013). The purpose of this chapter is to discuss and reflect on our process of studying the institutional setting of crisis management training and how it has been informed by a close collaboration with the studied community and the decisions we have made along the way. We illustrate how carrying out research in this context has required us to rethink our position as researchers and to apply EMCA in ways that partly differ from its traditional starting points.

The EMCA methodological procedure is in many ways unique and different from other approaches that study social interaction, such as (socio)linguistics, mainstream sociology, and cultural anthropology. First, it typically entails working with video (or audio) recorded data from naturally occurring encounters from situations that take place regardless of the ongoing research. The start of the research process is, rightfully, the selection of a research site and data collection. The focus in the latter is often on the equipment and decisions regarding their placement in order to get the best possible quality data. Second, a key feature in EMCA is the role of the researcher in the field, which is to be an observer of the events without an attempt to participate in them. Third, the analysis itself has multiple stages: it starts when the data is transcribed (i.e., the first-stage analysis) and with what is called "unmotivated looking" into the recordings (ten Have, 2007). The purpose of this "empirical bite" (Clift, 2016) is to remain as objective as possible and refrain from making deductions based on anything but the recorded data. Originally, "purist" CA scholars were sceptical about the role of contextual knowledge in all stages of the work (ten Have, 2007). However, when conducting research on work communities with distinctive routines and characteristics, the reasoning of what occurs in an interactional event may need to be complemented and enriched with additional information. Gaining *ethnographic* knowledge from study participants that adds to what can be learned from the video recordings has been found beneficial, if not crucial, in some cases: It is "required for entry into settings that are generally inaccessible, for the understanding of local activities, for the identification of what has to be recorded, and also for the arrangement/positioning of the recording device(s)" (Mondada, 2013, p. 37; see also Maynard, 2006). In addition, as Lindholm (2016) notes, researchers who have collected their own data may begin to identify the focal phenomena of their research already during the data collection and write about them in their field notes. In applied CA in particular, the role of observation and ethnographic knowledge has been recognised and appreciated during the past years (e.g., Antaki, 2011).

Researcher positionality, including the use of additional data and the researcher's role during fieldwork, has been addressed by many EMCA scholars (e.g., Hoey & Kendrick, 2017; Maynard, 2006; Peräkylä, 2004; ten Have, 2007). The most recent work has touched upon participation in the interactional events of the recording, challenging the way the researcher's role has been traditionally enacted (see, e.g., Hofstetter, 2021; Katila et al., 2021; Pehkonen et al., 2021). One aspect that has not been comprehensively described nor discussed in previous EMCA literature is: how the researcher's contextual knowledge, deriving from experiences and observations during the data collection phase and the relationships built with the community members, informs the identification of research topics and the formation of research questions, and how it helps to analyse the data (but see Lindholm, 2016; Waring et al., 2012). Peräkylä (2004), for example, highlights the importance of gathering additional information on the research site through ethnographic observation, interviews, and questionnaires. This information can then be used "to contextualise the CA observations, in terms of the larger social system of which the tape-recorded interactions are apart", as well as to "offer information without which also the understanding of tape-recorded interactions may remain insufficient" (Peräkylä, 2004, p. 169).

In this chapter, our aim is to reflect on our own experiences conducting research on the context of UN Military Observer training courses. We discuss how studying this unique setting has required us to take a more participatory approach to EMCA, including a multi-phase data collection process, upholding continuous dialogue with the studied community, and gaining a unique kind of membership in it. In this chapter, we introduce the ways in which collecting and using complementary data have become constitutive elements at different stages of the research project and helped us refine our research questions and objectives along the way. Furthermore, we will discuss the practical, theoretical, and methodological aspects concerning the process and our way to adapt the "conversation analytic mentality" (Schenkein, 1978), and what it has meant to us and how we have reflexively developed it. We revisit the core EMCA concepts of *inductivity* and *unmotivated looking* regarding the data collection and analysis and consider how they can, or sometimes cannot, be adhered to in the investigation of all contexts. We also highlight the significance of accumulated ethnographic knowledge in reaching a sufficient level of competency, or "unique adequacy" (see Garfinkel, 2002; Garfinkel & Wieder, 1992; Jenkings, 2018), which is needed to understand the study participants' locally produced actions. Finally, we propose that such ethnographic knowledge and researchers' lived experiences during fieldwork can comprise what we call *proto-data*. Proto-data informs our in-situ analyses of the observed interactional situations and can help to identify and establish topics and foci already before the start of the video-based micro-analysis. The chapter is ordered chronologically: We first explain the initial steps of the project and the work done to understand the setting, and then move on to discuss the different stages of data collection, and how we got from the point of unmotivated looking to a more informed data collection and analysis. Lastly, we illustrate how the knowledge gained during the whole process has helped us make valid arguments on the video recorded data, which would have not been possible without it.

Reviewing the concepts of *unmotivated looking* and *inductive approach*: fieldwork observations as *proto-data*

Our project investigates interaction in multinational crisis management training, which encompasses diverse course designs and team configurations as well as both military personnel and trainees, and civilian participants. This chapter concerns our study of, and involvement in, a UN military observer course, which trains officers from multiple nationalities to work as unarmed military observers in various peace operations around the world. UN military observers' (UNMO) main task is to patrol crisis areas and identify and verify military activity. While patrolling crisis areas, demilitarised zones, or their surroundings, they observe minefields, troops, weapons, artillery, and military vehicles. They may have prior knowledge about the ongoing military activity in the area, or they may encounter it by surprise. When UNMOs encounter troops, their task is to collect and report facts about activities that violate or may lead to violations of ceasefire agreements. The collected information is reported to the UN, and it can be used by the mission headquarters, head of the mission, or the UN Security Council in negotiations with the conflict parties. The UN military observer course is organised by the Finnish Defence Forces International Centre (FINCENT) and consists of two parts: a one-week theoretical part where the trainees participate in lectures and small-group work, and a one-and-a-half-week field exercise, where they learn their future work through practical training and tasks in a simulated operation area (Figure 8.1). The research process has involved close collaboration with the community and various visits to the field, and the research topics and ideas have developed, transformed, and been refined through continuous dialogue with the course organisers and instructors. Furthermore, the planning and execution of data collection have been informed and shaped by this dialogue and by our own observations and experiences in the field.

What we propose in this chapter is broadening some of the EMCA core concepts, namely *unmotivated looking* and *inductive approach*, and how they could be developed to apply to the pre-analytic process and combined with ethnographic observation as part of data collection. Traditionally, unmotivated looking has been referred to as an "open-minded approach" (ten Have, 2007, p. 121) to the recorded data, treating anything and everything one sees and hears as a possible research interest. We, however, address unmotivated looking as part of the researchers' mentality already during data collection, when entering a completely new environment without a clear idea or understanding of the interactional phenomena. We also argue that such situations necessarily require a certain level of inductivity, concerning not only the data itself but also the research process as a whole. We introduce a multi-layered, multiphase approach to conducting EMCA research and propose that, in some cases, the real-life and real-time "first-hand" experiences of us researchers are needed to understand the interactional context well enough to carry out an informed data collection and accurate analysis (see also Edmonds, 2021). We treat our experiences and different forms of ethnographic

FIGURE 8.1   A realistic UN base in the simulated operation area.

knowledge, such as extensive observation, field notes, and the continuous dialogue with the studied community, as elements of *proto-data* that can contribute to identifying research foci already prior to the start of the video analysis (cf. Lindholm, 2016). During the video analysis phase, these same observations and experiences are used as ethnographic data alongside the recordings. The role of accumulated knowledge has been fundamental, since it has guided us to see potential research topics, refine our research questions and do initial analyses already from what we observed around us during the preliminary stages of data collection. Furthermore, access to such ethnographic data has been key in making valid deductions based on the video recordings, which would otherwise be rather impenetrable. In this section, we will further elaborate on the key concepts and the overall progression of our work (Figure 8.2).

FIGURE 8.2   Visualisation of the research process.

Preparing for data collection: from first contact to first visit to the field

EMCA research on institutional contexts may have different kinds of starting points and motivations, which are often driven by the researcher's own interests. However, they may also be affected or even instigated by the needs of the studied community, which has increasingly been the case with research on professional settings (see e.g., Heath et al., 2003; Hindmarsh & Pilnick, 2007; Mondada, 2013). In our case, the collaborating party raised matters that our research could address from the beginning and at different organisational levels. In 2018, two of us researchers took part in a management-level meeting, the purpose of which was to strengthen the role of scientific research in the development of crisis management training. It was during this meeting, when the then-Commandant of FINCENT first brought up the military observer course. As part of the course, the trainees rehearse car patrolling in independently operating pairs or groups of three, and at certain points in the exercise many of them end up "getting killed." Since in that specific part of the course the teams operate independently without an instructor present, the instructors have no access to what happens inside the vehicles prior to these incidents, apart from the trainees' accounts afterwards. Our video-based research was seen as a possible solution to this problem. Thus, already at this time, the focus of the first data collection and a possible wider research question started to be composed based on the course organisers' "substantive concerns" (Maynard, 2006, p. 70).

In his seminal paper on the interplay between CA and ethnography, Maynard (2006, p. 59) describes how he got interested in the phenomenon of delivering diagnostic news in clinical settings through unmotivated listening of pre-recorded audio tapes he had received, and reading of the transcripts that came with them. In an endnote, he compares his approach to the data collection with the ethnographic strategy of "hanging out" (Dingwall, 1997, p. 53 as cited in Maynard, 2006) in a setting "to experience the people and the social situation, avoiding prior questions and letting the situation pose its own questions" (Maynard 2006, p. 83, fn1). This made it possible for him to begin collecting new data with a focused phenomenon in mind. In our case, the first discussion led to the first researcher visit in the autumn of 2018, where the objective was to get to know the course and the setting and make observations for planning the data collection on the following course. This also functioned as an important first experience and a step towards gaining the knowledge needed about the practices of the studied community.

The visit took place during the field exercise part when the trainees were conducting their first simulated tasks. Although we had been previously presented with one question to seek answers to, we had also been given a more or less free rein to study whatever we might find interesting. Thus, we were invited to take part in the course at first as observers, in order to get to know the course, its surroundings, and contents, and identify potentially interesting parts of the course that might include topics for our research. In other words, our aim during the first visit was to *hang out* and look for different "interactional hot spots" (Jordan & Henderson, 1995, p. 43). The course director introduced us to the basic structure and objective of the course and presented the various tasks and exercises the trainees perform during the course. We had the possibility to inspect and document the vehicles and the bases, which helped us in planning and, later, building the camera systems. By that time, we had already decided to record in-car interaction, and therefore the focus was on what possibilities and limitations we had for installing the equipment. Once we saw the activities that took place in the bases and other buildings, such as negotiation and mediation exercises, lessons, briefings, and planning, we also started to plan different options to record in some of those spaces. We were also given some suggestions about where to look by the course teachers and instructors, who already had a good professional understanding of the different interactionally challenging tasks and exercises of the course, and who were also just interested in hearing interaction researchers' – that is, our – views on some course-related issues. During the visit we also got to sit in the cars during patrolling exercises, which gave us insights into the practicalities and contents of the tasks and was an eye-opener into the various events and challenges that the trainees face during patrolling. We were provided yellow "invisibility" vests that the instructors also used, which indicated that we did not exist in the training scenario.

The first visit gave us several preliminary ideas for possible research topics, especially related to patrolling exercises, and it afforded us with the first possibility to gain and begin to utilise proto-data for future data collection and analyses. In this respect, the preparation and observation phases were key in the research process, as they set the basis for the data collection on the next course. By taking an inductive and open-minded approach, we were able to reflexively identify spaces and activities that could become sites for interesting interactional practices and phenomena. Our approach thus resembles the ethnography of nexus analysis (Scollon & Scollon, 2004; see also Raudaskoski, 2010) in that our aspiration was to engage and create the kind of a zone of identification that enabled us to see which phenomena were the most interesting ones.

Data collection: Part one

Scholars in diverse fields of study, such as social psychology, communication, sociology, and linguistic anthropology, have advocated combining naturalistic perspectives, that is, gaining an insider's perspective, with ethnomethodological social constructivism when collecting and analysing recorded data from authentic interactions (e.g., Duranti, 1997; Goodwin, 1990; Gumperz, 1992; Potter, 1997). Maynard (2006, p. 62) describes how ethnography can be used to differing extents within EMCA, making a distinction between "limited affinity" and "mutual affinity". In the former, ethnography is used as a resource to complement interactional analysis in the shape of descriptions of settings and identities of parties, when explicating words, utterances, or courses of action potentially unfamiliar to an investigator or reader, and explaining "curious" patterns that the analysis reveals. In the latter, a more profound insider's perspective is sought through active participation in the ongoing activities and *membership* in the studied community. What seems to drive the decision on the linkage of the two approaches are their affordances and limitations; on the one hand, limited affinity facilitates retaining analytical control regarding the arguments made on interactional data, while on the other hand, mutual affinity can result in data loss due to its aspiration to take into consideration the wider institutional structures (Maynard, 2006, p. 66).

Our research is somewhere in between the two affinities: both planned and spontaneous discussions and dialogue with the course organisers, instructors, and trainees at different phases as well as carrying out *increased participant observation* (see also Edmonds, 2021) have provided us access to not only information on specific contexts of interaction but also continuous analysis of "lived-in data". The multiphase data collection process has also afforded us the opportunities to gain membership in the community. Our membership is not that of a course trainee, nor is it that of an instructor or a teacher, but instead it is of a unique kind in the sense that it contains aspects of both the aforementioned. As researchers, we have both gained and been given access to the inner workings of organising the course, as well as information on the events that will take place during different parts of the practical exercises that the trainees do not have. However, we lack the same level of course-related experience and the expertise of the instructors and, being non-military, also the professional knowledge of the trainees (cf. Jenkings, 2018). At the same time, we have still experienced the course for the first time in a similar way as the trainees do, but from our own professional perspective as interaction researchers. This unique constellation of enacting the role of a researcher and a participant has helped us make informed decisions (e.g., on what data to include and how) along the way.

On the following course, in the spring of 2019, the first data collection was executed based on the pre-planning during the first visit. This time, one researcher participated in the theoretical part of the course from the first day onwards and began compiling extensive field notes (Emerson et al., 2011). She thereby got an opportunity to get to know the trainees and the instructors and to follow the lessons and exercises. This proved to offer valuable information about the learning contents and objectives of the course, but even more of the participants, their development, expertise, and the overall dynamics.[1] Before the second week, when the trainees arrived at the field exercise area, two researchers went ahead and installed the recording systems as planned after the first visit.

During the first data collection, car patrolling became a central focus of our attention because we were offered an opportunity to join the patrol teams as backseat passengers and record their in-car interactions with hand-held GoPro cameras. In other words, at this point the different forms and levels of dialogue and the "substantive concerns" (Maynard, 2006, p. 70) raised earlier, in the very first meeting, had led us researchers there. As "invisible" passengers in the patrol cars, we had no idea when to turn on our cameras and record, nor did we yet have portable power supplies with us. As a result of the inductive approach to the first data collection, we could not record much, but instead, the recording was more *reactive*, and the cameras were turned on only when something that we perceived as potentially interesting happened. Although this reactiveness often led to the lack of footage of the build-up to the recorded event, the gained first-person perspective (Edmonds, 2021) allowed us to learn from the recordings which then helped with the preparation for the next part of our work. As opposed to the first visit, when we were taking part (as passengers) in the patrolling exercises during which the instructors gave us a discrete heads-up to indicate good timings to start recording, this time we were more independent and made a comprehensive amount of field notes to which we were able to resort later.

During the second visit, the instructors approached us frequently with topics related to their work and posed specific questions for us to consider, which indicated that they now treated us as members of the community (see, e.g., Marttila, 2018). This mainly happened when the cameras were not recording, showing the participants' orientation to our varying roles in the course. This first data collection could be characterised as an extended observation phase during which we recorded anything and everything we deemed interesting through *unmotivated looking*. Based on our observations during the course, we were then able to develop even more refined ideas of what we could focus on more in depth.

Data collection: Part two (informed data collection)

The process from the first data collection to the second one entailed refinement of the research problems and specific interactional phenomena. Before entering the field again, we were able to go through a process of selecting the locations of interesting contexts and make plans accordingly, and thereby orientate ourselves towards a more informed data collection. The decision-making was partly practical; not having the equipment to record everything, it would be more reasonable to focus on particular parts of the exercise. Some places were also more difficult to record (due to, e.g., lighting, sound, visibility, or mobile participants), while others included activities that were less relevant for our overall aims (e.g., situations where there were recruited actors who had a central role). Our decisions were also informed by the interests of the training community (i.e., instructors, course director, and the Commandant) and the aspects that had been brought up in earlier discussions.

Through an inductive process, that is, the reflection on the observations we made in/of our proto-data during and after the previous data collection, we had decided to investigate specific activities and tasks during car patrolling. Comparing the initial research questions and foci that were formed during the first visit, relating to the trainees' potential interactional challenges, we were now able to direct our focus to readily identified phenomena, such as practices and routines of navigation (see next section). Furthermore, we were able to zoom into specific parts of the final patrolling exercise, where we knew the trainees would have to solve practical problems in collaboration *in situ*. For one, we had identified two specific parts of the final patrolling exercise where the teams encounter sudden and unexpected situations, and we discussed them with the instructors. These turned out to represent the incidents during which the teams consistently ended up getting "killed", which was mentioned by the Commandant of FINCENT in our very first discussion with him. Our decision was now to systematically record all the teams' actions on these two sites in and outside the vehicles (Figure 8.3), which also helped us start forming a *collection* of cases already during the fieldwork.

We attended the course for a second time in the autumn of 2019. The practical troubles we had encountered previously were taken into consideration, and some changes were made in the recording setup. Furthermore, we now had two independently operating in-car camera systems and multiple GoPro cameras with spare batteries and memory cards for handheld recording. Two researchers accompanied the trainee patrols during the final exercise and recorded their interactions from the backseat, whereas one researcher moved between two predefined locations in the field to record the outside-the-car activities of the patrols in the autonomously recording vehicles. This second, more focused, and informed

FIGURE 8.3   Collecting data in the field (image from recording a task outside the vehicle).

data collection was crucial in building more comprehensive collections for our respective studies. In addition, it afforded us a deeper understanding of the course and its contents, which helped validate our arguments in the upcoming analyses.

Using accumulated ethnographic knowledge in the recognition and analysis of interactional phenomena

In this section, we illustrate how the above discussed overall procedure has helped us in the recognition of interactional phenomena and their detailed analyses. What follow are brief descriptions of the processes through which central research themes were identified, and how these involved the development of unmotivated looking (i.e., towards more motivated looking) and reaching an in-depth understanding of the task-specific goals. The first interactional context is noticings during car-patrolling, the second one decision-making in sudden situations, and the third one routines and practices of navigation talk.

Noticing actions as part of military observation in car patrolling

The UNMOs' successful observation task is made possible by the timely production of one social action, the noticing action, and by how it is produced and what happens after it. Noticing actions are part and parcel of UNMOs' work and very frequent. In EMCA, noticing is considered a perceptual and visual action that identifies and makes public some aspect of the environment (Schegloff, 2007). The design of the noticing turn (or embodied action) offers an interpretation of the noticed feature; noticings also invite a co-participant's attentional shift to the noticed feature and prompt a transition to a new activity. Detailed analysis of noticing actions in the context of UNMOs' work (e.g., Haddington, Kamunen & Rautiainen, 2022) shows how the "professional vision" (Goodwin, 1994; Nevile, 2013a, 2013b) of the trainees is manifest in how they formulate the seeing of a feature that is relevant for their task and how the team members respond to the noticing in ways that ensure the appropriate advancement of the observation task.

In the context of military observation, the first elements, which prompt the noticing action and are consequential for its design, are usually invisible to the camera and thereby inaccessible to the analyst from the recordings. Access to "proto-data" made it possible to gain first-hand information on the tasks and on what the trainees were supposed to notice, without which it would have been impossible to understand the "correct procedure" in these situations. Furthermore, proto-data made the analysis of the responses to noticing actions more specific and accurate. Schegloff (2007, p. 219) and Stivers and Rossano (2010, p. 27) have noted that in mundane interactions, noticing actions have low response relevance and do not prescribe a specific action in response. Indeed, some noticings never receive an uptake, and a non-response is not necessarily treated as accountable. However, responses to noticing actions in the context of military observer training come in many forms, displaying the range of meanings that the noticings may construct. Sometimes they are verbal acknowledgements, such as expressions that build a context for continued scanning of the environment but with no reportable details, or actions that actively progress the observation activity, such as listing observations for reporting purposes. When studying noticings, access to knowledge about the organisation of these moments and about the sociomaterial and semiotic fields (Goodwin, 2000) around or within the car (e.g., maps, notebooks, aide-mémoires, compasses, satellite navigators), namely what the trainees see and experience, provided us with crucial information about the consequentiality of the noticing actions: how they are produced and interpreted in the moment.

Decision-making in sudden situations

As mentioned earlier, the issue of UNMO trainees "getting killed" in certain parts of the final exercise was brought to our attention by the Commandant of FINCENT already before any data collection began. Therefore, this was one of the issues we were interested in examining in our research from the beginning. It was, however, not specified to us which incidents this was in reference to, but rather it was left for us (intentionally or not) to discover. During the first data collection, we identified three incidents that were designed to be unexpected and sudden for the teams, in two of which they had some agency over the outcome. One incident was selected for closer inspection: a task during which the patrol teams encounter a simulated situation where another UN peacekeeper patrol has driven their car off the road and exploded a landmine. As the studied context was identified already during the first data collection phase, a collection of 11 cases was quickly formed of all the teams' encounters with the incident. The first data collection also informed the process of collecting data from the next course where one of the researchers was present in the field to record the teams' activities also outside the cars that had autonomous recording systems.

Some of the trainees' challenges with the incident became evident already during the first data collection. The most noticeable difficulty in their work regarded the identification of what the simulated scene is supposed to represent, which was a reoccurring phenomenon in almost all of the recorded team interactions. The repeated viewings of the recordings of each team after the data collection was guided by a more motivated looking, which revealed aspects of the incident that had not been spotted in the field. One of the key findings of the study was that in several of the cases, the trainees made references to some earlier event, such as "another one", "this again", and "they need help again", as they had arrived at the scene and were still working to make sense of what was going on in front of them (Kamunen et al., 2022; see Figure 8.4). These references were found to be related to a prior task that each of the teams had encountered a couple of hours earlier, in which they had to provide first aid at a traffic accident site, which also involved another UN peacekeeper team and was very similar to the mine accident in its

FIGURE 8.4   Illustration of the mine incident case (from Kamunen, Haddington, & Rautiainen, 2022).

layout. While this detail is also available in the data, it is rather far away from the mine incident, and the connection between these two setups is not explicitly verbalised by the participants in any of the cases. Watching the recordings of these moments evoked a memory of the first-aid task while being present in the exercise throughout the patrol route and helped to quickly make the connection to it, without the need to comb through the tapes in order to identify the referent incident. Overall, having knowledge not only about the interactional context under scrutiny but also about past events proved invaluable for us researchers in identifying the problem and potential reasons for its reoccurrence in the teams.

Routines and practices of navigation

At the early stages of the research process, attention was also paid to themes that felt at the time somewhat irrelevant with respect to the training community's main interests. Their focus seemed to be on particular action points during the training, but we also became interested in actions that take place in between those points, when "nothing is going on". Since we had an open mandate to explore whatever we found interesting, attention was also turned to all interaction regarding teamwork, be it planning, executing, or assessing the team's tasks. Furthermore, our understanding of the course and UNMOs' work was very limited to begin with but developed as we followed the trainees and watched them execute their tasks during the first visit and data collection. This knowledge offered us the opportunity to form an understanding of what patrolling is and how it is structured. All the activities in the car were recorded without any presumptions about what might be interesting. During the second data collection, spending some additional time observing the teams caused one of us to focus on navigation and navigational talk. The significance of the routines really became highlighted later when examining recordings of other teams, specifically when coming across a team that really struggled with navigating, and forming and maintaining its routines.

Our understanding of the routines and practices of navigation developed out of the perception that navigation and talk related to it takes up a notable amount of time in the patrolling vehicle (Rautiainen, 2021). Even when everything goes smoothly, patrolling is a continuous progression from waypoint to waypoint, and navigating and following the route structures all other task-related activities, making navigation and navigational talk ubiquitous for patrolling. The experiences with and observations of the first followed team were the starting point that led to examining other teams and their actions. The objective was to find out how the teams "do navigating" and how they achieve a smooth progress that enables performing various other tasks, such as documenting and reporting events, simultaneously with navigating.

To conclude, accumulated ethnographic knowledge, aspects of "proto-data", and developing unmotivated looking throughout the process, namely prior to and during the recording phase, and before the actual analysis, have formed key elements in all stages of our work. Their role has also been substantial, or even required, in gaining "unique adequacy" and when identifying and analysing the interactional phenomena: noticings, decision making, and navigation talk, which cannot be fully understood in their respective environments and as part of the military observer training context without complementary information.

Discussion and concluding remarks

In this chapter, we have discussed a multi-phase participatory approach to EMCA research and considered the role of extended observation, contextual knowledge, inductivity and unmotivated looking. We have addressed our positioning and procedures in contrast to traditional EMCA and raised the question of what constitutes the beginning of the analysis. In our reflections on fieldwork and the experiences of collecting data in a highly specified and immersive training environment, we have argued for the relevance of supplementary data and knowledge that are sometimes needed for informed data collection and analyses. Through entering the studied environment as newcomers, we were able to get a similar (but not the same) first-hand experience on the course and its contents as the trainees, who were also experiencing everything for the first time. In this sense, we were basically living in our (future) data for the period of time we were collecting it and looking at it from the inside, making observations. Therefore, we have argued that contextual knowledge, including a researcher's own subjective experience of the studied context and events, can function as proto-data that guide and inform the identification of interactional phenomena and the development of research questions. Whereas studies that are more grounded in ethnography treat field-notes and researcher observations as equally valid data with photographs and video-recordings, in EMCA, these phenomena and questions will nevertheless have to be studied objectively through what the method treats as the primary data: video recordings of naturally occurring interactions (see, though, Stevanovic this volume).

We hope the experiences presented in this chapter become an incentive for further discussion in EMCA and thereby contribute to possible reviewing, or even redefining, of the conversation analytic research process. Whereas previous literature has included many studies regarding complex settings, utilising longitudinal data and comprising ethnographic aspects (e.g., Maynard, 2006), there are only a few methodological descriptions of "pre-analytic" processes, and how they have, or have not, impacted the analyses or the results of the studies (e.g., Finlay et al., 2011). We have aimed to show how gaining a member's perspective on locally produced social actions may sometimes require additional work to get a sufficient amount of knowledge of the setting and the phenomena, and thereby to meet the "unique adequacy requirement" (Garfinkel, 2002; Garfinkel & Wieder, 1992; Jenkings, 2018). To reach this goal, our study has looked into methodological procedures and practices that go beyond traditional EMCA. Furthermore, it has meant the utilisation of other research methods, such as ethnography, and taking an inductive approach to a multilevel and multiphase data collection and analysis. Our approach resembles prior research in which EMCA has been complemented with more participatory methods or practices (e.g., Hofstetter, 2021; Katila et al., 2021; Maynard, 2006), as well as some aspects of nexus analysis (Scollon & Scollon, 2004), but it has its distinctive characteristics. Whereas Maynard (2006) discusses his ethnography from the starting point of limited affinity, referring to the use of other methods as something that complements or deepens understanding of what happens in video data, our experience has been more immersive. Instead of merely taking advantage of ethnographic knowledge in order to gain a better understanding of the studied context, our ethnographic experiences as researchers had a more profound impact on our research process.

A part of our ethnographic approach has been finding the balance between analytic control and reaching "the right kind of" inductivity. The cumulating knowledge gained through ethnographic observations has helped us outline our focus and extend unmotivated looking into the phase of fieldwork. At the same time, we have been interacting with the studied community who have also motivated our views of what should or could be investigated. Along with our multi-layered, multiphase approach to carrying out EMCA research, involving multiple occasions of data collection and developing an in-depth understanding of the course and its contents, we have had to define which topics or ideas have been identified in ways that comply with the research mentality and, indeed, which topics or ideas *can be studied* through EMCA. This has led us to situations where we have had to negotiate with the course organisers and instructors about some of their wishes for the research and the questions they would want answers to, and to build a shared understanding of what can and what cannot be achieved through our method.

The purpose of this discussion is by no means to say that the traditional understanding and definition of the conversation analytic process is outdated or wrong. On the contrary. We are all currently going through the various, previously unviewed data (as there are plenty) in an unmotivated way to find new research topics. Nevertheless, some contexts, such as the military observer course, are too complex and multifaceted by their nature to be understood without the accumulated knowledge and researcher participants' perspective. However, there are some methodological "risks" involved in the kind of fieldwork described in this chapter. Leaning too far into the subjective observation of the studied environment can lead to jumping to conclusions; what might seem and feel like one thing in the moment, can actually be proven to have been something else entirely once examined through watching the recordings (which is, of course, one of the main arguments for using EMCA in institutional and professional settings). Another possible risk factor is the bias that can come from having gotten to know the participants during the fieldwork. While having information on, for example, individual participants' personalities, expertise, and past experiences can give us explanations for some specific moments or actions, this knowledge can only be allowed to inform the analyses when it becomes evident in the recorded interactions. Remaining conscious of these risks, we nevertheless see value in broadening the conversation analytic scope by combining in-situ observations and the information gained through ethnographic knowledge gathering and incorporating them as part of the analyses that show how the situation at hand developed for *all* its participants, including those who, for some of the time, were researchers.

Acknowledgments

We wish to thank all the course participants, especially the trainees and the instructors, for letting us get a glimpse of their important and valuable work. We also thank FINCENT and the Finnish National Defence University, Academy of Finland (project numbers 287219 and 322199), Eudaimonia Institute at the University of Oulu for their help and support. We extend our special thanks to Antti Siipo from the LeaF infrastructure, who worked as our technician in the data collection process.

Note

1 In our overall research process, we recognise the connection with the ethnography of nexus analysis (Scollon & Scollon, 2004) which takes into account the participants' individual experience, skills and capacities (the historical body), as well as the shared social space in which the interactions take place (discourses in place).

References

Antaki, C. (2011). Six kinds of applied conversation analysis. In C. Antaki (Ed.), *Applied conversation analysis: Intervention and change in institutional talk* (pp. 1–14). Springer.
Arminen, I. (2005). *Institutional interaction: Studies of talk at work*. Ashgate.

Clift, R. (2016). *Conversation analysis*. Cambridge University Press.

Day, D., & Kjaerbeck, S. (2013). 'Positioning' in the conversation analytic approach. *Narrative Inquiry*, 23(1), 16–39. https://doi.org/10.1075/ni.23.1.02day

Dingwall, R. (1997). Accounts, interviews and observations. In G. Miller & R. Dingwall (Eds.), *Context & method in qualitative research* (pp. 51–65). Sage.

Drew, P., & Heritage, J. (1992). *Talk at work: Interaction in institutional settings*. Cambridge University Press.

Duranti, A. (1997). *Linguistic anthropology*. Cambridge University Press.

Edmonds, R. (2021). Balancing research goals and community expectations: The affordances of body cameras and participant observation in the study of wildlife conservation. *Social Interaction: Video-Based Studies of Human Sociality*, 4(2). https://doi.org/10.7146/si.v4i2.127193

Emerson, R. M., Fretz, R. I., & Shaw, L. L. (2011). *Writing ethnographic fieldnotes* (2nd ed.). *Chicago guides to writing, editing, and publishing*. University of Chicago Press.

Finlay, W. M. L., Walton, C., & Antaki, C. (2011). Giving feedback to care staff about offering choices to people with intellectual disabilities. In C. Antaki (Ed.), *Applied conversation analysis* (pp. 161–183). Palgrave advances in linguistics. Palgrave Macmillan. https://doi.org/10.1057/9780230316874_9.

Garfinkel, H. (2002). *Ethnomethodology's program: Working out Durkheim's aphorism*. Rowman & Littlefield.

Garfinkel, H., & Wieder, D. L. (1992). Two incommensurable, asymmetrically alternate technologies of social analysis. In G. Watson & R. M. Seiler (Eds.), *Text in context: Contributions to ethnomethodology* (pp. 175–206). Sage.

Goodwin, C. (1994). Professional vision. *American Anthropologist*, 96(3), 606–633.

Goodwin, C. (2000). Action and embodiment within situated human interaction. *Journal of Pragmatics*, 32(10), 1489–1522.

Goodwin, M. H. (1990). *He-said-she-said: Talk as social organization among Black children*. Indiana University Press.

Gumperz, J. J. (1992). Contextualization and understanding. *Rethinking context: Language as an interactive phenomenon*, 11, 229–252.

Haddington, P., Kamunen, A., & Rautiainen, I. (2022). Noticing, monitoring and observing: Interactional grounds for joint and emergent seeing in UN military observer training. *Journal of Pragmatics*, 200, 119–138.

Heath, C., Knoblauch, H., & Luff, P. (2003). Technology and social interaction: The emergence of 'workplace studies'. *British Journal of Sociology*, 51(2), 299–320.

Hindmarsh, J., & Pilnick, A. (2007). Knowing bodies at work: Embodiment and ephemeral teamwork in anaesthesia. *Organization Studies*, 28(9), 1395–1416.

Hoey, E., & Kendrick, K. (2017). Conversation analysis. In A. M. B. De Groot & P. Hagoort (Eds.), *Research methods in psycholinguistics and the neurobiology of language: A practical guide* (pp. 15–173). John Wiley & Sons.

Hofstetter, E. (2021). Analyzing the researcher-participant in EMCA. *Social Interaction: Video-Based Studies of Human Sociality*, 4(2). https://doi.org/10.7146/si.v4i2.127185

Jenkings, K. N. (2018). Unique adequacy in Studies of the military, militarism and militarisation. *Ethnographic Studies*, 15, 38–57. https://doi.org/10.5281/zenodo.1475771

Jordan, B., & Henderson, A. (1995). Interaction analysis: Foundations and practice. *Journal of the Learning Sciences*, 4(1), 39–103.

Kamunen, A., Haddington, P., & Rautiainen, I. (2022). "It seems to be some kind of an accident": Perception and team decision-making in time critical situations. *Journal of Pragmatics*, 195, 7–30.

Katila, J., Gan, Y., Goico, S., & Goodwin, M. H. (2021). Researchers' participation roles in video-based fieldwork: An introduction to a special issue. *Social Interaction: Video-Based Studies on Human Sociality*, *4*(2). https://doi.org/10.7146/si.v4i2.127184

Lindholm, C. C. (2016). Keskustelunanalyysi ja etnografia. In T. M. Stevanovic & C. C. Lindholm (Eds.), *Keskustelunanalyysi. Kuinka tutkia sosiaalista toimintaa ja vuorovaikutusta* (pp. 331–348). Vastapaino.

Marttila, A. (2018). Tutkijan positiot etnografisessa tutkimuksessa – Kentän ja kokemuksen dialoginen rakentaminen. In P. Hämeenaho & E. Koskinen-Koivisto (Eds.), *Moniulotteinen etnografia* (pp. 362–392). Ethnos-toimite 17.

Maynard, D. W. (2006). Ethnography and conversation analysis. In S. N. Hesse-Biber & P. Leavy (Eds.), *Emergent methods in social research* (pp. 55–94). Sage.

Mondada, L. (2013). The conversation analytic approach to data collection. In J. Sidnell & T. Stivers (Eds.), *The handbook of conversation analysis* (pp. 32–57). Wiley-Blackwell.

Nevile, M. (2013a). Collaboration in crisis: Pursuing perception through multiple descriptions (how friendly vehicles became damn rocket launchers). In A. De Rycker & Z. Mohd. Don (Eds.), *Discourse and crisis: Critical perspectives* (pp. 159–183). Benjamins.

Nevile, M. (2013b). Seeing on the move: Mobile collaboration on the battlefield. In P. Haddington, L. Mondada, & M. Nevile (Eds.), *Interaction and mobility: Language and the body in motion* (pp. 153–177). Walter de Gruyter.

Pehkonen, S., Rauniomaa, M., & Siitonen, P. (2021). Participating researcher or researching participant? On possible positions of the researcher in the collection (and analysis) of mobile video data. *Social Interaction: Video-Based Studies of Human Sociality*, *42*(2). https://doi.org/10.7146/si.v4i2.127267

Peräkylä, A. (2004). Conversation analysis. In C. Seale, D. Silverman, J. Gubrium, & G. Gobo (Eds.), *Qualitative research practice* (pp. 165–179). Sage.

Potter, J. (1997). Discourse analysis as a way of analysing naturally occurring talk. In D. Silverman (Ed.), *Qualitative research: Theory, method and practice* (pp. 144–160). Sage.

Raudaskoski, P. (2010). "Hi Father", "Hi Mother": A multimodal analysis of a significant, identity changing phone call mediated on TV. *Journal of Pragmatics*, *42*(2), 426–442.

Rautiainen, I. (2021). Talk and action as discourse in UN military Observer Course: Routines and practices of navigation. In I. Chiluwa (Ed.), *Discourse and conflict: Analysing text and talk of conflict, hate and peace-building* (pp. 381–412). Palgrave.

Schegloff, E. A. (1996). Turn organization: One intersection of grammar and interaction. In E. Ochs, E. A. Schegloff, & S. A. Thompson (Eds.), *Interaction and grammar* (pp. 52–133). Cambridge University Press.

Schegloff, E. A. (2007). *Sequence organization in interaction: A primer in conversation analysis*. Cambridge University Press.

Schenkein, J. N. (Ed.). (1978). *Studies in the organisation of conversational interaction*. Academic Press.

Scollon, R., & Scollon, S. W. (2004). *Nexus analysis: Discourse and the emerging Internet*. Routledge.

Stivers, T., & Rossano, F. (2010). Mobilizing response. *Research on Language and Social Interaction*, *43*(1), 3–31.

Stivers, T., & Sidnell, J. (2005). Introduction: Multimodal interaction, *156*, 1–20. https://doi.org/10.1515/semi.2005.2005.156.1

ten Have, P. (2007). *Doing conversation analysis*. Sage.

Waring, H. Z., Creider, S., Tarpey, T., & Black, R. (2012). A search for specificity in understanding CA and context. *Discourse Studies*, *14*(4), 477–492.

9

A SATELLITE VIEW OF SPATIAL POINTS IN CONVERSATION[1]

*Joe Blythe, Francesco Possemato, Josua Dahmen,
Caroline de Dear, Rod Gardner, and Lesley Stirling*

The video recordings of the extracts in this chapter may be accessed through Figshare using the QR below or the following link: https://doi.org/10.25949/18133682

Introduction

When using video to record conversational interaction, we often observe participants pointing to locations that are not within their immediate vicinity; the targets of these points extend beyond the scene being captured by the video cameras. This is not a members' concern for participants that share knowledge of their local environment, but for the external analysts unacquainted with the local topography, it can pose a methodological challenge. We try to level this imbalance by considering the wider spatial context in which locational points are produced.

DOI: 10.4324/9781003424888-12

This chapter presents a *geospatial framework* that supports EMCA investigations of naturally occurring locational points during occasions of place reference in conversation. The approach was developed by the authors through our work on the *CIARA* project.[2] Using Geographic Information System (GIS) software and Global Positioning System (GPS) metadata we superimpose video stills from our recordings onto satellite images of the locations where the conversations were conducted. When we rotate the satellite images to replicate the angular bearings of the video cameras, we visualise directional points as though filmed from above. This allows us to identify probable targets of these points and to determine where the angular vectors are oriented with respect to the local topography. As well as micro-considerations such as the alignment of points with parts of speech, or their placement within sequences of actions, the layering of video onto satellite imagery gives our multimodal analyses a grand vista onto conversational interaction. This panoramic view goes some way towards incorporating the totality of the environments that participants inhabit into the analysis of ordinary conversation.

The geospatial approach provides a set of procedures for acquiring, annotating, and managing geographically enriched conversational data. We demonstrate these procedures using extracts from multiparty conversations recorded in the Australian outback, conducted in three Aboriginal languages (Gija, Murrinhpatha, and Jaru) as well as English. The analyses show how analytic efforts aimed at describing endogenous practices occasioned by place reference in interaction can benefit from considerations that are exterior to the proximal interactional scene, and that – quite literally – surround it. Shifting scale from local scene to absolute space can advance our understanding of how locational points emerge and are understood within everyday interactions. Furthermore, a geospatial approach to pointing can uncover the complex relationships between locational gestures, language, and interaction with the wider environment, and what this might reveal about spatial cognition. Such an approach can facilitate systematic comparisons of pointing styles across languages, contexts, and cultures, and support investigations into the universals of human conduct.

Our interest in geospatial explorations of locational points stems from considerations surrounding the ways in which participants understand *where* speakers are talking about in conversation. In line with the conversation analytic interest in exploring participants' sense-making practices in ordinary interactions, we are mainly concerned with referential practices which participants treat as *adequate* for the purpose of the interactional task at hand (Garfinkel, 1967, pp. 7–9), rather than *accurate* in absolute geospatial terms. Repeated observations of the multimodal practices employed by speakers during place formulations, particularly when referring to distant locations, have highlighted the analytic import that geospatial data may add to the analyses of talk and embodied conduct in interaction. Thus, this geospatial framework aims at facilitating analyses of place reference and locational pointing practices in everyday conversation.

The integration of geographic information into the methodological toolkit of research in social sciences and the field of linguistics is not new. Both linguists from various fields and researchers of language and spatial cognition have long drawn upon geographical data for their analyses and linguistic mapping (see, e.g., Auer et al., 2013). More recently, there has been a renewed interest in spatial and topographical considerations of language use, and the extent to which environmental features correlate with the observed crosslinguistic diversity in spatial language (e.g., Palmer et al., 2017; Palmer et al., 2018). However, GPS-informed naturalistic studies on spatial referencing strategies and co-occurring embodied practices remain scant. Notable exceptions are Haviland's (1993, 2000, 2003) studies on pointing gestures in narratives by speakers of the Australian language Guugu Yimidhirr and the Mexican Mayan language Tzotzil, a recent study on the interrelation of demonstrative expressions and pointing gestures in large-scale space in the indigenous Mexican language Quiahije Chatino (Mesh et al., 2021), and a study by de Dear et al. (2021) which employs the geospatial methodological approach discussed herein.

We conceptualise locational pointing in line with Enfield, Kita and de Ruiter (2007), who define pointing gestures as "communicative bodily movement which projects a vector whose direction is determined, in the context, by the conceived spatial location, relative to the person performing the gesture, of a place or thing relevant to the current utterance" (p. 1724). Following Le Guen (2011, p. 272), we consider points to be comprised of the four components illustrated in Figure 9.1. The vector is a semi-axis projected from the *origo* (O), the origin of the point. The vector then passes through an *anchor point* (A) which is articulated either with a body part (e.g., a finger, a hand, the head, the lips, or the eyes) or with an artefact (e.g., a stick). The *anchor point* indicates the angular orientation of the point. The vector is then projected towards the *target* (T) – the entity being pointed at.

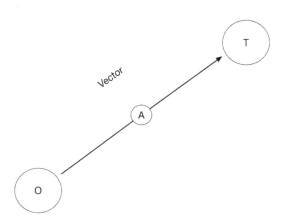

FIGURE 9.1   Main point components (adapted from Le Guen, 2011, p. 272).

This chapter demonstrates how GPS-derived information and GIS visual representations of the geospatial environment can be integrated into multimodal studies of interaction in order to capture and visualise the directionality of locational pointing gestures, particularly when studying conversational place reference and spatial language and cognition. The geospatial approach offers a new analytic tool for the investigation of pointing practices in interaction. While the multimodal approach to conversational data (cf. Goodwin, 2012; Mondada, 2014; Mondada, 2019b; Stivers & Sidnell, 2005) allows analysts to uncover the relationship between the multisemiotic resources that participants recruit when doing locational reference, the geospatial framework enhances and expands the domain of talk-in-interaction by facilitating the incorporation of the wider spatial context in which the locational points are produced. The methodological procedures are intended to provide researchers with a systematic account for the analysis of pointing gestures relative to parts of speech, sequences of actions in interaction, and the wider geographic environment in which the pointing gestures occur.

The chapter is structured as follows. The next section offers an outline of the existing research on locational pointing and the different methodologies employed in the literature. We then illustrate the step-by-step procedures that are used to identify, code, and visually represent pointing gestures in order to verify their directional accuracy. The following section demonstrates how geospatial considerations are integrated into the interactional analysis by presenting a geospatial analysis of pointing gestures in four excerpts of conversation conducted in typologically distinct languages from the *CIARA* corpus: the Aboriginal languages Murrinhpatha, Gija, and Jaru, as well as Australian English spoken by non-Aboriginal people in Halls Creek in the north of Western Australia (see Figure 9.2). We conclude with a discussion of the prospects and implications for the study of naturally occurring locational pointing practices and spatial language.

Space, language, and locational pointing

Referring to places is a fundamental activity in social interaction (Enfield & San Roque, 2017; Levinson, 2003; Schegloff, 1972). While the grammatical options for expressing spatial relations differ across languages (Levinson, 2003; Levinson & Wilkins, 2006), the tendency to utilise embodied resources in conversation appears to be universal (Enfield, 2013; Schegloff, 1972). In fact, embodied action in the context of place reference has the potential to replace verbal formulations entirely (Schegloff, 1984).

One such embodied action is pointing, which is largely considered a foundational human gesture (Tomasello, 2008, p. 62) across human societies (Kita, 2003a), typically developing in early infancy (e.g., Filipi, 2009). Pointing gestures have galvanised cross-disciplinary interest for centuries (Kendon, 2004). However, in more recent years interest in pointing has been particularly concentrated within

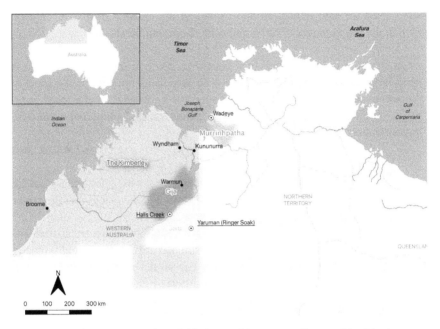

FIGURE 9.2   The CIARA Project field sites and languages discussed in this chapter.

the fields of psychology and cognitive sciences, psycholinguistics, language acquisition, semantics, semiotics, pragmatics, and ethnography (cf. Enfield, 2009 and references therein), as well as Conversation Analysis.

A considerable amount of research on locational pointing has been conducted by comparative researchers working on linguistic and spatio-cognitive variation within the realms of pragmatics and semantics (cf. Kita, 2009 for an overview). Cross-cultural and cross-linguistic investigations of spatial language and spatial Frames of Reference (FoR) (Levinson, 2003) – namely the cognitive strategies speakers use to conceptualise space – have examined the links between spatial language and non-linguistic behaviour (i.e., gesture). Much of the research on FoRs suggests that linguistic methods for encoding space might account for FoR "dominance" across language groups (e.g., absolute vs. relative vs. intrinsic).[3] It must be noted, however, that studies in comparative pragmatics and semantics have instead largely relied on stimuli within task-based experiments (Levinson, 1996, p. 200; Levinson et al., 2002; Levinson & Wilkins, 2006, pp. 8–13). Rotational tasks have been used to expose "dominant" FoR and a proposed correlation between cognitive and linguistic methods of encoding space (e.g., Majid et al., 2004; Pederson et al., 1998). Within this line of research, Le Guen's (2011) comparative study has made a significant contribution to the development of the geospatial methods presented in this chapter. Using both naturalistic and experimental data from two speech communities (Yucatec Maya and French), Le Guen examines pointing gestures used for path indication and signalling the location of distant entities. Central to the development of our framework, he recommends that:

> when studying pointing when the geocentric frame of reference is used it is necessary for the researcher to always be able to identify the orientation of the scenes described, i.e., to have an extensive knowledge of the local geography, objects, and manmade things (roads, houses, etc.) using maps and GPS measurement.
>
> *(Le Guen, 2011, p. 301)*

We believe that our geospatial approach provides a means of better understanding the physical environments inhabited by participants, and the places that they refer to within it.

Research on Australian Aboriginal languages has also investigated spatial language and gesture use, but predominantly within narrative contexts and typically in languages considered to have a "dominant" absolute FoR (Green, 2014; Green & Wilkins, 2014; Haviland, 1993; Haviland, 1998; Levinson, 1996; Levinson, 1997; Wilkins, 2003). Most research on Australian Aboriginal narrative has relied on elicitation techniques, recollection tasks, and stimuli. Central to the development of our geospatial framework, Blythe et al. (2016) utilise an interactional experiment to demonstrate the possibilities of GPS and GIS-derived information to examine the connection between demonstratives and pointing gestures in Murrinhpatha. Building on Blythe et al.'s (2016) methods, a recent study by de Dear (2019) uses the geospatial approach presented in this chapter to investigate conversational place reference and pointing in Gija conversations, while de Dear et al. (2021) use the same approach to compare pointing gestures across Gija, Murrinhpatha, and Australian English spoken in remote regions.

A related line of research proposes a sociotopographic account of spatial language diversity both across languages and within language communities. The close connections between culture, topography, and spatial language that are drawn out in this research (Palmer, 2015; Palmer et al., 2017, 2018) resonate with the development of our geospatial approach, especially with regard to incorporating participants' surrounding environments (cf. also de Dear et al., 2021) into the analyses. While sociotopographic considerations of spatial language and gestures support the relevance of geographical data for linguistic analyses, these studies are primarily experimental and do not consider naturally occurring conversational data.

Although research on pointing has been predominantly (quasi-)experimental to date, socio-interactional lines of inquiry – with which our approach aligns – consider pointing gestures as a locally situated practice (Goodwin, 2003, 2006). Unlike cognitively oriented research, socio-interactional studies observe pointing gestures captured in video recordings as per conversation analytic methods. For instance, Enfield (2009) and Enfield et al. (2007) investigate pointing gestures in semi-structured "locality interviews", as well as in naturally occurring Lao conversations. Similarly, Kendon (1992, 1995, 2004) draws on informal conversations, (semi-)institutional interactions, and elicited talk, to closely examine the interactional and pragmatic aspects of pointing. In another study, Kendon and Versante (2003) describe and compare six distinctive types of deictic manual gestures produced during occasions of place and person reference using naturally occurring video recorded Italian conversations. Socio-interactional research on the coordination of pointing gestures and speech has also combined various methods – i.e., experimental and naturalistic data – in an effort to complement psycholinguistic conceptualisations of pointing gestures with interactional perspectives gleaned from the analysis of everyday talk (e.g., Kita, 2003b).

Interactional research informed by Ethnomethodology (Garfinkel, 1967) and CA has systematically investigated interactants' embodied conduct and its relationship with turns-at-talk (Schegloff, 1984), with a focus on the sequential organisation of actions in interaction (for an overview, cf. Deppermann, 2013; Nevile, 2015) and on the relationships between grammar and embodied actions (e.g., Couper-Kuhlen, 2018; Iwasaki, 2009, 2011; Keevallik, 2018). Over the past thirty years conversation analytic research has demonstrated the complexities of pointing and its finely tuned coordination with talk. Conversation analysts have explored pointing in a variety of contexts, including work meetings (Mondada, 2007), archaeological field excavation (Goodwin, 2003), parent–child interactions (Filipi, 2009), interactions involving aphasic participants (Goodwin, 2003; Klippi, 2015), and children with Down's syndrome (Wootton, 1990). Moreover, a recent special issue of *Open Linguistics* on place reference in interaction (Enfield & San Roque, 2017) includes analyses of pointing behaviour (Blythe et al., 2016; Sicoli, 2016; Williams, 2017).

Although the fine details of interaction and matters such as temporal and sequential relations have traditionally been at the centre of conversation analytic research (e.g., Deppermann & Streeck, 2018; Mondada, 2016; Mushin & Doehler, 2021; Streeck et al., 2011), the relationship between locational gestures, the wider space, and geography has regularly been overlooked (however, see Auer et al., 2013). With some exceptions (e.g., Stukenbrock, 2014), conversation analytic studies have generally considered the immediate interactional context, describing the ways in which participants may orient to specific interactional affordances offered by the surrounding environment, artefacts, and other local referents. While our geospatial framework aligns with the temporal and sequential conventions of orthodox CA, the GIS and GPS technologies allow us to incorporate the wider spatial context into the analysis, allowing a more holistic view of the environment, extending it beyond the very proximal setting in which face-to-face interaction transpires. This allows the external analyst to visualise, from space, the local topography, and thus gain familiarity with participants' backyards, which reduces the epistemic disparity between co-participants and external analysts. The utility of this framework lies not so much in establishing whether or not points are accurate (although our procedures are very helpful in this regard) but in understanding where events under discussion are alleged to have transpired. Conversational narratives often commence with place references and locational points may be part of how place references are formulated (Dingemanse et al., 2017). When place or person references are designed to be elliptical (especially for reasons of taboo) (Blythe et al., 2016), a geospatial view of locational points can help external analysts understand where participants are talking about and therefore what they are talking about, all of which is requisite information for most EMCA analyses.

Visualising geographically enriched conversational data

This section discusses the data collection procedures adopted in our framework (de Dear et al., 2021; Possemato et al., 2021; Stirling et al., 2022), and illustrates how the acquisition of geospatial information can yield spatial insight to support interactional analyses of locational points in conversation.

A central aspect of collecting conversational data for geospatial investigations is the geolocalisation of the recording location. An accurate geographical determination of the recording session site is critical for later determination of the directionality of pointing gestures, and for the positioning of the interactional scene within the wider topogeographical context. While exact coordinates can be gathered through a GPS unit[4], GPS derived information can be also imported and utilised for visualisation purposes in various Geographic Information System (GIS) software, such as Google Earth and QGIS. Once the geographical data are instrumentally acquired, the recording location can be found on a map using GIS software, such as Google Earth, where the recording place can be located, and a *placemark* or *pin* can be added to the satellite imagery (Figure 9.3). The recording location can also be saved and the associated spatial data can be stored, exported, and imported from and into other GIS software programs that can be later used for the mapping and visualization of geospatial data.

An equally crucial element for interactional analyses of locational pointing is the annotation of the relative bearings of the camera(s) used in the recording session. The alignment of the camera(s), expressed in degrees from true north, can be acquired through the use of a compass, a handheld GPS device, or a dedicated mobile application[5]. It is important to record the initial bearings of each camera, as well as any subsequent alignment changes during the session in order to accurately infer the pointing gestures' directionality. If the location is known but the bearing of the camera has not been recorded, it is possible to estimate the bearing (admittedly with less precision) based on the rooflines of any buildings that are visible within the satellite imagery, particularly in urban settings. The orientation of buildings can be measured using Google Earth's ruler tool (see below).

FIGURE 9.3   The placemark window.

The visual representation of space and locational pointing gestures

The graphics described in the present framework are realised through a process of geospatial information overlaying. This section outlines how to visually supplement interactional analyses of locational points in conversation.

Firstly, after identifying the locational points in the recording, a single frame of the gesture during the *stroke* phase[6] is captured, as shown in Figure 9.4. Here, Mabel is pointing with an elevated index-finger to the north-north-east.

We have found that when extrapolating the trajectory of the vector projected by the pointing gesture, and the resulting semi-axis orientation determined by the main articulator or anchor point (Le Guen, 2011, p. 272), reorienting the scene from another vantage point, such as a bird's-eye view (cf. Figure 9.5) can be helpful. Software such as Adobe InDesign or OmniGraffle can be used to model the

FIGURE 9.4   A still frame of a pointing gesture.

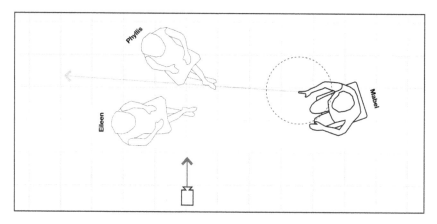

FIGURE 9.5   The scene reproduced from a bird's-eye perspective.

scene. In the graphic in Figure 9.5 the inferred pointing vector is represented by the long arrow, the camera position and its bearing are represented by the short arrow, and the pointing gesture is circled by a dotted line. It should be noted that the participants' spatial arrangement is inferred. By closely examining the video recorded interaction and/or pictures of the scene we are now able to extrapolate participants' relative positioning, which allows us to produce a sufficiently accurate visual representation.

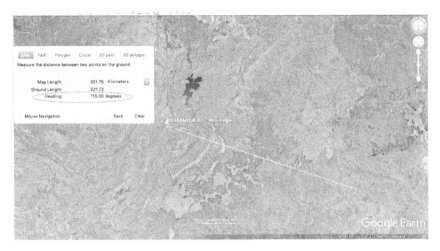

FIGURE 9.6   Using Google Earth's ruler tool to orient to landscape with respect to the absolute bearing of the video camera.

Next, the satellite imagery is rotated according to the camera bearing recorded in the appropriate metadata file (for this example, the satellite imagery is rotated 110° east-south-east)[7]. A method to ensure that this rotation corresponds with the camera bearing(s) is to use the *ruler* tool in Google Earth (cf. Figure 9.6). This will make it possible to draw a semi-axis with a precise heading measured in degrees, which should correspond with the bearing of the camera recorded in the metadata. In other words, the line projected from the pinned recording location represents the direction toward which the camera is pointing. After saving the line, the compass on the top right-hand side of the screen (circled) can be rotated until it is aligned vertically (see Figure 9.7).

A snapshot of the rotated satellite image displaying the recording location is then captured and imported into a digital illustration software, where the origo (O) of the point as well as its intended targets (T_n) are marked (in this case the target communities are Kununurra, WA, and Wadeye, NT). A compass is also included for reference (Figure 9.8).

A still frame of the stroke of the pointing gesture, including an arrow indicating the direction of the point and the names of participants can then be overlaid onto the map. The extrapolated vector is signified by a solid arrow that has been pivoted to correspond with the point from the still frame of the pointing gesture. This arrow can be duplicated and re-sized to use as a reference on the compass. When participants point somewhat inaccurately to a target location, an idealised vector connecting the origo with the true target(s) – represented here by a barred line – is then added to the image, as shown in Figure 9.9.

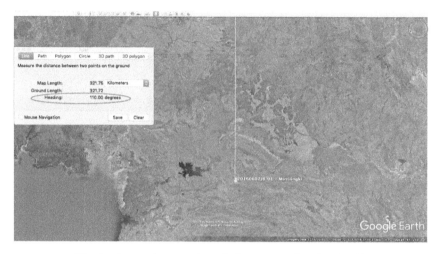

FIGURE 9.7   The landscape is rotated until the camera bearing is aligned vertically toward the top of the image

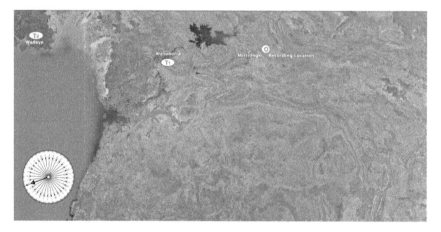

FIGURE 9.8   The rotated satellite imagery with Origo and Targets placemarked.

This procedure is a practical tool for the investigation of pointing direction-ality. By comparing the trajectories of participants' actual pointing vectors with corresponding ideal vectors where necessary, it is possible to calculate the approximate angular discrepancy between the two vectors, thus numerically deriving just how accurate participants are when pointing to distant locations. In the example illustrated in the figures above, we calculated the approximate

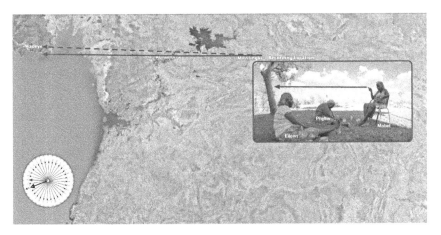

FIGURE 9.9   The satellite imagery showing actual and ideal pointing vectors.

angular discrepancy between Mabel's actual point (A) and the intended target(s) (T) to be 2°.

This process has illuminated the remarkable accuracy of interactants' locational pointing gestures, which is something that has continued to emerge in our research on spatial reference and pointing in conversations conducted in remote Aboriginal and non-Aboriginal Australian communities (de Dear et al., 2021; Stirling et al., 2022). It has also highlighted interactants' preference to maintain the relative distances between intended targets even when their points are somewhat inaccurate. Graphically representing ideal and actual vectors has rendered the acuity of locational points analytically accessible. Moreover, this procedure has the potential to yield significant quantitative insights especially when applied to large-scale cross-linguistic studies on the acuity of locational pointing gestures.

Transcription and coding

In line with conversation analytic procedures, the transcription of the talk follows the standard Jeffersonian conventions (Hepburn & Bolden, 2017; Jefferson, 2004), while an adapted version of Mondada's conventions (2019a) was employed for the annotation of pointing gestures. While transcripts are crucial for indicating the emergence (i.e., the *position*) of points within sequences of action in interaction, the development of an ad-hoc coding scheme enables the systematic description of their *composition*. In order to preserve the readability of the extracts, particularly those coming from languages with which the readers might not be familiar, we have decided to minimise the visual complexity of the transcripts[8]. Asterisks delimit the beginning and the end of the gesture transcribed, while hashtags indicate the moment where the screenshots – all representing the stroke phase of the points – were taken with reference to the talk (or absence thereof). It should also be noted that the morphological description of the pointing gesture, along with its directionality, has been incorporated in the relative figure caption. The coding of the pointing gestures was also informed by EMCA, and by recent work within Pragmatic Typology (e.g., Dingemanse & Enfield, 2015; Floyd et al., 2020). We do not discuss these here; however, see Possemato et al. (2021) for details.

The next section will show how geospatial methods can be employed to enrich interactional analyses of place reference and locational points. The four excerpts discussed here come from the *CIARA* corpus.

Geospatial analyses of pointing in conversation

The excerpts discussed in this section are part of a collection of place reference and locational points in multiparty conversations conducted (predominantly) in three typologically distant Australian languages, Murrinhpatha, Gija, and Jaru, and Australian English spoken in the Kimberley region of Western Australia (see Table 9.1). Note that in the Gija and Jaru corpora, participants frequently code-mix these languages with the local varieties of Kriol (an English-based creole language), as well as with neighbouring Indigenous languages (Dahmen, 2021; de Dear et al., 2020). While we have found many of the directional points in these corpora to be reasonably *accurate* (i.e., if the indicated vector lies within 30° of the target, de Dear et al., 2021), our principal concern here is whether co-partic-ipants orient to directional points as being sufficiently *adequate*, such that the reference is successful.

Our first extract comes from the Murrinpatha conversational corpus. Jim, Rob, and Ray have been looking out over the bay, imagining what it would be

TABLE 9.1 The languages from the CIARA Project corpus

Language	Murrinhpatha	Gija	Australian English	Jaru
Description	A Southern Daly language: head marking, polysynthetic, nominal classifiers	A Jarragan language: head marking, complex predicates	A Germanic language: SVO – remnant inflectional morphology	Ngumpin-Yapa language: dependent marking, complex predicates

like if white people were to settle in the area and develop a city or a town. They recall an old man at a meeting speaking out against possible development of the area.

Excerpt 1   Destroy the place (20190622JB_02 1201371_1229675)

```
1  Rob    Ma wurda mam wulmenyu; (0.3) mamwarda
           ma  wurda mam            wulmen =yu mam           -warda
           but no   3SG.S.say.NFUT old_man=CL 3SG.S.say.NFUT-TEMP
           But the old man said "no!" (0.3) He said

2          da wailwan kardamatha pirranannu.
           da      wailwan karda-matha  pirra        -nan  -nu
           NC:PL/T wild    PROX -INTS   3SG.S.stand.FUTIRR-2PL.DO-FUT
           "This is your wild place it should stand just like it is."

3          (.)

4  Ray    Mm Mm Berengundha wulmen; (0.3) ((Post-alveolar click))
           berengundha wulmen
           Alright     oldman
           The old man is alright.

5          (0.8)

6  Rob    Nyini damatha thama;
           nyini damatha thama
           ANAPH INTS    2SG.S.say/do.FUT
           That's right, you know!

7  Ray    Yu. Burrk nyini wulmen.
           yu   burrk nyini wulmen
           Yeah good  ANAPH old_man
           Yeah, {he's} good, that old man.

8  Rob    Mam merretjin manandjinukun.
           mam           merretjin ma- nandji=nukun
           3SG.S.say.NFUT medicine  NEG-NC:RES=FUT.IRR
           He said, "there'll be no {bush} medicine"

9          (0.3)

10 Rob    Merritjin ngarra kardu tjipmam manandjinukun.
           merritjin ngarra kardu   tjipmam ma- nandji=nukun
           medicine  LOC    NC:PERS black   NEG-NC:RES=FUT.IRR
           "There'll be no medicine for Aboriginal people."

11         (1.5)

12 Rob    damkardu.
           dam-ngkardu
           2SG.13.NFUT-look/see
           You know?

13         (0.9)

14 Rob    Da wailwan karrim kanyidamatha; (0.8) spiritwarda karrim kanyi
           da      wailwan karrim              kanyi-damatha
           NC:PL/T wild    3SG.S.stand.EXIST PROX -INTS
           spirit-warda karrim              kanyi
           spirit-TEMP  3SG.S.stand.EXIST PROX
           This is a wild place. There are spirits here.

15         (0.9)

16 Rob    [Da spirit karrim kanyi
           da      spirit karrim              kanyi
           NC:PL/T spirit 3SG.S.stand.EXIST PROX
           There are spirits in this place.
```

```
17 Ray    [Da murndak pubemarikerdektha ngarra nandji kanyi-
           da       murndak pube            -marikerdek-tha ngarra nandji kanyi
           NC:PL/T before  3PL.S.13.PST.IRR-finish  -PST LOC   NC:RES PROX
           They would have finished off this place before {like when}

18         *(0.7) #bam- ba(h)m-* pubammardurt nandji kanyi nawa.
           bam          bam          pubam       -ma -rdurt
           3SG.S.13.NFUT 3SG.S.13.NFUT 3PL.S.13.NFUT-APPL-find
           nandji kanyi na-wa
           NC:RES PROX  tag-EMPH
           they found this stuff {natural gas} here, hey.
    Ray    *------# Figure  9.10 ---*((Sagittally oriented LH small IF point
    WSW))
19         (.)
20 Jim     Yu.
           Yeah.
21         (0.9)
22 Rob     ku bangkengthaynime ku watjpalayu.
           ku   ba      -ngkengthay-nime ku    watjpala=yu
           NC:ANM 3SG.S.13.FUT-destroy   -PC.M.NSIB NC:ANM white_person=CL
           They will destroy it, the whitefellows.
23         (2.5)
24 Rob     Da ngalla kanyiyu.
           da      ngalla kanyi=yu
           NC:PL/T big    PROX=CL
           The whole place.
```

At lines 1 and 2 Rob recounts the old man's words as he urged his countrymen to
protect the country from destruction. From lines 4 to 7 Ray and Rob display their
agreement about the old man being a good man (and wise). At lines 8, 10 and 12
Rob again reports the man's oratory, where he pointed out that no bush medicine
would be growing in the area. He goes on to point out that the unspoilt country
has spirits in it (lines 14 and 16). At line 17 and 18 Ray makes the claim that if
white people had settled in this area, they would have ruined the country, as they
have done where they found natural gas. As he does this he points back over his
shoulder (Figure 9.10) in a west-south-westerly direction to the onshore gas processing plant near Yeltjerr beach where a pipeline brings in gas from a gas field in
the Joseph Bonaparte Gulf. Jim agrees with Ray's assertion at line 20. At lines 22
and 24 Rob then makes the seemingly justified claim that white people (if left to
their own devices) will destroy the whole country.

Ray's reference to natural gas in line 18 is vaguely composed of the "residue"
nominal-classifier *nandji* plus the proximal demonstrative *kanyi* ("this stuff").

FIGURE 9.10   Ray produces a sagittally oriented index-finger point behind his left shoulder, due WSW, towards the gas processing plant near Yeltjerr beach.

His equally vague place-reference is composed of the proximal demonstrative *kanyi* ("this" / "here") plus the point, which is accurate to within 40° of the gas processing plant. Importantly, Ray's references are adequately precise for his co-participants as the processing plant is the only industrial construction within this otherwise unspoiled area. This adequacy is evidenced by Rob's uptake at lines 20 and 22. The satellite image plainly reveals the scar on the landscape that Ray is referring to, thus providing the external analyst with a bird's eye view over the scenery under discussion; scenery that quite literally is part of the participants' shared common ground.

Our second extract comes from the corpus of Gija conversations. The participants Shirley, Mabel, Phyllis, and Helen are seated on an incline above the Bow River, in the East Kimberley region of Western Australia. The women have been discussing the notable absence of dingos (*marrany*, *Canis lupus dingo*). As the extract commences, Shirley shifts the topic to fish, which she notes also seem to have been depleted in numbers.

Excerpt 2   Cattle Creek (20170426_JB_01 00:18:42–00:18:48)

```
1  Shi   *tharrei gendoowa yooloo nathing na, #no: goorndarri,*
           tharrei gendoowa yoorloo    nathing na  no goorndarri
           DIST    upstream downstream nothing FOC no fish
           Over there upstream and downstream there is nothing now, no fish,
     Shi   *--------------------------------#1 Figure 9.11----*

2        (0.6)

3  Phy   wijeyi-
           Where-

4        (0.4)

5  Shi   *ngenengga gerloorr cat#tle creek  *
           ngenengga gerloowoorr cattle creek
           PROX.LOC  up          place_name
           Up here at Cattle Creek
     Shi   *----------------------#2 Figure 9.11*

6        (0.5)

7  Hel   eh,
           INTJ
           yeah,

8  Phy   .Hhh dama:nyji. (0.2) jirragem.
           da  -m -wanyji jirragi     -m
           that-NS-maybe  frog_species-NS
           .Hhh maybe those frogs

9        (0.2)

10 Shi   °mm°
           °mm°

11       (0.5)

12 Phy   ja- (0.2) janganyji boo:rroo:rn, hh
           jang-wanyji boorr-oorn
           eat -maybe  3NS.S-say/do_PRES
           may- maybe they eat hh

13 Shi   Mm.
           Mm.
```

While gazing to the east (inset 1, Figure 9.11[9]), Shirley produces a place refer-ence at line 1 which is comprised of a Kriol distal deictic *tharrei* ("that way/over there") plus two (apparently contradictory) Gija geocentric terms related to a river-drainage system: *gendoowa* ("upstream") and *yoorloo* ("downstream"). Phyllis,

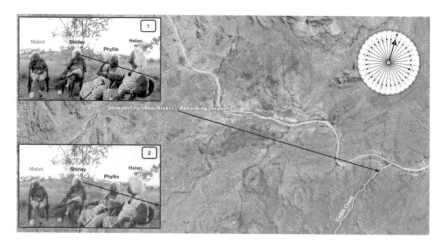

FIGURE 9.11   Shirley gazes and lip-points E.

who does not appear to have noticed Shirley's eastward gaze, initiates repair at line 3 with the Kriol question word, *wijeyi* ("where"). Shirley specifies the location at line 6, as "up here at Cattle Creek". This is composed of a proximal demonstrative (*ngenengga*), an elevational term (*gerloorr*, "up"), the English name of the creek, plus a lip-point to the east (inset 2, Figure 9.11). Helen displays apparent recognition of this location at line 7. Phyllis then goes on (at lines 12 and 14) to suggest that "these frogs" might account for the absence of fish in the creek. It is likely that Phyllis is here referring to Cane Toads (*Bufo marinus*), a highly poisonous feral toad that is having a devastating impact on the local fauna. Shirley's gaze is quite accurately directed toward Cattle Creek, a tributary of the Bow River that lies some 25 km from where the women are seated.

In the next extract from the Jaru corpus, the three participants, Juanita, Nida, and Ruby are sitting near the abandoned Gordon Downs homestead in the East Kimberley, where Nida and Ruby used to live when they were young. Just before the exchange in Extract (3), Nida explained that planes used to land at a nearby aerodrome to transport sick people. This prompts Juanita to ask where kids were born back in the day.

Excerpt 3   Wyndham (20181018JD 00:11:14–00:11:28)

```
1   Jua   en wanyjila ola kid ngalu bon yani, =
            en  wanyji-la ola      kid nga-lu   bon  ya-ni
            and which-LOC the.PL   kid CAT-3PL.S born go-PST
            and where were the kids born,

2   Jua   = most of them murlanguny.
            most of them murla-nguny
            most of them PROX-GEN
            most of them from here.

3         (0.6)
4   Nid   *Windum#dalu sam*bala [bon yanani. hhhm.
            Windum     -da -lu    sam -bala bon  ya-nani
            place_name-LOC-3PL.S some-NMLZ born go-PST.IPFV
            some of them were born in Wyndham. hhhm.
    Nid   *------#Fig9.12---*

5   Jua                       [Windumda sambala.
                               Windum    -da  sam -bala
                               place_name-LOC some-NMLZ
                               some of them in Wyndham.

6         (1.9)
7   Nid   en *murlawanalu Gudandanda sambala bon yanani*
            en  murla-wana-lu    Gudandan -da  sam -bala bon  ya-nani
            and PROX -PERL-3PL.S place_name-LOC some-NMLZ born go-PST.IPFV
            and some of them were born around here at Gordon Downs
    Nid      *elevated open hand fluttering ESE--------*

8         *rait dea. hh.
            rait  dea
            right there
            right there. hh.
    Nid   *elevated index finger ESE-->>

9   Jua   yea.
            yeah.

10        #(0.6)    * (0.3) *(0.3)
    Nid   #Fig9.13 --->*    *elevated index finger -->>

11  Nid   Gudandanda murlangga,*
            Gudandan -da  murla-ngga
            place_name-LOC PROX -LOC
            here at Gordon Downs,
    Nid                   --->*
```

In this question–response sequence, Juanita asks Nida where most of the children from Gordon Downs were born (lines 1–2), to which Nida responds that some of them were born in Wyndham (line 4). Wyndham is the northernmost town of the Kimberley region, located about 370 km in air distance from the recording location. As Nida utters the place name *Windum* ("Wyndham"), she gazes to her left side and points backwards with her thumb in a north-westerly direction to indicate the location of Wyndham (Figure 9.12). The direction of Nida's thumb-point lies within 35 degrees of the target location which is considerably accurate. At line 5 Juanita nods and repeats the place name Wyndham in sequential third position to overtly register Nida's response (cf. Schegloff, 1996, pp. 178–179). After 1.9 seconds of silence, Nida then adds that some children were also born at the Gordon Downs homestead, which is close to the recording location and within sight. At lines 7 through 11, Nida points with a fluttering open hand to the area of the homestead, followed by an index-finger point with a series of six pulses in the direction of an abandoned building that sits 240m in an east-south-easterly direction (Figure 9.13).

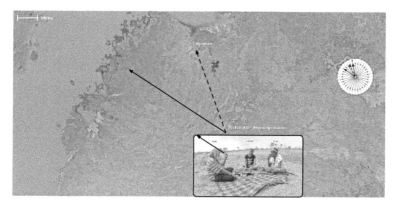

FIGURE 9.12   Nida thumb-points backwards NW to Wyndham and gazes sideways.

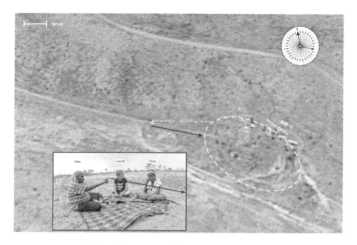

FIGURE 9.13   Nida points to Gordon Downs through an elevated index finger point ESE producing six consecutive pulses.

Although both Nida's place references to Wyndham and Gordon Downs involve a pointing gesture in combination with a place name, there is a crucial difference: The place reference to Wyndham is combined with a backward pointing gesture that does not invite the recipient(s) to re-direct their gaze; it is what has been described as a "secondary point" (Enfield et al., 2007). On the other hand, the reference to Gordon Downs indicates a location in the participants' vicinity and is combined with spatial deictic expressions, *murlawana* ("around here", line 7), *rait dea* ("right there" in Kriol, line 8), and *murlangga* ("here", line 11). The accompanying canonical pointing gesture to Gordon Downs conveys crucial locational information and invites the recipient(s) to look in the direction of the pointing gesture. While satellite imagery as presented in this chapter is especially powerful for the analysis of secondary points to distant locations, it can also provide analysts with geospatial information of more proximal locations that are the target of pointing gestures.

Our final extract comes from the Australian English corpus. The four participants Dave, Warren, Malcolm, and Jamie are seated near Halls Creek, in the East Kimberley. Dave asks Warren whether he knows a way to transport his timber factory to Adelaide "for nothing", hinting at the possibility of Warren helping him move the factory on one of his trips.

Excerpt 4   Adelaide (20180719LSJB_01 00:26:06–00:26:32)

```
1   Dave   warr^en,
2          (0.5)
3   Dave   you know a bit about- (0.4) you know a lot about (.) truck=an'
4          things like that don't [you.
5   Warr                          [o:h not really˘ .hmf °°i'm no-°°
6   Dave   $come o[n$]
7   Warr          [i-] i'm not a truckie mpf. he he h. hh.
8          (0.7)
9   Dave   nah but [shif]ting stuff around the place
10  Warr           [wh- ]
11  Warr   what do you- (.) what do you w^ant
12  Dave   w-
13  Warr   >what's happe[ning<]
14  Dave                [if i ] want to *shift the timber factory, (1.0)
    Dave                               *thumb-points behind --->>
15         from here* (0.9) #*down- (0.5) f- down*
    Dave        -->*      #1 Figure 9.14-------*
16         *(0.2) to adel#aide o- o- yeah adelaide will do,* (0.7) uhm f'r
    Dave   *------------#2 Figure 9.14--------------------*
17         nothing, >how would i do it<?
18  Warr   h. ha [ha ha
19  Malc         [ha [ha ha ha ha
20  Jam             [hh. ah ah [ah
21  Warr                       [>put it in< a wheelbarrow.
22         (0.2)
```

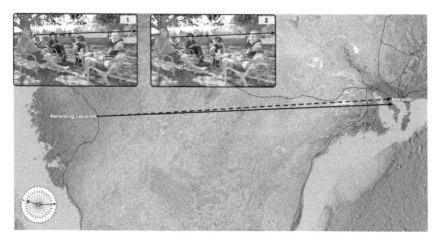

FIGURE 9.14 Dave points SSE to Adelaide (1) and (2).

After summoning Warren's attention (line 1), Dave produces a pre-request over lines 3, 4, and 9, to which Warren issues a go-ahead at lines 11 and 13. Between lines 14 and 17 Dave produces a seemingly tongue-in-cheek request for haulage advice – perhaps masking an actual request for haulage. After initially pointing with his thumb to the timber factory (lines 14 and 15), Dave produces a small index finger point south-south-east as he launches a word-search at line 15 (inset 1, Figure 9.14). At line 16 Dave again points in the same direction (inset 2, Figure 9.14), this time accompanied by the place name, Adelaide. Dave's points are remarkably accurate (to within 5 degrees). Adelaide is a city of 1.3 million people, located 2,133 km away from where the participants are seated.

It is worth noting that despite the enormous distance, Dave's points are small in scale and neither point is elevated. These gestures are anti-iconic in that they are inversely proportional in magnitude to vast distance being indicated (cf., Bauer, 2014; Le Guen, 2011; Levinson, 2003; Wilkins, 2003, inter alia). Warren, Jamie, and Malcolm do not need enlightening that Adelaide is a long way from Halls Creek. The tiny points may instead downplay the imposition of the request ("It's only a small way to go!") and thereby contribute toward prompting the co-partici-pants' joint laughter at lines 18–20. This laughter, along with Warren's dismissive suggestion that Dave haul his own factory in a wheelbarrow (line 21), demonstrate Dave's multimodal reference to this distant location to be more than adequate for his communicative objectives.

Conclusion

Place reference in conversation needs to be designed in a way to enable recipients' recognition of *where* a speaker is referring to. An EMCA approach to interaction offers a strong set of methodological and analytical procedures to develop an emic understanding of how place reference is locally achieved – through talk and other conduct – in interaction. Focusing on participants' location analysis (Schegloff, 1972) has the potential to reveal their intimate connections with the surrounding landscape – both proximal and distal – particularly in communities where land represents crucial sociocultural aspects of life. In order to ask *if* and *how* the interactional setting in which points are produced relates to the wider sociocultural and topographic environment, we need a framework capable of reconciling the knowledge imbalance between external observers (i.e., analysts) and the participants themselves.

This chapter presents a method for the analysis of locational pointing gestures in conversations, which was developed within the *CIARA* project. It outlines the procedures for collecting, managing and applying geographically-enriched interactional data. The resulting framework highlights the importance of incorporating data derived from satellite imagery-based programs such as Google Earth in the analysis of locational pointing practices in everyday conversations. While transcripts capture the temporal relationships between unfolding talk and gestural components, overlaid graphics create a visual representation of the "proximal scene" (i.e., the relative arrangement of the participants and the morphology of the point represented in its stroke phase), and also the "wider scene" (i.e., the terrain derived from satellite imagery, and the direction and acuity of vectors projected by the pointing gesture). The addition of superimposed graphics is crucial to multimodal transcriptions of talk and embodied behaviour, particularly when determining the direction and accuracy of points. Without geospatial information, the relevance of the topographic context and the ways in which it is referred to, invoked, and "used" in interaction would be lost, rendering an emic account of naturally occurring locational pointing ultimately unviable.

Notes

1 The methodological framework discussed here was first published in Possemato et al. (2021). This chapter reworks the procedures discussed in that article, re-presenting them for an EMCA audience – with altogether different data.
2 *Conversation Analysis in Aboriginal and Remote Australia* (CIARA) is a collaborative research project funded by the Australian Research Council (DP180100515, www.ciaraproject.com) that uses Conversation Analytic/Interactional Linguistic techniques to compare conversational interactions across different languages, cultures and geographic locations within the Australian outback.
3 For a critique of FoR models and Whorfian assumptions in studying naturally occurring points in interaction cf. de Dear et al. (2021).
4 It is worth noting that some cameras can mount GPS receivers or have in-built GPS. Various mobile phone applications, such as iOS Compass, and other GPS trackers can also be used for geolocalization purposes.
5 Compass sensors are usually integrated in GPS units and in GPS mobile applications.
6 Research on gesture describes points as generally articulated into three core distinct phases, namely preparation, stroke, and retraction (e.g., McNeill, 1992; Kita et al., 1998).

7 Only one camera was used during this recording session.
8 We have delved into the more fine-grained details of gestural components accompanying place reference in conversation elsewhere (Stirling et al. 2022; de Dear et al. 2021), while also adopting the present framework.
9 We recommend accessing the video-recording of this extract to fully appreciate the details of the points captured in insets 1 and 2.

References

Auer, P., Hilpert, M., Stukenbrock, A., & Szmrecsanyi, B. (Eds.). (2013). *Space in language and linguistics: Geographical, interactional, and cognitive perspectives.* De Gruyter.

Bauer, A. (2014). *The use of signing space in a shared sign language of Australia.* De Gruyter Mouton; Ishara Press.

Blythe, J., Mardigan, K. C., Perdjert, M. E., & Stoakes, H. (2016). Pointing out directions in Murrinhpatha. *Open Linguistics, 2*(1), 132–159. https://doi.org/10.1515/opli-2016-0007

Couper-Kuhlen, E. (2018). Finding a place for body movement in grammar. *Research on Language and Social Interaction, 51*(1), 22–25. https://doi.org/10.1080/08351813.2018.1413888

Dahmen, J. (2021). Bilingual speech in Jaru-Kriol conversations: Codeswitching, codemixing, and grammatical fusion. *International Journal of Bilingualism, 26*(2), 198–226. https://doi.org/10.1177/13670069211036925

de Dear, C. (2019). *Place reference and pointing in Gija conversation.* Macquarie University Master of Research. http://hdl.handle.net/1959.14/1284209

de Dear, C., Blythe, J., Possemato, F., Gardner, R., Stirling, L., Mushin, I., & Kofod, F. (2021). Locational pointing in Murrinhpatha, Gija and English conversations. *Gesture, 20*(3), 417–452. https://doi.org/doi.org/10.1075/gest.20035.dea

de Dear, C., Possemato, F., & Blythe, J. (2020). Gija (east Kimberley, Western Australia) – Language snapshot. *Language Documentation and Description, 17,* 134–141. http://www.elpublishing.org/PID/189

Deppermann, A. (2013). Multimodal interaction from a conversation analytic perspective. *Journal of Pragmatics, 46*(1), 1–7. https://doi.org/10.1016/j.pragma.2012.11.014

Deppermann, A., & Streeck, J. (Eds.). (2018). *Time in embodied interaction.* John Benjamins Publishing Company.

Dingemanse, M., & Enfield, N. J. (2015). Other-initiated repair across languages: Towards a typology of conversational structures. *Open Linguistics, 1*(1), 96–118. https://doi.org/doi:10.2478/opli-2014-0007

Dingemanse, M., Rossi, G., & Floyd, S. (2017). Place reference in story beginnings: A cross-linguistic study of narrative and interactional affordances. *Language in Society, 46*(2), 129–158. https://doi.org/10.1017/S0047404516001019

Enfield, N. J. (2009). *The anatomy of meaning: Speech, gesture, and composite utterances.* Cambridge University Press.

Enfield, N. J. (2013). Reference in conversation. In J. Sidnell & T. Stivers (Eds.), *The handbook of conversation analysis* (pp. 433–454). John Wiley & Sons, Ltd.

Enfield, N. J., Kita, S., & de Ruiter, J. P. (2007). Primary and secondary pragmatic functions of pointing gestures. *Journal of Pragmatics, 39*(10), 1722–1741. https://doi.org/10.1016/j.pragma.2007.03.001

Enfield, N. J., & San Roque, L. (2017). Place reference in interaction. *Open Linguistics, 3*(1). https://doi.org/10.1515/opli-2017-0029

Filipi, A. (2009). *Toddler and parent interaction: The organisation of gaze, pointing and vocalisation* (Vol. 192). John Benjamins.

Floyd, S., Rossi, G., & Enfield, N. J. (Eds.). (2020). *Getting others to do things: A pragmatic typology of recruitments.* Language Science Press. https://doi.org/10.5281/zenodo.4017493

Garfinkel, H. (1967). *Studies in ethnomethodology.* Prentice-Hall.

Goodwin, C. (2003). Pointing as situated practice. In S. Kita (Ed.), *Pointing: Where language, culture, and cognition meet* (pp. 217–242). L. Erlbaum Associates.

Goodwin, C. (2006). Human sociality as mutual orientation in a rich interactive environment: Multimodal utterances and pointing in aphasia. In N. J. Enfield & S. C. Levinson (Eds.), *Roots of human sociality* (pp. 96–125). Berg.

Goodwin, C. (2012). The co-operative, transformative organization of human action and knowledge. In *Proceedings of the 14th ACM international conference on multimodal interaction* (ICMI '12), 1–2. ACM.

Green, J. (2014). Signs and space in Arandic sand narratives. In M. Seyfeddinipur & M. Gullberg (Eds.), *From gesture in conversation to visible action as utterance* (pp. 219–243). John Benjamins Publishing Company.

Green, J., & Wilkins, D. P. (2014). With or without speech: Arandic Sign Language from Central Australia. *Australian Journal of Linguistics, 34*(2), 234–261. https://doi.org/10.1080/07268602.2014.887407

Haviland, J. B. (1993). Anchoring, iconicity, and orientation in guugu Yimithirr pointing gestures. *Journal of Linguistic Anthropology, 3*(1), 3–45. https://doi.org/10.1525/jlin.1993.3.1.3

Haviland, J. B. (1998). Guugu Yimithirr cardinal directions. *Ethos, 26*(1), 25–47. https://doi.org/10.1525/eth.1998.26.1.25

Haviland, J. B. (2000). Mental maps and gesture spaces. In D. McNeill (Ed.), *Language and gesture: Window into thought and action* (pp. 13–46). Cambridge University Press.

Haviland, J. B. (2003). How to point in Zinacantán. In S. Kita (Ed.), *Pointing: Where language, culture, and cognition meet* (pp. 139–169). Lawrence Erlbaum Associates.

Hepburn, A., & Bolden, G. (2017). *Transcribing for social research.* Sage Publications.

Iwasaki, S. (2009). Initiating interactive turn spaces in Japanese conversation: Local projection and collaborative action. *Discourse Processes, 46*(2–3), 226–246. https://doi.org/10.1080/01638530902728918

Iwasaki, S. (2011). The multimodal mechanics of collaborative unit construction in Japanese conversation. In J. Streeck, C. Goodwin, & C. LeBaron (Eds.), *Embodied interaction: Language and body in the material world* (pp. 106–120). Cambridge University Press.

Jefferson, G. (2004). Glossary of transcript symbols with an introduction. In G. H. Lerner (Ed.), *Conversation analysis: Studies from the first generation* (pp. 13–23). John Benjamins.

Keevallik, L. (2018). What does embodied interaction tell us about grammar? *Research on Language and Social Interaction, 51*(1), 1–21. https://doi.org/10.1080/08351813.2018.1413887

Kendon, A. (1992). Some recent work from Italy on "quotable gestures (emblems)." *Journal of Linguistic Anthropology, 2*(1), 92–108. https://doi.org/10.1525/jlin.1992.2.1.92

Kendon, A. (1995). Gestures as illocutionary and discourse structure markers in Southern Italian conversation. *Journal of Pragmatics, 23*(3), 247–279. https://doi.org/10.1016/0378-2166(94)00037-F

Kendon, A. (2004). *Gesture: Visible action as utterance.* Cambridge University Press.

Kendon, A., & Versante, L. (2003). Pointing by hand in Neapolitan. In S. Kita (Ed.), *Pointing: Where language, culture, and cognition meet* (pp. 109–137). Lawrence Erlbaum Associates.

Kita, S. (2003a). *Pointing: Where language, culture, and cognition meet.* L. Erlbaum Associates.

Kita, S. (2003b). Interplay of gaze, hand, torso, and language. In S. Kita (Ed.), *Pointing: Where language, culture, and cognition meet* (pp. 307–328). L. Erlbaum Associates.

Kita, S. (2009). Cross-cultural variation of speech-accompanying gesture: A review. *Language and Cognitive Processes, 24*(2), 145–167. https://doi.org/10.1080 /01690960802586188

Kita, S., van Gijn, I., & van der Hulst, H. (1998). Movement phases in signs and co-speech gestures, and their transcription by human coders. In I. Wachsmuth & M. Fröhlich (Eds.), *Gesture and sign language in human-computer interaction* (Lecture Notes in Computer Science) (pp. 23–35). Springer. https://doi.org/10.1007/BFb0052986

Klippi, A. (2015). Pointing as an embodied practice in aphasic interaction. *Aphasiology, 29*(3), 337–354. https://doi.org/10.1080/02687038.2013.878451

Le Guen, O. (2011). Modes of pointing to existing spaces and the use of frames of reference. *Gesture, 11*(3), 271–307. https://doi.org/10.1075/gest.11.3.02leg

Levinson, S. C. (1996). Language and space. *Annual Review of Anthropology, 25*(1), 353.

Levinson, S. C. (1997). Language and cognition: The cognitive consequences of spatial description in guugu Yimithirr. *Journal of Linguistic Anthropology, 7*(1), 98–131. https://doi.org/10.1525/jlin.1997.7.1.98

Levinson, S. C. (2003). *Space in language and cognition: Explorations in cognitive diversity.* Cambridge University Press.

Levinson, S. C., Kita, S., Haun, D. B. M., & Rasch, B. H. (2002). Returning the tables: Language affects spatial reasoning. *Cognition, 84*(2), 155–188. https://doi.org/10.1016 /S0010-0277(02)00045-8

Levinson, S. C., & Wilkins, D. P. (Eds.). (2006). *Grammars of space: Explorations in cognitive diversity.* Cambridge University Press.

Majid, A., Bowerman, M., Kita, S., Haun, D. B. M., & Levinson, S. C. (2004). Can language restructure cognition? The case for space. *Trends in Cognitive Sciences, 8*(3), 108–114. https://doi.org/10.1016/j.tics.2004.01.003

McNeill, D. (1992). *Hand and mind: What gestures reveal about thought.* University of Chicago Press.

Mesh, K., Cruz, E., van de Weijer, J., Burenhult, N., & Gullberg, M. (2021). Effects of scale on multimodal deixis: Evidence from Quiahije Chatino. *Frontiers in Psychology, 11,* 3183. https://doi.org/10.3389/fpsyg.2020.584231

Mondada, L. (2007). Multimodal resources for turn-taking: Pointing and the emergence of possible next speakers. *Discourse Studies, 9*(2), 194–225. https://doi.org/10.1177 /1461445607075346

Mondada, L. (2014). The local constitution of multimodal resources for social interaction. *Journal of Pragmatics, 65,* 137–156. https://doi.org/10.1016/j.pragma.2014.04.004

Mondada, L. (2016). Challenges of multimodality: Language and the body in social interaction. *Journal of Sociolinguistics, 20*(3), 336–366. https://doi.org/10.1111/josl.1 _12177

Mondada, L. (2019a). Conventions for multimodal transcription. https://www .lorenzamondada.net/_files/ugd/ba0dbb_986ddd4993a04a57acf20ea06e2b9a34.pdf

Mondada, L. (2019b). Contemporary issues in conversation analysis: Embodiment and materiality, multimodality and multisensoriality in social interaction. *Journal of Pragmatics*, *145*, 47–62. https://doi.org/10.1016/j.pragma.2019.01.016

Mushin, I., & Doehler, S. P. (2021). Linguistic structures in social interaction: Moving temporality to the forefront of a science of language. *Interactional Linguistics*, *1*(1), 2–32. https://doi.org/10.1075/il.21008.mus

Nevile, M. (2015). The embodied turn in research on language and social interaction. *Research on Language and Social Interaction*, *48*(2), 121–151. https://doi.org/10.1080/08351813.2015.1025499

Palmer, B. (2015). Topography in language: Absolute frame of reference and the topographic correspondence hypothesis. In R. De Busser & R. J. LaPolla (Eds.) *Language structure and environment: Social, cultural, and natural factors* (pp. 177–226). John Benjamins.

Palmer, B., Gaby, A., Lum, J., & Schlossberg, J. (2018). Socioculturally mediated responses to environment shaping universals and diversity in spatial language. In P. Fogliaroni, A. Ballatore, & E. Clementini (Eds.), *Proceedings of the 13th international conference on spatial information theory (COSIT 2017)* (pp. 195–205). Springer.

Palmer, B., Lum, J., Schlossberg, J., & Gaby, A. (2017). How does the environment shape spatial language? Evidence for sociotopography. *Linguistic Typology*, *21*(3), 457. https://doi.org/10.1515/lingty-2017-0011

Pederson, E., Danziger, E., Wilkins, D., Levinson, S. C., Kita, S., & Senft, G. (1998). Semantic typology and spatial conceptualization. *Language*, *74*(3), 557–589.

Possemato, F., Blythe, J., de Dear, C., Dahmen, J., Gardner, R., & Stirling, L. (2021). Using a geospatial approach to document and analyse locational points in face-to-face conversation. *Language Documentation and Description*, *20*, 313–351. https://doi.org/10.25894/ldd54

Schegloff, E. A. (1972). Notes on a conversational practice: Formulating place. In D. Sudnow (Ed.), *Studies in social interaction* (pp. 75–119). The Free Press.

Schegloff, E. A. (1984). On some gestures' relation to talk. In J. M. Atkinson & J. Heritage (Eds.), *Structures of social action: Studies in conversation analysis* (pp. 266–296). Cambridge University.

Schegloff, E. A. (1996). Confirming allusions: Toward an empirical account of action. *American Journal of Sociology*, 161–216. https://doi.org/10.1086/230911

Sicoli, M. A. (2016). Formulating place, common ground, and a moral order in Lachixío Zapotec. *Open Linguistics*, *2*(1), 180–210. https://doi.org/10.1515/opli-2016-0009

Stirling, L., Gardner, R., Blythe, J., Mushin, I., & Possemato, F. (2022). On the road again: Place reference in multiparty conversations in the remote Australian outback. *Journal of Pragmatics*, *187*, 90–114. https://doi.org/doi.org/10.1016/j.pragma.2021.10.026

Stivers, T., & Sidnell, J. (2005). Introduction: Multimodal interaction. *Semiotica*, *156*(1/4), 1–20.

Streeck, J., Goodwin, C., & LeBaron, C. (Eds.). (2011). *Embodied interaction: Language and body in the material world.* Cambridge University Press.

Stukenbrock, A. (2014). Pointing to an 'empty' space: Deixis am Phantasma in face-to-face interaction. *Journal of Pragmatics*, *74*, 70–93. https://doi.org/10.1016/j.pragma.2014.08.001

Tomasello, M. (2008). *Origins of human communication.* MIT Press.

Wilkins, D. P. (2003). Why pointing with the index finger is not a universal (in sociocultural and semiotic terms). In S. Kita (Ed.), *Pointing: Where language, culture and cognition meet* (pp. 171–215). Lawrence Erlbaum Associates.

Williams, N. (2017). Place reference in Kula conversation. *Open Linguistics*, *3*(1). https://doi.org/10.1515/opli-2017-0028

Wootton, A. J. (1990). Pointing and interaction initiation: The behaviour of young children with Down's syndrome when looking at books. *Journal of Child Language*. *17*(3), 565–589. https://doi.org/10.1017/S0305000900010886

Abbreviations

ALL: allative, ANAPH: anaphoric demonstrative, APPL: applicative, CAT: catalyst, CL: clitic, DIST: distal demonstrative, DO: direct object, EMPH: emphatic, EXIST: existential, FOC: focus, FUT: future, GEN: genitive, IMPV: imperfective, INTS: intensifier, INTJ: interjection, IRR: irrealis, LOC: locative, M: masculine, NC:ANM: 'animate' noun classifier, NC:PERS: 'person' noun classifier, NC:PL/T: 'place/time' noun classifier, NC:RES: 'residue' noun classifier, NEG: negator, NFUT: non-future, NMLZ: nominalizer, NSIB: non-sibling, NS: non-singular, PC: paucal, PERL: Perlative, PL: plural, PRES: present tense, PROX: proximal, PST: past, S: subject, SG: singular, TEMP: temporal adverbial.

10

EMCA INFORMED EXPERIMENTATION AS A WAY OF INVESTIGATING (ALSO) "NON-ACCOUNTABLE" INTERACTIONAL PHENOMENA

Melisa Stevanovic

Ethnomethodological conversation analysis (EMCA) constitutes a break from the traditional social scientific approaches. While Parsons explained the orderliness of social action in terms of the socialisation of actors into the values and norms of their society, EMCA researchers explain social order with reference to the mundane practices by which members make sense of the world and act in it (Heritage, 1984). What is thus demanded of social science, and what EMCA aims to do, is to document "the processes by which social life is constituted rather than treating social phenomena as given objects in the world" (Hammersley, 2003, p. 755). This is also my aim in this chapter. Albeit deviating from some principles of EMCA, I seek to contribute to a better understanding of how the social world comes into being.

The chapter has the following structure. First, I will describe the methodological commitment of EMCA to "ontological muteness" regarding those aspects of social reality that go beyond what may be seen as the publicly observable, accountable features of interaction. Then, I introduce two interactional phenomena – prereflective mirroring mechanisms and the physiological underpinnings of interaction – which call for deviation from this insight. Thereafter, I will discuss the experimental induction of social actions and sequences of action as a way of empirically investigating these two topics. Finally, I will explain the research process associated with an EMCA informed experimental research endeavour and draw certain overall conclusions from the discussion.

DOI: 10.4324/9781003424888-13

Revisiting the ontological assumptions of EMCA

Social constructionism and the EMCA commitment to ontological muteness

Some of the central tenets of EMCA can be clarified with reference to the broad field known as social constructionism (Burr, 2015). Historically, both EMCA and social constructionism draw from the phenomenological approach by Berger and Luckmann (1967), which stresses the central role of human interpretation and communication in the constitution of social realities. This key notion of social constructionism is shared by all branches of EMCA – discursive psychology (Edwards & Potter, 1992; Wiggins, 2017), micro sociology (Goffman, 1967), and interactional linguistics (Couper-Kuhlen & Selting, 2001). Some EMCA scholars have nonetheless actively opposed the idea of their research representing social constructionism (see e.g., Watson, 2000; Wowk, 2007). A key point where EMCA has been seen to deviate from social constructionism is epistemology. While social constructionism is generally critical towards knowledge (Burr, 2015, pp. 2–3), the EMCA rhetoric, in which the researcher can "sit back and observe the structuring quality of the world as it happens" (Boden, 1994, p. 74), presupposes a view in which social reality is researchable in some objective form (Burr, 2015, p. 183).

Certain principles of social constructionism are, however, subscribed to by virtually every EMCA scholar. For example, this holds for the notion of performativity in language use. Words are used to do things (Austin, 1962), which means that, as social action, words have concrete consequences (Burr, 2015, p. 10). Furthermore, EMCA is consistent with the social constructionist view of the social world being constantly constructed and maintained in and through social processes (Burr, 2015, pp. 4–5). This principle fits seamlessly with the EMCA principle of refraining from taking any sociolinguistic variables or social identity categories as a starting point for the analysis of interactional phenomena (Drew & Heritage, 1992, p. 17). Instead, for an EMCA researcher, these aspects of social reality are *interactional achievements*, which are constructed by participants rather than being stable, pre-existing structures (Svennevig & Skovholt, 2005). Finally, EMCA shares the methodological commitment of social constructionism to "ontological muteness" regarding those aspects of social reality that go beyond the publicly observable features of interaction. The analysis should focus solely on how the participants *themselves* interpret each other's behaviours as "morally accountable" (Garfinkel, 1967) actions, and the researcher is not supposed to produce any ontological claims detached from the participants' own interpretations.

The EMCA focus on participants' own publicly displayed orientations as a sole basis for making analytic claims on what is happening in the interaction has been criticised on various grounds. For example, some critics have invoked the notion of the social world being intertwined with power relations, which affects what different people can do in their interactions with others and how they can legitimately treat their interaction partners (Burr, 2015, p. 5). Indeed, there are many situations in which a researcher could have compelling reasons to assume that the participants' relationship is in some way fundamentally unequal or unbalanced (e.g., sexual harassment and violence), in which case the sole focus on the participants' publicly displayed orientations leaves the researcher at the risk of disregarding those aspects of interaction that are particularly relevant for the participants themselves (Wetherell, 1998; Billig, 1999).

In this chapter, I will describe EMCA informed research that deviates from the ontological muteness characteristic for this field of inquiry. I will describe EMCA informed research on two interactional phenomena that go beyond people's publicly displayed, accountable conduct – the prereflective human mirroring mechanisms and the physiological underpinnings of social interaction. Although these phenomena are likely to evade EMCA analytic tools, I still assume these phenomena to play a key role in what EMCA is generally interested in – that is, in how social interaction is organised as actions and sequences of action.

Phenomenon I: Prereflective human mirroring mechanisms

Mirroring is common in various domains of human behaviour: People have been found to copy each other's lexical choices (Garrod & Anderson, 1987), to mimic each other's facial expressions (Lundquist & Dimberg, et al., 1995), to imitate each other's body postures, movements, and gestures (Chartrand & Bargh, 1999; Kimbara, 2006; Shockley et al., 2007), and to entrain to the melodic and rhythmic features of each other's speech (Gorisch et al., 2012; Stevanovic & Kahri, 2011). While the human mirroring mechanisms range from intentional to prereflective (automatic), here I will focus on the prereflective tendency of humans to synchronise their bodily behaviours with those of each other. Such spontaneous synchrony has been observed, for example, when pairs of people walk (Zivotofsky & Hausdorff, 2007), swing pendulums (Schmidt & O'Brien, 1997), or sit in rocking chairs (Richardson et al., 2007). Prereflective mirroring mechanisms have been shown to exist already early in infancy (e.g., Condon & Sander, 1974).

Extensive literature points to the social meaningfulness of the prereflective mirroring mechanisms. These mechanisms play a significant role in the degree to which individuals are perceived as a social unit or entity (Hamilton & Sherman, 1996; LaFrance, 1985; Marsh et al., 2009). They have also been suggested to facilitate communication by helping the alignment of mental and affective states (Cross, 2005; Frith & Frith, 2006). More specifically, empirical studies have shown, for example, that synchrony in body movements increases compassion (Valdesolo & DeSteno, 2011), trust (Launay et al., 2012), rapport (Miles et al., 2009), affiliation (Hove & Risen, 2009), cooperation (Wiltermuth & Heath, 2009), generalised prosociality (Reddish et al., 2014), and empathy (Rabinowitch et al., 2013).

The positive social consequences of prereflective mirroring have been shown to be sensitive to the participants' more specific conversational activities and the requirements of the setting (e.g., Shockley et al., 2003). For example, Paxton and

Dale (2013) found significantly less bodily synchrony within a dyad during argumentative settings, compared to affiliative ones. Fusaroli & Tylén (2012) found that when dyads were making joint decisions in a psychophysical task, the degree to which the participants matched each other's task-relevant expressions correlated positively with their task performance, whereas the indiscriminate matching of all expressions had a negative effect on the task performance. Findings such as these suggests that people's behaviours vary with respect to when they mirror each other's behaviours and when not. Some researchers have even suggested that it is precisely the alternation between mirroring and non-mirroring that drives the interaction and makes it interesting (Beebe & Lachman, 2002; Fuchs & De Jaegher, 2009). These ideas highlight the relevance of prereflective mirroring from the EMCA perspective (Stevanovic, Himberg et al., 2017; Stevanovic & Himberg, 2021). If people do not mirror each other's behaviours all the time, the EMCA researcher asks: "Why that now?" – that is, what it is in the situation at the moment that makes mirroring more or less relevant. Even if the prereflective mirroring behaviours go beyond people's publicly displayed accountable behaviors, it is still possible that these behaviours somehow contribute to people's interpretations of actions and sequences of action.

In our EMCA informed experimental study on dyadic joint decision-making interaction (see Stevanovic, Himberg et al., 2017), we compared the degree of similarity in the participants' body sway during sequential continuations and sequential transitions, finding that the instances of highest body-sway synchrony occurred during the sequential transitions. In my view, this finding suggests that it is specifically at those moments of interaction when a close coordination is critical – for example, when the participants need to reach and display a common understanding that a joint decision has been reached – that the prereflective mirroring mechanisms can become consequential for the sequential organisation of action. From this perspective, the phenomenon becomes a topic of EMCA informed inquiry.

Phenomenon II: physiological underpinnings of social interaction

While the prereflective human mirroring mechanisms go beyond people's publicly displayed accountable behaviours, the situation is even more so for the participants' physiological, affective, psychological, and experiential realities. Phylogenetically, many human mental characteristics have been suggested to have evolved specifically to meet the needs of social interaction (Levinson, 2006; Scott-Phillips, 2014). This has led some researchers to ask how the core topics of EMCA – actions and sequences of action – are underpinned by these processes. Here I will discuss the participants' physiological responses to interactional events.

Human physiological responses are varied. Electrodermal activity has often been used as a measure of emotional arousal, and increased activity has been linked to various social and emotional stimuli (e.g., DiMascio et al., 1957; Khalfa et al., 2002; Marci et al., 2007; Stark et al., 2005). Other physiological response variables that have been associated with specific social and affective processes are heart rate (Konvalinka et al., 2011), breathing (McFarland, 2001), and facial electromyographic activity (Deschamps, 2012). Measuring these physiological responses requires technical equipment other than video recordings, which is new to EMCA but has played a central role in psychological research.

One set of studies on the physiological underpinnings of social interaction has focused on the degree of *synchrony* in the physiological changes in the interacting participants (Feldman et al., 2011; Konvalinka et al., 2011; Marci et al., 2007). In these non-EMCA studies, physiological synchrony has come across as a feature of intense social interaction, which may range from competitive computer games (Sovijärvi-Spapé et al., 2013) to fire-walking rituals (Konvalinka et al., 2011). Consistently with this insight, our own EMCA informed experimental study on joint decision-making interaction (Stevanovic et al., 2021) showed physiological synchrony to be higher during proposal sequences, compared to the other types of sequences constituting the participants' conversational activity.

Another related set of studies has focused on how social-interactional events relate to *increases* or *decreases* in the physiological indicators of participants' arousal. For example, in an early study, DiMascio and colleagues (1957) examined psychotherapy sessions with reference to the categories of Bales' Interaction Process Analysis (Bales, 1950), finding that the categories "showing tension", "showing tension release", and "showing antagonism" were reflected in the participants' heart rates in systematic ways. This type of focus has also characterised some recent EMCA informed experimental studies on the physiological underpinnings of interaction (Koskinen et al., 2021; Peräkylä et al., 2015; Stevanovic et al., 2019b, 2021, 2022; Voutilainen et al., 2014, 2018a). For example, focusing on storytelling and story reception, Peräkylä and colleagues (2015) found that an increased level of affiliative story reception is associated with a decrease in the storyteller's arousal and an increase in the story recipient's arousal, as indicated in the participants' SC (skin conductance) response during the storytelling episodes (see also Stevanovic et al., 2019b). The authors interpreted this finding by drawing on the dyadic systems theory by Beebe and Lachmann (2002), which postulates that the system by which participants regulate their affective arousal is bidirectionally connected to the system by which participants regulate the unfolding of social interaction.

From the perspective of EMCA, the dyadic systems theory by Beebe and Lachmann (2002) offers an important insight. It suggests that, even though one-half of this entire big picture escapes publicly displayed moral orientations (self-regulation of arousal), the understanding of the entire picture is necessary to get a deeper understanding of the other half of the system – the one that is governed by the mechanism of moral accountability (regulation of interaction) and constitutes the focus of traditional EMCA inquiry.

Towards the experimental induction of actions and sequences of action

EMCA has emphasised close observation and rigorous descriptions of the structures of social interaction, as these become visible in naturally occurring interactional encounters, and excluded experimental and laboratory studies from its traditional scope (Kendrick, 2017). Laboratory experiments have been argued to transform the dynamics of interaction into forms that are not anymore relevant for social scientific inquiry (Schegloff, 1996b, p. 28). Unlike the physical and material world, which may be investigated experimentally, human activity has been argued to be quite different in a laboratory than in real life situations (Levitt & List, 2007). Thus, the results obtained in a laboratory study are likely to suffer from problems of ecological validity and thus not generalise to the world outside the lab. In addition, experimental research has also been criticised for sticking to the prevailing preconceptions of human activity rather than being genuinely curious about what people do (Schegloff, 2004).

However, every social interactional encounter is embedded in some *context*. While this holds for all encounters taking place within various naturally occurring settings, this holds also for interactions in a laboratory. While EMCA rejects the "bucket theory of context" (Goodwin & Heritage, 1990, p. 286; Heritage, 1987) in which pre-existing circumstances are seen to determine the interaction from above, this also means that the consequentiality of the laboratory context for the participants' interaction should not be taken for granted. Instead, just like in the analysis of everyday encounters, it is important to observe the extent to which participants themselves display their orientations to various features of the context and consider their relevance for research on this basis (see Schegloff, 1991, 1997). From this perspective, no tenable distinction between "natural" and "contrived" data can be made (Speer, 2002).

How should one then best induce the interaction phenomena of interest in the distinctive context of the laboratory? The answers vary, as has been demonstrated in EMCA informed experimental studies conducted during the last years. For example, if we want to study people's perceptions of social-interactional stimuli, this can be done by studying one participant at a time (see e.g., De Ruiter et al., 2006; Hirvenkari et al., 2013; Roberts et al., 2006, 2011). However, if we want to examine how participants in interaction react to social-interactional stimuli in situ, we should design experimental tasks that allow the generation of repeated instances of such reactions (Bavelas et al., 2000; Clark & Krych, 2004). Also, if we want to learn about people's interactional use of gestures, we cannot attach their hands to many wires and sensors that could change the trajectories of their hand movements (see e.g., Bavelas et al., 2008, 2014; Holler & Wilkin, 2011). But then again, if we want to make use of contemporary measurement technologies (e.g., eye-tracking, breath tracking, motion capture) to get detailed information about those behaviours that cannot be reliably investigated with the help of video recordings alone, we may need to use some measuring equipment attached to the participants' bodies (see e.g., Stevanovic & Himberg et al., 2017; Holler & Kendrick, 2015; Torreira et al., 2015;). This is also the case for physiological measurements, which typically limit the participants' physical freedom (see e.g., Koskinen et al., 2021; Peräkylä et al., 2015; Stevanovic et al., 2019b, 2021; Voutilainen et al., 2014, 2018a). Hence, whether and how experimentation would make sense as a means of investigation must always be assessed in the light of the specific questions that one wants to study.

EMCA informed experimental research may be motivated by various reasons. First, one might want to assess the generalisability of certain findings obtained in the qualitative data-driven scrutiny of naturally occurring interactions. The possibility of inducing repeated instances of those actions and sequences of action that one has previously studied on a case-by-case basis and subjecting the observations to quantification and statistical analysis might come across as a natural next step in one's attempts to better understand these interactional phenomena. Second, one might be interested in comparing the interactional practices of different participant groups (e.g., participants with various clinical conditions). Given that such differences cannot be considered as absolute and static but as subject to high interindividual and intraindividual variation, analytic claim must be done based on a larger collection of parallel cases than would be possible to obtain by using naturally occurring data only.

Third, as has been highlighted in this chapter, one might want to examine social-interactional phenomena, such as the prereflective human mirroring mechanisms and the physiological underpinnings of interaction, which can best be technically measured in laboratory conditions. This is not only due to the possibilities of using measurement technologies in the lab, but also due to the nature of the phenomena as going beyond publicly displayed accountable behaviours. To accept the possibility that the construction of actions and sequences of action could be also informed by interactional phenomena that the participants are not reflexively aware of makes it relevant also for the researcher to accept the possibility that not every single case in the data can be accounted for in similar terms. In other words, the EMCA principle involving the need to account for all the so-called "deviant cases" must be relaxed and replaced by effective ways of separating the generic patterns of action construction from what may now be regarded as "noise". Such separation necessitates larger amounts of comparable data (with parallel actions and sequences of action) than one might be able to obtain in natural settings.

Research process associated with EMCA informed experimentation

The experimental method has a long history in the natural sciences, where it has been specifically associated with testing hypotheses derived from existing theories and illustrating the consequences of manipulating individual variables. This is radically different from the inductive EMCA enterprise with "unmotivated look-ing" of naturally occurring interactions as a starting point. The EMCA informed way of conducting experiments must therefore be conceived as a compromise between these two entirely different ways of carrying out research.

I suggest that the research process associated with EMCA informed experi-mentation encompasses the following five steps: (1) theorizing the interactional target phenomenon, (2) inventing the social interaction tasks, (3) running the experiments, (4) coding or rating and checking for inter-coder reliability, and (5) statistical analysis and the interpretation of results. In what follows, I will briefly discuss each step separately, pointing to certain complications and concerns that an EMCA researcher might experience during them.

Theorising the interactional target phenomenon

The first step in an EMCA informed experimental research process involves theo-rising about the interactional target phenomenon. From the EMCA perspective, this idea is contradictory. EMCA has traditionally been sceptical about social scientific theories and conceptualisations of social interaction, which have been considered not to do justice to the complexities of human interaction but rather to mislead researchers (ten Have, 2007 [1999]), pp. 29–31). Simultaneously, EMCA literature itself contains many concepts that are necessary for any EMCA finding to get formulated, although the status of these concepts as *theoretical* ones has seldom been discussed.

The EMCA informed way of conducting experiments must be cognisant of the immense theoretical substance of the EMCA approach (see Heritage, 2009) and the researcher must be willing to explicate the phenomena that this specific theo-retical understanding of social interaction can help to elucidate. The core EMCA assumption about conversation constituting an institutional order of its own involves several sub-assumptions that can inform empirical inquiry and motivate the generation of hypotheses. First, the organisation of *turn-taking* is assumed to be elementary in the management of the entire interaction order. EMCA informed experimental research can then make use of the concepts of "turn constructional units", "transition relevance places", and "turn allocation" (Sacks et al., 1974), and the taxonomies of different types of "overlaps" (Jefferson, 1984) to construct hypotheses about the specific practices that participants engage in when alter-nating with their spoken utterances (see e.g., De Ruiter et al., 2006; Hirvenkari et al., 2013). Moreover, social interaction is assumed to be underpinned by the organisation of utterances and expressions into chains of initiating and responsive utterances in terms of *sequence organisation* (Schegloff, 2007). Here, for exam-ple, the notion of "preference" and its associated practices provide a rich source of hypotheses for experimental research (see e.g., Bögels et al., 2015; Roberts et al., 2006, 2011). In addition, hypotheses may be drawn from the EMCA literature on *repair* (Schegloff et al., 1977), *turn-design* (Lerner, 1995), *epistemics* (Heritage,

2013), and *deontics* (Stevanovic, 2018), although not much has yet been done in this respect.

Notably, theorising interactional phenomena must not be exclusively based on EMCA literature. In addition, the EMCA informed theorising of actions and sequences of action may be augmented by using theories from other fields, such as psychology (De Ruiter & Albert, 2017). It is from this perspective that also questions about "non-accountable" interaction phenomena surface. As traditional EMCA operates on ontological and epistemological assumptions that are not compatible with this view, some researchers might be inclined to deny the EMCA informed nature of research on such questions. However, solely the idea of social action and its multiple resources and configurations in chains of initiating and responsive actions is essentially *informed* by EMCA. In my view, it is only right and just to acknowledge this source of inspiration when theorising social interaction, as it motivates asking questions that have not been asked by researchers from other fields of inquiry.

Inventing the social interaction tasks

The next step in designing an EMCA informed experimental study is to invent social interaction tasks and task instructions that would lead the participants "spontaneously" to produce those actions and sequences of action that one wants to investigate. This aim is characterised with an inherent tension between two goals. One the one hand, it will be elementary to come up with ways of invoking the relevant actions and sequences maximally, naturally. The task instructions should thus be generic enough not to directly influence the precise forms in which the relevant actions and sequences are realised during the task. On the other hand, specifically to deal with "noise" associated with the analysis of pre-reflective and "non-accountable" phenomena, it will be important to design the task in such a way that each dyad or group of participants will necessarily have produced repeated instances of the target phenomenon by the completion of the task. While the balancing between the two above-mentioned goals is challenging, it is not impossible. As pointed out by Schegloff (1991, p. 54–57), some tasks may generate modifications to how participants normally interact, but there can also be other tasks that preserve the dynamics of the turn-by-turn sequential unfolding of naturally occurring interaction.

When planning the experimental tasks, it is useful to anticipate later steps in the research process. Specifically, the coding of interaction (see below) will be easier if the key events that the study focuses on are easily and reliably identifiable from the data. Thus, for example, in our studies on joint decision-making sequences (Stevanovic & Himberg, 2017; Stevanovic et al., 2021), we wanted to make sure that transitions from a decision-making sequence to a next one would be realised as unambiguously as possible. Thus, we ended up using a task, in which the participants were given a series of eight letters in alphabetical order (e.g., H, I, J, K,

L, M, N, O), and then asked to select eight adjectives that would start with these letters, and describe a fictional target (e.g., Donald Duck). As a motivation for the task, the participants were told to imagine being editors of a children's book, teaching the alphabet by featuring the target character with a series of adjectives. The participants carried out the task entirely without experimenter intervention. Once a decision for one letter was reached, the dyad moved on to the next letter in the alphabet, which means that the typical practice by which a transition to a new sequence was constructed was the mentioning of the next relevant letter (e.g., "and then K"). As indications of transitions, such utterances were easily and reliably identifiable from the data.

Running the experiments

Running the experiments can be a relatively straightforward task for a researcher that inherits the experimental setup and can continue the research done by their predecessors. In contrast, building an experimental setup from scratch is a formidable task, which might discourage the EMCA researcher who wants to try something new for a change. The possibility of collaborating with researchers from other fields (e.g., psychology, cognitive science, and neuroscience) is therefore worthwhile.

Recruiting participants to the experiments is somewhat different from recruiting them to a typical EMCA study. On the one hand, the recruitment may be considered easier in that the researcher is not imposing their (video camera) presence on any naturally occurring setting but asks for volunteers to participate in a setting created solely for research purposes. On the other hand, the idea of testing specific EMCA driven hypotheses necessitates care in the selection of the participants. Because an EMCA researcher typically wants to focus on interactional phenomena, and not person-specific individual-level variables, the latter need to be controlled as far as possible. Given the size of the data set that one might be able to realistically obtain, the best way to control for these variables is to delimit the population that the participant sample represents. In our own studies, we have set criteria for the participants' age, gender, mother tongue, educational level, and work experience, which could have most likely interfered with those physiological responses that we were specifically interested in. Unless a candidate fitted to a specific participant profile, they were excluded from the study.

In the EMCA studies, the unique context of each conversational contribution is taken into consideration in the analysis of the participants' conduct. However, in the experiments that target prereflective and "non-accountable" interactional phenomena, it is important to keep the amount of unintentional contextual factors that could influence the results (e.g., changes in illumination, room temperature, and humidity) to a minimum. From the perspective of social interaction, the delivery of the task instructions necessitates specific care, as most subtle differences in the ways in which the task is explained to the participants may reflect on their entire conversation. Also, in case the experiment consists of several tasks to be conducted during a single laboratory session, it is important to have the order of the tasks counter-balanced across the different sessions.

Coding or rating of interaction and checking for inter-observer reliability

Next, the interactions induced through the experimental tasks must be *coded* for their relevant features to enable their quantification and statistical analysis. This part of the research process is the same, independent of whether the research is interested in "non-accountable" phenomena or those that are subject to participants' moral orientations. While also classical CA work is compatible in spirit with certain aspects of quantitative methodology, specifically when it comes to identifying, categorising, and counting instances of a phenomenon (Stivers, 2015), in formal coding, the categorisation process is more transparent, as the categorisation criteria must be made explicit in a coding scheme. The basic idea of the coding scheme is that, in principle, any researcher following the scheme would end up categorising the target phenomena in the same way. The statistical testing of whether the categorisation criteria are clear enough, which is typically done by using Cohen's kappa coefficient (Cohen, 1960), will then become a critical part of the process. Reaching a sufficient level of inter-observer agreement is necessary to be able to proceed with the analysis.

One persistent challenge in the attempts to code social interaction has to do with the fact that many aspects of human behaviour may be better understood as continuous than as categorical (Stivers, 2015). Therefore, another possibility to quantify social-interactional phenomena is to *rate* those dimensions with reference to which participants' behaviours appear continuous. Such dimensions include, for example, empathy (Peräkylä et al., 2015; Voutilainen et al., 2018b), dominance and affiliation (Stevanovic, Henttonen et al., 2017; 2019a; 2019b), and the level of participation or responsiveness (Stevanovic et al. 2020). An advantage of rating over coding is the possibility of using multiple "naïve" raters to observe the same interactional phenomena, while the intraclass correlation coefficient (ICC) may be used to assess agreement between the raters (Koch, 1982). Instead of designing a detailed coding scheme, the raters may be instructed to rely on their own culturally based intuitions on what behaviour constitutes, for example, an affiliative response in different types of contexts.

Statistical analysis and the interpretation of results

The purpose of coding and rating is to help capture the complexities of social interaction in numbers. Numbers enable not only the scrutiny of the distributions of the relevant phenomena but also the examination of the relationship between these phenomena and other numerical variables – be they social, behavioural, affective, experiential, or physiological in nature.

A central task of the researcher is to determine which variables are to be seen as predictors and which as outcomes. From the EMCA perspective, this assignment of roles is not intuitively straightforward. Our own study on body sway during sequential transitions (Stevanovic, Himberg et al., 2017) is a case in point. The study was motivated by the idea of sequential transitions as *interactional achievements* that the participants' synchronised body sway could contribute to. A successful sequential transition thus appeared as an *outcome* of what participants manage to do. From the perspective of statistical analysis, however, the reasoning worked the other way around. We had previously divided the participants' conversations into two different types of segments: sequential continuations and sequential transitions. To test our hypothesis, we treated the variable "segment" as a predictor variable, to see whether it would be able to predict the level of "body sway synchrony" as an outcome variable. While the statistical analysis showed that the participants' levels of body sway synchrony were higher during the sequential transitions, compared to the sequential continuations, and that this pattern was unlikely to be a co-incidence, we obtained no information about the mechanisms or causal relationships underlying this pattern. Instead, it was our EMCA informed understanding of social interaction and of sequential transitions as *interactional achievements* (i.e., "outcomes" of interactional practices) that allowed us to interpret the result and expand our understanding of the resources that participants use for this purpose.

Conclusions

In this chapter, I have described EMCA informed experimentation as a way of addressing social-interactional phenomena that go beyond people's publicly displayed accountable behaviors, but which may still be ontologically real and somehow relevant for how social interaction ends up becoming organised as actions and sequences of action. I have given two examples of such phenomena: the pre-reflective human mirroring mechanisms and the physiological underpinnings of social interaction.

The investigation of "non-accountable" interactional phenomena is challenging from the EMCA perspective. Such investigation emphasises the need to use quantification to distinguish between the basic and non-basic patterns of interaction and involves a relaxation of the requirement to account for "deviant cases". While researchers in other fields are used to dealing with "noise" in the data, for an EMCA researcher such an idea is hard to reconcile with the notion of "order at all points" (Sacks, 1984, p. 22). EMCA informed experimental research thus involves various complications and concerns that are likely to arise during the research process. In addition, publishing the results may involve a further risk: I once had a paper submitted to a journal for nine months, after which the editor returned the submission stating that that they had been unable to find reviewers for the paper.

Despite the above-mentioned difficulties, I believe that many different types of complexities of human social interaction must be further investigated and new ways of grasping them must be developed. EMCA has been elementary in shedding light on those actions and sequences of action by which the social world comes into being. EMCA informed experimentation is about doing the same from a different perspective.

References

Austin, J. L. (1962). *How to do things with words*. Harvard University Press.

Bales, R. F. (1950). *Interaction process analysis: A method for the study of small groups*. Chicago: University of Chicago Press.

Bavelas, J., Coates, L., & Johnson, T. (2000). Listeners as co-narrators. *Journal of Personality and Social Psychology, 79*(6), 941–952.

Bavelas, J., Gerwing, J., & Healing, S. (2014). Effect of dialogue on demonstrations: Direct quotations, facial portrayals, hand gestures, and figurative references. *Discourse Processes, 51*(8), 619–655.

Bavelas, J., Gerwing, J., Sutton, C., & Prevost, D. (2008). Gesturing on the telephone: Independent effects of dialogue and visibility. *Journal of Memory and Language, 58*(2), 495–520.

Beebe, B., & Lachmann, F. (2002). *Infant research and adult treatment: Co-constructing interactions*. The Analytic Press.

Berger, P. L., & Luckmann, T. (1967). *The social construction of reality: A treatise in the sociology of knowledge*. Harmondsworth: Penguin Books.

Billig, M. (1999). Whose terms? Whose ordinariness? Rhetoric and ideology in conversation analysis. *Discourse and Society, 10*(4), 543–558. https://doi.org/10.1177/0957926599010004005

Boden, D. (1994). *The business of talk: Organizations in action*. Polity Press.

Bögels, S., Kendrick, K. H., & Levinson, S. C. (2015). Never say no… How the brain interprets the pregnant pause in conversation. *PLOS One, 10*(12), e0145474. https://doi.org/10.1371/journal.pone.0145474

Burr, V. (2015). *Social constructionism* (3rd ed.). Routledge.

Chartrand, T. L., & Bargh, J. A. (1999). The chameleon effect: The perception–behavior link and social interaction. *Journal of Personality and Social Psychology, 76*(6), 893–910. https://doi.org/10.1037//0022-3514.76.6.893

Clark, H. H., & Krych, M. A. (2004). Speaking while monitoring addressees for understanding. *Journal of Memory and Language, 50*(1), 62–81.

Cohen, J. (1960). A coefficient of agreement for nominal scales. *Educational and Psychological Measurement, 20*(1), 37–46. https://doi.org/10.1177/001316446002000104

Condon, W. S., & Sander, L. W. (1974). Synchrony demonstrated between movements of the neonate and adult speech. *Child Development, 45*(2), 456–462. https://doi.org/10.2307/1127968

Couper-Kuhlen, E., & Selting, M. (2001). Introducing interactional linguistics. In M. Selting & E. Couper-Kuhlen (Eds.), *Studies in interactional linguistics* (pp. 1–22). John Benjamins.

Cross, I. (2005). Music and meaning, ambiguity and evolution. In D. Miell, R. MacDonald, & D. J. Hargreaves (Eds.), *Musical communication* (pp. 27–43). Oxford University Press.

De Ruiter, J. P., & Albert, S. (2017). An appeal for a methodological fusion of conversation analysis and experimental psychology. *Research on Language and Social Interaction*, *50*(1), 90–107. https://doi.org/10.1080/08351813.2017.1262050

De Ruiter, J. P., Mitterer, H., & Enfield, N. J. (2006). Projecting the end of a speaker's turn: A cognitive cornerstone of conversation. *Language*, *82*(3), 515–535. https://doi.org/10.1353/lan.2006.0130

Deschamps, P. K. H., Schutte, I., Kenemans, J. L., Matthys, W., & Schutter, D. J. L. G. (2012). Electromyographic responses to emotional facial expressions in 6–7 year olds. *International Journal of Psychophysiology*, *85*(2), 195–199. https://doi.org/10.1016/j.ijpsycho.2012.05.004

DiMascio, A., Boyd, R., & Greenblatt, M. (1957). Physiological correlates of tension and antagonism during psychotherapy: A study of "Interpersonal Physiology". *Psychosomatic Medicine*, *19*(2), 99–104.

Drew, P., & Heritage, J. (1992). Analyzing talk at work: An introduction. In P. Drew & J. Heritage (Eds.), *Talk at work: Interaction in institutional settings* (pp. 3–65). Cambridge University Press.

Edwards, D., & Potter, J. (1992). *Discursive psychology*. Sage.

Feldman, R., Magori-Cohen, R., Galili, G., Singer, M., & Louzoun, Y. (2011). Mother and infant coordinate heart rhythms through episodes of interaction synchrony. *Infant Behavior and Development*, *34*(4), 569–577. https://doi.org/10.1016/j.infbeh.2011.06.008

Frith, C. D., & Frith, U. (2006). How we predict what other people are going to do. *Brain Research*, *1079*(1), 36–46. https://doi.org/10.1016/j.brainres.2005.12.126

Fuchs, T., & De Jaegher, H. (2009). Enactive intersubjectivity: Participatory sense-making and mutual incorporation. *Phenomenology and the Cognitive Sciences*, *8*(4), 465–486. https://doi.org/10.1007/s11097-009-9136-4

Fusaroli, R., & Tylén, K. (2012). Carving language for social coordination: A dynamical approach. *Interaction Studies*, *13*(1), 103–124. https://doi.org/10.1075/is.13.1.07fus

Garfinkel, H. (1967). *Studies in ethnomethodology*. Prentice Hall.

Garrod, S., & Anderson, A. (1987). Saying what you mean in dialogue: A study in conceptual and semantic co-ordination. *Cognition*, *27*(2), 181–218. https://doi.org/10.1016/0010-0277(87)90018-7

Goffman, E. (1967). *Interaction ritual: Essays on face-to-face interaction*. Anchor Books.

Goodwin, C., & Heritage, J. (1990). Conversation analysis. *Annual Review of Anthropology*, *19*(1), 283–307. https://doi.org/10.1146/annurev.an.19.100190.001435

Gorisch, J., Wells, B., & Brown, G. J. (2012). Pitch contour matching and interactional alignment across turns: An acoustic investigation. *Language and Speech*, *55*(1), 57–76.

Hamilton, D. L., & Sherman, S. J. (1996). Perceiving persons and groups. *Psychological Review*, *103*(2), 336–355. https://doi.org/10.1037/0033-295X.103.2.336

Hammersley, M. (2003). Conversation analysis and discourse analysis: Methods or paradigms? *Discourse and Society*, *14*(6), 751–781. https://doi.org/10.1177/09579265030146004

Heritage, J. (1984). *Garfinkel and ethnomethodology*. Polity Press.

Heritage, J. (1987). Ethnomethodology. In A. Giddens & J. Turner (Eds.), *Social theory today* (pp. 224–272). Polity Press.

Heritage, J. (2009). Conversation analysis as social theory. In B. Turner (Ed.), *The new Blackwell companion to social theory* (pp. 300–320). Blackwell.

Heritage, J. (2013). Epistemics in conversation. In J. Sidnell & T. Stivers (Eds.), *Handbook of conversation analysis* (pp. 370–394). Wiley-Blackwell.

Hirvenkari, L., Ruusuvuori, J., Saarinen, V.-M., Kivioja, M., Peräkylä, A., & Hari, R. (2013). Influence of turn-taking in a two-person conversation on the gaze of a viewer. *PLOS One*, *8*(8), e71569. https://doi.org/10.1371/journal.pone.0071569

Holler, J., & Kendrick, K. H. (2015). Unaddressed participants' gaze in multi-person interaction: Optimizing recipiency. *Frontiers in Psychology*, *6*, 98. https://doi.org/10.3389/fpsyg.2015.00098

Holler, J., & Wilkin, K. (2011). An experimental investigation of how addressee feedback affects co-speech gestures accompanying speakers' responses. *Journal of Pragmatics*, *43*(14), 3522–3536. https://doi.org/10.1016/j.pragma.2011.08.002

Hove, M. J., & Risen, J. L. (2009). It's all in the timing: Interpersonal synchrony increases affiliation. *Social Cognition*, *27*(6), 949–960. https://doi.org/10.1521/soco.2009.27.6.949

Jefferson, G. (1984). Notes on some orderlinesses of overlap onset. In V. D'Urso (Eds.), *Discourse analysis and natural rhetoric*, (pp. 11–38).

Kendrick, K. H. (2017). Using conversation analysis in the lab. *Research on Language and Social Interaction*, *50*(1), 1–11. https://doi.org/10.1080/08351813.2017.1267911

Khalfa, S., Isabelle, P., Jean-Pierre, B., & Manon, R. (2002). Event-related skin conductance responses to musical emotions in humans. *Neuroscience Letters*, *328*(2), 145–149. https://doi.org/10.1016/S0304-3940(02)00462-7

Kimbara, I. (2006). On gestural mimicry. *Gesture*, *6*(1), 39–61. https://doi.org/10.1075/gest.6.1.03kim

Koch, G. G. (1982). Intraclass correlation coefficient. In S. Kotz & N. L. Johnson (Eds.), *Encyclopedia of statistical sciences* (pp. 213–217). Wiley.

Konvalinka, I., Xygalatas, D., Bulbuliac, J., Schjødt, U., Jegindø, E.-M., Wallotd, S., Van Ordend, G., & Roepstorff, A. (2011). Synchronized arousal between performers and related spectators in a fire-walking ritual. *PNAS*, *108*(2), 8514–8519. https://doi.org/10.1073/pnas.1016955108

Koskinen, E., Tuhkanen, S., Järvensivu, M., Savander, E., Valkeapää, T., Valkia, K., Weiste, E., & Stevanovic, M. (2021). The psychophysiological experience of solving moral dilemmas together: An interdisciplinary comparison between participants with and without depression. *Frontiers in Communication*, *6*, 17. https://doi.org/10.3389/fcomm.2021.625968

LaFrance, M. (1985). Postural mirroring and intergroup orientation. *Personality and Social Psychology Bulletin*, *11*(2), 207–218. https://doi.org/10.1177/0146167285112008

Launay, J., Dean, R. T., & Bailes, F. (2012). Synchronization can influence trust following virtual interaction. *Experimental Psychology*, *60*(1), 53–63. https://doi.org/10.1027/1618-3169/a000173

Lerner, G. H. (1995). Turn design and the organization of participation in instructional activities. *Discourse Processes*, *19*(1), 111–131. https://doi.org/10.1080/01638539109544907

Levinson, S. C. (2006). On the human "interaction engine". In N. J. Enfield & S. C. Levinson (Eds.), *Roots of human sociality* (pp. 39–69). Berg.

Levitt, S. D., & List, J. A. (2007). What do laboratory experiments measuring social preferences reveal about the real world? *Journal of Economic Perspectives*, *21*(2), 153–174. https://doi.org/10.1257/jep.21.2.153

Lundquist, L. O., & Dimberg, A. (1995). Facial expressions are contagious. *Journal of Psychophysiology*, *9*, 203–211.

Marci, C. D., Ham, J., Moran, E., & Orr, S. P. (2007). Physiologic correlates of perceived therapist empathy and social-emotional process during psychotherapy. *Journal of Nervous and Mental Disease, 195*(2), 103–111. https://doi.org/10.1097/01.nmd.0000253731.71025.fc

Marsh, K. L., Richardson, M. J., & Schmidt, R. C. (2009). Social connection through joint action and interpersonal coordination. *Topics in Cognitive Science, 1*(2), 320–339. https://doi.org/10.1111/j.1756-8765.2009.01022.x

McFarland, D. H. (2001). Respiratory markers of conversational interaction. *Journal of Speech, Language, and Hearing Research, 44*(1), 128–143. https://doi.org/10.1044/1092-4388(2001/012)

Miles, L. K., Louise, K. N., & Macrae, C. N. (2009). The rhythm of rapport: Interpersonal synchrony and social perception. *Journal of Experimental Social Psychology, 45*(3), 585–589. https://doi.org/10.1016/j.jesp.2009.02.002

Paxton, A., & Dale, R. (2013). Frame-differencing methods for measuring bodily synchrony in conversation. *Behavior Research Methods, 45*(2), 329–343. https://doi.org/10.3758/s13428-012-0249-2

Peräkylä, A., Henttonen, P., Voutilainen, L., Kahri, M., Stevanovic, M., Sams, M., & Ravaja, N. (2015). Sharing the emotional load: Recipient affiliation calms down the storyteller. *Social Psychology Quarterly, 78*(4), 301–323. https://doi.org/10.1177/0190272515611054

Rabinowitch, T.-C., Cross, I., & Burnard, P. (2013). Long-term musical group interaction has a positive influence in empathy in children. *Psychology of Music, 41*(4), 484–498. https://doi.org/10.1177/0305735612440609

Reddish, P., Bulbulia, J., & Fischer, R. (2014). Does synchrony promote generalized prosociality? *Religion, Brain and Behavior, 4*(1), 3–19. https://doi.org/10.1080/2153599X.2013.764545

Richardson, M. J., Marsh, K. L., Isenhower, R. W., Goodman, J. R. L., & Schmidt, R. C. (2007). Rocking together: Dynamics of intentional and unintentional interpersonal coordination. *Human Movement Science, 26*(6), 867–891. https://doi.org/10.1016/j.humov.2007.07.002

Roberts, F., Francis, A. L., & Morgan, M. (2006). The interaction of inter-turn silence with prosodic cues in listener perceptions of "trouble" in conversation. *Speech Communication, 48*(9), 1079–1093. https://doi.org/10.1016/j.specom.2006.02.001

Roberts, F., Margutti, P., & Takano, S. (2011). Judgments concerning the valence of inter-turn silence across speakers of American English, Italian, and Japanese. *Discourse Processes, 48*(5), 331–354. https://doi.org/10.1080/0163853X.2011.558002

Sacks, H. (1984). Notes on methodology. In J. M. Atkinson & J. Heritage (Eds.), *Structures of social action: Studies in conversation analysis* (pp. 21–27). Cambridge University Press.

Sacks, H., Schegloff, E. A., & Jefferson, G. (1974). A simplest systematics for the organisation of turn-taking for conversation. *Language, 50*(4), 696–735. https://doi.org/10.1016/B978-0-12-623550-0.50008-2

Schegloff, E. A. (1991). Reflections on talk and social structure. In D. Boden & D. H. Zimmerman (Eds.), *Talk and social structure: Studies in Ethnomethodology and Conversation Analysis* (pp. 44–70). Polity Press.

Schegloff, E. A. (1996b). Issues of relevance for discourse analysis: Contingency in action, interaction and co-participant context. In E. H. Hovy & D. R. Scott (Eds.), *Computational and conversational discourse* (pp. 3–35). Springer. https://doi.org/10.1007/978-3-662-03293-0_1

Schegloff, E. A. (1997). Whose text? Whose context? *Discourse and Society, 8*(2), 165–187. https://doi.org/10.1177/0957926597008002002

Schegloff, E. A. (2004). Experimentation or observation? On the self alone or the natural world? *Brain and Behavioral Sciences, 27*(2), 271–272. https://doi.org/10.1017/S0140525X0431006X

Schegloff, E. A. (2007). *Sequence organization in interaction: A primer in conversation analysis.* Cambridge University Press.

Schegloff, E. A., Jefferson, G., & Sacks, H. (1977). The preference for self-correction in the organization of repair in conversation. *Language, 53*(2), 361–382. https://doi.org/10.1353/lan.1977.0041

Schmidt, R. C., & O'Brien, B. (1997). Evaluating the dynamics of unintended interpersonal coordination. *Ecological Psychology, 9*(3), 189–206. https://doi.org/10.1207/s15326969eco0903_2

Scott-Phillips, T. (2014). *Speaking our minds: Why human communication is different, and how language evolved to make it special.* Palgrave Macmillan.

Shockley, K., Baker, A. A., Richardson, M. J., & Fowler, C. A. (2007). Articulatory constraints on interpersonal postural coordination. *Journal of Experimental Psychology: Human Perception and Performance, 33*(1), 201–208. https://doi.org/10.1037/0096-1523.33.1.201

Shockley, K., Santana, M.-V., & Fowler, C. A. (2003). Mutual interpersonal postural constraints are involved in cooperative conversation. *Journal of Experimental Psychology: Human Perception and Performance, 29*(2), 326–332. https://doi.org/10.1037/0096-1523.29.2.326

Spapé, M. M., Kivikangas, J. M., Järvelä, S., Kosunen, I., Jacucci, G., & Ravaja, N. (2013). Keep your opponents close: Social context affects EEG and fEMG linkage in a turn-based computer game. *PLOS One, 8*(11), e78795. https://doi.org/10.1371/journal.pone.0078795

Speer, S. A. (2002). "Natural" and "contrived" data: A sustainable distinction? *Discourse Studies, 4*(4), 511–525. https://doi.org/10.1177/14614456020040040601

Stark, R., Walter, B., Schienle, A., & Vaitl, D. (2005). Psychophysiological correlates of disgust and disgust sensitivity. *Journal of Psychophysiology, 19*(1), 50–60. https://doi.org/10.1027/0269-8803.19.1.50

Stevanovic, M. (2018). Social deontics: A nano-level approach to human power play. *Journal for the Theory of Social Behaviour, 48*(3), 369–389. https://doi.org/10.1111/jtsb.12175

Stevanovic, M., Henttonen, P., Koski, S., Kahri, M., & Voutilainen, L. (2019a). Affiliation and dominance in female and male dyads: When discoordination makes happy. *Gender Issues, 36*(3), 201–235. https://doi.org/10.1007/s12147-018-9218-0

Stevanovic, M., Henttonen, P., Koski, S., Kahri, M., Voutilainen, L., Koskinen, E., Nieminen-von Wendt, T., Tani, P., & Peräkylä, A. (2017). On the Asperger experience of interaction: Interpersonal dynamics in dyadic conversations. *Journal of Autism, 4*(2). http://doi.org/10.7243/2054-992X-4-2

Stevanovic, M., Henttonen, P., Koskinen, E., Peräkylä, A., Nieminen von-Wendt, T., Sihvola, E., Tani, P., Ravaja, N., & Sams, M. (2019b). Physiological responses to affiliation during conversation: Comparing neurotypical males and males with Asperger syndrome. *PLOS One, 14*(9), e0222084. https://doi.org/10.1371/journal.pone.0222084

Stevanovic, M., & Himberg, T. (2021). Movement synchrony as a topic of empirical social interaction research. In J. Lindström, R. Laury, A. Peräkylä, & M.-L. Sorjonen (Eds.), *Intersubjectivity in action* (pp. 229–346). Benjamins.

Stevanovic, M., Himberg, T., Niinisalo, M., Kahri, M., Peräkylä, A., Sams, M., & Hari, R. (2017). Sequentiality, mutual visibility, and behavioral matching: Body sway and pitch register during joint decision-making. *Research on Language and Social Interaction*, *50*(1), 33–53. https://doi.org/10.1080/08351813.2017.1262130

Stevanovic, M., & Kahri, M. (2011). Puheäänen musiikilliset piirteet ja sosiaalinen toiminta. [Social action and the musical aspects of speech.]. *Sosiologia*, *48*, 1–24.

Stevanovic, M., Tuhkanen, S., Järvensivu, M., Koskinen, E., Lindholm, C., Paananen, J., Savander, E., Valkeapää, T., & Valkia, K. (2022). Making food decisions together: Physiological and affective underpinnings of relinquishing preferences and reaching decisions. *SAGE Open*. https://doi.org/10.1177/21582440221078010

Stevanovic, M., Tuhkanen, S., Järvensivu, M., Koskinen, E., Savander, E., & Valkia, K. (2021). Physiological responses to proposals during dyadic decision-making conversations. *PLOS One*, *16*(1), e0244929. https://doi.org/10.1371/journal.pone.0244929

Stevanovic, M., Valkeapää, T., Weiste, E., & Lindholm, C. (2020). Joint decision making in a mental health rehabilitation community: The impact of support workers' proposal design on client responsiveness. *Counselling Psychology Quarterly*. https://doi.org/10.1080/09515070.2020.1762166

Stivers, T. (2015). Coding social interaction: A heretical approach in conversation analysis? *Research on Language and Social Interaction*, *48*(1), 1–19. https://doi.org/10.1080/08351813.2015.993837

Svennevig, J., & Skovholt, K. (2005). The methodology of conversation analysis – Positivism or social constructivism? Paper presented at the 9th International Pragmatics Conference, July 10–15, 2005.

ten Have, P. (2007 [1999]). *Doing conversation analysis: A practical guide*. Sage.

Torreira, F., Bögels, S., & Levinson, S. C. (2015). Breathing for answering: The time course of response planning in conversation. *Frontiers in Psychology*, *6*, 284. https://doi.org/10.3389/fpsyg.2015.00284

Valdesolo, P., & DeSteno, D. (2011). Synchrony and the social tuning of compassion. *Emotion*, *11*(2), 262–266. https://doi.org/10.1037/a0021302

Voutilainen, L., Henttonen, P., Kahri, M., Ravaja, N., Sams, M., & Peräkylä, A. (2014). Affective stance, ambivalence, and psychophysiology. *Journal of Pragmatics*, *68*, 1–24. https://doi.org/10.1016/j.pragma.2014.04.006

Voutilainen, L., Henttonen, P., Kahri, M., Ravaja, N., Sams, M., & Peräkylä, A. (2018a). Empathy, challenge, and psychophysiological activation in therapist–client interaction. *Frontiers in Psychology*, *9*, 530. https://doi.org/10.3389/fpsyg.2018.00530

Voutilainen, L., Henttonen, P., Stevanovic, M., Kahri, M., & Peräkylä, A. (2018b). Nods, vocal continuers, and the perception of empathy in storytelling. *Discourse Processes*, *56*(4), 310–330. https://doi.org/10.1080/0163853X.2018.1498670

Watson, R. (2000). The character of institutional talk: A response to Hester and Francis. *Text and Talk*, *20*(3), 377–389. https://doi.org/10.1515/text.1.2000.20.3.377

Wetherell, M. (1998). Positioning and interpretative repertoires: Conversation analysis and post-structuralism in dialogue. *Discourse and Society*, *9*(3), 387–412. https://doi.org/10.1177/0957926598009003005

Wiggins, S. (2017). *Discursive psychology: Theory, method, and applications*. Sage.

Wiltermuth, S. S., & Heath, C. (2009). Synchrony and cooperation. *Psychological Science*, *20*(1), 1–5. https://doi.org/10.1111/j.1467-9280.2008.02253.x

Wowk, M. T. (2007). Kitzinger's feminist conversation analysis: Critical observations. *Human Studies*, *30*(2), 131–155. https://doi.org/10.1007/s10746-007-9051-z

Zivotofsky, A. Z., & Hausdorff, J. M. (2007). The sensory feedback mechanisms enabling couples to walk synchronously: An initial investigation. *Journal of NeuroEngineering and Rehabilitation*, *4*, 28. https://doi.org/10.1186/1743-0003-4-28

PART 4

Enhancing transparency of analytical processes

11

BEYOND VIDEO

Using practice-based VolCap analysis to understand analytical practices volumetrically

Paul McIlvenny and Jacob Davidsen

Introduction

In this chapter, we propose a general approach we call *practice-based volumetric capture analysis* (PBVCA) that uses Virtual Reality (VR) technology to better understand and support the practices by which scholars collaborate over time to develop an analysis of a complex event recorded with multiple cameras. What is novel in this approach is the virtualisation of two sets of practices, namely (a) the viewing and manipulation of mediated representations of complex time-based audio-visual data, and (b) the *ethno-scenography* of analytical performances of observation, demonstration, and analysis.[1] To virtualise both, we combine a powerful digital tool (AVA360VR) for immersion within a virtual spatial environment and another tool (VolCap) to capture and re-enact live actions *volumetrically*. This chapter explores the practices in which these digital tools and virtualisations come to make sense for the participants (for us as analysts) as they work towards an analysis of socio-interactional phenomena. We also consider if the "heuristic handicap" of collaboratively working with the digital tools entails a methodological bonus or are these tools mere supplements, conveniences, or distractions, from the perspective of ethnomethodology (EM) and ethnomethodological conversation analysis (EMCA).

Beyond video in EM and EMCA

Before we turn to our methodological and analytical practices, we first situate this chapter within the literature on audiovisual data, technologies, and methods in EM and EMCA.

DOI: 10.4324/9781003424888-15

Ethnomethodology, audiovisuality and method

Even though Garfinkel (2002) affirmed that "audio-visual documents are premier resources", most EM analysis usually involves a researcher-member who engages in the topicalised practice to reveal how it is methodically accomplished. Eisenmann and Lynch (2021, p. 14) contend that "Garfinkel's field is a field of embodied actions, in the thickness of lived space and time, populated by things, irreducibly intersubjective, infused with language, inhabited by the presence and absence of other beings." Studying members' ethno-methods using audio-visual documents should *not only* be restricted to the careful analysis of talk-centred transcripts; we also need to develop practices and tools that allow us to study this "field", that get at other dimensions of the *thickness* of lived space and time, such as volumetricity. Even more importantly, we need to find ways of showing how we as researchers make sense of this "field" and to document more immersively how we "work with the data". Watson (1999, p. 57) warns that unreflective studies of a video-based data corpus

> might seduce one into thinking that they are, de facto, more sensitive to inter-subjectively-based interaction than are projects based on other forms of data. In fact, unless the conceptual approach that informs this video-based analysis adopts a coherent alignment towards members' *in situ, in vivo*, intersubjectively-based practices, video-data only operates as part of the theory, corroboratively reproducing any incoherences the theory itself espouses.

A corollary is that the affordances of new technologies should, in fact, highlight and remind us of the analytical mentality of EM, so we are not just blindly adopting technologies in our analytical work. For instance, Smith (2020) highlights the methodological troubles that can occur when attempting to analyse the collaborative and praxiological accomplishment of perception-in-action, such as interpretations of the saliency of phenomena shown in video recordings, by addressing both members' and researcher-as-member's orientations. He hints at the need for a focus on varieties of "instructed viewing" within and as professional and lay practices.

EMCA and the praxeology of "doing analysis"

In contrast to most (conceptual) EM studies, EMCA relies heavily on audio-visual resources to gain empirical access to human sense-making practices. While the use of audio-visual data is widespread, only a few attempts have been made to make visible, or reflexively supplement, the practice of recording video data (Mondada, 2019) and doing an EMCA analysis. For example, there are several studies of the social interactional practices of learning and sharing how to do research as researchers while participating in the "data session" genre (Antaki et al., 2008). In their analysis of the complementary professional visions of conversation analysts doing video-based "microanalysis", Katila and Raudaskoski (2020) argue that their co-produced practices of analytical sense-making are embodied and locally managed. In a sophisticated, but technologically dated, reflection on the "hidden" work of doing conversation analysis based on a tape recording of an event, Ashmore and Reed (2000) present a reflexive account of the complex cycles of hearing versus listening and reading versus seeing that take us back and forth from recording an event through working on a transcript, to doing an analysis, which ends up in a publication.

Practice-based video analysis (PBVA)

Suggesting a different direction, Sormani (2014) has experimented with using video itself as a methodological probe in EM studies of scientific work. He talks about video recording a scientific experiment (and its failures) in order to learn how the experiment was constructed and achieved by re-enacting it and filming that re-enactment. In his respecification of a lab ethnography, Sormani (2014) describes in detail his *three*-step practice-based video analysis. To paraphrase the steps involved:

1. Video recording (A) the task undertaken by the scientist or trainee
2. Video recording (B) of the re-enactment of the task at hand (by the analyst) based on experience in the lab and replaying the first video recording (A)
3. A detailed reconsideration of both video clips (A and B) to recover the missing practices that EMCA and EM "two-step" methods elide

The (point-of-view) video recording (B) serves as both a "heuristic handicap" to disclose some of the disjunctions in the practices of the practitioner and those of the analyst/novice, and as a documentation for presentational purposes later. Sormani (2016, p. 103) notes that "'practice-based video analysis', then, stands for an ethnomethodological approach that makes explicit the analyst's practical experience in the technical practice that his or her video analysis bears upon".

Sormani's PBVA approach could also be re-characterised as practice-based *re-enactive* analysis because the "video" in PBVA is only one of many technologies that could pose as the spur to re-enact the topicalised practice for the approach to work. Alternatively, we could characterise this as PBXA, where X is any suitable representational technology (e.g., motion capture, eye-tracking, volumetric capture). The key is that although video per se serves as an instructive documentation on the basis of which re-enactment (Tutt & Hindmarsh, 2011) can be staged (and productively fail), it is not the only possible source (X) for re-enacting the practice. It is the re-enactment, via a reactivation, that counts, not video per se.[2]

Volumetric capture and virtual collaborative practices

One important question that arises in this chapter is whether or not (and how) EMCA methods can be enhanced by novel practices using new technologies and software, such as 360-degree cameras or VR. Indeed, there are new ways of collecting audio-visual data that need *digital tools* to be developed to support *immersive qualitative analysis* of that data. Those tools should support a richer method of archiving the embodied business of doing analysis for the purposes of aiding critical reflection in the future. *AVA360VR* (Annotate, Visualise, Analyse 360 Video in VR) is a Windows-based software package that we developed to support the analysis of complex video archives consisting of synchronised 360-degree video (see Raudaskoski, this volume), 2D video, and spatial audio recordings in an immersive virtual environment.[3] It offers a range of tools affording sophisticated re-visualisations and annotations of simultaneous video and audio streams (McIlvenny, 2018). Most importantly for this chapter, it also supports the volumetric capture (*VolCap*) of an analyst's use of the tool for performative immersive *RePlay* at a later date (McIlvenny, 2020b).[4] This is a unique feature built into *AVA360VR* for the express purpose of asynchronously collaborating spatially with others. Later, we document how we used the software package *AVA360VR* to share and expand our emerging analyses of social, embodied, and spatial interaction. Below we summarise the aims of, and support for, volumetric capture with software in VR, which *AVA360VR* implements within its own interactive scenography.

Volumetric capture describes a set of tools that attempt to capture the complete volume in which physical or virtual events take place, so that they can be reconstructed from any spectator standpoint in the scene in terms of visual and/or aural events. Besides the implementations of some form of capture in video games (e.g., Machinima), early scholarly approaches to capture and replay of computer-supported activity can be found in pioneering systems such as *Digital Replay System* (DRS) (Crabtree et al., 2015). VolCap in *AVA360VR* is our implementation of the volumetric capture of an analyst (in our case, an EMCA researcher using the virtual tools to construct an analysis) in VR, so that the event of analysis can be reconstructed and *RePlayed* (reactivated) immersively from any position in the scene captured. This includes the voice of the analyst, as well as the tracked head and hand movements logged by the VR headset and controllers. When a VolCap is RePlayed at a later point, the RePlayer should experience immersively what the original analyst (VolCapper) was doing virtually in three-dimensions with six-degrees-of-freedom. Hence, RePlay is *not* a passive spectatorial experience, such as going to the cinema or watching a video clip.[5]

Practice-based VolCap analysis

VolCap supports the notion that an archive can be created of "all" the virtual events that take place while using *AVA360VR* such that the archive can be used at a later date to reactivate the performance of the virtual events *as if* they were taking place "exactly" as they did in the "original" event. As RePlayers and practical analysts, we have to find sense in what the VolCapper is doing. Indeed, our experience of RePlaying VolCaps, with the incipient troubles one has to follow talk and action, make clear some aspects of the missing "whatness" of the bodies of practices in the virtual (Kovács & McIlvenny, 2020).

In regard to the method of practice-based video analysis (PBVA), VolCapping was not available to Sormani, but we can still entertain the possibility that a candidate for the X in PBXA is volumetric capture (e.g., VolCap), but with added complexity. In *our* version of PBVCA, which we call "practice-based VolCap analysis", there are four basic steps:

1. VolCapping the task undertaken by an analyst or trainee in *AVA360VR*, who is analysing video recordings of an event
2. (Videoing) Reactivations (RePlays) of the VolCap by the meta-analyst (who is studying the analyst or trainee) in *AVA360VR*
3. VolCapping re-enactments of the analysis task-at-hand by the meta-analyst in *AVA360VR*
4. A detailed reconsideration of the original VolCap (step 1), with the supplement that a *practice-based* reactivation and re-enactment give that a one-time through video withholds

In Figure 11.1, the complex relationship between the embedded layers of PBVCA is shown. On the left is indicated the relationship between the original event, the recording of the event, and the VolCap of the ongoing analysis of the event via the recording (step 1). On the right, that VolCap becomes fodder for the meta-analyst to reactivate and re-enact the analysis-at-hand (steps 2–3). Step 4 involves reflecting from the perspective of the right side as a "heuristic handicap" to uncover the "missing whatness" of the ongoing analysis on the left side. Indeed, each VolCap is "another next first time" with the data, which is also evident in any reactivation of the VolCap.[6] It is in the re-enactments of the analysis in the RePlays of VolCaps (steps 2–3) that the "missing whatness" is recoverable, *not in the VolCaps*

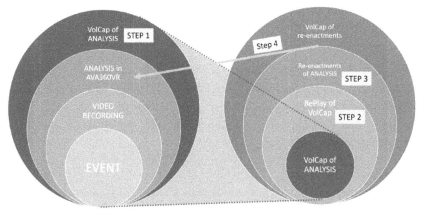

FIGURE 11.1   Diagram showing four steps of PBVCA

themselves. Rather than just watching the recorded analysis, the meta-analyst can re-enact the analysis and pose alternative analyses as an embodied experience. Moreover, with two analysts sharing VolCaps, then PBVCA becomes collaborative and incremental.

The interactional scenography of a VolCap

Within professional practices, video has a clear role as an instructional medium (Evans & Lindwall, 2020; Johansson et al., 2017). There are also a small number of studies of instructed action in 2D YouTube videos that focus on, for example, the practical use of the video player while following the instructions, such as pausing, for a variety of practical purposes (Heinemann & Möller, 2016; Tuncer et al., 2020). However, in these studies, there is understandably little concern with the scenography of such 2D videos on their own terms, let alone within the setting in which it is placed. Traditionally, scenography is concerned with the *mise-en-scène*, the staging of a theatrical performance, such as lighting, props, theatre space, and costumes. Indeed, there is a scenographic element to every VolCap that is staged for a future RePlayer to inhabit. This is constituted not only in and through the body and talk of the analyst, but also with the assemblage of the user interface tools and video/audio objects for an instructed viewing in a re-enactment. Rather than the VolCapper constructing the scenography of action for a static or mobile 2D camera (viewer), the scenography is for an embodied other (a RePlayer) who "inhabits the same virtual space" for all practical purposes, but in the future. However, VolCaps are not only scenographic, they are also interactable. The RePlayer can also interact with the tools and the VR interface during the RePlay because the RePlay is reactivating the same 3D tools as used in the original. Thus, VolCaps provide a perspicuous setting for insights into embodied, scenographic practices.[7] They help reveal the work of sense-making that the embodied eyes do, even in virtual 3D space, with the achievement of bodies of practices, namely that "these bodies have eyes that are skills; eyes that are skills in the ways that eyes do looking's work" (Garfinkel, 2002, p. 210).

Data

In this section, we give some information on our video data collected in a specific setting, as well as our recording practices to document the event in question. We also outline how we captured and archived VolCaps and RePlays of researchers analysing this video data using *AVA360VR*.[8]

Arch1 data

The *Arch 1* data stems from a large archive of recordings following architecture and design students as they make physical models of their designs. It was recorded

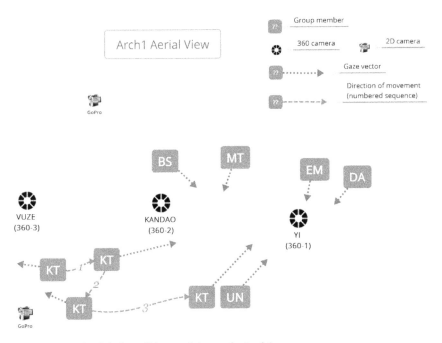

FIGURE 11.2   Aerial plan of the participants in Arch1

with three different 360-degree cameras and two GoPro 2D cameras positioned statically at different locations in the workshop area (see Figure 11.2).

The student group consists of six members, who are working in a distributed manner on different smaller parts of their shared presentation. They are working together in clusters (e.g., EM/DA, BS/MT and UN/KT) to put together the physical materials into three different versions of their design. In Figure 11.2, an aerial view shows the location of the group members, their gaze direction, and the movements of KT, as well as the positions of the relevant cameras. In Figure 11.3, the talk and embodied actions of the main participants in Arch1, which feature predominantly in all our VolCaps, are represented much simplified in a comic panel sequence (see Laurier & Back, this volume). The panels contain images from the anonymised original video recordings of the event (e.g., shots from 360-1, 360-2, and GoPro-2).

In the nine-panel comic transcript, the key participants and actions are shown. In panels 1–3, we see EM and DA engage with UN about their newly discovered problem, while KT works at the other side of the room. In panel 4, UN responds to the report of the problem, after which KT turns around and responds verbally in panel 5. In panel 6, UN turns to look at KT while BS turns to glance at KT in panel 7. In panel 8, KT starts to move towards UN and arrives next to UN in panel 9.

The phenomenon that is the locus of the researcher's analytical attention with respect to the original event described above is what we might call a "huddle",

FIGURE 11.3 Comic panel sequence for short excerpt from Arch1

namely an unplanned, temporary assembly of a smaller group or cluster from a larger group who are engaged in some distributed, collaborative work practice (Goffman, 1963, p. 95). However, in this chapter we only document how our approach to PBVCA shaped how we discovered, shared, modified, and contested a proto-analysis in VR of the practices of coming together in a "huddle".

VolCaps as data

For us as qualitative analysts, VolCapping has become an important tool to demonstrate an observation or an analysis in the act of doing an observation or analysis. We do that analysis using the range of tools offered by *AVA360VR* within the 3D space in which the original recorded data is inhabited spatially. However, VolCaps are data of a different order than legacy video recordings, such as Arch1. A VolCap is a camera/spectator-independent representation, and the actual capture files are primarily time-based primitives in code that are only renderable in 3D by the original object-oriented software. Thus, the VR software is also an essential part of the archive. The consequence of this is that there is *not* a camera-dependent, flat, 2D, pixel-based, hard-coded representation present in the VolCap archive (McIlvenny, 2020b). Nevertheless, for those without access to the VR software, we are obliged to make a 2D video rendering of the RePlay for readers to be able to easily view and hear a unique rendering of the VolCap on their desktop computer. The reader should not assume that the video clips rendered from the RePlays can substitute for the VolCaps themselves. They are a pale imitation of the immersive experience of *AVA360VR* in virtual reality.

In Figure 11.4, the basic elements of a RePlay are shown in a 3-D representation.

The original VolCapper (J) is represented virtually by an avatar head (blue) and the RePlayer (P) by another avatar head (green). The VR controllers that the VolCapper uses are also visible; see the inset decontextualised image in which the right controller has a raycast (blue line) used by J for pointing, selecting, and moving. J and P are present virtually in three-dimensional space, but not co-present temporally. The current master 360-degree video (360-1) is projected onto a sphere around them, and they are at the centre of that sphere. The VolCapper and RePlayer are both looking in the direction of one of the student clusters (EM/DA) on the 360-degree video. The *AVA360VR* tools (e.g., Timeline) appear in 3-D close to their virtual embodiments.

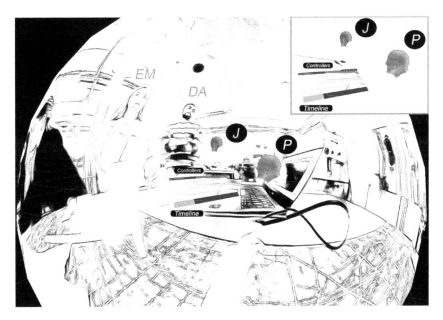

FIGURE 11.4   A rendering of a VolCap RePlay scene in VR

The RePlayer is currently positioned behind the VolCapper but can teleport to any position on a horizontal plane. The RePlayer can record the view from a selection of virtual cameras simultaneously, such as the VolCapper's and the RePlayer's viewports (see the figures in Example 2 that show the two viewports side-by-side).[9]

Some readers may ask why we did not just use a standard video camera to record the EMCA analysts together in the same room analysing the event recorded above on a 2D display. That would have been easier, but it would have missed the volumetric phenomena that we analyse below. Because we capture volumetrically the work of analysing video recordings in VR, we can repeatedly revisit those practices *volumetrically*. Alternatively, we would have loved to capture volumetrically co-present analysts at work, but this is not yet technically feasible in *natural* settings. We did record ourselves using a live collaborative prototype of *AVA360VR* that allowed us to annotate, visualise, and analyse the data in VR simultaneously, but it is *not* yet possible to do a VolCap of that scenario for later analysis in RePlay. Note that we are *not* claiming that the analysis using VolCaps *in VR* is equivalent to (or a proxy for) *co-present* analytical work; both are legitimate analytical practices.

With several cases of VolCap and one case of RePlay, we illustrate some aspects of our analytical "workflow" as we pursue an analysis of how "huddles" are socially accomplished in our Arch1 data.

1. *Arch1-RePlay1* – a recording of a specific RePlay by Paul of a VolCap created by Jacob concerning his observations on Arch1.
2. *Arch1-VolCap2* to *VolCap5* – a series of VolCaps by Paul and Jacob that cumulatively reactivate and respond to prior VolCaps concerning an emerging proto-analysis of Arch1.

Notes on Transcripts

In this chapter, we use a specific set of multimodal transcription conventions.[10] Our modifications include an action sub-tier type naming system for explicitness, as well as a transcoding of numbered time intervals into strings made up of symbols (each representing 0.1 second, e.g. ▫▫▫▫ = 0.4) to better show visually the passing of time in a manner that is comparable to the graphemic representation of the temporal stream of speech.[11] The shaded boxes in the transcripts indicate the talk and actions *in the video recording* of the students at work (Arch1), whereas the non-shaded sections are related to the talk and actions of the VolCapper and Replayer *in VR*.[12]

Analysis

The analysis that follows focuses on a *practice-based VolCap analysis* (PBVCA) of our own collaborative practices of assembling tangible observations and proto-analyses of complex data. This involves inspecting the digital traces of our working practices in the acts of documenting, archiving, observing, and analysing that VolCapping facilitates (mainly the right side of Figure 11.1).

Analysis of Arch1-RePlay1

The first case we explore is a specific segment (12:45–15:53) of a rendering of a RePlay by Paul (P) of a VolCap created by Jacob (J) in May 2021. The source VolCap that is RePlayed is identical to Arch1-VolCap5 that is analysed later in this chapter, though the segment of the VolCap that is RePlayed here is 8:04–9:16. J is observing the scene of the recorded event from the perspective of the 360-degree camera (360-2) in the middle of the room (see Figure 11.2). It is possible for J to see KT, UN, and BS, but a large foam block on the table in the middle of the room is obstructing J's view of EM, DA, and MT.

In Example 1, we see how J provides an instructed viewing *and* hearing for a future RePlayer (the RePlayer in this case is P).

Example 1 – Instructed viewing and hearing.

```
 6 BS:        &{begyn mæ at sæt          }{↑sidderne på}
              begin with putting          the sides on
 7 DA:        {>ja det har de da godt nok<}
              yeah they really have been
 8 J:                                   {when she is } &orienting
    P/view:   -->&.................................................&KT-->

 9 BS:        {{eller } hva gør jeg}
              or what do i do
10 UN:        {hva så}
              what's
11 J:         {{orient}ing        } towards the group

12 UN:        hvad har i gjort
              what have you done

13 MT:        %{prøv at spørg} de andre%
              try to ask the others
14 J:           {and she says }
    J/view:   -->%......................%TML-->

15 EM:        {[>det er det vi %ikke ] ved<}
              that is what we do not know
16 DA:        [de er bar for  %korte]
              they are just too short
17 J:         {is it            }& an%{noy}ing,
18 BS:                             %{hva}
                                    what
    J/view:              -->%...............%TRN-->
    P/view:                 -->&..J-->
```

VolCappers are continually faced with giving accounts for their past, present, and future actions and observations in relation to the video data that is presented scenographically and temporally in *AVA360VR*. In this case, J has already started playing the 360-degree video and gives a running commentary that anticipates what KT will do and say next. He is orienting to what a RePlayer must attend to in order to observe the same phenomenal details of an unfolding action – an *instructed viewing* for a future RePlayer. In a delicate dance with the recalcitrant video playback, J says "when she is orienting orienting towards the group and she says is it annoying" (lines 8, 11, 14 and 17). However, in the viewable playback so far, KT has neither turned to orient to the group nor spoken. Therefore, we can see and hear that J's embodied talk and action is *prospectively oriented to a known, but not yet shared, seeable and hearable whose occurrence and course of action are unfolding.* During this example, P shifts gaze to KT (line 8) and then back to J (line 18).

Often when RePlaying a VolCap, it becomes difficult to follow the pace of the VolCapper's reorientations – such as pointing, glancing, and checking – in 360-degrees. This is a practical problem facing a RePlayer who is trying to follow a VolCapper, which is exacerbated by spatial positioning. Hence, with the PBVCA method, we can enquire into how the *immersive practices* of using *AVA360VR* and VolCapping reshapes how the RePlayer comes to see a spatial referent (in the 360-degree video) in common with the VolCapper. Moreover, we can experience this phenomenon for ourselves by RePlaying the VolCap, an embodied experience of a practice that is *not* available with a *video recording* of a RePlaying of a VolCap, nor in a *video recording* of someone trying to follow an analysis by someone else. In the examples above, and below, both the VolCapper and Replayer accomplish the scenic and sonic intelligibility of action in 360-degrees volumetrically.

In Example 2, we see a more complex case of the practical work of following an instructed viewing.

Example 2 – Following BS or the mirror cam.

```
30 J:            %■■■ a:nd #if we% look ■■■
   J/view:    -->%..............%BS-->
                         #fig1

     fig1

31 J:            &maybe we %should %just&
   J/view:            -->%.......%TRN-->
   P/view:    -->&....................&-->

32 J:            @pull up& the #mirror @cam &act@ually&
   J/CLeft:   @CREA---------------@FILE----@TIME-->
   P/view:        -->&BS----------------&.........&J-->
                         #fig2

     fig2

33          ■■■■■■■■■■■@■■■■■■■■■■■@■■■■■@
   J/CLeft:        -->@FILE------@CAMR-@

34          %&£■■■■■  £■■■■■■■■■■■■■■■■■■■■■■■■■■■£
   J/CRight:     £SEL/MCAMEGrip.Move-----------------£
   J/view:   -->%MCAM-->
   P/view:   -->&MCAM-->

35 J:            ah that's going to £be: pre:tty:£:
   J/CRight:          £Zoom........£
```

In the unfolding instructed viewing of an observation, J glances at BS (line 30; see J's viewport in the left frame of #fig1) in the 360-degree video as he says "and if we look", but in lines 31–32 he pivots back to the direction of KT and the 3D tools (see J's viewport in the left frame of #fig2) to begin to load the mirror cam tool using his left controller (CLeft).[13] However, when J glances at BS, P is still looking at KT (see P's viewport in the right frame of #fig1). Then, as J indicates a better solution to an as of yet undeclared task-at-hand (line 32), P belatedly turns to gaze at BS (see P's viewport in the right frame of #fig2), which means he no longer sees J's avatar (nor KT) in the scene. J searches for the right tool on the controller menus (lines 32–34), saying "pull up the mirror cam". As he is searching, P turns back to look at J (the end of line 32). As the tool window appears visually in the 3D scene, J and P both look towards the window. For J, the gaze shifts are part of the search for the ongoing inspectability of the immersive image for its recognisability as a snapshot of the unfolding action in a sequence involving KT and BS. For P, it is to find the intelligibility of the instructed viewing by J in progress.

An *instructed viewing* is finally accomplished, but for what purpose? On lines 34–35, J repositions and zooms the mirror cam to feature BS in the window while he is looking at KT, and then he goes on to lock the mirror cam so that the view remains unchanged no matter where it is moved. This is part of the *progressive and emerging juxtaposition* by J of alternative views of the two participants in the 360-degree video, namely KT and BS, that is particular to the position of the 360-degree video camera in the unfolding scene (and not to the relative position and gaze of the two participants themselves). To accomplish this juxtaposition, at least *three correspondences* have to be accomplished by J in the course of the instructed viewing, namely, (i) that what anyone can see in the 360-degree video and in the mirror cam window are identical moments in the event, (ii) that anyone can see that the juxtaposition of the two videos side-by-side is *as if* one were simultaneously viewing the participants as recorded spherically in the 360-degree video, and (iii) that the juxtaposition of these two views has an epistemological relationship to what the spatially embodied participants themselves can see, which should be available to any competent sighted member. Given that for each of these correspondences there is a potential distortion or disruption of some expectable visual order (scenic intelligibility), then work has to be done to elide those or pass over them for-all-practical-purposes. For instance, in regard to (ii), the juxtaposition of KT and BS by J results in temporal parity but spatial discontinuity because KT's and BS's gaze vectors are no longer in the same contiguous space. What is beginning to emerge in the proto-analysis by J in this VolCap is an interest in recipiency in relation to whether or not KT first orients to the troubles-talk of BS and MT. That is, although BS and UN turn to look towards KT almost in synchrony, BS's glance is not reciprocated, and then KT is moving towards UN (see Example 3 for what happens at the end of the sequence). This phenomenon is only available through the embodied practices to accomplish the instructed viewing of *apposite alternative perspectives* on the 360-degree video.

In *AVA360VR* generally, and when making a VolCap, the analyst is always roughly at the centre of the 360-degree video sphere (see Figure 11.4), but in a VolCap Replay, the RePlayer can teleport to any point on a horizontal plane within a large circular region around the VolCapper. The 360-degree video appears the same for all practical purposes, but the tools and windows as well as the VolCapper's avatar are always relative. In Example 3, P is currently positioned behind and to the left of J, with the tools opened by J reasonably visible to P.

Example 3 – Repositioning to achieve co-viewing.

```
40 J:           we can se£e:
   J/CRight:         -->£

41 KT:          #&█£§@det jer    & ‡(em$#ma)§█   $‡
                     it  you       (emma)
   KT/gaze:     -->§,,,,,,,,,,,,,,,,,,,,,,,,,,§
   KT/body:         @turns away-->
   KT/hand:                       ‡drop.foam----‡
   J/CRight:        £PLY-->
   P/view:      -->&glance down-up&
   P/CRight:                         $teleport$
                #fig1                 #fig2
```

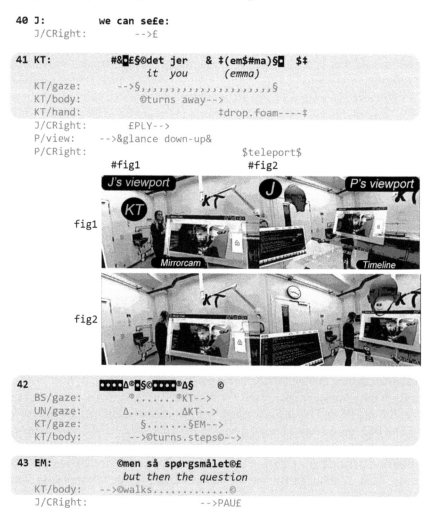

```
42              ■■■■Δ®█§@■■■■®Δ§    @
   BS/gaze:         ®........®KT-->
   UN/gaze:         Δ.........ΔKT-->
   KT/gaze:         §.......§EM-->
   KT/body:         -->@turns.steps@-->

43 EM:          @men så spørgsmålet@£
                but then the question
   KT/body:     -->@walks............@
   J/CRight:                   -->PAU£
```

In the course of his instructed viewing, J has primed the seeability of some phenomenal detail which is as yet unspecified: "we can see" (line 40). Just prior, J adjusted the mirror cam and then repositioned the window slightly to the left so that KT is no longer occluded from his point of view (see J's viewport in the left frame of #fig1). Unbeknownst to J, who made the VolCap in the past relative to P, this causes an occlusion problem in the RePlay for P *now*. The repositioning of the mirror cam by J results in P no longer being able to see KT on the 360-degree video (see P's viewport in the right frame of #fig1). As P glances down (to his controller?) in line 41, J restarts playback of the 360-degree video from his vantage point. P then teleports to a position almost directly behind J to see from the same angle as J sees the scene unfolding with KT visible again (see P's viewport in the right frame of #fig2). P has achieved a co-viewing (in lines 42–43) of what transpires to be a demonstration by J using the mirror cam of BS's non-reciprocated glance at KT (see gaze shifts by BS, UN and KT on line 42) after her question.

Analysis of Arch1-VolCaps

With the help of four interconnected VolCaps (Arch1-VolCap2 to VolCap5), the initial analysis was developed by the authors (P and J) of how KT comes to notice, and announce her noticing, of trouble resulting from the public work of EM and DA (see Figure 11.3). To reach this stage of proto-analysis, P and J have iteratively and collaboratively developed a set of observations of the event through re-activating each other's VolCap. Each VolCap is a new capture by J or P created after RePlaying prior VolCaps.

Arch1-VolCap2

In Example 4 from Arch1-VolCap2, while creating the VolCap in *AVA360VR*, J is observing the scene of the recorded event from the location of the 360-1 camera on the table near the cluster EM and DA (see Figure 11.2).

Example 4 – Scanning for a phenomenon.

```
1                    ▣▣£
  J/CRight:     £PLY-->

2 UN:          °uh: o[h::°          ]
               °uh oh::°

3 KT:              [irriterer §©det] jer ‡(emma)§▣ ‡
                    does it irritate you   (emma)
  KT/gaze:                 -->§,,,,,,,,,,,,,,,,,§
  KT/body:                     ©turns away-->
  KT/hand:                               ‡drop.foam‡

4                    ▣▣£
  J/CRight:     -->PAU£

5                  ▣▣▣▣▣£
  J/CRight:     £PLY-->

6 J:           she'sΔ actuallyΔ§©£ putting something back on the table
  UN/gaze:          Δ.........ΔKT-->>
  KT/gaze:                   §..EM-->>
  KT/body:              -->©turns towards main table-->
  J/CRight:         -->PAU£

7 J:           oh and £then
  J/CRight:         £PLY-->

8 EM:          ©{ så må vi bar skær dem her til så }{den sidder der   }©£
                  the we just cut the them here like this one here

9 MT:                                             {det der er væggen}
                                                   that is the wall

10 J:              {she's walking to the main table    }
   KT/body:    -->©walks towards UN---------------------------------------©
   J/CRight:                                                 -->PAU£

11 J:          ·KFFUH so %▣▣▣▣▣ my analysis here is %▣▣ %is m- %▣▣i- i start to think that
   J/view:         -->%KT---------------------%.MT%......%KT-->

12 J:          %s'first% ▣▣ she is concerned with er bee ess and kay er: and em tee
   J/view:     -->%.......%MT+BS-->

13 J:          %and then %while she's standing there in the £middle of the er room
   J/view:     -->%.........%KT-->>
   J/CRight:                                                 £REWIND-->
```

From this camera position, it is possible for J to see everyone except BS because a large foam block on the table in the middle of the room is obstructing the camera's view. J focuses on the troubles identified by the cluster BS and MT and suggests that KT is also searching for what their trouble might be (lines 11–12). In earlier research, not in this chapter, we primarily analysed how the cluster EM and DA tried to solve their problem, but we did not focus on the cluster BS and MT. Both clusters at the table are experiencing troubles with their task at hand, and they are hearably stating that they are experiencing troubles. In this VolCap, J plays the "uh oh" sequence and provides a running commentary. Just after KT finishes her turn (line 3), J pauses the video to mark this sequence as an observable. Then J plays a little more while commenting on what KT is doing (lines 6–7). There is a sense of surprise ("oh") in the way that J is commenting on the interaction (e.g., "she's actually putting something back on the table oh and then" on lines 6–7) to do with a noticing in the video as it was replaying. J is *scanning for visible evidence of a phenomenon* in the playback that the VolCap documents. J continues playback and observes that KT is walking to the main table (line 10). J pauses the video, and makes a claim that KT is at first concerned with what the cluster BS and EM are saying and then shifts to another focus while standing in the middle of the room (lines 11–13). This claim in J's VolCap2 is what P's argument in VolCap3 below focuses on (made after P has RePlayed J's VolCap2).

Arch1-VolCap3

In Example 5, P makes a new VolCap to provide a counter-observation to J's claim in VolCap2 above using the different 360-degree views afforded by the locations of the 360-1 and 360-2 cameras that recorded the Arch1 event.

Example 5 – Zooming in on what bodies do.

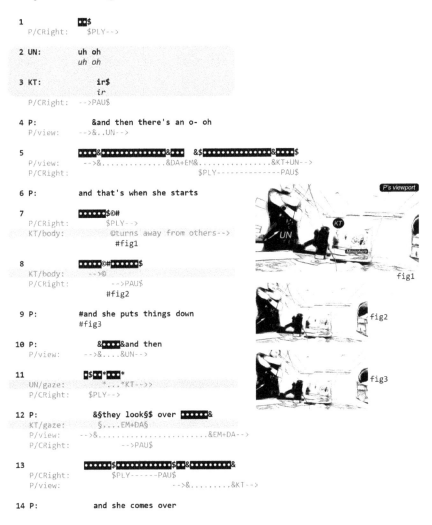

```
1              ■■$
   P/CRight:   $PLY-->

2 UN:          uh oh
               uh oh

3 KT:            ir$
                 ir
   P/CRight:   -->PAU$

4 P:             &and then there's an o- oh
   P/view:     -->&..UN-->

5              ■■■■&■■■■■■■■■■■■■■&■■■   &$■■■■■■■■■■■■■■■&■■■■$
   P/view:     -->&.............&DA+EM&..............&KT+UN-->
   P/CRight:                          $PLY-------------PAU$

6 P:           and that's when she starts

7              ■■■■■■$@#
   P/CRight:   $PLY-->
   KT/body:    @turns away from others-->
              #fig1

8              ■■■■■@#■■■■■■$
   KT/body:    -->@
   P/CRight:   -->PAU$
              #fig2

9 P:           #and she puts things down
               #fig3

10 P:             &■■■■&and then
   P/view:     -->&....&UN-->

11             ■$■■*■■■*
   UN/gaze:       *...*KT-->>
   P/CRight:   $PLY-->

12 P:             &§they look§$ over ■■■■■■&
   KT/gaze:       §....EM+DA§
   P/view:     -->&.....................&EM+DA-->
   P/CRight:                 -->PAU$

13             ■■■■■$■■■■■■■■■■$■■&■■■■■■■■■&
   P/CRight:   $PLY------PAU$
   P/view:                   -->&.........&KT-->

14 P:          and she comes over
```

fig1

fig2

fig3

P's viewport

KT

UN

Minisphere

P's counterpoint is to show that KT is establishing a sightline to EM and DA, and that she is not looking at what BS and MT are doing, which is J's initial claim above. The repeated use of play and pause by P in lines 1–3, 5, 7, 8, 11, 12 and 13 fragments the scene and renders it intelligible in a new way that contrasts with VolCap2. One result is that it is not possible to hear in situ what KT is saying clearly (heard on line 3 in Example 5). Nevertheless, in playing and pausing the 360-degree video, the *phenomenal details of "bodies in practices"* become the primary observables for P. P notes the "uh oh" (line 2) to begin his analysis of how KT is positioning her body spatially to establish a sightline to EM and DA. Then, while incrementally playing small snippets of the video, P conjoins a running commentary on what the embodied participants (see #fig1, #fig2, and #fig3) have just done in the prior snippet, e.g., "and that's when she starts" (line 6), "and she puts things down" (line 9), "and she comes over" (line 14), etc. The commentary does not include a reference to the cluster BS and MT. Instead, for P, it is UN's "uh oh" that leads to KT turning and then walking over to UN. By repeatedly turning to look at the cluster EM and DA (lines 5 and 12), P visibly orients to that cluster (and not BS and MT) as the action source that UN and KT are both responding to.

Unlike in VolCap2, P is not doing a play-through of the complete 'uh oh' sequence. Instead, P is narrating the analysis and adding relevant contextual details for the observation-at-hand that are not present in the play-through of the video. Also, in this VolCap, the analytical focus has shifted to the bodily positioning of KT in relation to EM and DA. While the observation by J in VolCap2 was oriented towards what KT does individually (talking and putting down foam pieces on the table), the focus in VolCap3 is directed by P towards how KT establishes with her body a participation framework that includes EM and DA.

Arch1-VolCap5

In a new VolCap4, not analysed here, J begins to integrate the counter-observation made by P in VolCap3. The final VolCap5 is also by J, and it completes the collaborative proto-analysis. In Example 6, the commentary by J is spatially conditioned by the different views of the event afforded by the 360-degree cameras (see Figure 11.2). At an earlier point in the VolCap, J transitioned from the 360-2 to the 360-1 camera view.

Example 6 – Back where we started.

```
 1 J:           %and we will just change position
   J/view:    -->%EM-->
   KT/gaze:   >>UN-->

 2             ██£██              £██████████
   J/CRight:    £Jump to 360-2£

 3 J:           %so: now we are back % where we started%
   J/view:    -->%VID-SPHERE----------%.................%KT-->

 4 J:           ·hhh and you see that em er:: kay tee is walking

 5 J:           ███% er:: %in █████
   J/view:    -->%......%UN..-->

 6 J:           %£©into the room©███████████©█████████
   J/view:    -->%KT-->
   J/CRight:    £PLY-->
   KT/body:         ©steps--------©steps-----©turns-->

 7 UN:         °uh: o[h::°          ]
               °uh oh::°

 8 KT:         [irriterer §©det] §    ©£
               does it irritate
   KT/gaze:        -->§,,,,,,§
   KT/body:        -->©turns away©
   J/CRight:            -->PAU£

 9             %██████%
   J/view:    -->%......%UN-->

10 J:          and ¤then she's ¤saying ██████████¤
   J/laser:     ¤..........¤VID-SPHERE.MOV--¤

11 J:          ¤er: does it bother you or ¤is it% annoying %you or what
   J/view:                    -->%KT........%UN-->
   J/laser:    ¤POINT.TRN----------------¤
```

When J says "we will just change position" (line 1) and transitions from the 360-1 to the 360-2 camera view, he orients to a future RePlayer who will also be automatically transported to the viewpoint of the new camera in their RePlay of this VolCap. Moreover, after the transition, he says "now we are back where we started" (line 3), orienting to the *scenic and scenographic intelligibility* of a visual sequence that is spatially located in the same scene ("back there"), yet at the current frame in the timeline (not "back then"). For J, the paused 360-degree video (line 3) provides sufficient resources for an observation to be partially formulated about the anticipated movement and interaction that is about to be re-activated shortly when playback resumes. The hesitation by J before completing the observation of the direction of movement indicates the practical ambiguity of the *static* video. It might happen now or later; it might be that she steps back or forward (at some point she does both). The precise timing and direction of the movement is only seeable once the video is playing. After playback resumes (line 6), the movement of KT is punctuated by J's syntactic addition of the complement, namely (walking) "into the room". Playback continues and the "uh oh" sequence is seen and heard in full. After the video is paused at line 8, J re-enacts the verbal interaction, prefaced by "and then she's saying" (line 10) in reference to an earlier ambiguous English translation in the already open transcript window. With VolCaps in *AVA360VR*, the source video(s) can be played and reactivated repeatedly to make bodily actions visible for a RePlayer. In this case, it is used by J to re-enact a playthrough and instructed viewing that aligns *for another next first time* with the ongoing proto-analysis from VolCap2 to VolCap4.

Conclusion

The chapter has documented the emerging analyses of a video-recorded event within practices that use the functionality of *AVA360VR*, specifically volumetric capture (VolCap) and RePlay. Using practice-based VolCap analysis (a version of PBVCA), we have discovered some of the missing phenomenal details of "bodies of practices" of "doing analysis for another member" by attempting to follow "the analysis" *volumetrically* in and as the artful production of a spatial field unfolding in RePlay. We documented the crucial role of the body and space in resolving for-all-practical-purposes the indexicality of instructed viewing, such as the practices of accomplishing co-viewing in 360-degrees, the instructed viewing of apposite alternative perspectives on the 360-degree video, and spatial repositioning to achieve co-viewing. We have also discovered some of the missing phenomena of practices of "doing analysis" by re-enacting "the analysis" by another member in and through reactivating it in RePlay, such as scanning for a phenomenon, zooming in on bodies of practices and bodily actions, and achieving the scenic and scenographic intelligibility of a visual sequence. This can only be undertaken volumetrically by reactivating and re-enacting an earlier VolCapped analysis or by viewing the RePlay and proactively redoing the analysis and creating alternative analyses by VolCap. We argue that VolCap – and the analytical possibilities afforded by taking a "scenographic turn" to video analysis (McIlvenny & Davidsen, 2017) – expands the range of abductive–inductive analytical potentials that lie between collecting data and finalising a robust analysis. We have demonstrated how the combination of VolCap and RePlay is negotiated as an analyst's resource for the performance of enhanced visual and spatial argumentation, accountable in terms of a praxeology of evidential adequacy and critical reflexivity. As an alternative to traditional EMCA data sessions, it leads to a complementary mode of performing, engaging, sharing, collaborating, and archiving with respect to mixed video data recorded at sites of social conduct.

This chapter has gone some way to determining the *contingencies* of the production of a VolCap that have to be *erased* to enable the VolCap *to act as* the "data" (with steps towards its naturalisation). We have also learnt from documenting how we come to share viewings, seeings, and hearings of audio-visual "data" within specific *interactional scenographic* practices that we need to reflect more on the relationships between (i) the original Event, (ii) the recordings of the Event, (iii) replaying audio-visual recordings of the Event, (iv) RePlaying VolCaps of the Event of analysis of the recordings of the original Event, and (v) the reflexive practices of analysis itself (see Figure 11.1). This is especially true if we are aiming to demonstrate a specific enhanced practice of working with complex data using *AVA360VR*, which is designed to support an alternative infrastructure for practice-based qualitative research *beyond* video (McIlvenny, 2020a).

In relation to the praxeology of VolCap reactivation, we can see interesting correspondences between Garfinkel's articulation of "another next first time" (Garfinkel, 2002) and (a misreading or at least an oversimplification of) Derrida's conceptual discussion of "signature event context" (Derrida, 1988). For Derrida, for a signature as an act to be authentic, for instance, it must, of necessity, be both repeatable and perceptually different on every event of its reduplication. If not, then it cannot function as a signature without the *iterability* of difference. Derrida writes: "In order to function, that is, to be readable, a signature must have a repeatable, iterable, imitable form; it must be able to be detached from the present and singular intention of its production" (Derrida, 1988, p. 20). Likewise, for Garfinkel every action is both undertaken as if for a first time, but inevitably it must be recognisable from earlier occasions as a similar or same action. Replays of a VolCap are reactivations that are recognisably of the same event as earlier reactivations, and yet they are understood in practice as different or unique for the specific project under way. While each next RePlay may have unique properties, the "same" VolCap event must continually reproduce recognisably the "same" properties. In this chapter, we hope to have given some insight into how VolCaps as "signatures" are in practice accomplished each next first time.

Notes

1 By *virtualisation* we mean that each and every activation of a video record or a volumetric capture is an abstract distillation of the event captured. With complex video data (and VolCaps), each virtualisation is more and more obviously never identical.

2 In performance studies, Auslander (2009: 85) suggests that "each reactivation discloses the original, but discloses it under different circumstances."

3 *AVA360VR* was officially released on 20th May 2021 by the BigSoftVideo team after several years of development and beta-testing. The software is free to use and is available to download from GitHub: github.com/BigSoftVideo/AVA360VR/.

4 We use the terms *VolCap* and *RePlay* to distinguish the specific implementation of volumetric capture and replay in *AVA360VR*.

5 Because a VolCap is camera/spectator-independent, and although in a RePlay a member has to continuously, without a timeout, find the scenic intelligibility of the 3D scene unfolding, it is *not* comparable to repeatedly viewing the unchanging 'continuous shot' found in a documentary film (Macbeth, 1999). Instead, it is much closer to the practices of the cameraperson in rendering live that 'continuous shot' in the first place.

6 Rawls (2002: 30) notes that "'Each next first time' signifies that while each next case of action is different, each next case of a particular recognizable sort of action must also be 'another' one of something that has been recognized before."

7 Garfinkel (2002: 181) clarifies that "a perspicuous setting makes available, in that it consists of, material disclosures of practices of local production and natural accountability in technical details *with which to find, examine, elucidate, learn of, show, and teach the organizational object as an* in vivo *work site*."

8 A data archive can be downloaded from the long-term *Open Science Foundation* repository: osf.io/w7h38/. In the archive, there are anonymised videos of the original event (from Arch1) and RePlays of the VolCaps analysed in our Examples. There is also an *AVA360VR* project containing versions of one or more anonymised VolCaps, so that inquisitive readers can use their own VR headset and controllers to RePlay the VolCaps and 'inhabit' our audio-visual data as we did.

9 A viewport shows approximately what someone in VR can see of the 3D scene in which they are immersed. It is rendered as a 2D frame that displays what a camera would see with an 80-degree horizontal field of view from the current head position of the user. Note that in VR, one can see a richer binocular view that affords stereoscopic depth in 360-degrees.

10 The latest version (v5.0.1) of the Mondadian multimodal transcription conventions: www.lorenzamondada.net/multimodal-transcription.

11 Examples that illustrate the similarities and divergences of our variant of the Mondadaian system can be found on a versioned 'fork': skandilocks.github.io/multimodal-transcription-fork.

12 Abbreviations found in the transcripts: TML (timeline), TRN (transcript), CREA (create menu), TIME (time menu), FILE (file menu), CAMR (camera menu), SEL (select), MCAM (mirror cam), PLY (play), PAU (pause), VID (video) and MOV (move).

13 The mirror cam is a window that displays an alternative view of the 360-degree video displaced elsewhere in the scene by the VolCapper.

References

Antaki, C., Biazzi, M., Nissen, A., & Wagner, J. (2008). Accounting for moral judgments in academic talk: The case of a conversation analysis data session. *Text and Talk*, *28*(1), 1–30. https://doi.org/10.1515/text.2008.001

Ashmore, M., & Reed, D. (2000). Innocence and nostalgia in conversation analysis: The dynamic relations of tape and transcript. *Forum: Qualitative Social Research*, *1*(3). https://doi.org/10.17169/FQS-1.3.1020

Auslander, P. (2009). Reactivation: Performance, mediatization and the present moment. In M. Chatzichristodoulou, J. Jefferies, & R. Zerihan (Eds.), *Interfaces of performance* (pp. 81–93). Ashgate.

Crabtree, A., Tennent, P., Brundell, P., & Knight, D. (2015). Digital records and the digital replay system. In P. Halfpenny & R. Proctor (Eds.), *Innovations in digital research methods* (pp. 193–220). Sage.

Derrida, J. (1988). *Limited Inc*. Northwestern University Press.

Eisenmann, C., & Lynch, M. (2021). Introduction to Harold Garfinkel's ethnomethodological 'misreading' of Aron Gurwitsch on the phenomenal field. *Human Studies*, *44*(1), 1–17. https://doi.org/10.1007/s10746-020-09564-1

Evans, B., & Lindwall, O. (2020). Show them or involve them? Two organizations of embodied instruction. *Research on Language and Social Interaction*, *53*(2), 223–246. https://doi.org/10.1080/08351813.2020.1741290

Garfinkel, H. (2002). *Ethnomethodology's program: Working out Durkheim's aphorism*. Rowman & Littlefield Publishers.

Goffman, E. (1963). *Behavior in public places*. Free Press.

Heinemann, T., & Möller, R. L. (2016). The virtual accomplishment of knitting: How novice knitters follow instructions when using a video tutorial. *Learning, Culture and Social Interaction*, *8*, 25–47. https://doi.org/10.1016/j.lcsi.2015.11.001

Johansson, E., Lindwall, O., & Rystedt, H. (2017). Experiences, appearances, and interprofessional training: The instructional use of video in post-simulation debriefings. *International Journal of Computer-Supported Collaborative Learning*, *12*(1), 91–112. https://doi.org/10.1007/s11412-017-9252-z

Katila, J., & Raudaskoski, S. (2020). Interaction analysis as an embodied and interactive process: Multimodal, co-operative, and intercorporeal ways of seeing video data as complementary professional visions. *Human Studies*, *43*(3), 445–470. https://doi.org/10.1007/s10746-020-09553-4

Kovács, A. B., & McIlvenny, P. (2020). BreachingVR. *QuiViRR: Qualitative video research reports* (Vol. 1). QuiViRR. https://doi.org/10.5278/ojs.quivirr.v1.2020.a0002

Macbeth, D. (1999). Glances, trances, and their relevance for a visual sociology. In P. L. Jalbert (Ed.), *Media studies: Ethnomethodological approaches* (pp. 135–170). University Press of America.

McIlvenny, P. (2018). Inhabiting spatial video and audio data: Towards a scenographic turn in the analysis of social interaction. *Social Interaction: Video-Based Studies of Human Sociality*, *2*(1). https://doi.org/10.7146/si.v2i1.110409

McIlvenny, P. (2020a). New technology and tools to enhance collaborative video analysis in live 'data sessions'. *QuiViRR: Qualitative Video Research Reports*, *1*, a0001. https://doi.org/10.5278/ojs.quivirr.v1.2020.a0001

McIlvenny, P. (2020b). The future of 'video' in video-based qualitative research is not 'dumb' flat pixels! Exploring volumetric performance capture and immersive performative replay. *Qualitative Research*, *20*(6), 800–818. https://doi.org/10.1177/1468794120905460

McIlvenny, P., & Davidsen, J. (2017). A big video manifesto: Re-sensing video and audio. *Nordicom Information*, *39*(2), 15–21. https://www.nordicom.gu.se/sites/default/files/kapitel-pdf/mcilvenny_davidsen.pdf

Mondada, L. (2019). Practices for showing, looking, and videorecording: The interactional establishment of a common focus of attention. In E. Reber & C. Gerhardt (Eds.), *Embodied activities in face-to-face and mediated settings* (pp. 63–104). Springer.

Rawls, A. W. (2002). Editor's introduction. In H. Garfinkel & A. W. Rawls (Eds.), *Ethnomethodology's program: Working out Durkheim's aphorism* (pp. 1–64). Rowman & Littlefield Publishers.

Smith, R. (2020). Seeing the trouble: A mountain rescue training scenario in its circumstantial and situated detail in three frames. *Ethnographic Studies*, *17*, 41–59. https://doi.org/10.5281/ZENODO.4050536

Sormani, P. (2014). *Respecifying lab ethnography: An ethnomethodological study of experimental physics*. Routledge.

Sormani, P. (2016). Practice-based video analysis: A position statement. *SocietàMutamentoPolitica*, *7*(14), 103–120. https://doi.org/10.13128/SMP-19698

Tuncer, S., Lindwall, O., & Brown, B. (2020). Making time: Pausing to coordinate video instructions and practical tasks. *Symbolic Interaction, 44*(3), 603–631. https://doi.org/10.1002/symb.516

Tutt, D., & Hindmarsh, J. (2011). Reenactments at work: Demonstrating conduct in data sessions. *Research on Language and Social Interaction, 44*(3), 211–236. https://doi.org/10.1080/08351813.2011.591765

Watson, R. (1999). Driving in forests and mountains: A pure and applied ethnography. *Ethnographic Studies, 3,* 50–60.

12

RECURRENT PROBLEMS AND RECENT EXPERIMENTS IN TRANSCRIBING VIDEO

Live transcribing in data sessions and depicting perspective

Eric Laurier and Tobias Boelt Back

Introduction – tracing back to Jefferson

In Ethnomethodology and Conversation Analysis (EMCA), Gail Jefferson's conventions for transcribing talk are widely considered the default transcription system (Ayaß, 2015), the one that most trained conversation analysts routinely turn to in transcribing talk-in-interaction. Getting acquainted with how to write and read the Jeffersonian format has long been considered an important first step on the road to becoming competent in "the ways of the CA tribe" (ten Have, 2007, p. 11). Over the years, these conventions have been continuously reworked and developed to represent newfound and increasingly complex phenomena. In this chapter, we try to recapture the spirit of Jefferson's transcribing as a way of attending to features that are overlooked by other forms of transcription. EMCA has its own peculiarities in transcribing because its analysts aren't sure what to transcribe at the outset, given its ethos of unmotivated attentiveness. The unmotivated ethos allows our attention to be caught by other things than those which the "literature" has found to be significant and would guide us to scrutinise. The task of EMCA transcribing is itself inescapably inventive in offering solutions to the problem of rendering newly relevant phenomena found in flight.

Although Jefferson's formats for marking details of talk are well known to scholars in EMCA, that she was experimenting and also attempting to capture the specifics of embodied action has been largely overlooked (though, see Albert et al., 2019; Hepburn & Bolden, 2017). As Charles Goodwin recalled, during their data sessions in the 1970s Jefferson would put a piece of transparency over a TV screen and outline prominent bodily features and experiment with adapting existing dance notation systems (Goodwin & Solomon, 2019). These attempts offer us an inkling of Jefferson's open-ness to alternatives to the line-by-line, ASCII

DOI: 10.4324/9781003424888-16

standard characters, text-based format that she became better known for. In the digital realm, the current generation of EMCA researchers have used screen grabs as their way of tracing embodied action from video screens.

In this chapter, we will return to Jefferson's warrants for changing existing transcription formats and reflect on the abiding problems of transcribing in EMCA studies. We will compare the Jefferson format with the graphic transcript and present our experiments with using the graphic transcript for transcribing "live" during data sessions, as well as for documenting social phenomena in final publications. The graphic transcript foregrounds other phenomena and in different ways than the Jeffersonian system, particularly visually and spatially available phenomena of order: bodily actions, objects, movements, environmental features, etc. As Jefferson did, we will raise the problems that we have faced in transcribing while also working through cases of phenomena that show how and why we shape and reshape the forms of our transcripts.

A short history of transcription conventions and their abiding problems

> While those of us who spend a lot of time making transcripts may be doing our best to get it right, what that might mean is utterly obscure and unstable. It depends a great deal on what we are paying attention to. It seems to me, then, that the issue is not transcription per se, but what it is we might want to transcribe, that is, attend to.
>
> *(Jefferson, 1985, p. 25)*

The Jeffersonian breakthrough was in transcribing as a means of becoming more attentive to orderliness in otherwise heard-but-un-noticed elements of talk, both for researchers and for their readers. Indeed, she asked us not to become overly fixated on the transcript itself because its rightness remains "utterly obscure and unstable". In practice this meant that when she noticed an un-noticed thing in talk such as a speaker saying "nyem", she did not follow the convention to correct it as a defectively spoken "yes" or "no" or "ehm" (Jefferson, 1978). Thereby she created a new translatable entity from the hearable details of speech into the textual details of a transcript. She compared and evaluated what she was creating with the renderings of speech in standard and dialect orthographies in newspapers, novels, and theatre scripts, showing that these formats missed variation in the use of "dialect signatures" (Jefferson, 1983, p. 9) and pronunciation: variation which was relevant, accountable, and reportable yet unnoticed by linguists, sociologists, anthropologists, etc. The point, then, was not to conform to existing standards for representing speech nor to iron out its wrinkles but to listen first to speakers' voices and then work out how to register what was hearable in order to reveal the orderliness of those wrinkles.

Mondada's amendment and supplementation of the Jeffersonian transcription system was in itself quietly radical. It not only revealed but also departed from several assumptions of transcripts of audible speech. In Jeffersonian transcripts, speakers and their speech appear as a next line or sentence (in fact, this is the case for almost all transcription formats). The line-by-line format itself neatly fits with the rule used by speakers: one person speaks at a time. The transcriber and analyst need only attend to one person's actions at a time. Phenomena that break that rule, overlapping speech being the most common, are notated and easily visible in Jeffersonian transcripts. It was never the case, of course, that all action from other parties halts while one person is speaking. What Mondada's (2018) system showed, from the outset, were the gestalts of doing things together, in which speaking was but one part. While a person speaks, other parties to the event would be, for example, frowning in time to an announcing of bad news, halting their walking at the place name just mentioned, picking up a pencil to establish themselves as a potential next speaker, and so on.

Relatedly, by registering non-verbal actions Mondada's system displaced speech itself, the feature which the Jeffersonian format assumed to be "the main course of action" (Mondada, 2018, p. 98). Her augmentation shifted analytic attention toward embodied actions of all sorts. For example, Mondada transcribed a video recording of a team of three people carrying around heavy paintings during the preparations of an art exhibition at a museum. As shown by her transcribing, one staff member lifts a large object. In response, another member of the staff assists him to lift the object via the haptic initiation, sensed through the object, without a word (a word being more than un-necessary). The transcribing reveals a course of haptic action which is being analysed by its recipient and their relevant response – help – is given. Moreover, Mondada's transcribing shows the party assisting the lifter in a timely way and the very absence of a verbal request for help produces a distinctive accountability to their help. To have asked "do you need a hand?" would have had its distinct accountabilities in being understood, for example, to have avoided immediate assistance or implying that a hand was not really needed.

Mondada is clear that a central quality of the transcript that she retains from the Jeffersonian format is time and timing and, in the example above of lifting an object, we can understand why. Her format maintains the use of bracketed numbers for marking the length of actions in tenths of seconds. Without each line of action being registered in parallel timelines, as lines of text, we could not see timing as one of the measures for producing and recognising the promptness or lateness of actions. Our first example is of two occupants of a car during a journey and it is an example we will look at first in Mondada format and then later as a graphic transcript.

In Transcript 1, line 01 the driver's inspection of his instruments lasts six tenths of a second, while the passenger brushing his trousers continues for 2.6 seconds plus the 0.6 seconds of the driver's inspection. Mondada's orthography adds complexity to the reading of the text when the reader seeks to assemble the timings shown via the brackets of clock-time measures, inserted symbols, and parallel formulations of non-verbal actions. The transcribers' continuing achievement is

TRANSCRIPT 1   Example of Mondada transcript created by Eric (with help from
              Mondada & Deppermann) from Deppermann et al. (2018).

```
01              ^(0.6)^                    (2.6)%
       dri:    ^inspects instruments^
       pas:    >> brushing trousers ------------%

02              * (1.6) +(1.2)+ (0.2)*
       dri:            +gz rvm+
       pas:    *gz PAS window-------*

03              (0.3)*(0.7)+ (0.6)*(0.5)+
       dri:                 +gz rsm------+
       pas:          *gz F window-* *gz PAS window---->> (5.8)

04              (0.9)+    (1.8)      +
       dri:            +gz instruments+
```

to render the relative timings of actions so that we can recover just when actions
start, their duration, and their temporal trajectory.

However, to only focus on Mondada's supplement to the existing Jeffersonian
format would lead us to miss that, like Jefferson, she has led EMCA's experiments and creativity in transcribing outside of that format. For example, she
hosted a workshop in Rome in 2017 bringing together artists, graphic designers, and EMCA researchers, including Eric, to experiment with distinct diagram-
matic, graphic, and other ways of transcribing action that extended beyond ASCII
text and figures. In her work, she continues to experiment with alternatives that
would help us register phenomena in other ways than our conventional text-based
transcripts.

Alongside bodily actions, the Mondada orthography deals with what we might
broadly call the material environment or, as Mondada sometimes calls it, the *local
ecology* of objects, technologies, architecture, vegetation, etc. Accompanying
the addition of the local ecology is a further choice about what features to render, which "are potentially infinite because they exceed conventional forms and
include situated, ad hoc resources that depend on the type of activity and its specific ecology" (Mondada, 2018, p. 95). There is always a tension between the infinite elements, the *plenum* as Garfinkel might put it, the absences of the recording,
and the desire to transcribe what the recording has preserved in a "similar, coher-
ent and robust way that is essential for systematic analyses" (p. 95).

Reflections on hiding, estranging, and formulating things when transcribing

There are four central problems of transcription in EMCA that we want to consider ahead of reflecting on our own graphic transcription practices. The first:
detail, is its seeming strength, and one of the earliest sustained reflections on the

problem of excessive detail in CA transcripts, was David Bogen's (1992, 1999). Bogen argued that Jeffersonian transcripts feature in a complementary literary pairing with the main text where, at one level, they serve a mimetic effect to achieve the sense that events recorded in this way, really happened in this way. In this sense, the transcript's purpose is no longer to narrate the earlier events but, instead, to provide an orthographic emplotment of the relevant acoustic (and, by extension, videographic) details. The literary pairing is manifest in the task of the text, accompanying the transcript, to help the reader recognise in the "hyperabundance of transcriptural detail what is significant about the original event" (Bogen, 1999, p. 203). The problem that Bogen identified was that as the level of detail increases it begins to obscure rather than show the phenomenon, after which, the trick of the analyst becomes to reveal the relevant feature for the reader which has become hidden in amongst the sea of details.

Defending Jeffersonian detailing, Hepburn and Bolden (2017) argued that Bogen, in his 1992 paper, did not prove that his criticisms of transcription diminish the findings from its use. They stressed the need for continuing to include hearable intricacies of recorded phenomena in transcripts, in part, because "a good, precise transcript is a display of quality, of taking the words and actions seriously" (Hepburn & Bolden, 2017, p. 192). Disagreeing with Bogen's characterisation of the Jeffersonian transcript, they argued that the features transcribed are warranted as being those which co-participants demonstrably find consequential in the course of interaction. Hepburn's (2004) work on crying and Glenn's (2010) and others' work on laughter, demonstrating the Jeffersonian spirit of transcribing as a way of attending to features that members are attending to. Crying and laughter's identifying details are absent from, or are caricatured in, their conventional renderings in literature, newspapers, and, of course, most work in psychology, linguistics, sociology, etc. In transcribing significant details EMCA researchers become all the more intimate with their logics and uses, even as the familiar features of laughter or tears are rendered in ways that seem strange, as texts, to their original producers. Yet Bogen does not exclude attention to details of speech or gestures per se but leaves us instead wondering about how to transcribe in ways that do not obscure the phenomena, and perhaps might even preserve its familiarity without the requirement of the analyst to recover it. Though, as we will discuss later, graphic transcripts become just as entangled in this thicket around detail, strangeness, and literary pairings.

Our second reflection on transcribing emerges around the problems of how we are inevitably categorising and formulating members and their actions when we are transcribing. With no god's eye perspective for us, as transcribers, we are partial and we are always, also, finding and losing the phenomenon. Rod Watson (1997) reminded us that the convention of presenting a speaker by the same identification (e.g., "dri", an abbreviated "driver", for Transcript 1) at every transition relevance place is at odds with the shifting identities emerging from the very activities transcribed. For example, for events happening in a vehicle we label its occupants in the transcript unchangingly even though, as the actions unfold, various pairings will become relevant: adult + child, aunt + nephew, driver + passenger, driver + navigator, etc. The salience of category identification is particularly marked in workplace settings, yet, of course, applies in other settings as well. As Watson puts it, these speaker formulations are "categorical-incumbency-as-transcribed" and "[t]he very transcription procedures for such occasions of speech exchange indicate a background reliance on the provision of membership categories" (1997, pp. 51–52). As such, the speaker's categorisation as e.g., "TV producer" precedes the transcribed action and thereby the transcript steers its readers to "hear" each turn-of-talk as tied to the category in the identification.

Our third reflection builds on Watson's categorisation problems but in relation to transcribing non-verbal action, given each non-verbal activity requires formulation for transcribing it. Again, it steers the reader toward what kind of action they should understand the person, or other agent, as doing. For example, in Transcript 1, Eric transcribed the driver's action as "inspecting instruments" rather than "glances at radio" or "looks down", etc. Equally, in line 2, the use of "gz" (an abbreviated "gaze") selects amongst the possible practices of looking. It occurs to us that we have come to use "gz" commonly in transcribing because it serves as a placeholder term for practices of looking, which leaves what kind of looking it is to be specified in the paired text. Trying to use more neutral or generic identifications of non-verbal actions does not solve the problem. Inevitably they lose the local recognisability and availability of the participants' ongoing production of their actions with their eyes, heads, hands etc.

Our fourth reflection on non-verbal action is around the granularity we use in describing embodied actions in transcripts where "gz" is itself a case in point. In their study of instructional demonstrations, Lindwall and Lymer (in press) build on Schegloff's (2000) analysis of the granularity of descriptions as a member's concern and resource. According to Schegloff, "[k]nowing how granularity works matters then not just substantively, but methodologically" (p. 719) because EMCA descriptions of practices stand in contrast to other social sciences' representations, in their greater attentiveness to identifying locally relevant details. Schegloff's point is that what details to include and when to be more or less detailed, should be tied to the level of detail being used by participants. Lindwall and Lymer contrast videos of instructions by medical professionals for students with Youtube instructional videos for a general audience. Via that comparison, they show that to standardise the level of detail in the transcriber's description then misses the divergent levels of detail the instructed actions provide and that characterises them. In short, transcripts that have built on Jefferson's pioneering work are not without problems that are internal and of abiding interest to EMCA. They should not be seen as the endpoint for our efforts to depict practices, document action, and do justice to the voices of others.

Transcribing with the comic strip form does not dissolve the problems of transcribing

It might appear that by reminding us of these four problems facing transcribers we are going to offer the comic strip form as a solution to those problems. We are not. Transcribing actions building on comic strip conventions provides us with distinct responses to those problems rather than solutions. Perplexingly for those hoping to escape the betrayals of transcription, our experience is that they add further problems for the analyst. A first place to begin is that, in Western popular culture, the comic strip form is associated with the trivial, the informal, and the fun. It stands in sharp contrast to the technical aesthetic of Jeffersonian and Mondada transcripts.

Or does it? In the early days of Jefferson's experiments, she contrasted what she was trying out with the existing transcription systems in linguistics:

> Phonetic transcripts are not accessible to most readers. And the sort of "comic book" orthography I use (e.g., for "What are you doing?", "Wutche doin?") is considered objectionable in that it makes the speakers look "stupid"; it seems to caricature them rather than illuminate features of their talk.
>
> *(Jefferson, 1983, p. 3)*

In a first look at a graphic transcript (Transcript 2) of the recording transcribed in Transcript 1, comic strip orthography, compared to a traditional CA transcript, caricatures the participants and their activities simply by resembling a comic. It seems also to have lost detail, particularly the details that were registered in the text in Transcript 1.

Jefferson (1983) balanced the risk of caricaturing speakers and their speech against the gain in accessibility of her "comic book" orthography. Her complaint was similar to Bogen's, but about phonetic transcription, which Jefferson argued was obscuring rather than showing identifying details. More than that, she showed that what might at first seem to be a trivial feature of speech, such as a "nyem" or

TRANSCRIPT 2 Graphic transcript of recording transcribed in Transcript 1.

the details of laughter particles, are deeply consequential for what is meant and done by participants in interaction. In publications, the seriousness of what the graphic transcripts is showing, is similarly vouched for in the accompanying analysis that reshapes first impressions of them as trivialising human affairs. Though, as we noted earlier, the association between comics and the inconsequential, and readers' expectations and conventions for reading them are variable across cultures of reading. At this point, it might still seem as if comic strips will be more fun to read, but the graphic transcript is by no means as captivating and vivid as classic comics. As with any type of transcribing, there is a meeting between the need for under-appreciated detail and the potential lack of imagination in depicting that detail. Part of our criteria in producing graphic transcripts, keeping in mind Bogen's complaint, is to show rather than obscure what is happening ahead of returning to it, as a members' accomplishment, in our analysis. There is a familiar grammar of comic strips for the EMCA scholar to draw on and adapt (see McCloud (1993) for an exemplary and fun guide). It is more than a visual grammar, it is what Grennan (2017) calls a *lexicogrammar*, which has distinct ways of representing speech, timing, time, actions, motion, etc., yet one that is familiar as part of, not just its use in comic strips, but also in the many advertisings, instructions manuals, etc. that share its grammar.

Perhaps the most central problem of graphic transcripts is the loss of a singular sense of, and measure of, the relative timing of actions. As mentioned above, a unitary measure of timing is implicit and explicit in the Jeffersonian format. The length of the line of ASCII text provides a measure of its timing, with variations on that measure marked in slower or faster delivery (e.g., '<slower>' and '>faster<'). There are ways to try and establish a graphic transcript with a comparable measure of timing, for example, you can add time markers explicitly in captions (see further experiments in showing time measures in Back, 2020; Laurier, 2019). In reflecting on the problem of showing a measure of timing, it is not that a sense of timing is missing from the comic strip form. The temporality of, and across, panels has always been multiple because they have the timing associated with the actions depicted in the image, the duration added by speech bubbles or other sounds, and the caption box's use in both timing of the panel as well as placing it in the past or future (see Laurier, 2014a, 2019). The lack of a single measure is also a possibility. Multiple temporalities are produced, drawn upon, recognised, etc. by members in and as part of multiple courses of action. Those multiple timings are a challenge in transcribing that Mondada (2018) also responds to.

The problem of timing takes a further twist in the graphic transcript. To provide for their intelligibility to readers as singular images in a panel, actions are routinely captured from video recordings at a moment in their course that makes them most recognisable as what they are seen to be by the analyst (Jayyusi, 1993). Actions' trajectories are broken into stages, which is more often in relation to their iconic recognisability than the shape of their trajectory, or they may be selected to represent other features of analytic interest visible in their course. However, in trying to show trajectories, they are captured at the points when they start (for example, at their "home position"), at a mid-point, then again at their completion (for example, a return to home position). In selecting for their representativeness in any panel, they run into Jefferson's original complaint over stereotyping in transcription. Yet, one development of the comic strip EMCA has pursued is using distinctive images, the equivalent of Jefferson's *nyem*, to help show a thing found in the recording that a comic strip writer would discard as ambiguous or unrecognisable. The way those ambiguities of the screen capture are routinely resolved is by captioning the image (e.g., "inspects instruments" in Transcript 2) in order to instruct the reader on how to see specific features of the image (Lindwall & Lymer in press). Such a caption, of course, leads us back to the categorisation and formulation problem of embodied actions that besets transcripts, so reflection is required on the warrants for categorisations formulated by the analyst.

To balance out what will likely sound like an overly cautious introduction we will now offer succour by considering our recent experiments in transcribing. Firstly, we will introduce a data session transcribing technique that displaces the typical pairing of a Jeffersonian or Mondada transcript with playing video recordings. Secondly, we will describe how a graphic transcript has served us well, if not better than a textual transcript in showing phenomena related to visual perspectives.

Live transcribing in data sessions via rapid triptychs

One of the great strengths of the line-by-line Jefferson transcript is its flexibility to serve as a worksheet in data sessions. It roughly follows the timeline of the video and is correctable, augmentable, and annotatable (see for example: Antaki et al., 2008; Bolden & Hepburn, 2017; Laurier, 2014b). By contrast, over the past decade we, Eric and Tobias, had come to accept that crafted graphic transcripts were almost always considered useless for the annotation and note-taking of data session participants. It appeared to us that the kind of video annotation tools being developed were, in fact, the more promising avenue for supporting video data sessions (Albert et al., 2019; McIlvenny, 2021). Our understanding was that having graphic transcripts at hand distracted from paying unmotivated attention to the video materials, and that these transcripts best arrived late in the day, long after the first noticings of things.

As part of the background work to writing this chapter, we began experimenting with graphical transcribing "live" during data sessions. To share their noticings, participants were asked to make three-panel strips, or a *triptych*, though they were left with the freedom to have more panels if they wished. Using this many panels was a suggestion rather than a prescription. A pair of panels could work, or they could have experimented with many more panels than three. Data sessions routinely vary in how many noticings are suggested by each person, according to local rules of thumb, numbers of analysts present, time available, etc. While we did not exclude transcribing by drawing from the video, or, in a nod to Jefferson, tracing paper over video screens, the fastest process was to frame-grab from the video recording (which is also the easiest way to re-grab and replace an image). For making the images, providing individual copies of the video was the only practical solution we could find[1]. We shared templates in Comic Life, PowerPoint, and Keynote formats for making comic strips. Participants, once they had made a preliminary noticing, would depict the thing which they noticed using three or more panels.

In one data session, we used video data of public transport during the coronavirus pandemic. Transcript 3 was made by a participant in that session. The session was used to explore how passengers select seats on a train as part of the joint accomplishment of following pandemic restrictions. Every other seat on the train had a *non-seating* sticker on it, serving as a resource and reminder for passengers of distancing guidelines. The sketch filter was applied to the original video for anonymisation purposes rather than during the transcribing in the data session. The transcript was used by the participant to support their describing of how seat-selecting and seat-proposing is divided between the passengers.

In the data session, each analyst usually only had time to produce one graphic transcript. These were sketches toward analyses. Even in that short time, the sketching routinely involved several grabs at the video frame to represent not just for each individual panel, but also, participants re-grabbed images for their fit in building sequences across the panels, thereby creating the narrative of the practice. Participants cropped to focus (e.g., panel 3 in Transcript 3), they broke up actions into shorter or longer durations across and within the panels, as ways of attending to different kinds of details and temporalities.

The participants reported that the depictional work of grabbing frames and captioning them shifted their attention toward the embodied, visual, and spatial aspects of the video recorded event. From the outset, in roughing out the transcripts, participants were inspired to pursue more adequate renderings of the embodied practices that they had become interested in. There was a stimulating dis-satisfaction with what they could render. At the same time, and in a limited

TRANSCRIPT 3   Three-panel noticing from data session in a graphic transcript workshop in June 2021.

time, the very process of producing the three-panel renderings became an occasion for the participants' initial noticings to foster more noticings at the point of documenting, as is so often the case in transcribing. Indeed, transcribing was fruitful rather than mechanical. For example, when Transcript 3 was produced, one researcher noted how, in cropping the video-grabs to focus on gaze and hand gesture, his attention was drawn to the literal *foot work* of the three passengers as part of proposing where to sit. To shift perspective to the feet was going to require cropping the image to foreground the feet of the passengers while also grabbing a differently timed set of frames from the video. Thus, the data-session graphic transcript was not an endpoint and instead pushed the participants through revealing recurrently what was missing. Live graphical transcribing altered other practices of the data session as well. Participants shifted away from replaying the source video, using their transcript to show the phenomena that they were talking about. This sharing of the document rather than replaying the video, lessened the time taken for each person to present in our online data sessions, though this will vary dramatically depending on local ecologies of room hardware and software for sharing screens, projecting video, etc. However, the change in presenting material was at the expense of staying with the video, with the attendant risk that transcripts supplanted the finding of details in the video recording.

One of the overlooked qualities of transcripts in data sessions is that they are usually passed back by members of the data session to the presenter as part of the sharing of collective analyses. The passing back shows the organisation and accountability of the workplace in terms of whose data it is and who should one day make something from the session. The multiple graphic transcripts continued to support this practice of passing back, yet as a different sort of resource. In a simple sense they were digital documents rather than paper, which fitted well to the fact that the sessions were online during the COVID pandemic. More significantly, they provided parallel, sometimes convergent, sometimes divergent, iterations of the very transcription process, rather than the one stabilised transcript with each member's annotation. The destabilisation was falling on a different side of the tensions between standardisation and inventiveness in transcribing. The presenter, at the end of a data session, had not only community noticings to draw on but also a portfolio of ways of representing the thing being analysed.

Depicting perspectives

When narratives of comic strips are drawn, rather than created with screen grabs, shifts of perspective are used to both show a perspective on things, people, and places and, relatedly, to show perspective as the perspectives of particular characters in the narrative. When we transcribe from the given perspectives of cameras, our ability to show different perspective is limited. In what follows we will, in that Jeffersonian spirit, use an analysis of perspectives to consider how it is more than simply the angle and location of the camera. The recognising, sharing, and diverging of perspectives are at the heart of the spatialising of members' sense-making and organisation of their action and so, in itself, showing see-able perspectives requires Jeffersonian experimentation with the comic strip form.

Perspective is an optical matter and an analytic one. It encompasses the use of different angles of lenses from 45 degree to 360 degree, the location of single or multiple cameras, what view into a setting is being presented, the use of close-ups, mid-shots, and wides. All of which are compositional and narrative matters, not just in cinematography but also in video recordings of activities for analysis in EMCA (Heath et al., 2010; Mondada, 2014). Cinematography has developed visual (and audio) perspective as a resource and grammar for indexing experience, character, opinion, and more. If we take this meaning of perspective further, it brings us to more familiar EMCA concepts of stance, orientation, alignment, and so on. Moreover, as we ourselves produce transcripts that are derived from single or multiple cameras' perspectives, we quickly come to guide the reader's recognition through instructed seeing of the preceding recordings (Goodwin, 2000; Lindwall & Lymer, in press).

As we have said, graphic transcripts are both able to draw upon and find themselves limited by the field of view and location of the video camera or multiple cameras. Luff and Heath (2012) remind us that rather than being simply a practical and technical concern, the task of placing a camera, and thus selecting its point-of-view as well as its point-viewed-from, "uncovers methodological concerns that reveal the distinctive demands that video places on researchers concerned with the detailed analysis of naturally occurring social interaction" (p. 257). Shooting with a camera is, as Mondada (2014) argues, a "proto-analysis" of the phenomenon. Working from what is shot may or may not be convergent with that proto-analysis. The question here is something of a practical one. How do we then use given perspectives either way? As transcribers we do not share the illustrator's luxury of being able to freely select amongst possible perspectives, yet the production of the graphic transcript need not be simply subservient to the details captured by a video recording. As we have hinted already, whenever we are working with screen grabs, we can crop the still image; with multiple cameras we can select between their perspectives and locations. The 360-camera provides further possibilities in showing perspective because we can select from a complete circle of view around the camera, even if the viewpoint's point of origin remains the same. The 360-camera effectively displaces the selection of what angle to look at, from the event of recording, to the event of viewing the recording and, of course, widens the perspective selection possibilities for the transcriber.

Selecting and sequencing images from video recordings

Transcript 4 draws upon the camera-perspectives available from a dashcam in order to show members' perspectives as a matter of concern for these members and how perspectives are produced via their actions on the road. The dashcam

TRANSCRIPT 4   Transcript from Laurier et al. (2020) dashcam with conventional perspective pairings.

has two lenses, one showing the occupants of the car (panel 1) and one showing part of the view out of the front of the car (panels 2–6). In a sense it prefigures the 360-camera given that many 360-cameras end up being edited or rendered to produce dashcam grammars of forward and backward perspectives (see CAVA360VR in McIlvenny, 2021). The dashcam has a fixed position within the vehicle on the dashboard, which means that the forward camera perspective is moving when the vehicle itself is moving. The graphic transcript was produced to show an event that helps us understand how the beeps from car horns are produced to be hearable by other road users.

The transcript uses a single image of the occupants from the rear-facing camera in panel 1 to provide the reader with a sense of *whose* perspective they will come upon in the next frame. As we have noted earlier, perspective provides more than locating where we are looking from, it is to whom this view belongs. The pairing of perspectives of a scene with its members looking, is routinely used in comic strips and film editing to show the subject and afterwards show what they are looking at. The graphic transcript builds on that adjacently-paired perspective relationship. Panel 1 provides more, an excess, yet one that is a relevant resource. It is the driver's perspective but also visible in the image is a front seat passenger and a child in the rear, all looking ahead. In the following sequence of video frames, it shows the visual perspective as a member's concern and practical accomplishment.

The analytic phenomena that Eric sought to show in creating Transcript 4, for the publication on driving-in-traffic, was what he had from the recording: the use of the car itself as a perspective producing device. The auto-rickshaw in front of the car is positioned, for the driver, as an obstacle to looking ahead. When the driver alters the car position as shown in panel 3, we can see, as the driver can see, a lack of vehicles ahead on the pavement side. In panel 5 we can see, through the graphic transcript, how returning to the middle of the dual lanes shows the view ahead for the slot to be overtaken into but that the view of the pavement side has been obscured again. The transcript is seeking to show the driver's work of finding perspectives into the traffic ahead. Eric selected the video-stills in panel 2 and 3 to show that gap, and for a certain perspective to be visible in its pairing with the image before and after it.

The sequencing in Transcript 5 is similar to that in Transcript 4. We see a passenger leave the train station platform, walk through a staircase to an underground tunnel while being interviewed about his daily commuting during COVID-19. The frames are grabbed from a 360-degree camera recording, which allowed Tobias to crop from a full sphere. The aim of the transcript is to show, from the passenger's perspective, the distribution of co-passengers in a shared space. Showing the

TRANSCRIPT 5   Building a passenger's perspective (Back, 2021).

passenger-interviewee looking and pointing towards the tunnel in panel 1, accompanied by his continuous voice-over in the connected speech bubbles throughout the subsequent panels, establishes him as the one to whom the perspectives in panels 2 and 3 belong.

An earlier version of Transcript 5 included the passenger from panel 1 in all three panels walking down the stairs on the right side of each panel (similar to the composition of panel 1). However, the analysis shifted from a concern with the multiactivity of walking and talking as intersubjective practice to the formations of the group of co-passengers walking in front of the camera and the interviewee. Consequently, Tobias re-cropped the panels to exclude the talking passenger and guide the reader's attention towards the group of passengers.

As with the auto-rickshaw, the moving passengers are recognisably the same across the three panels. The changing environments: the railway platform in panel 1, the stairs in panel 2, and the underground level in panel 3 are seen as sequentially related. They show the reader, from the interviewee's perspective, how the passengers ahead move together across the three sites, while maintaining some degree of social distancing due to COVID-19 regulations. The reader's attention is redirected from timing as a member's resource, as emphasised in the line-by-line transcript, to spacing. That is, the transcript focuses its reader's attention on the relative location of bodies from one site to the next and within those sites. The recognisability of each scene as a next, but not incrementally progressing, does however produce a sense of the longer stretches of time between each panel. The interviewee's words are read in terms of how and when he sees the spatial distribution of co-passengers from panel to panel and site to site, progressing from the reader seeing the crowd as dense as "herrings in a barrel" in panel 2 to revealing the later assessment of the interviewee on the number of passengers in the tunnel as "not so bad" in panel 3. Given the different ways of assessing the busy-ness of public spaces during the COVID pandemic, it is possible that our interviewee would have seen even a small group like the one shown as too dense for him to feel comfortable.

From panel to panel there are undoubtedly other elements to the participants' work of seeing what is happening: glancing to the sides, drivers using their mirrors, drivers and walkers looking over their shoulder, noticing co-passenger formations, etc. Being tied to the footage, graphic transcripts sometimes produce strange and ambiguous visual sequences. Their strangeness requires the use of caption boxes and further instruction through the accompanying text to help the reader make sense of unconventional perspective pairings which again returns us to the problems of analysing the category organisation of the scene.

In re-examining the work of the graphic transcript, we can begin to understand not just that it allows for complex assemblies of members' practices but also that multiple perspectives and temporalities are at work where those perspectives and temporalities are relevant to members' practices. Our concern has been to show how we might try and address those via the renderings of the graphic transcript.

What we want to remind you of, before concluding, is that the transcripts in this section were, of course, the result of a number of versions where different grabbed images were tried, various layouts, speech bubbles shifted around, etc.

Conclusion

In opening this chapter, we examined, at some length, the reasons for and some of the abiding problems of transcription in EMCA studies. We considered the introduction of "live" graphic transcribing in data sessions as a novel way of showing what each analyst had noticed. We underlined how rendering a video recording as a comic strip shifted the analysts' attention toward the embodied, visual, and spatial aspects of members' practices and how it changes the sharing of noticings with the presenter. In a further reflection on our recent experiments in transcribing, we demonstrated how, in finalising our transcripts for publication, we responded to the phenomena of visual perspective and the intimately related problem of reproducing members' perspectives from the perspective(s) of our cameras.

As we argued, in the comic strip form, we have distinct possibilities to respond to the action formulation and actor categorisation problems: For example, in relation to *gaze*, by showing direction of view, and to whom a specific view belongs, rather than merely describing who is looking/gazing at what when. We have shown how transcribing using comic strip conventions hybridised with transcription criteria was shaped around particular analytic foci. We used the case of perspective as one such spur to us, as part of participants' sense-making and action production, finding perspectives into traffic, guiding a co-passenger through a crowded tunnel, distributing seats on a train, etc. As Jefferson herself showed, this required both drawing upon and disrupting existing conventions for exhibiting phenomena.

Transcribing, in the comic strip form, shares EMCA's commitment to transcription as a way of highlighting and pointing up practices. As John Heritage recalls the 1970s, when Jefferson first circulated her recording and transcripts:

> [T]he transcripts highlighted features of the recordings that we might have otherwise overlooked, and pointed up practices in the talk which turned out to be highly relevant to our analyses. Because the tapes and transcripts were quite widely circulated, they contributed to a 'culture of transcribing', to the development of a set of common standards that we learned to share, and tried to live up to. The standards allowed us to recognize failure – our own and other people's – as well as success.
>
> *(Heritage quoted in Hepburn & Bolden, 2017, p. 181)*

While Heritage's comments emphasise the common standards, transcribing has also always been a site for supplementing or altering those standards when we reveal further orders of social practices. What we would urge caution around is reproduced standardised forms being the criteria that we use to recognise

Jefferson's rightness ahead of inquiries that are "utterly obscure and unstable". Indeed, we do not wish to propose a fixed set of standards for the many elements of the graphic transcript (e.g., panels, captions, textualised speech, layout of bubbles). For us, the Jeffersonian breakthrough emerged from questioning the existing and dominant traditions of representation of hearable and consequential speech. Even as Jefferson was building a new system because existing representations of talk were ignoring the hearable and accountable features of speech, she was wary around how speakers might then be caricatured in her transcribing. There is no existing standard for graphic transcript orthography in EMCA that we wish to depart from, it is already a departure from Jeffersonian and Mondada formats. Building graphic transcripts for EMCA inquiries remains instead, as it shouldn't surprise EMCA scholars to learn, an ad hoc endeavour.

Our aim here has not been to pull you into a puzzling transcription procedure, a tutorial of a primary problem in EMCA studies, that any recording and any transcript misses the haecceities of the thing. Garfinkel (2002) taught us that lesson in his summoning phones tutorial, where transcribing was instructively impossible and the tutorial in transcribing was at best a secondary one for his students and, more likely, a useful ruse. Our aim instead has been to help EMCA researchers develop their craft in good-enough representations of events, weighing the balance between their identifying details and gratuitous granularity. Elsewhere, Garfinkel did not abandon attempts to show phenomena via vivid ethnographic descriptions, diagrams, photographs, and re-use of members' own representations of a phenomenon. Our warrant for experimenting with graphic transcripts is to maintain the Jeffersonian spirit of showing what is missed or otherwise caricatured. Using the comic strip's forms of panels, speech bubbles, etc. is a different way of picking up Jefferson's pencil and tracing paper to settle upon what we are attending to.

Note

1 Depending on the sensitivity of the materials, this may not be possible and/or may require trusting members to destroy their copies of the video at the end of the session.

References

Albert, S., Heath, C., Skach, S., Harris, M. T., Miller, M., & Healey, P. G. T. (2019). Drawing as transcription: How do graphical techniques inform interaction analysis. *Social Interaction: Video-Based Studies of Human Sociality*, 2(1). https://doi.org/10.7146/si.v2i1.113145

Antaki, C., Biazzi, M., Nissen, A., & Wagner, J. (2008). Accounting for moral judgments in academic talk: The case of a conversation analysis data session. *Text and Talk*, 28(1), 1–30. https://doi.org/10.1515/TEXT.2008.001

Ayaß, R. (2015). Doing data: The status of transcripts in conversation analysis. *Discourse Studies*, 17(5), 505–528. https://doi.org/10.1177/1461445615590717

Back, T. B. (2020). *One more time with feeling: Resemiotising boundary affects for doing 'emotional talk show' interaction for another next first time* (ISBN 978-87-7210-627-4) [PhD Thesis, Aalborg University]. Aalborg University Press.

Back, T. B. (2021). *Building a passenger's perspective.* [Unpublished transcript from the project 'Travelling Together']. Aalborg University. Copies available from the author.

Bogen, D. (1992). The organization of talk. *Qualitative Sociology, 15*(3), 273–295. https://doi.org/10.1007/BF00990329

Bogen, D. (1999). *Order without rules.* Suny Press.

Deppermann, A., Laurier, E., Mondada, L., Broth, M., Cromdal, J., De Stefani, E., Haddington, P., Levin, L., Nevile, M., Rauniomaa, M. (2018). Overtaking as an interactional accomplishment. *Gesprachsforschung - Online-Zeitschrift zur verbalen Interaktion, 19*, 1–131.

Garfinkel, H. (2002). *Ethnomethodology's program.* Rowman & Littlefield.

Glenn, P. J. (2010). *Laughter in interaction.* Cambridge University Press.

Goodwin, C. (2000). Practices of seeing: Visual analysis - An ethnomethodological approach. In T. v. Leeuwen & C. Jewitt (Eds.), *Handbook of visual* (1st ed., pp. 157–182). Sage Publications.

Goodwin, C., & Salomon, R. (2019). Not being bound by what you can see now. Charles Goodwin in conversation with René Salomon. *Forum: Qualitative Social Research, 20*(2). https://doi.org/10.17169/fqs-20.2.3271

Grennan, S. (2017). *A theory of narrative drawing.* Springer.

Have, P. t. (2007). *Doing conversation analysis, A practical guide.* Sage.

Heath, C., Hindmarsh, J., & Luff, P. (2010). *Video in qualitative research: Analysing social interaction in everyday life.* Sage Publications.

Hepburn, A. (2004). Crying: Notes on description, transcription, and interaction. *Research on Language and Social Interaction, 37*(3), 251–290. https://doi.org/10.1207/s15327973rlsi3703_1

Hepburn, A., & Bolden, G. B. (2017). *Transcribing for social research.* Sage Publications.

Jayyusi, L. (1993). The reflexive nexus: Photo-practice and natural history. *Continuum: The Australian Journal of Media & Culture, 6*(2), 25–52. https://doi.org/10.1080/10304319309359397

Jefferson, G. (1978). What's in a `Nyem. *Sociology, 12*(1), 135–139. https://doi.org/10.1177/003803857801200109

Jefferson, G. (1983). Issues in the Transcription of Naturally-Occurring Talk: Caricature versus capturing pronunciational particulars. *Tilburg Papers in Language and Literature, 34*.

Jefferson, G. (1985). An exercise in the transcription and analysis of laughter. In T. A. Van Dijk (Ed.), *Handbook of discourse analysis* (pp. 25–34). Academic Press.

Laurier, E. (2014a). The graphic transcript: Poaching comic book grammar for inscribing the visual, spatial and temporal aspects of action. *Geography Compass, 8*(4), 235–248. https://doi.org/10.1111/gec3.12123

Laurier, E. (2014b). The lives hidden by the transcript and the hidden lives of the transcript [Unpublished manuscript].

Laurier, E. (2019). The panel show: Further experiments with graphic transcripts and vignettes. *Social Interaction: Video-Based Studies of Human Sociality, 2*(1). https://doi.org/10.7146/si.v2i1.113968

Laurier, E., Muñoz, D., Miller, R., & Brown, B. (2020). A bip, a Beeeep, and a beep beep: How horns are sounded in Chennai traffic. *Research on Language and Social Interaction, 53*(3), 341–356. https://doi.org/10.1080/08351813.2020.1785775

Lindwall, O., & Lymer, G. (in press). Detail, granularity, and laic analysis in instructional demonstrations. In M. Lynch & O. Lindwall (Eds.), *Instructed and instructive actions.* Routledge.

Luff, P., & Heath, C. (2012). Some "technical challenges" of video analysis: Social actions, objects, material realities and the problems of perspective. *Qualitative Research, 12*(3), 255–279. https://doi.org/10.1177/1468794112436655

McCloud, S. (1993). *Understanding comics: The invisible art.* Kitchen Sink Press.

McIlvenny, P. (2021). New Technology and Tools to Enhance Collaborative Video Analysis in Live 'Data Sessions'. QuiViRR: Qualitative Video Research Reports, 1. https://doi .org/10.5278/ojs.quivirr.v1.2020.a0001

Mondada, L. (2014). Shooting as a research activity studies of video practices. In M. Broth, E. Laurier, & L. Mondada (Eds.), *Studies of video practices: Video at work* (pp. 33–63). Routledge.

Mondada, L. (2018). Multiple temporalities of language and body in interaction: Challenges for transcribing multimodality. *Research on Language and Social Interaction, 51*(1), 85–106. https://doi.org/10.1080/08351813.2018.1413878

Schegloff, E. (2000). On granularity. *Annual Review of Sociology, 26*(1), 715–720. https:// doi.org/10.1146/annurev.soc.26.1.715

Watson, R. (1997). Some general reflections on 'categorization' and 'sequence' in the analysis of conversation. In S. Hester & P. Eglin (Eds.), *Culture in action: Studies in membership categorization analysis* (pp. 49–76). University Press of America.

INDEX

aboriginal languages 10, 172, 174, 176, 184–90

accountability 1, 4, 77, 113, 115, 126, 203, 247, 255

affordance 8, 96–101, 106, 111, 128–9, 133, 138, 160, 177, 222

avatars 112–29, 139, 229, 233–4

camera: 360-degree 5, 10, 117, 132–46, 224, 227, 231–42, 256–8; handheld 134–5, 162; static 9, 86–8, 90, 93, 96, 106, 226; wearable 9, 85–87, 90, 96, 101–107

camera perspective 5, 106, 115, 231, 234, 240, 255–7

camera view 87, 96, 100, 106, 135–46, 172, 187, 233,

captioning 252–4, 259

coding 7, 38, 183–4, 206–7, 209

comic strips 6, 11, 227–8, 251–7, 260–1

communicative gestures 9, 24, 37, 173

contextual configuration 64, 75, 111–12, 115, 125–7, 145

co-presence 85, 87–8, 91, 93, 95, 98, 125, 129, 229–30

distributed bodies 112, 125–6

double membership 132, 143, 145

dual embodiment 111–15, 118–22, 125–9

embodiment 5, 11–12, 47, 112, 229

ethnographic knowledge 12, 77, 132, 154–7, 163, 166–8

ethnomethodology 4, 65, 76, 146, 177, 221–2, 245

experimentation 7, 22, 109, 205–6, 210–11, 256

geospatial framework 172, 174, 176–7

GIS 172, 174, 176–8

GPS-derived data 172–4, 176–8

graphic transcripts 246–9, 251–61

human-robot interaction 9, 42–4, 47, 58

individual activity 90–1, 93, 96

inductivity 2, 153, 155–6, 159, 161, 166–7

involvement 88, 93, 98

locational pointing 171–5, 178–9, 183–4, 193

longitudinal data 26, 31, 146, 167

member's perspective 3, 8–11, 24, 26, 63–4, 67–9, 75, 77, 153, 167

mirroring 11, 199, 201–2, 205, 210

mobile groups 132–5, 138, 142, 145–6

mobility 65, 71, 76, 85, 106, 134

motion capture 113, 125, 204, 223

multiactivity 68, 90, 96, 106, 259

naturalness 86, 89, 101, 106

next-turn proof procedure 2–3, 23–4, 37–8, 43, 55, 57, 127

non-accountability 10, 199, 207–10
non-human interaction 6, 8–9, 21–2, 24, 26–7, 37–8, 47, 57, 66

observability 45, 47, 55, 63, 67, 71, 73–6, 85–6, 88, 97, 134, 136, 144, 199–200, 237
ocularcentrism 8–9, 63–8, 70–8

participation 8–9, 12, 43–5, 57–8, 64, 74, 93, 132–5, 137, 144, 146, 154, 160, 209
participation framework 9, 58, 63–78, 87, 111–12, 125–7, 238
physiological signal analysis 11, 199, 201–3, 205, 208–10
place reference 172, 174, 176–7, 184, 187–8, 191, 192–3
pointing 10, 71, 75, 86, 96, 98–101, 113, 122–3, 171–184, 191, 192–3, 232, 259
practice-based video analysis 223, 225
practice-based VolCap analysis 224–5, 230, 240
private actions 3, 7–8, 10, 96, 127
proto-data 10, 155–7, 158, 161, 163, 166

rating 206, 209
recording equipment 68, 86–7, 89, 101, 105–7
researcher positionality 154
robots 6, 8–9, 42–58, 63, 66–74

screen capture 85–7, 90, 93, 95–6, 101, 103–5, 107, 116–17, 253
sequence organisation 28, 37, 206
smartphone 85–8, 90–8, 101, 103, 105–7
social action 1, 3–4, 6–8, 22–3, 25, 113, 115, 125–6, 128, 163, 199–200, 207
space 4, 29, 47, 58, 71, 74, 111, 116, 127, 172–5, 179, 222, 240, 258; virtual 111–2, 115–7, 226, 229
speech bubbles 252, 259–61
statistical analysis 205–6, 209–10

temporality 90–1, 98, 252
topography 171–2, 176–7
transcription 9, 42–3, 45, 47–54, 57–8, 230, 245–251, 253, 255, 260–1; Jeffersonian 6, 11, 183, 246–9, 251–3, 261; Mondada 48, 90, 183, 246–8, 251–3, 261

unique adequacy 3, 6, 22, 77, 155, 166–7
unmotivated looking 134, 143, 145, 154–6, 161, 163, 166–7, 206

VE see virtual environment
virtual: environment 5, 10, 111–12, 114–15, 118, 121–2, 125, 127, 129, 221, 224; reality 11, 112, 116, 122–3, 138, 221, 229
visual impairment 63, 65–6, 71, 73, 76
volumetric capture 221, 223–5, 240–1
VR see virtual reality
vulgar competence 3, 58, 77